Tarzan and Jane's
Guide to Grammar

Books by Mark Phillips

Metallica Riff by Riff
Guitar for Dummies
Honeymooners Trivia
Sight-Sing Any Melody Instantly
Sight-Read Any Rhythm Instantly
The Wizard of Oz Vocabulary Builder
The Pinocchio Intermediate Vocabulary Builder

Tarzan and Jane's Guide to Grammar

Mark Phillips

Based on characters from and including material from
Tarzan of the Apes
by Edgar Rice Burroughs

A. J. Cornell Publications
New York

Tarzan and Jane's Guide to Grammar

For information address:
A. J. Cornell Publications
18-74 Corporal Kennedy St.
Bayside, NY 11360

Cover illustration by Debbie Phillips
Cover design by Jonathan Gullery

Library of Congress Control Number: 2005900721

ISBN-13: 978-0-9727439-3-8
ISBN-10: 0-9727439-3-6

Printed in the Unites States of America

Note: *American Monthly* is a fictitious magazine. It is not meant
to represent any actual publication, past or present.

CONTENTS

Chapter 1: Jane's Idea

I first met Tarzan when he rescued me from the clutches of a savage gorilla. Now it was a day later and we were seated across from each other at the crude wooden table in his jungle cabin.

"First of all," I said, looking at the tall, strikingly handsome, shirtless, muscular, dark-haired young man across from me, "I want to thank you for saving me from that awful gorilla yesterday. He would have killed me. I was scared to death."

"Tarzan save."

Neither of us said anything for a few seconds, and then Tarzan blurted out, "Me Tarzan; you Jane."

"That's right," I said patiently. "Your name is Tarzan and my name is Jane. Jane Porter. I'm a reporter for a magazine called *American Monthly*. I've come here to Africa to write a series of articles about you for my magazine. I've traveled all the way from Baltimore."

"Baltimore?"

"Yes. It's a city in Maryland. You see, *American Monthly* is published there. If you want to know the truth, no one really wanted this assignment, because Africa is so far away and the jungle is so unpleasant with its sweltering temperatures, wild beasts, and disgusting insects."

"Insects?"

"Yes. Anyway, because I'm the newest and youngest journalist at the magazine—I just finished school, really—I got stuck with this assignment."

Tarzan just stared at me. He stared as if he'd never seen a girl before. Well, come to think of it, he probably hadn't. After all, he'd been raised by apes in the jungle. I could see myself reflected in the pupils of his eyes—a girl of nineteen, slim, five-foot-three, long dark hair. I know that description sounds like something from a personal ad, but perhaps that's fitting because Tarzan was looking at me with love in his eyes. I'm young, but I can tell when a guy likes me.

I said, "Tarzan, would you like to help me write some articles about your unusual life for my magazine?"

"Magazine?"

"You know what a magazine is, don't you? It's like a newspaper, but it has a shiny cover and more pictures."

"Pictures? Tarzan help."

I'd known Tarzan for only one day and already he was driving me nuts with two of his habits of speech. One was that he seemed to an-

1

swer everything simply by repeating the last word I'd said, but as a question. If I say "I'm from Baltimore," he says "Baltimore?" I don't know if by that he means "Oh, really? That's interesting. Go ahead," or if, like a parrot, he repeats it with no idea of what I'm talking about.

The other thing he does that gets on my nerves is that he always uses his name. He says "Tarzan eat," "Tarzan save," "Tarzan help." Things like that. I think to myself: My goodness! Can't he ever use the word *I?* Didn't he ever hear of a pronoun? Can't he ever say "*I* eat" or "*I* save"?

"Tarzan," I said, "let me tell you more about these articles. You see, my magazine is published once a month. My boss wants me to write a series of twenty-four articles, which would be published over a two-year period. During those two years, the American readers would become more and more fascinated by you and your story. At the end of the two years, we would bring you to the United States and put you on display in New York City. Does that appeal to you?"

"New York City?"

"Yes, it's the biggest city in America."

Tarzan didn't answer.

"Hey, wait a second," I said. "Do you know what? I have a wonderful idea. I think that instead of *me* writing the articles, you should write them yourself."

"Tarzan write?"

"Yes. Don't you see? That way they would be more authentic; they would grab the reader's attention."

"Attention?"

"Yes. Oh, it will be wonderful! What do you say? Do you want to give it a try?"

"Tarzan try."

Of course, I knew that Tarzan couldn't write a magazine article at a level appropriate for publication. He would need help. A lot of help.

I said, "Tarzan, here's what I propose—"

Just then a long snake slithered into the cabin! As I drew back in horror, Tarzan casually picked it up by the tail and flung it out the window. I heard it make a dull thud on the ground outside.

When my heart started beating again, I continued, "As I was saying, what I propose is that for the first few articles, you tell me your story out loud, and I'll put it into writing myself. Then I'll show you what I've written, and you'll approve it or suggest changes."

"Changes?"

"Yes. If there's something inaccurate, or if there's something you don't want published, you'll let me know, and we'll change it. Okay?"

"Tarzan change."

"But here's the best part. We can use those first few articles to teach you the basics of English grammar. Then you'll be able to write the remainder of the articles yourself!"

"Grammar boring."

"Grammar usually is boring. But don't you see? You'll be reading about yourself! What could be more interesting to someone than his own life story? And in your case, it's such an amazing story. Believe me, you won't be bored."

Tarzan didn't answer, so I hurried on. "Look, this will work out beautifully. The articles will be riveting, because they will have been written in the first person."

"First person?"

"Yes. What I mean is that instead of the first article beginning something like "Tarzan was born in the jungle," it would start "I was born in the jungle." It would be you talking directly to the reader. That's what I meant by *first person*. And, as I said, we'll use the articles to teach you proper grammar."

"Proper grammar?"

"Yes. You see, I'll point out the rules of grammar to you by using sentences from your articles as examples and illustrations. For instance, I'll show you how a pronoun relates to its antecedent. Things like that."

"Pronoun? Antecedent?"

"Oh my, you're right! You don't even know what those things mean. How can I teach you grammar if you don't the meanings of the various grammatical terms?"

"Grammatical terms?"

"Yes. Grammatical terms, like *noun, verb, clause, phrase,* and so on."

We were both silent awhile. I became aware of the jungle noises outside the cabin: the hum of insects, the rustle of leaves, the growl of some unseen animal. I became aware of the hot, sticky air in the cabin and the perspiration forming on my face. Tarzan, I noticed, continued to stare at me with a gleam in his eyes.

"Let me think," I went on. Then, after a few seconds I said, "I know; we'll do it this way: We'll use the first few articles, the one's that I ghostwrite—"

"Ghostwrite?"

3

"I mean the ones I write for you, but under your name."

"Tarzan understand."

"So, we'll use the first few articles not to teach you the *rules* of grammar, but to teach you the *terms* of grammar, the *vocabulary* of grammar. Then, we'll use the articles you write yourself to teach you the rules of grammar. And the rules of punctuation and capitalization, too."

"How teach rules?"

"We'll do it the most natural way there is—through writing! I'll read what you write, and I'll point out your grammatical errors. Then I'll explain the reason for the error and give you a rule to follow so that you'll never make that error again."

"How many terms? How many rules?"

"I don't know. Maybe about forty terms and a hundred rules. Do you think you can handle that? Let's say I'll write the first five articles, based on what you dictate to me. We'll use those five articles to teach you the meanings of the grammatical terms. Then we'll use the other nineteen articles, the ones you write yourself, to teach you the actual rules of grammar. But that will work—and don't take this the wrong way—only if you manage to make every possible grammatical error there is in the course of those nineteen articles. Do you think you can do that?"

Tarzan stared at me with a dopey grin. I didn't know if that meant that he was willing to try to learn grammar or if he simply had a big crush on me. Can you believe what we journalist have to go through?

Chapter 2: The First Lesson

Judging from his speech, I didn't have any doubt that in writing, Tarzan would make every grammatical error under the sun. I was pleased with my plan.

The next day I said, "Tarzan, before you begin telling me—I mean writing—your life story, there's something else we should talk about, and that's basic *syntax*."

"Syntax?"

"Yes. The way words are put together in the correct order to make a sentence. Before you start writing your life story for *American Monthly*, you have to learn how to speak like a normal human being, not like someone raised by apes. Do you understand?"

Tarzan looked like he was about to cry, but he murmured, "Tarzan understand."

I felt guilty for having offended him. "I didn't mean anything by that," I said. "You really speak very well for someone . . ." I didn't know how to finish that, so I just let it hang there.

I worked with Tarzan over the next several weeks on basic sentence structure. He was a very fast learner. I think he inherited excellent genes—his father was one of the brightest men in England. Anyway, after a while, Tarzan was speaking pretty much the way normal people do, and we were able to carry on normal conversations.

Finally the day came when we started to work on the first article. But instead of talking about himself, Tarzan spoke about his parents.

"Why is this entire article about your parents?" I asked. "Don't you think people will be more interested in hearing about you?"

"But people need to know about my parents to understand how I came to be an orphan in Africa." (Do you see what I mean about his learning to speak like a normal person?)

"Okay," I said. It was too hot to argue, and he was probably right.

Tarzan told me all about how his parents left England for Africa, and when he was finished I began to write. It was an easy article to write because the subject matter was really very interesting.

When I showed him my finished version, he didn't suggest a single change!

The following is the text, in Tarzan's voice (but ghostwritten by me), for the first of the twenty-four articles.

Article 1: "Cast Ashore"

For many years I believed that my parents were apes of the jungle and that I was a skinny, hairless ape. But after I taught myself to read, I discovered my father's diary and learned that my parents, whose names were John and Alice Clayton, were really human beings from England! In fact, my father was a nobleman!

Before I was born, the English government sent my parents by sailing ship to central Africa to investigate a theft of rubber and ivory in a European-held territory. The officers and crew of the ship they sailed on hated each other, and after about a week at sea, the crew, who were a bunch of thugs, revolted and took over the vessel. The mutineers killed all the officers, but since they liked my parents, they allowed them to live. However, they didn't want any witnesses to the mutiny, so they put my parents ashore with their possessions and a supply of food and tools.

Watching the large ship sail away, my father and mother realized that they were now all alone at the edge of an endless, unexplored jungle filled with wild beasts.

"Oh, John," my mother cried, "the horror of it. What are we to do? What are we to do?"

"There is but one thing to do, Alice," my father answered calmly, "and that is work. We mustn't give ourselves time to think, for that would drive us mad. Our ancient ancestors faced the same problems we must face, possibly in this very jungle. That we are here today is proof of their ultimate victory. We can do what they did. And we can do it more easily, for we are armed with ages of superior knowledge and technology. What they accomplished, Alice, with stone instruments and weapons of bone, surely we can also accomplish."

"Okay, Tarzan," I said with a smile, "are you ready to start learning grammar?"

"Tarzan ready," he said.

I was shocked; was he really going back to speaking like a—

"I was kidding!" he said. "Yes, I'm ready. Go ahead and teach me; I want to learn."

I decided to start with the definitions of the various parts of speech.

"Tarzan," I said to the eager young man sitting across from me, "the words of the English language fall into various categories, depending on how they function in a sentence."

"What do you mean by 'how they function'?"

"Well, I mean that certain words name things, other words describe things, still other words describe actions, and so on. Each category is known as a "part of speech." Can you say "part of speech"?

"Jane, you're talking down to me. I heard you; I don't have to repeat it."

He was being touchy, I thought. But then, maybe I *was* talking down to him. I felt bad about that. While I was trying to decide how to handle the situation, he suddenly said, "So what are the names of these parts of speech?"

That brought me back to the moment and I decided to forget about the "talking down" issue and simply continue with the lesson. "Well, don't try to memorize this now, because we're going to take them one at a time, but the parts of speech are *noun, pronoun, adjective, verb, adverb, preposition, conjunction, interjection,* and *article.*

"That's a lot. How many is that?"

I had to count them on my fingers. "I guess that's nine. But like I said, we'll take them one at a time. Let's start with the noun, okay?"

"Okay."

"You see, a noun is a word that—"

Just then my body froze because a truly enormous, hairy spider was crawling up the table leg. I let out a scream that must have been heard for miles around. Tarzan was momentarily startled, but when he spotted the creature he grabbed a knife and slit the thing in half. Then he carried both halves outside.

When he came back and sat down I seemed to be breathing fairly normally again, so I continued, "Basically, a noun is a word that names something. It can name a thing, a person, a place, an idea, or an action. Let me give you some examples. Words like *jungle, tree,* and *ape* are nouns because they name things. Words like *mother, father, Tarzan,* and *Jane* are nouns because they name people. Do you understand?"

"Yes, that's easy. Let me try making up examples of nouns that name places, okay?"

"Sure. Go ahead." (He was such a good student!)

"How about the words *England* and *Africa?*"

"That right! Very good!" I exclaimed. "Now here are some nouns that name ideas: *strength, courage,* and *bravery.* Now it's your turn. Give me some words that name actions—or activities."

He thought for a moment and then said, "*Hunting, swimming,* and *eating.*"

"Tarzan, you're a genius," I found myself saying. "Okay, now that you get that, here's your first assignment. Take the first paragraph of Article 1 and underline all the nouns."

"Okay. Let me see it." Tarzan took the piece of paper with Article 1 and stared at the first paragraph for a while. Then he underlined some of the words and handed it back to me. It looked like this:

For many <u>years</u> I believed that my <u>parents</u> were <u>apes</u> of the <u>jungle</u> and that I was a skinny, hairless <u>ape</u>. But after I taught myself to read, I discovered my <u>father's</u> <u>diary</u> and learned that my <u>parents</u>, whose <u>names</u> were <u>John</u> and <u>Alice Clayton</u>, were really <u>human beings</u> from <u>England</u>! In fact, my <u>father</u> was a <u>nobleman</u>!

"Tarzan, that's excellent! I think you've got it.

He beamed with pride.

"Now let's go into a little more detail about these nouns," I said. "Did you know that a noun can be either *singular* or *plural?*"

"Um . . ."

"Well, look at the first three words you underlined. They're all plural because they refer to more than one of something—not one year but many *years;* not one parent but both *parents;* not one ape but a certain number of *apes.*"

"I think I see. Since the words are plural, the nouns are called *plural nouns,* right?"

"Right! Now look at the next two words, *jungle* and *ape.* There you're talking about just one jungle and just one ape, so those two are *singular nouns.* Now here's a little tip: If you see the word *the* or *a* before a noun, you know that the noun is singular."

8

"Because those words—*the* and *a*—refer to one of something, right?"

"Yes, yes, yes! Tarzan, you are an excellent student!"

Again he beamed.

"Okay," I said, "we've talked about nouns being singular or plural. Now let's talk about nouns being either *common case* or *possessive case.*"

He stared at me expectantly.

"If a word simply names something, it's called a *common-case* noun. For example, the word *lion* is a common-case noun. But if a noun shows ownership or possession of something, then it's called a *possessive-case* noun. For example, if I say "lion's claw," the word *claw* is common case but the word *lion's*—which is really just the word *lion* with an apostrophe and an *s* added to it—is *possessive-case.* Why? Because it shows possession; the claw belongs to the lion. Do you see?"

"Yes. In that first paragraph I underlined 'father's diary.' The word *father's* is a possessive noun; it shows ownership of the diary. The diary belonged to my father."

"Good! Can you make up another example of a possessive noun?"

Tarzan looked around his cabin and then said, "If I say 'hunter's knife,' the word *hunter's* is a possessive noun. The knife belongs to the hunter."

"Good. Okay. Now, one more thing about nouns. Did you know that nouns can be either proper or common?

"Um . . ."

"You see, certain nouns identify names or titles that are always capitalized when you write or spell them."

"Such as?"

"Well, such as the names of people or countries. In that first paragraph, you underlined *John, Alice, Clayton,* and *England.* Those are the names of people or places that are capitalized, so they are *proper nouns.* Any noun that is not capitalized is called a *common noun.*"

"Hey, just a minute! Before you said that a common noun is one that is not *possessive.* Now you're saying that a common noun is one that is not *proper.* Which is it?"

"I agree that it's a bit confusing. But remember, a noun that is not possessive is called a common-*case* noun. On the other hand, a noun that is not proper is called a *common* noun. You see, one's called *common case,* and the other is just called *common.*"

9

"Oh." Then Tarzan asked an insightful question. "How many cases are there? You already named the possessive and common cases. Are there others?"

"Actually, that's all there are. And do you know what? Hardly anyone even talks about a noun as being "common case." If a noun is possessive, people say that it's a possessive-case noun. But if a noun isn't possessive, its case is usually not even mentioned.

"Hmm . . ." Tarzan considered this awhile and then asked, "What about proper and common nouns? Do people talk about those?"

"Well, yes. But again, they often speak of a capitalized noun— *Africa*, for example—as being a proper noun. But if a noun isn't capitalized, they usually don't bother mentioning that it's a common noun.

"Hmm . . ."

"Tarzan, let's look at one other word you underlined. When you underlined the word *human* in the phrase *human being*, did you think that the word *human* was a noun? You know, some people would say that the noun is the word *being* and that the word *human* simply describes the *type* of being."

"I thought about that, but I decided that the whole phrase, *human being*, even though it's two words, should be considered as a single unit. So I underlined the whole thing. Was I right?"

I was beginning to think that this guy was as smart as he was handsome, strong, and brave. I was nearly speechless. "Um, y-yes. You could look at it that way," I stammered.

Chapter 3: Tarzan and Jane Plan a Picnic

The next day, after a breakfast of fresh tropical fruit that Tarzan had gathered from somewhere or other, we continued the lesson. We were in our accustomed seats, across from each other at the wooden table. On the floor, out feet were about three inches away from each other. No harm in that.

"Okay," I began, "today we're going to talk about another part of speech, the *pronoun*. Now, a pronoun—"

All of a sudden, an enormous head with two bony bumps at the top floated in the air directly between our *own* heads! Because this seemed to defy the laws of gravity, I was too shocked to be afraid. Then I saw that the head was connected to a very long brown and yellow spotted neck, and that the neck passed through the open window to a body. It was a giraffe that, perhaps, was looking for some leftover fruit! Because I know that giraffes don't bite people, I was more amused than afraid. Tarzan barked something to it in what sounded like a strange foreign language and the animal quickly withdrew. With its head and neck once again outside the cabin, the thing ran off.

"Wow!" I thought. "Who is this guy, Dr. Dolittle? Can he speak every animal language?" Then I wondered whether each animal language—if such things existed—had its own rules of grammar. Then I wondered whether Tarzan knew those rules.

But these thoughts were getting out of hand. Better get back to the English grammar lesson.

"Anyway, about these pronouns—"

"Right, the pronouns," he said.

I noticed that on the floor under the table our feet were now only about *two* inches apart. No harm in that.

"Do you remember," I began, "when I told you that you don't always have to say your name when you talk about yourself? For example, instead of saying 'Tarzan likes to swim,' you could say 'I like to swim.' In that sentence, the word *I* is a pronoun."

"It is?"

"Yes. You see, a pronoun is a word—such as *I, me, you, he, she, him, her,* or *it*— that takes the place of a noun. It substitutes for a noun. Do you see?

"Yes, but why do you need to use a substitution? Wouldn't it be clearer if you just say the names of the people you're talking about? If

I say "he told him about her," you wouldn't know which people I'm talking about."

I thought about pointing out to him that he'd just used some pronouns himself—*you* and *I*, for example—without even realizing it. But I decided not to get into that. Instead I said, "You're right, that would be confusing. You should use pronouns only when their meaning is obvious."

"How do you do that?"

"Well, let's take the sentence 'Tarzan walked into his cabin.' The pronoun in that sentence is *his*, and it's obvious that *his* refers to *Tarzan*. If you really want to get technical, the term for the word that a pronoun refers back to—or substitutes for—is *antecedent*. Can you say . . ." I stopped myself there because I remembered that he gets touchy if I talk down to him.

Was it my imagination, or under the table, was his foot pulled back from mine a bit more? Oh well. "Anyway," I continued, "you should use a pronoun only if it's clear what the antecedent is; only if it's clear which noun the pronoun substitutes for or refers to."

Then Tarzan asked another of his insightful questions. "Do you remember," he said, "when you told me that nouns have different cases, such as possessive and common? And how nouns can be proper or common? What about pronouns? Do they have different cases? Are there different types."

I thought to myself: Now he's opened a can of worms. "Actually, pronouns are more complicated than nouns. First of all, there are different types of pronouns."

"Such as?"

"Well, there are *personal* pronouns, such as *I*, *me*, and *you*."

"I get that. Those substitute for people's names."

"Right. Then there are *relative* pronouns, such as *who*, *that*, and *which*."

"What do those do?"

"Well, those are usually used to begin a portion of a sentence, but they also refer back to an antecedent. For example, if I say 'Jane traveled to Africa to meet Tarzan, who is a very nice man,' the word *who* refers to Tarzan and introduces the second portion of the sentence."

Instead of commenting on that, Tarzan blushed a little.

"That part about you being a very nice man was just an example," I said with a smile. "Okay, let's see . . . we've already talked about personal and relative pronouns. Also, there are *interrogative* pronouns, such as *what* and *whose*."

"What do they do?"

"Those are used to begin a question, such as 'Whose cabin is this?' or 'What would you like to do this afternoon?'"

"Do you know what I'd like to do this afternoon? I'd like—"

"No, no, I was just saying that to show you how to use an interrogative pronoun."

"I know, but still, I want to tell you what I'd like to do. Let's go for a swim in the river."

It was awfully hot, and a swim sounded inviting. But I had two concerns. First, did I want Tarzan to see me in a bathing suit? And second, what about crocodiles? "Um," I said, "let's continue working on grammar until lunch. Then after we eat, let's see how we feel and we'll decide. Okay?" That was really just a stall for time because I couldn't make up my mind about the swim.

"What should we have for lunch?" he asked.

"Let's have bananas and coconuts. But first let's finish talking about types of pronouns."

"Tarzan hungry," he joked.

"I know, but just hold on. We're almost done. In addition to personal, relative, and interrogative pronouns, there are *indefinite* pronouns, such as *each, none,* and *everybody.*"

"What do they do?"

"Instead of referring to *specific* people or things, they refer to people or things in general. In the sentence 'Everybody likes coconuts,' the word *everybody* is an indefinite pronoun."

"Because it doesn't refer to any specific person, right?"

"Right. Okay, two more. There are pronouns that have the syllable *self* or *selves* added to them, such as *myself* and *themselves.*"

"What do you call those?"

"Well, that's a little complicated. Some people call them *compound personal pronouns*—compound because they're made up of two parts, such as *my* and *self.* But sometimes they're called *reflexive* pronouns, if they express an action that "reflects" back on the person you're talking about. And sometimes they're called *intensive* pronouns, if they serve to intensify or emphasize the person you're talking about."

"I don't understand."

"Well, let me give you some examples." I thought of two examples. One was sort of flirtatious and might make Tarzan blush again. The other was about food and might make Tarzan even hungrier for lunch. I decided to take a risk.

"Well," I said, "in the sentence 'I consider myself lucky to have met a nice man like Tarzan,' the word *myself* is a reflexive pronoun. It 'reflects' back on the word *I*."

Tarzan blushed. And I think that under the table, his foot moved back to where it was before.

"And in the sentence 'Tarzan and Jane gathered the bananas and coconuts themselves,' the word *themselves* is an intensive pronoun. It *emphasizes* who gathered the fruit."

"Okay, I get it. Now let's eat."

"Wait. One more type of pronoun. There are *demonstrative* pronouns, such as *this, that,* and *those*. They refer to particular *things*, not to particular people. In the sentence 'This is fun!' the word *This* is a demonstrative pronoun."

"And when we finally eat," Tarzan said, "and I say 'These coconuts are delicious,' the word *These* is a demonstrative pronoun, right? Look, I'm starving. Let's go gather the fruit. Then let's eat it on the riverbank so that, if we feel like it at the time, we can go swimming afterwards."

It was so hot that I didn't argue about swimming. Nor did I mention that my mother always told me that I should wait thirty minutes after eating before swimming—so I wouldn't get a cramp. "Okay," I said, "it's lunchtime and we'll eat on the riverbank. But before we swim, we have to talk about the three *cases* of pronouns."

"I thought we already did that."

"No, we talked about *types* of pronouns. But pronouns also have *cases*, which include the *subjective* case, the *objective* case, and the *possessive* case."

"You're kidding, right?"

"No, really. Do you see why I said that pronouns are more complicated than nouns? I know you're too hungry to learn about all that now. Let's eat first, at the riverbank. Then we'll learn about the cases of pronouns, and after that we'll swim, okay?"

"Okay!"

Chapter 4: Tarzan and Jane Swim in a River

We gathered our lunch together, but Tarzan really did all the work. In a flash he had filled a basket with ripe bananas and coconuts. When we arrived at the riverbank I think I was just as hungry as he was.

After we had stuffed ourselves with fruit, Tarzan said, "How about some berries for dessert?"

"Okay, I said, but don't pick the poisonous ones." I don't think he knew whether or not I was kidding. Actually, I was only half kidding. Who knew what kinds of things grew out here?

We each ate a handful of plump red berries. I don't know what kind they were, but they were delicious.

"Now let's swim," said Tarzan, standing up.

"No, first we have to finish our pronoun discussion."

"Okay, but make it fast because I'm hot."

"I'll tell you what, we can sit with our feet in the water while we talk. That should cool us off."

We walked to the edge of the river, sat down, and submerged our feet in the cool water. I forgot to worry about crocodiles.

"Do you remember," I said, "how some nouns are in the possessive case?"

"Yes, as in 'hunter's knife.' The word *hunter's* is a possessive noun."

"Right. And pronouns can also be in the possessive case. In the sentence 'The hunter took out his knife,' the word *his* is in the possessive case."

"That's easy. The word *his* is a pronoun because it stands for "hunter," and it's possessive because it shows ownership of the knife. It's *his* knife."

As Tarzan said that, I noticed a hippopotamus in the middle of the river! I had never seen one before, and I was amazed. "Look! A hippopotamus!" I shrieked.

"So?" Tarzan replied calmly. "There are always hippos around here. They won't bother you."

"Bother me? I didn't think that they—" Then I remembered the crocodiles and pulled my feet from the water. "Tarzan, are there any crocodiles in this river?"

"I don't know. Maybe. But tell me about those other cases of pronouns you mentioned back at the cabin. What did you say they were called?"

I backed away from the water a little more. "One is called the *subjective* case—but that one can also be called the *nominative* case. It has two names. The other is called the *objective* case."

"How do you use those?"

"Tarzan, wait. I'm afraid of crocodiles. I don't want to be killed. Let's go back to the cabin and I'll tell you there."

"Jane, we made an agreement to go swimming and a deal is a deal. Besides, I'm hot. If a crocodile attacks, I promise to protect you, okay?"

I may be crazy, but I agreed to stay by the river. I guess I thought that he really could protect me. He *did* save me from that fierce gorilla the day we met. It occurred to me that we were a bit like Lois Lane and Superman—you know, from the comic books. I was a reporter, like Lois, and he seemed to have superhuman strength, like Superman.

"Well . . . okay," I said uncertainly. I tried to force myself to concentrate on pronouns. Tarzan waited patiently. He seemed to be staring at the river.

"What you have to understand is that a noun or pronoun is sometimes used as the *subject* of a sentence. By that I mean that a word like *hunter* or *Tarzan* is what the sentence is about; it's the hunter or Tarzan who does something or other. But other times a noun or pronoun is the *object* of a sentence. By that I mean that it's the hunter or Tarzan who has something happen to him. Do you see? Instead of Tarzan doing something, as in 'Tarzan saved Jane,' Tarzan is the object of some action, as in 'Jane likes Tarzan.'"

"Tarzan likes Jane!"

"Well, okay. In that sentence, *Tarzan* is the subject and *Jane* is the object.

"But what difference does that make? The word *Tarzan* is the same whether it's the subject or the object. There's no difference."

"You're right. There's no difference with nouns. But with pronouns there *is* a difference. For example, if you're talking about yourself, you use the word *I* for the subjective case, as in 'I like Jane,' but you use the word *me* for the objective case, as in 'Jane likes me.'"

"I see. So it would be wrong to say 'me likes Jane' or to say 'Jane likes I.'"

"That's right. I mean it would be wrong."

"What are some other subjective-case pronouns?"

"Well, there's *he, she, we,* and *they.*"

"And what are some objective-case pronouns?"

"Him, her, us, and *them."*

"So," said Tarzan, "you can say 'he likes her' and 'they like them' but you can't say 'him likes she' or 'them likes they.' Is that it?"

"Exactly. But I have to tell you one more thing. Some pronouns are the same in both cases—you know, just the way nouns are. For example, you use the pronoun *you* and the pronoun *it* for both subjective and objective cases.

"So if I want to say that you're afraid of a crocodile, I could say '*you* are afraid of *it*' or I can say '*it* scares *you.*' In both cases I use the word *you* for both the subjective and objective case and the word *it* for both the subjective and objective case."

"Very good. You've got it. Now let's get out of here before a crocodile really *does* attack."

"Not until after we've had our swim."

I really didn't want to go in the water.

"Wait," I said, my voice rising. "I have to test you on pronouns first. Remember how you underlined all the nouns in the first paragraph of the first article? Now you're going to underline all the *pronouns* in the second paragraph."

"No. Now I'm going to go for a swim." And with that he stood up and waded out into the water. In a moment he was swimming briskly away from me. He was an excellent swimmer; in fact, he was a better swimmer than any athlete I'd ever seen. I yelled to him, "Okay, but as soon as you come out, you have to underline those pronouns!"

While I waited for him to finish his swim I grew hotter and hotter. I don't know if it was from the tropical heat or if I was getting overly nervous about crocodiles lunging at me, but I started to break out in a sweat. The cool river water looked irresistible. I had my bathing suit on under my clothes. Tarzan had swum far enough away that he wouldn't be able to see me very well from where he was. I quickly removed my outer garments and submerged myself in the water. It was deliciously cool and invigorating.

"Hey there!" he called. "How's the water?"

"Wonderful!" I yelled back as I searched for any sign of crocodiles. Not wanting to risk my luck, I decided to get out. I sat on the riverbank and waited for Tarzan to return.

All of a sudden there he was standing over me, dripping wet and smiling. "Nice bathing suit," he said.

Oh my! I'd forgotten that I didn't want Tarzan to see me in my bathing suit. Oh well. What's done is done. Besides, back in America

I used to go to the Maryland beaches and people saw me in my bathing suit all the time. No big deal, I guess.

"Thanks," I said. "Now are you ready to underline those pronouns in that paragraph? I brought the article and a pencil with me; they're right here." I handed him the pencil and paper.

"Okay. Let me see this." Then Tarzan sat down and studied the article. After a while he underlined some of the words and handed it back to me. This is what it said:

Before <u>I</u> was born, the English government sent <u>my</u> parents by sailing ship to central Africa to investigate a theft of rubber and ivory in a European-held territory. The officers and crew of the ship <u>they</u> sailed on hated <u>each other</u>, and after about a week at sea, the crew, <u>who</u> were a bunch of thugs, revolted and took over the vessel. The mutineers killed all the officers, but since <u>they</u> liked <u>my</u> parents, <u>they</u> allowed <u>them</u> to live. However, <u>they</u> didn't want any witnesses to the mutiny, so <u>they</u> put <u>my</u> parents ashore with <u>their</u> possessions and a supply of food and tools.

"Tarzan, I think you got them all! Now let's review a little. Give me an example of a *personal* pronoun in that paragraph."

"In the first sentence the word *I* is a personal pronoun."

"Right. How about a *relative* pronoun?"

"The word *who*, which introduces 'who were a bunch of thugs.'"

"Good! Now how about an *indefinite* pronoun?"

"I think *each other* serves that purpose. Am I right?"

"Yes, I can see that. It's two words, but it does serve that purpose. Okay, now let's talk about case. Show me a pronoun in each case—the objective case, the subjective case, and the possessive case."

"Okay. Where it says 'my parents,' the word *my* is possessive case. Also, where it says 'their possessions,' the word *their* is possessive case."

"Good. What about objective and subjective cases?"

"Where it says 'they allowed them to live,' the word *they* is subjective case and the word *them* is objective case."

"Why?"

"Because *they* is the subject of the sentence. *They* performed the action—of allowing, I mean. And *them* is the object of the sentence. They allowed *them* to live.

18

"Excellent." There were other examples of subjective case and objective case pronouns in the paragraph, but I knew that he understood, so I didn't bother asking him to identify them. Then suddenly I realized that I'd forgotten to teach him one thing about pronouns.

"Tarzan, there's one more thing you have to know about pronouns."

"What's that?"

"Pronouns can be either singular or plural."

"What do you mean?"

"I mean that if you're talking about just one person, you use a singular pronoun, such as *I, me, he,* or *him.* But if you're talking about two or more people, then you use a plural pronoun, such as *we, us, they,* or *them.*"

"Let me guess. You want me to point out examples of singular and plural pronouns in the paragraph. Okay, in the first sentence, *I* is singular. And where it says 'the ship they sailed on,' *they* is plural."

"You're really very good at this," I told him. "In another life you could have been a grammarian!"

He smiled, obviously pleased with himself.

"Let's go back to the cabin," I said.

We began to walk back up the bank toward Tarzan's cabin. We walked in silence, aware of each other and of the natural activities of the jungle—insects buzzing about, birds flying overhead, monkeys swinging from branch to branch. The thought entered my head that Tarzan might take my hand in his as we strolled. If he did, I didn't know what I would do. As his grammar improved, I kept liking him more. But when we got back to the cabin, each of us still had our hands to ourselves.

19

Chapter 5: Tarzan and Jane Climb a Tree

The next morning it was drizzling, and I knew that we'd be having our grammar lesson indoors. I had decided that the next part of speech I'd talk about was the *adjective*, but I had a vague feeling that something about pronouns had been left unsaid. At first I couldn't put my finger on what it was, and it annoyed me. But after a while it came to me.

As soon as we'd finished breakfast, I said to Tarzan across the table, "I have to tell you one more thing about pronouns. No, actually two things. The first is kind of simple, but the second is a little more complicated."

"Okay."

"Do you remember that I said that pronouns can be either singular or plural, and that they can be in either the subjective or objective case, and so on? Well, there's still another thing they can be. They can be either *masculine* or *feminine*. In other words, they have what is called *gender*."

"What do you mean?"

"I mean that if you're talking about a man or boy, you use pronouns like *he, him,* and *his*. And if you're talking about a woman or girl, you use pronouns like *she, her,* and *hers*. For example, since you're a man, you'd say 'Tarzan walked into *his* cabin,' not 'Tarzan walked into *her* cabin.'"

Tarzan seemed about to say something, but I went on, "But you also have to understand that not *all* pronouns have gender. For example, if you're referring to a *thing*, like, say, a knife, you use what's known as a *neutral* pronoun, such as *it*, and you say 'That's a nice knife; let me see *it*,' not 'That's a nice knife; let me see *him*.'"

"But all that seems so obvious!"

"I know. Anyone who grew up where the English language is spoken would use the correct gender naturally—because it just sounds right. But for people who learned some other language as a child, it might not be so obvious. Also, there are exceptions to the rule. For example, for some reason, sometimes a ship or a country is referred to as *she* instead of *it*."

"Oh."

I was glad Tarzan didn't ask me why ships and countries are sometimes considered feminine, because I didn't know the answer. "Anyway," I continued, "the other thing I mentioned that's a little more complicated is the concept of *agreement*."

20

"Do you mean whether you and I *agree* if we should swim first or eat first? Something like that?"

"No, I'm talking about agreement between a pronoun and its antecedent. You see, a pronoun and the word it stands for must always agree with each other in number and gender."

"They must?"

"Yes. For example, if an antecedent is singular, the pronoun must also be singular. That's why you say something like 'Tarzan saw *himself* reflected in the water,' not 'Tarzan saw *themselves* reflected in the water.' Why? Because *Tarzan* is singular, and so is *himself*. Do you see? And if an antecedent is, let's say, feminine, the pronoun must also be feminine. That's why I say 'Jane likes *her* friend Tarzan,' not 'Jane likes *his* friend Tarzan.' Because Jane is a female—I mean, I'm a female. Do you see?"

I knew very well that whenever I offered a grammatical example that could be taken as a flirtatious remark, Tarzan either blushed or moved his foot closer to mine under the table. This time I chose not to look at his face or feet but to keep my eyes glued to the tabletop. Was it my imagination, or was his hand suddenly awfully close to mine? I interlocked my fingers and placed my hands on my lap, out of sight. "So," I continued, without looking at him, "do you see what I mean about agreement?"

"Sure. And I *agree* that it's an important rule!" he said, smiling.

I felt better, now that I'd discussed with him the concepts of gender and agreement. If there was anything he still didn't understand about pronouns, that would become apparent, I imagined, once he began writing his own articles. Now it was time to move on to the next part of speech, the adjective.

"Tarzan, are you ready to begin learning about another part of speech—the adjective?"

"Is that an easy one, like the noun, or a hard one, like the pronoun?"

"Well, I think it's pretty easy."

"Good."

Just then a ray of morning sunlight fell upon the table between us.

"Look," Tarzan exclaimed, "it's stopped drizzling and the sun has come out!" Let's have our lesson on adjectives up in a tree."

"A tree?" I thought he was kidding. "You're kidding, right?"

"No, really. Oh Jane, it's so beautiful up in the trees! You feel like you live in the sky, like a bird."

"But don't monkeys swing on branches up there? What if they bang into us and we fall?"

"I've been climbing trees my whole life! I promise that nothing bad will happen."

Tarzan stood up and put out his hand to me. I got up, took his hand and let him lead me out of the cabin.

Even though we walked through the jungle holding hands, I didn't think of that as something romantic. I told myself that Tarzan was simply leading me to an appropriate tree for climbing. As I was thinking about that, he suddenly he lifted me in one arm and I felt both of us rise through the air! He had an amazing knack for grabbing vines and swinging from one to another, like an ape. Well, I guess that's why he's known as Tarzan the Ape Man. We actually flew upward from vine to vine, seemingly defying gravity. In a moment we were seated on a thick branch at the top of a tall tree. The view was magnificent! To the east I could see the blue waters of the Atlantic Ocean, and to the north, west, and south I could see miles of jungles and plains.

"Wow!" I said. "This is amazing! I know we're here to talk about adjectives, but let me look around a bit first."

"Okay."

I couldn't stop thinking about how tall this tree was and how beautiful the view was, and those words—*tall* and *beautiful*—got me thinking about adjectives. I looked at Tarzan and said, "Okay, let's talk about adjectives."

"Okay. What's an adjective?"

"Well, it's a word that modifies a noun."

"What do you mean? I thought to *modify* something is to change it."

"Well, usually that's what *modify* means, but in grammar the word *modify* has a special meaning. If you say that an adjective *modifies* a noun, you usually mean that it describes it; it makes it more specific."

"What do you mean?"

"For example, if I say the word *tree*, you don't really know what kind of tree I'm talking about. Is it large or small? What color is it? But if I say *tall, green tree*, then I'm being more specific. Do you see? Adjectives are words that make nouns more specific by describing them."

"I see. So if I say 'The view from up here is beautiful,' the word *beautiful* is an adjective because it describes—I mean *modifies*—the word *view*."

"Very good! The word *beautiful* is an adjective."

"Jane is beautiful."

"Um—"

"That was just an example to show you that I know how to use an adjective."

"Oh." I could feel my face getting hot and I knew I must be blushing a little. I didn't want him to notice, so I pretended to gaze at the view behind me.

Then I heard Tarzan say, "I like adjectives. Tell me more."

"Well," I said, turning back around, "did you know that an adjective is often placed before the noun it modifies, but it can also be placed after it?"

"It can?"

"Yes. For example, if you say 'tall tree,' the word *tall*, which is the adjective, comes *before* the noun *tree*. But if you say 'the view is beautiful,' the word *beautiful*, which is the adjective, comes *after* the noun *view*."

"But if it comes after, then you need to connect the noun and adjective with a word like *is*, right? The view *is* beautiful. You couldn't just say 'the view beautiful,' right?"

"Right." I was about to mention that that's how he *used* to speak when we first met, but what would be the point? It would only hurt his feelings.

Just then I felt something tingly on my thigh and I was horrified to see a huge caterpillar crawling on it! I screamed and automatically flicked it off with the backs of my fingernails. But in doing so I must have moved on the branch, because I started to lose my balance.

"Steady there!" Tarzan's strong arm pulled me back into position.

I was breathing hard. If I had fallen, that would have been the end of me!

"Tarzan, let's go back down to the cabin."

"You're okay now. You're safe. It's nice here. Let's stay."

"But . . . but I was going to ask you to underline all the adjectives in the third paragraph of Article 1, to show that you understand what an adjective is. But we left the paper and pencil in the cabin. So you see, we *have* to go back."

"Just take a deep breath and you'll be fine. I promise I won't let anything happen to you."

"But—"

"I'll make you a deal. If you've told me everything there is to tell about adjectives, we'll go back to the cabin right now and I'll underline the words. But if there's more to tell, tell me here in the tree."

I could have told Tarzan then and there that I'd already told him everything about adjectives, and we could have gone back to the cabin. But something was gnawing at me. I felt the lesson wasn't really complete. And I couldn't be dishonest.

"Well—" I began.

"Aha!" he exclaimed. "I knew there was more."

"Okay, I *will* tell you a bit more. But what I have to tell you isn't really that big a deal."

"What is it?"

"Well, there are two things. First, I want to make sure that you understand that some adjectives don't actually *describe* nouns. I mean, they don't tell you what the noun looks like. Sometimes, instead, they limit or identify nouns."

"What do you mean?"

"I mean that usually you think of words like *tall* and *beautiful* as adjectives because they tell you what something looks like. They describe nouns."

"You mean they *modify* nouns."

"Right. They modify nouns by describing them. But if you say 'we ate two coconuts,' the word *two* modifies coconuts by *limiting* it—that is, by telling how many. Do you see? The word *two* doesn't tell you what the coconuts look like, but it still modifies the noun *coconuts* by limiting it. It tells you *two* coconuts, not some other number of coconuts."

"And that makes it an adjective?"

"Yes. And if I say 'we're sitting in this tree,' the word *this* modifies tree—not by describing it, but by *identifying* it; *this* tree, not some other tree."

"I think I see. It's a little tricky. I'll just have to remember that *modify*—as in *an adjective modifies a noun*—doesn't simply mean describe; it means describe, limit, or identify, right?"

"That's right. Now tell me the truth. Don't you think grammar is fun?"

"Um, I guess. Kind of."

"I'm glad you said that, because now I'll tell you one last thing about adjectives. You see, sometimes people compare things."

"What do you mean?"

24

"Well, if I say "Tarzan is taller than Jane,' I'm comparing our heights. And if I say 'Tarzan is the strongest man in the world,' I'm comparing your strength to that of every other man."

"But what does that have to do with adjectives?"

"Well, sometimes you have just a regular adjective, like *strong*. But when you make comparisons, adjectives have special forms."

"What are those called?"

"Well, when you compare only two things, you use what's called the *comparative* form. To change an adjective from its regular form to its comparative form, you usually just add the letters *er* to the word. For example, *tall* becomes *taller*; *strong* becomes *stronger*. Tarzan is *taller* than Jane. Tarzan is *stronger* than Jane. Do you see?"

"Yes. Jane is *smarter* than Tarzan."

"I wouldn't necessarily say —"

"No, that was an example. I used the comparative form of *smart* to make a new adjective: *smarter*."

"That's very good. I'm glad you're not trying to flatter me."

"I wouldn't do that," he said with a twinkle in his eye.

"Good. Okay. Now that we have that settled, let's talk about comparing *more* than two things. When you compare *three* or more things, you use what's called the *superlative* form. To change an adjective from its regular form to its superlative form, you usually just add the letters *est* to the word. For example, *fast* becomes *fastest*. Tarzan is the *fastest* runner in Africa. Do you get it?"

"Well, there are a lot of animals that can run faster—hey! I just used the *comparative* form of *fast!*—than I do, but I see what you mean. Now, let me see if I understand this. Are there two forms—comparative and superlative, or are there three forms—regular, comparative, and superlative?"

"Um—" That was actually a very tough question, and I wasn't entirely sure of the answer. "Um, I think that real grammarians like to talk about three degrees of comparison; for example, tall, taller, tallest."

"But if you just say *tall*, about a tree, for example, you're not really comparing anything. Or are you?"

"I guess you're kind of comparing that tree to other trees in general. So it's kind of comparative. But grammarians don't call the first form *regular*; for some reason they call it *positive*. So adjectives can have three degrees of comparison: *positive*, *comparative*, and *superlative*."

"And in every case you just add *er* for comparative and *est* for superlative? Like *tall, taller, tallest?*"

"Well, that's what makes it tricky. It doesn't work in every case. For most short words you can just add *er* or *est*: *high, higher, highest; warm, warmer, warmest.* But for longer words, you usually leave the adjective in its regular—I mean *positive*—form, but add the word *more* or *less* before it for comparative and the word *most* or *least* before it for superlative. For example: *beautiful, more beautiful, most beautiful; interesting, less interesting, least interesting.*"

"Well, if you're talking about yourself, I agree that you are the most beau—"

"I wasn't!"

"And if you're talking about grammar, I don't agree that that it's less interesting than something else. I'm starting to find it very interesting."

"Good, because I have to tell you one more thing about comparisons. With some adjectives, you can't add *er* or *est*, and you can't add the word *more, less, most,* or *least.*"

"Why not?"

"Well, some adjectives show comparison by what are called *irregular* forms. I mean, their changes in form don't seem to follow any rules."

"For example?"

"Well, the three forms of the word *good* are *good, better, best*—not *good, gooder, goodest,* and not *good, more good, most good.*"

"Well, how can I know which words are irregular like that?"

"That's hard to say. I think you learn it just from being exposed to the English language. From hearing it or reading it."

"Well, that doesn't help me much right now. Tell me another of those irregular forms."

"If I do, will you take me down from this tree? Will you take me back to the cabin? Will you underline the adjectives in the third paragraph of Article 1?"

"Yes, yes, and yes!"

"Okay. The three forms of the word *bad* are *bad, worse, worst.* Now let's get down from this tree and go back to the cabin before another bad caterpillar crawls on my leg!"

"You're right. What could be badder than that? I mean, what could be *worse* than that?"

"Very fun—" I suddenly felt Tarzan's arm around my waist and I was lifted off the branch. As he swung from vine to vine, the two of us gently floated downward until we were firmly on the ground.

"I know that you don't know your way back to the cabin from here," he said, "so I'll lead the way." He put his hand out to me, and I took it.

As we walked back to the cabin, out hands seemed to swing forward and backward in an exaggerated, playful motion, forming huge semicircles in the air. But neither of us mentioned anything about it.

In the cabin I let go of his hand and picked up the paper with Article 1. "Okay," I said, "now that you know all about adjectives, let's see if you can underline them in the third paragraph."

He looked at the paper and said, "But the third paragraph is so short!"

I looked at it. "You're right. The third and fourth paragraphs are both very short. Why don't you underline all the adjectives from the beginning of the third paragraph until the end of the article. Okay?"

"Okay. Let me see it."

I handed it back to him. We both sat in our accustomed chairs at the table. He studied the paper awhile, then took a pencil and underlined some of the words. He handed it back to me. It looked like this:

Watching the <u>large</u> ship sail away, my father and mother realized that they were now all <u>alone</u> at the edge of an <u>endless</u>, <u>unexplored</u> jungle filled with <u>wild</u> beasts.

"Oh, John," my mother cried, "the horror of it. What are we to do? What are we to do?"

"There is but <u>one</u> thing to do, Alice," my father answered calmly, "and that is work. We mustn't give ourselves time to think, for that would drive us <u>mad</u>. Our <u>ancient</u> ancestors faced the <u>same</u> problems we must face, possibly in <u>this</u> <u>very</u> jungle. That we are here today is proof of their <u>ultimate</u> victory. We can do what they did. And we can do it more easily, for we are armed with ages of <u>superior</u> knowledge and technology. What they accomplished, Alice, with <u>stone</u> instruments and weapons of bone, surely we can also accomplish."

Before I could tell him what a good job he'd done, Tarzan said, "Do you see that I underlined the word *one* in the phrase *one thing to do*? That's an adjective that limits rather than describes. And do you see that I underlined the word *this* in the phrase *this very jungle*? That's an adjective that identifies rather than describes."

"Very good! That's right! Now, what about the other adjectives you underlined?"

"Well, those describe things: *large* ship, *unexplored* jungle, and so on."

"That's very—"

"Hey! Wait a minute!" Tarzan almost shouted. He seemed upset.

"What's the matter?" I asked. I had no idea what was bothering him.

"Are you trying to trick me or something?"

"What do you mean? I'm not trying—"

"Don't you remember? The other day you told me that the word *this* was a kind of pronoun—a *demonstrative* pronoun. You said that it's used to stand for a particular thing rather than a particular person. As an example, you used the sentence 'This is fun.' I don't think it's very nice of you to try to—"

"I'm not trying to trick you. I swear."

"Then why did you tell me the word *this* is a pronoun and now you're telling me it's an adjective?"

My oh my. This Ape Man was about as smart, or smarter, than anyone I'd ever met. And what a memory he had! He seemed genuinely hurt, as if I'd tried to make fun of him by tricking him.

"Tarzan—sweetie—I'm not trying to trick you. Maybe I should have mentioned this to you earlier, but I guess I forgot. You see, sometimes a particular word can be more than one part of speech."

"It can?"

"Yes. It depends on how it's used. For example, take the word *stone*. In the last paragraph of Article 1, you underlined the word *stone* in the phrase *stone instruments*, because the word *stone* described the type of instruments—*stone* instruments, not metal instruments or some other kind of instruments. It was an adjective. Right?"

"Right," he answered uncertainly.

"But if I say that I tripped over a stone on the ground, then what part of speech is the word *stone*?"

"Well, in that case it's a noun."

"Why?"

"Because it names a thing—a stone."

"Good. So do you see? Depending on how you use a word, its function in a sentence can change. And its part of speech changes as well."

"But what about the word *this*? How can that be a pronoun *and* an adjective?"

"Well," I explained, "if you say 'Let's climb this tree,' you're modifying the word *tree* by identifying it. *This* tree, not some other tree. You're using the word *this* as an adjective—not an adjective that describe or limits, but an adjective that identifies. Do you get that?"

"Yes."

"But if you use the word *this* by itself—that is, without a noun following it—as in 'Let's climb this,' then you're using *this* to stand for some particular thing—some noun—that you want to climb, like a mountain, a ladder—"

"Or a tree!" Tarzan finished. "I see. The word *this* is being used to stand for a particular thing, so it's a pronoun—a demonstrative pronoun! It's not an adjective in that case!"

"That's right! Very good! So you see, I wasn't trying to trick you."

He looked at me and I stared into his eyes. "I would never do anything like that . . . to you," I said.

He gave me a big dopey grin, and I considered our lesson on adjectives finished.

Chapter 6: Tarzan and Jane Swim in a Pond

The next day the weather was splendid. The morning sun made the edges of all the leaves sparkle. I was getting used to the heat, and I was actually developing a tan!

I decided that the next part of speech I would teach Tarzan about was the *verb*. I was worried that it might prove a bit difficult because of the different tenses—you know, like past, present, and future: *I ate, I eat, I will eat*—and because of the different forms a verb takes depending on who's performing the action: *I am, you are, he is*. Stuff like that.

But then I realized that Tarzan and I couldn't discuss verbs immediately because we'd already used up the entire first article underlining nouns, pronouns, and adjectives. We'd have to write our second article first.

I was looking forward to working on this second article with Tarzan because I couldn't wait to hear what had happened to his parents, John and Alice, who were stranded in the jungle.

We met, as usual, at the table in his cabin. I said, "Tarzan, before we learn anything else about grammar, we have to write our second article. Are you ready?"

"Yes, but where should we work? It's too nice out to stay indoors."

"You're right. Where should we go? We've already gone to the river and to the top of a tree. I don't want to go back to the river because I'm afraid of crocodiles."

"Well, there are a lot of nice places we could go. There's a pretty pond not too far from here. We can sit by its edge and eat breakfast while we talk."

"That sounds perfect."

I gathered my notebook and pencils—I'd decided that from now on I'd keep the articles in a notebook instead of on loose pieces of paper—and walked with Tarzan through the cabin door and into the jungle. Suddenly he seized me in one arm and took to the trees. We swung from vine to vine for about three or four minutes, landing finally at the edge of a lovely pond.

"Wait here a second," Tarzan said.

I knew he'd gone to pick some fruit for our breakfast. While he was away I thought a little about verbs and a little about his parents being all alone and afraid in an unexplored jungle.

In a moment he was back with an armful of fruit. They were not fruits I was familiar with; they looked strange and exotic.

"What are those?" I asked.

"I don't know what they're called because I've never seen pictures of them in any of my father's books. But they're delicious. Here, try one."

"I was hungry. I took a somewhat square-shaped green one from him and bit into it. At first the flavor was strange, but after a few seconds it changed into something very pleasant. I took another bite. I liked it!"

Tarzan was eating a round red one. "Let me try that one," I said.

He handed it to me and I took a bite. This one was different from anything I'd ever tasted, but it was delicious. "Okay," I said, very happily, "why don't you tell me what happened to your parents in the jungle, and I'll just listen and munch on these fruits." Few things in life are better than hearing a good story and eating tasty food at the same time!

"Okay. But as soon as we finish the article, we'll take a swim in the pond. The water's nice and warm."

I walked to the edge of the pond and tested the temperature with my foot. He was right; it was warm, but not too warm. It was very inviting.

"Are there any crocodiles in this pond?" I asked. You can't be too careful.

"No."

"Is there anything bad in there?"

"Well, maybe a few snapping turtles."

"Really? How big are they."

"Oh, they're pretty big. And they snap pretty hard."

It occurred to me that he might be teasing me.

"Are there really snapping turtles in here? Tell me the truth."

"No. I was joking. It's perfectly safe to swim here. There are only a few small fish—like guppies.

"Okay," I said, leaning back against a rock. "Tell me all about your parents being stranded in the jungle."

While Tarzan spoke I listened and ate one piece of unusual fruit after another. When he finished, he ate while I wrote in my notebook. After a while we had finished our second article. I kept it kind of short on purpose because the readers of *American Monthly* don't have very long attention spans. That's what kind of magazine it is, if you want to know the truth. Anyway, the article looked like this:

31

Article 2: "Shelter"

My father's first thought was to arrange a sleeping shelter for the night—something that might serve to protect them from prowling beasts. He opened the box containing his rifles. He handed one to my mother and kept one for himself, so that they might both be armed against possible attack while at work. Then together they searched for a suitable spot for their first night's sleeping place.

A hundred yards from the shore was a little level spot, fairly free of vegetation. Here they decided to construct a little platform in the trees out of reach of the larger beasts. My father selected four trees that happened to form a rectangle about eight feet square. Cutting long branches from other trees, he soon built a framework around them about ten feet above the ground, securely fastening the ends of the branches to the trees by means of a rope that was among their supplies. Across this framework he placed other smaller branches quite close together. Finally, he paved this platform with the huge, thick leaves of the jungle.

Seven feet higher he constructed a similar, though lighter platform to serve as a roof, and from the sides of this he hung a sailing cloth for walls. When completed, he had a rather snug little nest, to which he carried their blankets and some of the lighter supplies.

All during the day excited birds and chattering monkeys watched these new arrivals and their wonderful nest-building operations with interest and fascination.

It was now late in the afternoon, and the rest of the daylight hours were devoted to the building of a crude ladder by means of which my mother could climb to their new home. Just before dusk my father finished the ladder and the two mounted to the comparative safety of their cozy little tree house.

"Well," I said, "your parents were certainly industrious—and clever! I can't wait to get to Article 3 to find out what happens to them. So! Are you ready to talk about another part of speech, the verb?"

Tarzan stared at the calm, sky-reflecting water of the pond awhile and then said, "Are verbs easy, like nouns and adjectives, or are they hard, like pronouns?"

"Well, understanding what a verb is is pretty easy. But using verbs properly can be pretty tricky."

"Why?"

"For one thing, verbs have to agree with—" But I was getting ahead of myself. "Wait a minute. Before we talk about what's tricky about verbs, let's just talk about what verbs are."

"Okay."

How could I explain this? Now I was staring at the water. In it I saw the reflection of a bird soaring overhead. I looked up to watch the actual bird. Tarzan's eyes followed mine.

"Birds fly," I said.

"I know. They fly."

"In that sentence, the word *fly* is a verb. You see, a verb is an action word—like *fly, eat, run,* and so on. It's a word that tells what someone is doing."

"But that's so easy!"

"I know. But using verbs can be tricky because verbs exist in various forms. As I started to say before, a verb has to agree with its subject—the person or thing doing the action—in *number* and *person* and *mood.*"

"Huh?"

"And verbs have to be in the correct *tense.*"

"Huh?"

"And verbs can be either *transitive* or *intransitive.*"

"Huh?"

"And verbs can be expressed in either the *active* or *passive* voice."

"Huh?"

"And sometimes verbs function as other parts of—"

"Wait a minute! I don't understand any of this! Slow down. Go back and start over."

I knew he was confused. But I wanted to get everything out on the table at once so he'd see what we were up against.

"Do you see what I mean when I say that verbs can be tricky?"

33

"Yes," he agreed. Then he said, "Okay, let's start over with the first thing you said, about agreement in *number*, *person*, and *mood*. What do you mean by *number*? Wait! Don't answer that yet. Let's talk in the water. Can you tread water?"

"Do you want to go in?" I asked.

"Yes. It'll be more fun than sitting here on the bank, roasting in the sun."

I was getting hot. "Are you sure there are no snapping turtles in there? Nothing bad?"

"Maybe a few leeches."

"You mean those things that attach to your leg and suck your blood!"

"Yes, those. But they probably won't bother you."

"Why not?"

"Because we won't stand on the bottom. We'll swim out to the deep part and tread water—or float on our backs."

"Okay. But if I get tired, we have to come back out. Okay?"

"Okay."

I was wearing a white sundress with a white bathing suit underneath. As I pulled the dress over my head, Tarzan discreetly kept his eyes fixed on the sky. Then the two of us ran into the water and started to swim toward the center of the pond. On the way, I swam underwater with my eyes open awhile to make sure there were no snapping turtles or leeches anywhere nearby. At least I didn't have to worry about crocodiles here. In a minute we were facing each other, treading water at the center of the pond. The water felt heavenly.

"How long can you tread water?" he asked.

"Did you ever hear of Deep Creek Lake?" I asked, my arms and legs gently fluttering to keep my head above water. "It's the largest lake in Maryland. When I was a kid, my family used to swim there, and I was able to tread water for a long time." My voice sounded slightly out of breath—as people's sometimes do when they're swimming or treading water. But I wasn't tired.

"I can tread water for a long time too," he said in a normal voice—not at all out of breath. "Now tell me more about verbs."

There was so much to tell that I knew I couldn't tell him everything without returning to shore. Well, I would tell him one thing, at least.

"Do you remember," I began, "when I said that a verb must agree with its subject in *number*?"

"Yes. What did you mean by that?"

34

"Well, I was talking about whether the subject of the sentence is singular or plural."

"Do you mean you were talking about the *number* of people that make up the subject?"

"Yes. If the subject is just one person, as in 'Tarzan swims,' the subject is singular. But if the subject is more than one person, as in 'Tarzan and Jane swim,' the subject is plural."

"I see. And the *number*—singular or plural—determines which form of the verb you use—*swim* or *swims*."

"Right!" I exclaimed, my arms and legs still fluttering to keep my body erect. "For singular you'd say, for example, 'Tarzan *swims*,' but for plural you'd say 'We *swim*.' So you see, depending on which—" All of a sudden my throat made a loud gasping sound as I involuntarily inhaled. It sounded like *grraaahh*.

"Are you okay? Are you getting tired?" he asked.

"Me? No . . . I mean yes. Let's sit on the shore awhile."

We swam back to shore, shook off the water that dripped from us, and sat down. Then I lay on my back, stared into the blue sky, and breathed deeply. After a few moments I sat back up.

"Okay!" I said. "Are you ready to continue?"

"Sure."

"Okay," I said, gazing at the water, "a verb also has to agree with its subject in *person*."

"What does that mean?"

"Well, do you remember when we first talked about writing these articles? I said that the articles would be more interesting if they were told from your point of view?"

"I remember," he said. "You said that instead of writing 'Tarzan was born in the jungle,' we would write 'I was born in the jungle.'"

"Right. If you say *I*, you're using *first person*."

"How many persons—I mean people—I mean persons—are there?"

"Well, there are three. There's *first person*, *second person*, and *third person*."

"Well, if I'm the first person, who's the second person and who's the third person?"

"Let's say that you're writing a story. If you're talking about yourself, by using pronouns like *I* and *me*, then *you're* the first person."

"Do you mean that whoever is referred to as *I* is the first person?"

"Yes. Now, the person you're talking to—the reader—is considered the second person."

"But if I'm writing a story, there's nobody else really there. I'm alone."

"I know, but you can pretend that the reader is there. You refer to the reader as *you*. For example, your story may begin "I was born in the jungle, even though you may find that hard to believe.""

"I think I get it. In that sentence, *I*—meaning Tarzan—is the first person, and *you*—meaning the reader—is the second person, right?"

"Right!"

"Then who's the third person. There isn't anyone else."

"But there is. Anyone you're talking *about*, other than yourself and the reader, is considered the third person. For example, if you say 'My father built a tree house,' *your father* is the third person."

"And if I say 'Jane visited Africa,' *Jane* is the third person."

"You've got it! Okay, that's pretty easy. But what you need to know is that these three *persons—first person, second person,* and *third person*—can be either singular or plural."

"How?"

"Well, sometimes when you talk about yourself, you talk about yourself as part of a group. For example, if you say 'We went swimming,' you're still talking about yourself, but as part of a group—so you're still using first person."

"Do you mean that *I* and *we* are both first person?"

"Yes. The difference is that *I* is considered *first person singular* and *we* is considered *first person plural.*"

"Oh."

Tarzan paused a moment while he absorbed this concept.

"What about second person?" he asked. "Does that come in singular and plural also?"

"It does. When you write or speak, you can be talking to just one person or to a whole group of people. But you use the same word—*you*—in both cases."

"You do?"

"Yes. The word *you* is used for second person singular *and* for second person plural."

"I think I see. So, like you said before, if I start a story by saying 'I was born in the jungle, even though *you* may find that hard to believe,' the word *you* could refer to just one reader or to a whole group of readers."

"Right. Good!" It crossed my mind that in the Southern United States, some people tend to say "you all" instead of "you" for second person plural, but I decided not to mention that because it wasn't

36

really standard English—it was just a regional quirk. He didn't need to about know that, did he? Besides, we weren't in the Southern U.S. We were in Africa.

"Okay," I went on, "now let's talk about third person."

"You mean about *third person singular* and *third person plural?*"

"Yes. You see, if you're talking about just one other person, you refer to him or her as *he* or *she.* That's *third person singular.*

"So," he said, "there are two forms of third person singular because of gender—*he* and *she.*"

"Right. But if you're talking about more than one person, you refer to them as *they.* That's third person plural."

"I see. And you use *they* for third person plural whether the people are male or female."

"Right. There's no difference."

"What if you're talking about a *thing*—like a tree or a knife—instead of a person. Does that count as *third person,* even though it's not really a person?"

"That's a good question. The answer is yes. If you're talking about a knife, for example, and you say 'it fell off the table,' the word *it* is considered third person."

"Third person singular, right?"

"Right."

"But something confuses me."

"What?"

"You keep mentioning *pronouns*—I, we, you, he, she, it—to demonstrate number and person. But do nouns have number and person too?"

"Well—"

"I mean, if I say 'Jane swims in the pond,' is *Jane* considered third person singular?"

"Absolutely. And if you say 'Jane and her sister swim in the pond,' then the subject of the sentence, *Jane and her sister,* is considered third person plural—because you're talking about more than one person."

"You have a sister?"

"No. I was just using that as an example. I'm an only child."

"Oh."

Tarzan was quiet for a while. Then he said, "What did you mean about a verb *agreeing* with its subject? Wait! Before you answer that, let's go back into the water. It's hot. Aren't you hot?"

I was. "Okay, but I can't tread water as long as you."

"Then we'll stand in the water up to our necks. That way we'll stay cool, but you won't have to exert yourself."

"But if we stand, the leeches might attach themselves to my legs. I've read that you can't feel them do that, and then they're very hard to get off. You have to burn them off or something."

"Then let's swim back out to the middle, and we'll float on our backs. That takes less effort than treading water."

"Okay," I said, somewhat doubtfully.

We swam to the center of the pond and started floating on our backs. He said something to me, but it was hard to understand. My nose and mouth were above water, but my ears were below.

"What?" I shouted.

He repeated it, but it still sounded like a faraway mumble.

"What?" I said again. I righted myself and began treading water. Before he could repeat what he'd said, I said, "Look, this isn't going to work. My ears are below water when I float. I can't hear anything you say."

"Wait here," he said.

He swam to shore and disappeared into the jungle. In a moment he reappeared pulling a huge log. He shoved it into the water and guided it to where I waited.

"Grab onto this," he said.

I put my hands on top of the log. It was like a life raft. I stayed afloat without effort. I kicked my legs a little anyway.

Tarzan faced me from the other side of the log, his hands next to mine. He kicked his legs a little, too, and said, "What I said was, What did you mean when you said that a subject and verb have to *agree* in number and person?"

"Oh, that. Well, for example, you would say I *swim* and you *swim*, but he *swims*. That shows that the form of the verb changes depending on the *person*. For first person and second person you use *swim*, but for third person you use *swims*. Do you see? Also, you would say he *swims*, but they *swim*. That shows that the form of the verb changes depending on *number*. For singular you say *swims*, as in *he swims*, but for plural you say *swim*, as in *they swim*."

"Well, how am I supposed to know which form of the verb to use? Is there a rule? Or am I supposed to remember, for every verb in the world, which form to use for each person and each number. That's impossible!"

"Isn't this log great?" I said. "It feels so good in the water. I could stay here all day."

"I know. But what about those verbs? It's too much to remember."

"Well, there are rules, but there are also exceptions. It's another one of those things that you just learn by ear from being exposed to the English language a lot. English-speaking children learn it automatically as they grow up. Some people, when they're in school, *conjugate* verbs."

"Conjugate?

"Yes. They take a particular verb and then they recite or write down the different forms of the verb, as determined by the number and person of the subject, in a fixed order. For example, for the verb *be* they would say or write: *I am, you are, he is, we are, you are, they are.*"

"I see. So the typical order, when you conjugate a verb, is *first person singular, second person singular, third person singular,* then *first person plural, second person plural, third person plural. I, you, he, we, you, they.* Is that right."

"Right. But for *he* you could also say *she* or *it,* because those are also third person singular. Why don't you try conjugating the verb *swim.*"

"Okay. *I swim, you swim, he—or she or it—swims, we swim, you swim, they swim.*"

"Good!"

"But that's an easy one because I love to swim and I talk about it a lot. But how do I learn how to make all the other verbs agree with their subjects in number and person?"

"Well, most verbs are not really difficult. Did you see how with the verb *swim* you used the same form of the verb for all instances except for third person singular? And there you simply added an *s. Swim* became *swims. He swims.* A lot of verbs work like that. You see, the simplest, most basic form of a verb is called the *infinitive.* The infinitive of the verb *swim,* for example is simply *swim* or *to swim.* Then there are other, more complicated forms or versions of *swim,* such as *swims, swam, swimming,* and so on. But those aren't infinitives because they're not the simplest form of the verb."

I kept kicking and enjoying the water. I saw a cute little guppy swim by.

"Anyway," I continued, "for a lot of verbs, when you conjugate them, you just use the infinitive, except for the third person singular. And for that you just add an *s;* for example: *I eat, you eat, he eats, we eat, you eat, they eat. But* sometimes you have to add *es* instead of *s,* as when a verb ends in *sh* or *ch* or something like that; for example: *I wash, you wash, he washes, we wash, you wash, they wash.*"

Now I saw about ten guppies swim by.

"Do all verbs follow that rule?" Tarzan asked.

"No, but most do. Verbs that follow that rule are called *regular* verbs. The ones that don't follow it, such as the verb *to be*, are called *irregular* verbs. Those are the tricky ones."

"What are some of the irregular verbs, besides *to be?*"

"Well, there's the verb *to have*: I have, you have, he has, we have, you have, they have. You see, for *he* I used *has—he has*. I didn't say *he haves*. It doesn't follow the rule; it's an irregular verb."

"How am I supposed to know if a verb is regular or irregular?"

Now I saw about a hundred guppies swimming all around me. Their backs reflected the sunlight.

"You'll learn it naturally as you hear English spoken—by me or by the people in America when we put you on display in New York." I was starting to think that putting Tarzan on display in New York might not be such a good idea, after all.

"Or you can find a book that shows the conjugation of every verb and study it. But I imagine that would be very tedious and boring. Don't worry; you'll get the hang of it."

Suddenly I was surrounded by about a thousand guppies, and they were making me nervous.

"Tarzan, let's swim to shore. I don't like all these guppies."

"Are you sure they're guppies?"

Oh my! Could they be something else? Like baby piranhas maybe? I swam to shore faster than I had ever swum in my life. I sat on the shore panting as Tarzan emerged from the water. He wore a smile and carried a turtle in his hand.

"Is that a snapping turtle?" I shrieked.

"No, it's a regular turtle. Isn't it cute?"

It was kind of cute. Tarzan let me pet it. Then we walked to the water's edge together and let the little guy swim away.

I suddenly realized that I was hungry. "It must be time for lunch," I said. "Are you hungry?"

"Yes."

"Okay. That's enough grammar for now. When we pick up next time, we'll talk about how a subject and verb agree in *mood*. But right now I'm not in the *mood* to talk about it." I was pleased with myself for having made a joke—even though Tarzan didn't laugh. "Can you find us some more of those strange-looking fruits?"

Chapter 7: Tarzan and Jane Dive from a Tree

We had a delicious lunch of fruits, nuts, and berries by the side of the pond. The overhead sun beat down on us, but every so often a cloud drifted in front of it, providing some shade. I watched the water lap the shoreline.

Suddenly Tarzan stood up and said, "Do you see that tree over there?" He was pointing to one that stood very close to the water's edge, about a quarter of the way around, going counterclockwise.

"Yes . . ."

"Do you see how its branches overhang the water? We can dive from them. Do you know how to dive? Are you a good diver?"

"Well, I'm not really very—"

"That tree," he said, "is perfect for diving. It has three thick branches that overhang the water—one about three feet high, one about ten feet high, and one about twenty feet high."

I was afraid that he was going to ask me to dive off each branch in turn, going higher and higher. But I really wasn't comfortable diving from anything higher than three feet. That's the height I usually dove from back at Deep Creek Lake in Maryland.

"Come on," he said. "Let's dive."

"Shouldn't we digest our food first?"

"We already have. Besides, we'll only be diving, not swimming—except a few feet back to shore after each dive. We won't be exerting ourselves very much."

"But I have to tell you about *moods*. About how nouns and verbs should agree in mood."

"Then tell me on the branch, before we dive. Come on."

He took my hand and led me to the tree.

"Okay, come on up," he said. We climbed onto the lowest branch—the one three feet above the water. Then, seated on the branch, we slid ourselves away from the tree's trunk until we were far enough out that the water directly below us would be pretty deep—at least ten feet or more.

Tarzan stood up, as if ready to dive.

"Wait," I said. "The moods."

"Oh, right. The moods." He sat back down. "I know what moods are. You can be in a good mood or a bad mood. Or you can be in the mood to do something—like dive from a tree!"

"But in grammar, the word *mood* means something a little different."

41

"Oh. What does it mean?"

"Well, first you should know that verbs can be expressed in three different moods—the *indicative* mood, the *subjunctive* mood, and the *imperative* mood."

"That sounds pretty complicated. It sounds like a lot to understand."

"Then let's take them one at a time."

"Do you know what? Let's take these branches one at a time. Let's dive off this one, then the higher one, and then the highest one."

"I'm glad to see that you remember your comparative and superlative forms of adjectives, but I'm afraid to dive from any higher than three feet. I'm not ashamed to admit it."

"Okay. Then let's start with that first mood—what did you call it, indicative? After you teach me about that, we'll dive off this branch. And then we'll see."

"Okay," I agreed. "You see, the form a certain verb takes sometimes helps show the attitude of the speaker."

"The speaker's attitude about what?"

"Well, it could show his attitude about how certain or uncertain he is about what he's saying, or how likely or unlikely his statements are to be true, or how desirous he is about something that he wishes for or imagines, or how emphatic or hesitant he is about what he's saying. Things like that."

"How can verbs show that?"

"By agreeing with their subjects in mood, like I've been trying to tell you."

"But can you be more specific? I still don't understand."

"Okay, we said we'd start with what's called the *indicative* mood. That's the easiest one to understand, because there's really nothing special to understand. You see, the indicative mood is what you might call the *normal* or *ordinary* mood. It's the mood you use to make an ordinary statement or ask a question. It's the mood you generally use all the time, without even thinking about it. For example, if I say 'Tarzan and Jane like to swim,' I'm using the indicative mood. Just think of it as your normal, everyday mood."

"That's so easy!"

"I know. There's nothing to it."

"Okay, now let's dive." He stood up.

"Okay," I said, "I'll dive from here. But first, I have to ask you something. Remember those little fish that were swimming all around me this morning? Were those guppies?"

"Of course. Couldn't you tell?"

"But you said—"

"I was kidding!"

"And what about the turtles? They don't snap?"

"No. I already told you. I was kidding about that too."

"All right, then," I stood next to Tarzan and we both looked down at the water. Suddenly he sprang from the branch, making a high arc in the air. He entered the water with his arms extended and his feet straight, making very little splash. In a moment his head bobbed above the surface and he called to me, "Okay, your turn!"

I looked down at the rippling water below. Even though the branch was only three feet high, it seemed higher from this vantage point—but not too high for me to dive. I bent my knees and then sprang from the branch. As I hit the water I closed my eyes and mouth and gently exhaled through my nose. The water engulfed me; it was delicious. I surfaced about two feet from Tarzan and wiped the hair from my eyes.

We stared at each other, and without saying a word, we swam together to shore.

"That was fun," he said. "Now let's dive from the middle branch."

"No. First I have to teach you about another mood."

"Which one?"

"The subjunctive."

"Okay, but tell me about it on the middle branch."

I knew what he was trying to do. He thought that if he could get me up on that branch, he'd be able to convince me to dive from it. But I'm not so easily fooled.

"Let's talk about it down here, under the tree," I said. "It's nice and shady."

"No, let's talk about it up on the branch."

This reminded me of some of the stupid conversations I used to have with my high school boyfriends.

"If we go up to the middle branch, do you promise not to try to make me dive?"

"I promise."

I trusted him, so I agreed. We climbed to the middle branch and sat side by side, gazing down at the water. A few clouds were reflected on its shimmering surface. Then suddenly I heard what sounded like a low growl coming from some bushes nearby.

"What was that?" I whispered. Call me paranoid, but I was afraid it might be a hungry lion or tiger. Well, it could have been.

"That was nothing," he said. "The jungle is full of noises like that. Don't even think about it."

Well, even if it was something bad, I knew that Tarzan would protect me.

"Okay," I said, "let's talk about the subjunctive mood. Generally, you use the subjunctive mood for statements that are contrary to fact."

"What do you mean?"

"For example, statements that involve wishes or suppositions."

"I still don't understand."

"Well, let's start with wishes. If I say 'I wish I were a bird so I could fly,' I'm making a statement that's a wish; it's contrary to fact, because I'm not a bird."

"So what makes that the subjunctive mood? It sounds like an ordinary statement."

"I know that it *sounds* like an ordinary statement, but since it concerns something contrary to fact, it's considered not ordinary. That's why I used the verb *were* instead of *was*. I didn't say 'I wish I *was* a bird . . .,' I said 'I wish I *were* a bird . . .'"

"What's so special about that?"

"It's special because normally—in the indicative mood, that is—after the word *I* you use the word *was*—because *I* and *was* agree with each other in number and person."

"You mean first person singular, right?"

"Right. As an example, I could say 'Fifteen years ago *I was* a four-year-old child.' That would be an example of indicative mood, and the subject and verb—*I* and *was*—agree with each other in the normal way. But in the subjunctive mood, the correct verb for first person singular isn't *was*, it's *were*. For example, I could say 'I wish I *were* a four-year-old child again.'"

"You do?"

"No, that was just an example."

"Oh. I think I see. You didn't say 'I wish I *was* a four-year-old child again' because in the subjunctive mood *I* and *was* don't agree; *I* and *were* agree. Is that it?"

"Exactly."

"And what were you saying about suppositions?"

"Well, suppositions—you know, statements that are in the nature of 'what if' and indeed often begin with the word *if*—are also contrary to fact and are in the subjunctive mood."

"For example?"

"Well, I could say 'If I were as strong as you, I wouldn't be afraid of that growling sound we heard before.' But I'm not as strong as you, so I'm not stating a fact; I'm making a supposition. I'm basically saying 'Suppose I were as strong as you' or 'What if I were as strong as you.'"

"I see. And because a supposition—a 'what if'—is in the subjunctive mood, you use *were* instead of *was* after the word *I*."

"Very good!"

"But how am I supposed to know which alternate verbs to substitute for the normal ones in the subjunctive mood? You gave me only one example: *were* substituting for *was*."

"Well, it's probably enough to know about that one. That's the one that goes along with wishing and supposing."

"But what if it's not first person singular, like in your example?"

I thought about that for a moment. "Okay," I said, "let's conjugate the verb *was* in the indicative and subjunctive moods and see what happens. First the indicative: *I was, you were, he was, we were, you were, they were.* Hey! In the indicative mood we're already using *were* and not *was* for everything except first person singular—I— and third person singular—he."

"Hey, that's right!"

"Now," I said, "let's conjugate *was* in the subjunctive mood: *If I were, if you were, if he were, if we were, if you were, it they were.* Do you see how in the subjunctive mood you use *were* in every case?"

"Yes. So the only time there is a difference is when the subject is *I* or *he*. *I was*, but *if I were*. *He was*, but *if he were*. For the others, there's no difference: *you were, if you were; we were, if we were; they were, if they were*."

"Good. But, of course, what applies to *he* also applies to *she* and *it*, because they are also third person singular. *If she were, if it were.* Now, can you make up an example of a 'what if' sentence that demonstrates that a subject and verb agree in mood?"

Tarzan thought a moment and then said, "If I were you, I'd work up the courage to dive off this branch."

You know, it didn't surprise me at all. Somehow I knew he'd get around to asking me to dive off the branch. "You want me to dive off the branch?"

"No, that was just an example of subject-verb agreement in the subjunctive mood."

"Good."

"Still, you might want to think about it. You'll like it."

45

"Me? No, I couldn't; it's too high." From the ground this branch seemed to be about ten feet above the water. But from up here, it seemed higher. "Besides, there's something I forgot to tell you about the subjunctive mood."

"What?"

"Well, sometimes something isn't definitely contrary to fact; sometimes something *might* be contrary to fact."

"What do you mean?"

"Well, for example, let's say that you said something to me and after you said it, you thought it might have been a rude thing to say."

"I wouldn't say anything rude to you."

"I know, but let's pretend. Let's say that you weren't sure if what you'd said was rude or not. You might then say to me, 'If I was rude, I apologize.'"

"But shouldn't it be 'If I *were* rude, I apologize'? It's a supposition, isn't it?"

"Not really. You see, if something is *definitely* contrary to fact, you use the *subjunctive* mood. You say 'If I *were* . . .' But if something *may or may not be* contrary to fact, such as whether or not you were rude, you use the *indicative* mood. You say, 'If I *was* . . .,' as in 'If I was rude, I apologize.'"

"Oh. Well, if I *was* being pushy when I asked you to dive from this branch, I apologize. But watch me; I'm going to dive."

Tarzan sprang from the branch and executed a perfect swan dive, just like the ones done by divers in the Olympics.

"Are you sure you don't want to give it a try?" he shouted from the water below.

I looked down at the water, which seemed to be far, far away. I was definitely too high to dive.

"If you don't want to dive," he shouted, "why don't you jump?"

That hadn't occurred to me. I realized that I probably *could* jump if I closed my eyes on the way down. Before giving myself time to change my mind, I held my nose and stepped off the branch.

On the way down, I imagined what it would feel like to be underwater. Then, suddenly there I was. I swam up to find Tarzan treading water next to me. We stared into each other's eyes and then wordlessly swan to shore.

As we shook the water from our bodies, Tarzan said, "Are you thinking what I'm thinking?"

"I think so. We have one more mood to discuss, the imperative mood, and there's one more branch to dive from, the highest one.

46

So you're thinking that we'll discuss that mood on the top branch and then dive from it. Am I right?"

"How did you know?"

"I'm getting to know you pretty well."

"Well, how about it? Shall we?"

I looked up at the branch. From down here it didn't look so high. And I knew that if I wanted to, I could jump, not dive. I guess I wanted Tarzan to think I was brave, so I agreed. Okay, call me foolish.

Instead of climbing the tree as before, this time Tarzan took me in an arm and swung us up to the top branch by means of hanging vines. I'll never understand how he does that.

"Okay," I said, sitting next to him, "let's talk about the imperative mood." I looked out over the water. The branch seemed much higher from up here. "Basically, the imperative mood is used for sentences that express a command or request."

"What do you mean?"

"Well, if I say 'Sit down!' I'm making a command. And if I say 'Please take a seat,' I'm making a request."

"So what? You said that a subject and verb must agree in mood. That's why you're teaching me about moods. Those sentences don't even have a subject."

"They *seem* like they don't have a subject, but the subject of each of those sentences is actually the word *you*."

"But the word *you* isn't even in the sentences."

"I know, but the subject is *understood* to be *you*, without its being stated. If someone yelled at you 'Sit down!' you'd know they were talking about you; it would be understood. In other words, from a grammatical point of view, there's no difference between 'Sit down!' and 'You sit down.' In each the subject is *you*, either understood or actually stated, and each is in the imperative mood."

"I get that, but I don't understand what that has to do with subject-verb agreement. Even in the normal—I mean *indicative*—mood, you would say *you sit* and *you take*. Are you saying that there's no difference in verb forms between the indicative and imperative moods?"

"Well, sometimes there isn't a difference. But sometimes there is. The only rule you have to remember is that in the imperative mood, you always use the *infinitive*."

"The infinitive?"

"Yes. Do you remember I said that the infinitive is the simplest, most basic form of a verb? I think I said that for *swim*, the infinitive is *swim* or *to swim*, and that there are other forms that are less basic, like *swimming* and *swam.*"

"I remember. But which is the infinitive: *swim* or *to swim?*"

"Either is considered the infinitive."

"You mean it doesn't make any difference whether or not you put the word *to* in front of it."

"No. You can call either one the infinitive. You can say 'Let's conjugate the verb *swim*' or 'Let's conjugate the verb *to swim*.' Anyway, like I said, the thing to remember about the imperative mood is that you always use the infinitive form of the verb. For example, let's look at the verb *to be.* When you conjugate it you get: *I am, you are, he is, we are, you are, they are.* Right?"

"Okay."

"But we just conjugated it in the *indicative* mood. In the *imperative* mood, using the infinitive each time, we get: *I be, you be, he be, we be, you be, they be.*"

"But that sounds so wrong!"

"Usually it sounds wrong, but not when the sentence expresses a command or request."

"For example?"

"For example, you might to say to someone 'I insist that you be on time.' Do you see? You wouldn't say 'I insist that you are on time.'"

"I think I see. Normally, you would say *you are.* But when you make a command or request, you say *you be,* as in 'I insist that you be on time.'"

"Right. Why?"

"Because in the imperative mood, you have to use the infinitive form of the verb; in this case, *be.*"

"Good! And did you notice that in that sentence, the subject, *you,* is actually stated and not merely understood?"

"Now that you mention it, yes."

"Similarly, you would say 'I insist that *he be* on time,' 'I insist that *we be* on time,' and 'I insist that *they be* on time.' For each *person*—first person, second person, and third person—whether singular or plural, you use the infinitive in the imperative mood."

He stared at me and said, "You're a very good teacher."

I stared back and said, "And you're an excellent student."

Then we stared into each other's eyes for a few seconds with silly grins on our faces.

He looked down at the water and said, "Do you want to dive from here?"

"It's way too high. I can't. Really."

"Do you want to jump, then?"

"Well—"

"What if I hold your hand and we jump together?"

Just then I heard that low growl again. It seemed to come from a bush not far from the foot of the tree. I imagined myself climbing down and seeing, waiting below, a lion or tiger with its mouth wide open and saliva dripping from its tongue.

"Okay, let's jump," I said. I counted "one, two, three," and on *three* we leaped hand in hand into the air. On the way down, the blue sky and green trees, and the reflection of those in the water, became a blur. Then suddenly we were deep underwater. We let go of each other's hand and began to do somersaults down there. Don't ask me why. Then, when our breath was nearly gone, we shot to the surface.

We treaded water awhile, smiling at each other. Then remembering the growling sound, I pointed to where we'd been sitting earlier in the day and said, "Let's swim back over there."

"Okay."

In a few moments we were on dry land shaking the water from our bodies like a couple of dogs.

"That was a good lesson today," I said.

"Are we finished with verbs now?"

"No, there's still more I have to tell you."

"Oh."

"But let's pick it up tomorrow. Now let's think about what we'd like to have for dinner."

Chapter 8: Tarzan and Jane Visit a Waterfall

The next morning, Tarzan and I met at the table in the cabin.

By the way, if you're wondering about our living arrangements, I'll tell you. When I first arrived in Africa, Tarzan was gracious enough to give me his cabin to live in. He said that he would live outside. Whether that meant that he lived in a tree house somewhere or that he'd built himself some kind of hut made of branches, twigs, and leaves, I really don't know. But I thought it would be okay for him to live outside because he was used to being among the animals. I certainly couldn't have lived outside, could I?

Anyway, like I said, we were at the table again, and we'd just finished breakfast.

"So, let's continue our discussion of verbs," I offered.

"That sounds good, but do you mean right here?"

"Why, is there somewhere you'd like to go?"

"Well, yesterday we went to the pond. I thought that today we could go to the waterfall and tomorrow to the cave."

I thought to myself: What waterfall? What cave? But I figured there must be a waterfall and a cave nearby. Actually, I love waterfalls.

"How far is this waterfall?"

"Not too far."

"Okay," I said. "Let's go."

We stood up and walked out the door. He took my hand and we began to stroll through the jungle; I followed his lead. All the while I scanned the area for snakes, spiders, and other such gruesome creatures.

Suddenly he said, "I know how we can get there faster." He grabbed me in an arm and took to the trees, swinging from vine to vine. Then, when we approached a clearing, we descended to the ground and began walking again, hand in hand.

I realized that I'd left my notebook in the cabin. Well, that was okay. I'd have him underline the verbs in the first paragraph of Article 2 when we got back.

"The thing about verbs I want to talk about today is *tense*."

"What does that mean?"

"Well, do you remember mentioning that yesterday we went to the pond, today we're going to the waterfall, and tomorrow we'll go to the cave?"

"Yes," he said, his voice rising toward the end of the word.

"Well, yesterday is the past, today is the present, and tomorrow is the future."

"So?"

"So, people use various *forms* of verbs to indicate the time of an action—to show whether a particular action takes place in the past, present, or future. Those different forms are the different *tenses* of a verb."

"I'm not sure I understand."

"Well, let's take the verb *go*. The infinitive—the simplest form—is *go*, or *to go*, right?"

"Right," he agreed, again with a rising pitch.

"If you're talking about yesterday, or any time in the past, you say *I went*, as in 'Yesterday I went to the pond.' And if you're talking about today—the present—you say *I go* or *I am going*, as in 'Today I am going to the waterfall.' And if you're talking about tomorrow, or any time in the future, you say *I will go*, as in 'Tomorrow I will go to the cave.'"

"I think I would naturally say it like that, even if I didn't know about tenses."

"That's wonderful. But tenses can become complicated."

"Why?"

"Well, the three main tenses—the three *principal* tenses—are the *past* tense, the *present* tense, and the *future* tense. Those are the ones I just illustrated: *I went, I go, I will go*. But there are many other tenses besides those three."

"There are? But how can there be? The past, present, and future are the only points of time that exist."

I thought about how to explain the other tenses to him. We continued walking through the clearing toward the waterfall, still holding hands.

"How much farther to the waterfall?" I asked.

"Not too much farther. Soon we'll see a great mist in the air."

"A mist caused by the waterfall?"

"Yes. A big white mist—a spray."

"How big is this waterfall?"

"It's huge—about a thousand feet high."

Wow, I thought. That's much higher than Niagara Falls in American. I couldn't wait to see it.

Then Tarzan unexpectedly said to me, "Do you know what a Venus flytrap is?"

"Do you mean one of those plants that captures a fly in its leaves and then digests it?"

"Right. But did you know that in Africa we have other, bigger, meat-eating plants?"

Was he kidding? "You're kidding, right?"

"No, really. There are certain meat-eating plant that actually live underground. Their tops sit about an inch below the surface."

"How can that be? Don't they need sunlight to survive?"

"I don't know. Maybe they're close enough to the surface that they do get a little light. But they mainly survive on meat."

"Meat? Where would they get meat?"

"Oh, a passing animal."

"You mean they actually reach up and grab it? And then pull it down, underground?"

"Yes, I've seen it. Once they have it underground, they digest it down there. That's how they stay alive."

"You mean they pull down a worm or a mouse? Something like that?"

"They could, but I've seen them pull down much larger animals too. Monkeys, lions—"

"Lions! How big are these plants?"

"There enormous. Their roots and branches spread all around under there."

I was starting to feel sick. "Why are you telling me about this now?"

"Well, these plants seem to like areas that are extremely humid. Maybe they compensate for their lack of sunlight by living near excessive moisture."

"Excessive moisture? Like a mist, or a spray?"

"Exactly."

"You mean they live near waterfalls!" I shrieked.

"That's what I'm trying to tell you. I'm just trying to say that as we approach the waterfall, be very careful where you step."

Now I was really sick.

"What do you mean be careful where I step! If these things are underground, I won't be able to see them!"

"But you can tell where they are. The ground is a little bumpy directly over them."

Thanks a lot, I thought. Couldn't the ground be bumpy from something else? Couldn't it be naturally bumpy? Could someone really tell where one of these gruesome meat-eaters waited for its next victim?

"Tarzan, let's go back. I don't have to see the waterfall."

"Look, I know how to avoid these things. Just stay right next to me and you'll be fine."

As much as I trusted him, I was still scared. "Tarzan, I—"

Suddenly he grabbed me and lifted me so that I was riding on his shoulders. My feet dangled near his waist. Then I saw a huge white mist in the air, straight ahead.

Tarzan began to run, swerving left and right, like a football player dodging opposing tacklers. Before I knew it we were standing on a rocky cliff. He put me down and said, "You don't have to worry. These are rocks. There are no plants here."

"Good!" I said. I was the one who was out of breath, even though it was he who did all the running.

Before us was an enormous chasm, the bottom of which was filled with violent whirlpools. Facing us, across the gulf, a thousand-foot vertical ribbon of water cascaded noisily, filling the air with white spray. Colorful birds dove and soared above. It was spectacular!

"Do you like it?" Tarzan asked.

"I love it!"

We stood awhile enjoying the view and the fresh smell. I made sure not to get too close to the edge of the cliff. If I fell into the churning waters below, I'd be finished.

Finally I said, "Let's sit right here on the rocks, okay?"

"Okay."

It was so misty that I thought it would be best if I removed my sundress and sat in my bathing suit, which, as usual, I wore underneath. I wasn't even embarrassed anymore; Tarzan had seen me in my swimsuit a number of times by now.

I removed the dress. The tingly, cool spray felt delicious on my skin. Tarzan was more accustomed to the jungle heat than I was, but I could tell he was enjoying it too.

At the same moment we each happened to turn our gaze from the waterfall and look at the other. We both started speaking at the same time. I don't know what he said, but I said, "Are you ready to continue our discussion of verb tenses?"

"That's what I was about to say!" he exclaimed.

"Good. Now, where were we?"

"You said that there are other tenses besides past, present, and future. Then I said that that can't be because those are the only points of time there are."

"Right. Now I remember. Okay. What makes verb tenses a bit complicated is that there are different forms of the past, present, and future. For example, there are what are called *progressive* forms, *intensive* forms, and *conditional* forms.

Tarzan sighed deeply but didn't say anything. He stared again at the rushing water before us.

"I know that sounds complicated, but it's really not. We'll take those forms one at a time, like we did before." Suddenly I remembered that the last time I wanted to teach him three things—the three moods of verbs—he wanted me to jump off higher and higher branches into a pond filled with leeches. I hoped he wouldn't try to pull a crazy stunt like that here. But what could he say? Before us was a chasm with deadly whirlpools at the bottom and behind us were those underground man-eating plants.

"Wouldn't you rather go swimming?" he said.

"You always want to go swimming."

"Don't you like to?"

"Yes, but how can we swim here? Are we supposed to make a thousand-foot dive off this cliff?"

"No. But do you see how the sides of this chasm are covered with plants and vines? And do you see how there are a number of rocky ledges on the way down?"

Against my better judgment I got up and walked closer to the edge of the cliff. I scanned the sides of the gorge. He was right. They were covered with plants and vines.

"Okay," I said, "I see the vines and the ledges, but that doesn't mean that we can get down to the water to swim. And even if we could, that water's too rough."

"First of all, we could get down there. I've done it before. I can swing on vines as easily as you can walk."

"But—"

"And about the water being rough: It's only rough at the surface. If you swim deep underwater, it becomes calm and peaceful."

"Deep underwater? But we couldn't stay there. We'd have to come up for air."

"Well, here's the best part. I know that you don't want to walk back the way we came because we'd have to pass those man-eating plants again. But if we swim deep enough underwater down there, we'll come to a narrow passageway that leads to a lake—a lake away from the man-eating plants. Once in the lake, we'll swim to shore and walk back to the cabin from there."

"A narrow passageway? Is it filled with air or water?"

"Water."

"Then how are we supposed to breathe?"

"I've done this once before so I know it's possible. What you have to do is take a very deep breath, then swim to the bottom of the chasm, through the passageway, into the lake, and then up to the surface. If we dive in from a ledge just above the whirlpools, it takes about ten seconds to swim down to the entrance to the passageway, thirty seconds to get through the passageway, and another ten seconds to get to the surface of the lake. All together, that's fifty seconds. It's possible."

All I had to do now was decide whether I'd rather be eaten by an underground plant or drowned in an underwater passageway. I should have listened to my mother when she told me not to major in journalism!

"Which side of the gulf is the lake on?" I said. "This side or the other side?"

"The other side."

Of course it was on the other side. Otherwise I would have seen it. "Then how are we supposed to get back?"

"If we walk along the edge of the chasm about a mile, we come to a fallen tree trunk that extends to the other side and serves as a bridge."

"You think I'm going to walk across a tree over a thousand-foot abyss? Are you crazy?"

"I've done it once before. It's a wide trunk. It's safe."

What have I gotten myself into? He was right about my not wanting to go anywhere near those man-eating plants. And the idea of an underwater passage seemed exciting. But could I hold my breath for fifty seconds? I thought back to my childhood, when I used to swim in Deep Creek Lake in Maryland. There was a floating dock about thirty yards from shore. It had a diving platform and a slide. One time I swam to it underwater. But did it take fifty seconds? Or was it less?

"Look," he said, "do you see that ledge down there?" He pointed to a sheet of rock about a quarter of the way down the side of the cliff, on the opposite side. "And do you see that series of vines hanging between here and there? I can swing us down there easily. If we sit there, we'll have a terrific view of the waterfall and you can tell me about those verb forms.

I may be crazy, but I was even more afraid of the man-eating plants. "Okay," I said, but hold me tight!"

He took me in one arm and then slid of the edge of the cliff, at the same time grabbing onto a vine. Then we were flying through the air, form vine to vine. At last we swung out in a huge arc, landing on the sheet of rock on the other side.

We were now actually *behind* the rushing waterfall. If I were to stand on the edge of the rock and put my hand out all the way, I could touch it. But I didn't. Suddenly I remembered that my dress was still up on the cliff. Well, I'd have to leave it there. But that was okay; I had others that I'd brought from America back at the cabin.

We enjoyed the invigorating sights and sounds all around us. Then we sat down with our backs against the edge of the cliff. The spray of the waterfall was wetter than ever.

"Okay," I said, "do you remember that I said there are different forms of the past, present, and future tenses? The first one I mentioned was the *progressive* form."

"What's that?"

"Well, the progressive form is the form you use to show that an action—or condition or situation—continues or is in progress. That's why it's called *progressive*—because it refers to an action that's in *progress*."

"What do you mean?"

"Well, I mean that the action goes on for a while instead of for only a moment. It continues."

"For example?"

"Well, let's take the present tense. I could say either 'I swim' or 'I am swimming.' The second one, 'I am swimming,' implies that the action is in progress; it's continuing; it's going on for a while. Do you see? So, you can call the first one, 'I swim,' the *present* tense and the second one, 'I am swimming,' the *present progressive* tense."

"Oh."

"And did you notice that—at least for the first person singular, like in the example I just gave—the present tense is the same as the infinitive, *swim*, but the present progressive tense isn't."

"Yes. The verb *am swimming* is not as basic as the infinitive."

"And we can talk about the progressive form of the past tense too. You can say either 'I swam' or 'I was swimming.' Do you see the difference?"

"I think so. 'I was swimming' implies that the activity continued for some time. If you say 'I swam,' it could've been for just a moment."

56

"Exactly! So 'I swam' is *past* tense, and 'I was swimming' is *past progressive* tense."

"Okay. But what about those other forms you mentioned?"

"Another form I mentioned is the *intensive* form."

"What's that?"

"Well, like its name implies, it's used to intensify something. To emphasize it."

"What do you mean?"

"Well, let's say that I said, 'Tarzan, did you throw out the garbage?' and you say, 'Yes,' and then I say, 'You *didn't* throw it away,' and you say 'I *did* throw it away.'"

"What garbage?"

"That was just an example. The point is, in order to emphasize the fact that you really threw away the garbage, you'd say 'I *did throw* it away' instead of simply 'I *threw* it away.' So, *I threw* is *past* tense, and *I did throw* is *past intensive* tense."

"Because I *intensified* what I was saying, right?"

"Very good! And you can have *present intensive* tense also."

"You mean like *I do swim*, right?"

"Right!"

"And what's the other form you mentioned?"

"It was the *conditional* form."

"What's that?"

"That's the form you use to indicate that some future event may or may not occur, depending on some condition. That's why it's called *conditional*, because it depends on some condition. Basically, you form the conditional tense by adding the word *would* before some other verb."

"I don't understand."

"Well, let's say that you say 'I would swim if I had the time.' You see, depending on whether or not you have the time, you may or may not swim. There's a condition—do you have the time, that is."

"I always have time to swim."

"I know, but that was just an example. The point is, *would swim* is the conditional tense."

"Oh."

"Anyway, there are lots of tenses. For example, we've already talked about such tenses as *I swim, I am swimming, I do swim, I will swim, I swam, I was swimming,* and *I did swim.* But remember, those examples all start with *I*; they're all first person singular. For each tense you can also talk about second and third person, singular and plural. Thinking about it all makes my *head* swim."

"But I think I understand it."

"But there are even more tenses than the ones I just mentioned."

"Really? Like what?"

"Well, I could say *I have swum, I had swum, I shall have swum,* or *I would have swum.*"

"Yikes. What do you call those tenses?"

"Do you really expect me to remember that? I haven't thought about that since my high school English class."

"You don't remember?"

I sat and thought about the names of the less common verb tenses. I watched the waterfall splash before us and listened to its rushing sound. I felt its spray tickle my skin.

I explored the deepest recesses of my mind. Slowly but surely, little sparks of memory began to flicker, then flash.

"Okay, I might know what they're called. Are you sure you want to know this?"

"Sure. Don't you think grammar is fun?"

I didn't know whether or not to take that last comment seriously, so I ignored it. "Okay, here's what I remember from high school English class. For each of those examples I just gave, I'll say the example and then I'll name the tense. Okay. Ready? *I have swum*—present perfect; *I had swum*—past perfect; *I shall have swum*—future perfect; *I would have swum*—conditional perfect. Okay? Are you happy now?"

"Well—"

"And don't forget," I said, my voice rising, "those example are only for first person singular, indicative mood. If I wanted to talk about, let's say, the subjunctive mood, I could say something like *if I should swim,* and that's even another tense; that's the future tense in the subjunctive mood!"

"Okay, you don't have to get touchy about it."

"But you want to know every single thing!"

"But isn't that the point of the lessons?"

"No. I mean yes. I mean I don't know. Nobody except grammar teachers knows every single term and rule. You have to know enough to speak and write properly and clearly. That's the main thing."

"Oh."

We were both silent awhile.

Finally he said, "Can I ask you one more thing?"

"What?"

"The four verb forms you just named all had the word *perfect* in them—present *perfect*, past *perfect*, and so on. What does that mean? What's so perfect about them?"

Oh my. Here we go again. "Okay," I said, "there's nothing perfect about them. In grammar, the word *perfect* refers to tenses that indicate actions that have been completed prior to some fixed point in time. For example, present perfect—*I have swum.* The action has already been completed, see?"

"Okay," he said weakly.

I think at this point he was afraid to ask me anything else because he could tell I was becoming irritated at having to remember the names of all those tenses. We were quiet for a while. We stared at the underside of the waterfall.

Then I thought of something that I thought he should know.

"I'm sorry I was cranky before. I didn't mean it."

"That's okay. I forgive you." He paused and then added, "I'd forgive you anything."

I looked at him and he looked as if he really meant it.

"That's sweet," I said. "But listen, there's something else you need to know about these verb tenses. Well, it's not about tenses exactly, but it sort of is."

"What?"

"Well, every verb has what's called its *principle parts.*"

"What does that mean?"

"You see, every verb has three principle parts—the present tense, the past tense, and the past participle."

"The past participle? What's that?"

"Well, it's a little hard to explain. It's a form of a verb that's used after a word like *have* or *had* to form various tenses."

"I don't think I understand."

"Well, let's take the verb *to go.* Now, its principle parts are *go, went,* and *gone.* The first principle part, *go,* is the present tense, which is the same as the infinitive. You use that to make ordinary present-tense sentences, such as 'I like to *go* swimming.'"

"That part I understand."

"Good. Now, the second principle part, *went,* is the past tense. You use that to make ordinary past-tense sentences, such as 'Yesterday I *went* swimming.'"

"I understand that too."

"Good. Now here's the tricky part. Sometimes you use a verb that's actually made up of two or more separate words."

"You mean as in 'Tomorrow morning we *will eat* breakfast'?"

"Exactly. Now, sometimes the first word of a two-word construction is the word *have* or *had*."

"What do you mean?"

"Well, as in 'I could *have gone*,' or 'I should *have gone*,' or 'If I *had gone*.' Do you see? I'm using two words—*have* and *gone*, or *had* and *gone*. In a construction like that, after the word *have* or *had*, you have to use the third principle part—the past participle."

"Do you mean it would be wrong to say 'I could have *went*'?"

"That would be wrong, because *went* is the past tense, not the past participle."

"Oh."

Tarzan seemed to think about this for a while. I used that time to enjoy the view from the ledge we sat upon. The waterfall rushed before us. Down below, the waters swirled and churned.

Finally Tarzan said, "But how am I supposed to know what the past participle is for every verb? Is there some kind of rule?"

"I admit it's a little tricky. Sometimes students memorize the three principle parts of various verbs and then recite them in order—present tense, past tense, past participle—to demonstrate that they know them."

"You mean out loud?"

"Yes, sometimes. For example, they might say: *swim, swam, swum; eat, ate, eaten; freeze, froze, frozen.* Things like that."

"So what's the rule?"

"There's no one rule, but I'll try to explain it the best I can. Often, the past participle is exactly the same as the past tense, and each is formed simply by adding *ed* to the present tense; for example, *hunt, hunted, hunted*—today I *hunt*; yesterday I *hunted*; I should have *hunted*."

I waited for Tarzan to make some comment or ask a question, but he didn't. I guess he understood that.

"But sometimes the past tense and past participle, even though they might be the same as each other, are *not* formed by adding *ed* to the present tense; for example, *win, won, won*—today I *win*; yesterday I *won*; I could have *won*."

Again Tarzan didn't say anything.

"Are you getting this?" I asked.

"Yes, completely. I just like listening to you talk. I like the sound of your voice."

"Oh." I think he was infatuated with me. Well, I liked him too.

"Okay," I continued, "sometimes you form a past participle simply by adding the letter *n* to the present tense; for example, *know, knew, known*. And sometimes you form it by adding an *n* to the *past* tense; for example, *speak, spoke, spoken.*"

"That's nice," he said.

"Tarzan, are you understanding this, or are you just listening to the sound of my voice?"

"I'm understanding it!"

"Okay. Now, sometimes the past participle is the same as not the *past* tense, but the *present* tense; for example, *run, ran, run*—today I *run*, yesterday I *ran*, I should have *run.*"

I decided to quiz him to see if he was really getting this. "Would it be correct to say 'If I had ran, I would have got there in time'?"

"No. You should say 'If I had *run* . . .'"

"Why?"

"Because after the word *had* you have to use the past participle. And the past participle of *run* is *run—run, ran, run.*"

"Very good!" Wow! I guess he *was* understanding this. "Now, sometimes all three principle parts are exactly the same; for example, *cut, cut, cut*—I like to *cut* ropes; yesterday I *cut* the rope; I should have *cut* the rope."

Again he didn't say anything. He seemed to be staring at my hair!

"What?" I nearly shouted.

"You have pretty hair."

Okay, he was infatuated with me. What was I supposed to do?

"Thank you. Anyway, here's the thing about past participles. Sometimes people use bad grammar because they don't know what the past participle of a certain verb is. And other times, they know what the past participle is, but they don't know that they're supposed to use it. So they make grammatically incorrect statements like 'I should have went,' 'If I had ran,' or 'I could have froze to death.'"

"But I still don't see how I'm supposed to know what the past participle is for every single verb. Do people memorize them by studying the dictionary?"

"Well, it's another one of those things that children learn by ear naturally as they grow up. But if someone's not sure about a particular past participle, he usually *does* look it up in a dictionary."

"Oh. But there's one thing I'm not clear about. If there's a *past participle*, why isn't there a *present participle?*"

"There is. It's just that it's not considered one of the three principle parts of a verb."

"Oh. Well, what is a present participle?"

"It's the ing form of a verb. For example, for the verb swim, the present participle is swimming. And for hunt, it's hunting."

'I see. You just add ing."

"Right."

"But how do you use it?"

"Well, remember we talked about the difference between the present tense and the present progressive tense?"

"Yes, I remember. The present progressive tense is used to indicate an action in progress—one that continues."

"Right. Well, that's where you can use the present participle. If you say 'I am swimming' you're using the present participle—swimming—to form the present progressive tense."

"Oh. Is that the only time you use the present participle?"

"Why are you staring at my lips?"

"You have pretty lips. I like them."

Oh brother! He had it bad. "Okay, that's enough about my lips! First it was my hair, and now it's my lips. What's next, my eyes?"

"Now that you mention it."

"Please. Concentrate on what I'm saying. Now you've made me forget where we were. What did you ask me?"

"I asked if you use the present participle for anything besides the present progressive tense."

Was it my imagination, or was he staring at my nose now? It was hard to tell. Maybe he was just waiting for my answer.

"You do. I know this might sound crazy, but sometimes you use the present participle as a part of speech other than a verb."

"How can that be?"

"Well, you can use it as a noun if it names some particular action or activity. For example, if you say 'Swimming is fun,' the word swimming is the name of an activity; it's a noun."

"That's weird."

"It's not so strange if you think about it. Actually, we spoke about it before—when we first talked about nouns. Remember that a noun names something. Here, it's the activity of swimming. And another thing you might be interested in knowing is that there's a special name for a present particle that functions as a noun."

"What?"

"It's called a *gerund*. I know that's a strange word, but it comes from a Latin word that means 'that which is to be carried on.' So it makes sense, actually."

"So if I say 'I enjoy fishing, hunting, sleeping, eating, and swimming,' each of those *ing* words is a *gerund?*"

"That's right. And here's another thing. Sometimes a present participle can function as an *adjective.*"

"An adjective? How can that be?"

"Well, let's say that I was speaking about a *falling* leaf or a *sinking* ship. *Falling* and *sinking* are *ing* forms of verbs, but they're being used to describe—or modify—a noun. A leaf that's falling—a *falling* leaf. A ship that's sinking—a *sinking* ship."

"I see. Those words are describing what kind of leaf, or what kind of ship. They're actually adjectives there."

He was quiet for a moment, and then he said, "You know, grammar really *is* interesting. I don't think it's boring at all."

"That's wonderful, but I'm getting a little tired of sitting on this ledge. If we expect to get back to the cabin before dark, we've got to head down toward that underwater passageway you talked about."

"You're right. See that ledge on the other side about halfway down? Hold on to me, and I'll swing us down there."

Tarzan grabbed me in one arm, and I put my arms around his neck. With his other arm he grabbed a vine and swung us out into the air. Then he let go and we simply flew downward. Suddenly another vine appeared, which he latched onto. Then by a series of deft maneuvers involving numerous vines and flexible branches, he swung us several hundred feet down until we gently landed on the sheet of rock on the opposite side that he'd pointed out from above.

You might think that I would have been utterly terrified by such a wild flight, but I wasn't because I trusted Tarzan so completely.

Now we settled on the ledge and had a look around. The top of the cliff was about five hundred feet above us and the swirling waters about five hundred feet below us. The waterfall, across from us now, tumbled and rumbled, spraying its white mist.

Finally I said, "There's something else about verbs you should know."

"What's that?"

"Did you know that verbs can be either *transitive* or *intransitive?*"

"What does that mean?"

"Well, do you know what it means to say that a verb can have an *object?*"

"No," he said, with that rising pitch he sometimes uses.

"Well, sometimes when you do something, you do it *to* something. For example, if I say 'I kick the ball,' the thing I'm doing is kicking. But the thing I'm doing it *to* is the ball. In that sentence, the verb is *kick*, and the object of the verb is *ball*. Do you see? The object of a verb is the thing that the action is being *done* to."

"I see."

"Let's try another one. I'll give you a sentence and you tell me the verb and the object of the verb."

"Okay."

"Here's one: 'Tarzan grabbed the vine.'"

That's easy. The verb is *grabbed* and the object of the verb is *vine*."

"Good! Okay. Now, some verbs *don't* have objects."

"How can that be?"

"Because sometimes you just do something—some activity—but you don't do it *to* anything. For example, if I say 'Tarzan runs,' you're not doing something *to* something else; you're just doing something. In that sentence, the verb is *runs*, and it *doesn't* have an object."

"Oh."

"Well, anyway, now that you understand that, I can explain about transitive and intransitive verbs. It's very simple, actually. A *transitive* verb is a verb that has an object, and an *intransitive* verb is one that doesn't have an object."

Tarzan thought about this awhile without saying anything. Then he said, "I get it. So if I say 'Jane brings fruit to the table,' *brings* is transitive because it has an object—*fruit*. But if I say 'Jane sleeps,' *sleeps* is intransitive because there's no object."

"Right. The only tricky thing is that sometimes a verb can be either transitive *or* intransitive."

"How?"

"Well, it depends on how you use it. Let's take the verb *sing*. If I say 'Tarzan sings,' then *sings* is *intransitive* because there's no object. But if I say 'Tarzan sings a song,' then *sings* is *transitive* because it has an object—*song*."

"I see. But I don't sing very much."

"You don't? Can you sing at all?"

"There's only one song that I sing. But it's really more like a yodel. I call it my jungle yell."

"Can you sing it for me?"

"Okay. It goes like this." Then Tarzan let out a ten-second ear-shattering scream that went low, then high, then low, with several quick yodeling sounds along the way.

"That was really something," I said. "Do you do that for enjoyment, or for some other purpose?"

"Sometimes I do it after I kill an animal for food."

"You kill animals?"

"Well—"

"Never mind. I don't want to hear about that."

We sat in silence for a while. Finally Tarzan said, "You're a good teacher. And a pretty one."

"That's nice. Now listen, we have to keep moving. There's only one more thing I want to tell you about verbs. Let's go down to that ledge that's just above the surface of the water." I pointed it out way down on the opposite side of the gorge.

"Okay." He grabbed me and flung us out into the air by means of a vine. We dropped quite a way before he grabbed another vine. The waterfall fell between us and the ledge.

"We'll have to swing *through the waterfall* to get to that ledge. Are you ready?"

"Okay. Go!"

As we swung through, the water ferociously beat down on our heads, our shoulder, and every part of us. The noise was ear-splitting. Then we suddenly came through to the other side, gently landing on the rock.

"Whew! That was amazing!" I exclaimed.

Just below us the waterfall and the churning whirlpools met.

"Okay! Just one more thing about verbs!" I was shouting because the rushing water was so loud.

"What did you say!"

"I said—!"

"What!"

I knew it was no use. The water was so loud down here that we couldn't hear each other. I decided that we should swim through the underground passageway to the lake, and then continue our discussion there, where it was quiet. But how could I indicate this to Tarzan?

I pointed down to the water below us and hoped that he'd understand what I had in mind. But he'd have to dive in before me, because I didn't know how to find the underwater passageway.

65

He looked down at the swirling water and then at me. Then he looked at the water again and at me again. I knew he understood. With his index finger he made a signal that said *follow me.*

We stood side by side at the edge of the rock. We were only about three feet above the water. The waterfall fell like thunder about twenty feet out from us.

He gave me a look to see if I was ready and I nodded.

He dove into the water. I filled my lungs with as much air as I could and followed right behind him. The water was colder than I expected.

I kept my eyes open so that I could follow him to the passageway. The water was rough but, like he'd said, the deeper we dove the calmer it became. After about ten seconds of swimming straight down, we came to an opening in the wall and he pointed to it. Then he swam into it.

I didn't hesitate because I knew that my breath would last only so long. I followed him into the passageway. What I didn't expect was how dark it would be in there. I could barely see Tarzan swimming ahead of me. Then soon, as we got further from the opening it became very dark. Then it became pitch black and I couldn't see Tarzan at all.

A panicky feeling started to engulf me. It was like claustrophobia plus a fear of the dark plus a fear of drowning. It began to overwhelm me. I wanted to cry out, but I knew that if I opened my mouth it would fill with water.

Something in me—survival instinct, I guess—forced me to fight the panic. I tried to reason with myself. I said: You'll be in this passageway for only about thirty seconds. Just keep swimming straight ahead and you'll be okay. Don't think about drowning or being buried alive. But it was so hard not to. I tried to focus on the thirty seconds. I thought if I counted the seconds, it would take my mind off everything else. I thought it might work even better if I counted backwards.

I was doing an underwater breaststroke, and each time I pulled my arms back and kicked my legs I ticked off, in my mind, another second. *Thirty, twenty-nine, twenty-eight* . . . When I got down to twenty I banged into a wall and lost my concentration. A wave of sheer panic washed over me. Keep going, keep going, I said to myself. It must just be the side of the passageway that I hit. I focused my thoughts and then continued counting backwards and swimming. *Fifteen, fourteen, thirteen* . . . When I got down to *five*, I felt as if I had no breath left.

But that survival instinct must have reared its head again, because I somehow kept on. *Four, three, two . . .* Then I saw light ahead. Suddenly I was out of the tunnel and at the bottom of the lake. I stopped counting seconds.

My lungs were ready to burst, and I still needed to get to the surface. I looked up and it seemed very far away. I knew I couldn't make it, and panic overwhelmed me again. Then Tarzan grabbed me and we both shot to the surface like a rocket. My head broke water, my mouth flew open, and air noisily entered my throat and lungs.

I gasped for air over and over. Then I must have fainted, because I don't remember the next part. When I woke up, I was lying on the shore with Tarzan at my side.

"Are you okay?" he asked, with genuine concern.

"What happened?"

"You passed out. I pulled you to shore."

"How long was I out?"

"Just a few minutes. How do you feel?"

I asked myself how I felt, but I didn't even know. "Just let me lie here awhile."

I lay there on my back and stared up at some white cumulus clouds in the sky. I inhaled and exhaled deeply. I remember thinking to myself: You know, my boss should give me overtime pay for this.

Finally I sat up and said to Tarzan, "What time is it?"

"What do you mean?"

Oh, right. He didn't really know about keeping time and wearing watches the way civilized people do. "Never mind."

I could see by the sun that we still had a couple of hours before dark. Should we finish the lesson on verbs or head back to the cabin, I wondered.

"Isn't it nice here?" Tarzan suddenly said.

"Yes, it's nice. But I nearly drowned! That was terrible!"

"I thought you said you could hold your breath for fifty seconds."

"I thought I could. Maybe I could when I was a kid. I'm not used to it now. And I didn't know it would be so dark in that tunnel."

"Oh. Well, I'm sorry it was so bad for you. Would you have rather walked back through the man-eating plants?"

"Aaahhhh!" I screamed. I didn't know how much more of this I could take.

"Listen," I said, "I need to take my mind off what just happened, though I do admit that the waterfall was beautiful."

Tarzan smiled.

"I think if I tell you that one last thing about verbs," I said, "it'll settle me down. I think it will be good for me."

"Okay."

"Let me just catch my breath."

I took a few deep breaths and tried to relax. Then I spent about another five minutes lying on my back and staring at the clouds in the sky.

Finally I sat back up and looked out over the lake. It was fairly large and nearly round and surrounded by trees.

"Okay," I said, "the other thing about verbs is something called *voice*. A verb can be in either the *active* or *passive* voice."

"What does that mean?"

"You know what? I can't do this now. I'm still too upset about almost drowning. Let's go back and we'll continue tomorrow."

"Okay." He stood up and held out his hand. I took it and he pulled me to my feet.

"Which way?" I said.

"Come on, this way." He led the way and I followed, thoroughly exhausted.

"Tarzan, I don't think I can walk all the way back."

"Okay, come on." He took me in an arm and then he took to the trees. He swung like an ape across the treetops for about a mile, then descended to the ground.

"Here's that tree trunk I told you about. We have to cross over the gorge."

Oh my! I had completely forgotten about that stupid tree trunk. The thought of having to cross over a thousand-foot drop made me dizzy and my head began to swim. I saw stars against a black background and I began to wobble.

The next thing I knew, we were on the other side of the gulf—the side toward the cabin.

"What happened? How did we get here?" I said.

"You passed out again. I carried you over the bridge."

I was glad to be back on our side of the gulf, but I didn't like the whole idea of the bridge crossing.

"Did anything happen during the crossing? Did you almost slip or fall?"

"Um . . . we—"

"Why did you hesitate? Something *did* happen! What was it?"

"What difference does it make if we're safe now?"

"Tell me!"

68

"Well, it's just that a bird flew very close to us and I nearly lost my balance. But I didn't."

Oh great, I thought. After nearly being eaten by a man-eating plant and nearly drowning, I nearly fell a thousand feet to my death.

"Tarzan," I said, "starting tomorrow we're going to play it safe. I know you want to go to a cave somewhere, but I don't know if that's such a good idea." I was already imagining deadly bats—or worse. "Now please just take me back to the cabin."

Tarzan grabbed me and took to the trees again. As we flew across the treetops I kept thinking: Don't let there be anything else bad on the way back. Don't let it start to rain. Don't let there be a poisonous snake in the trees.

Thankfully, nothing bad happened. Finally Tarzan swung down to the ground and deposited me at my doorstep.

"Why don't you get a good night's sleep," he said. "I'll see you to-morrow morning."

I didn't even answer. I just nodded and trudged inside. I collapsed onto the bed and fell into a deep sleep.

Chapter 9: Tarzan and Jane Visit a Cave

When I awoke the next morning everything that had happened the day before came back to me. I took a deep breath and vowed to avoid any dangerous places or activities from now on.

When Tarzan arrived, we sat at the table and ate breakfast—bananas. He was being unusually quiet, but eventually he said, "Did you know that mosquitoes are especially attracted to people who've just eaten bananas?"

"Why do you always do that?"

"Do what?"

"Tell me something when it's already too late to do anything about it. Like yesterday, you asked me if I knew what a Venus flytrap was—after we were already among the underground meat-eating plants. And now you tell me about mosquitoes and bananas after we've already eaten bananas? Do you think it's funny?"

"No. I just thought about the mosquitoes now. If I'd thought about them before, I would have told you then."

"Well, next time tell me sooner."

He didn't answer.

"Why do they like people who've just eaten bananas?" I asked.

"I don't know. Maybe banana juice gets into the blood."

"Banana juice?"

"I mean digested banana."

"That's disgusting. I don't want a mosquito sucking my blood so that it can get a drink of banana juice!"

Then I remembered that mosquitoes can carry disease. "Can't mosquitoes carry disease? You're the animal expert. What diseases can they carry?"

"Well, malaria and yellow fever mainly. But first they have to bite you."

"Well, now that we've eaten bananas, they will!"

He looked at me with a sad expression, as if he'd done something wrong.

"What happens," I said, "if someone catches malaria or yellow fever? I mean, what are the symptoms?"

"Mainly fever and chills." He paused a moment and then said, "And in severe cases, coma and death."

I glanced at the window of the cabin, which had no screen. Tarzan followed my gaze and said, "But you don't get sick from the bite of a healthy mosquito. You get sick from the bite of an infected mosquito."

"Infected?"

"One that has bitten someone who is already sick."

"You mean the mosquito picks up the disease from the blood of an infected person and then transfers it to the blood of a healthy person?"

"Right. But I don't think there are any infected people around here."

"But we ate bananas!"

"So what? Even if you get bitten, you probably won't get malaria or yellow fever."

"But I don't want to get bitten at all! Where can we go were we won't get bitten?"

Before Tarzan could answer I guessed what he would say. I was right.

"Well, there's that cave I mentioned. I don't think there are any mosquitoes in the cave."

No, just bats, I thought.

"How far is this cave?" I said.

"Not far."

"That's what you always say. How far?"

"I don't know how to explain it. Not as far as the waterfall, in another direction."

I was so afraid of malaria and yellow fever that I agreed to go to the cave—even though I didn't expect that to be totally safe either.

We began to walk through the jungle toward the cave. I kept listening for the hum of a mosquito near my ear.

"Let's hurry," I said.

We began to run through the jungle. For some reason, Tarzan didn't grab me and take to the trees. I guess he didn't feel like it that day.

After about ten minutes we arrived at the side of a large, rocky hill.

"There's the entrance to the cave," he said, pointing to an opening near the center.

When we got up close I saw that the opening led to a tunnel that sloped downward.

"Okay, now listen," I said. "The only reason I'm going into this cave is to get away from the mosquitoes—because I ate bananas. And I don't expect there to be anything dangerous or scary in there. And

71

don't ask me to do any crazy daredevil stunts either. Do you understand?"

"Okay."

"And once we get in there, I'm going to explain about how verbs can be in either the active or passive voice. By then, hopefully, the banana juice won't be in our blood any longer, and we can go back to the cabin. When we get there, you're going to underline all the verbs in the first paragraph of Article 2. Understood?" I was trying to sound firm. I think I succeeded.

"Okay."

We walked through the opening and started our descent into the cave.

"I've been in a cave before," I said.

"Really?"

"Yes. When I was little, my parents took me to a big cave in Kentucky."

"Kentucky?"

"That's a state in America, not too far from my home state of Maryland. Anyway, I think it was called Mammoth Cave. It has five different levels, and the bottom level has an underground river running through it."

"This cave is like that. It has lots of chambers on many levels. And the bottom level not only has an underground river, it has an underground lake!"

"Wow! Africa is amazing! It's just amazing!"

In spite of my determination to avoid potentially dangerous situations, I said, "Let's go down to the bottom level. I want to see the river and lake."

Tarzan took my hand and we walked farther and farther into the cave. Soon it became very dark.

"I can't see," I said.

"I know. The light doesn't get this far down. Come with me."

He took my hand and led me through a passageway to our right into a large chamber or "room." Large, icicle-like formations hung from the ceiling and strangely twisted coils grew from the walls.

"I can see! How come?"

"Glowworms," he said.

"Glowworms? What are glowworms?"

"They're fireflies without wings. Thousands and thousands of them live on the ceiling of the cave. They light up the whole thing."

"They don't fly?"

"No. They don't have wings."

"Good." I didn't like the idea of swarming fireflies. "Are there any other bugs in here."

"Yes, but they won't bother you."

"What are they?"

"Mostly crickets, beetles, centipedes, and spiders."

Yuck, I thought. I felt my skin crawl. Well, I thought, trying to be brave, I won't bother them, and they probably won't bother me.

"What else lives in here?" I asked.

"Some birds, lizards, and rats."

"Rats? Where are they?"

"You won't see them. They stay in the dark."

"What about bats."

"Bats sleep all day. They only come out at night–to hunt."

"Where are they?"

"They're deep in the cave. You won't see them."

To tell the truth, I wasn't too happy about the spiders and lizards and rats and everything else, but at least he didn't mention mosquitoes. And I *did* want to see the underground lake.

"Follow me," he said, and I'll lead you to the bottom level.

We passed from one room to another, each time going lower and lower. Some rooms had thin layers of water over the walls. Others had strange-looking mushrooms growing from the floor and walls.

Suddenly Tarzan startled me by letting out his jungle yell. It echoed off the walls several times.

"I was testing the echo," he explained.

"Next time warn me. You scared me half to death," I said.

Finally we arrived at the bottommost level, which was one enormous chamber. From the high ceiling, a stream of water–a waterfall, really–dropped into a round natural pool about thirty feet in diameter. From this flowed an underground stream.

"Let's get right next to the pool," I said, "where it flows into the stream.

We walked to the edge of the pool and found two flat rocks to sit on.

"This is amazing!" I said. "I've never seen anything like it!"

"It's pretty," he said.

"Can we swim in that water?" I asked, pointing to the pool.

"I don't know. I guess. It might be cold."

I put my foot in to test the temperature. It was chilly. But the pool was drawing me like a magnet. I felt an irresistible urge to swim in it. I had on my bathing suit under my dress, as usual.

"Hold this," I said, as I removed my sundress and handed it to him. "I'm going in."

"Isn't it too cold?"

"I don't care." I slid my body along the flat rocks that formed the bottom of the pool until I was halfway in. "It's freezing!" I shrieked.

"Come out, then."

"No, I want to swim!" I slid in up to my neck. Then I began to actually swim—first the backstroke, then the sidestroke, and then the breaststroke. "I'm getting used to it!" I called from the middle of the pool. "Are you coming in?"

He tested the temperature with his foot. "No, it's too cold."

"Okay. Let me swim around a little more, then I'll come out and tell you about the active and passive voice."

I don't know how long I stayed in there. I had become accustomed to the water temperature, so it no longer felt cold. It felt nice. The bottom level of the cave was like a magical wonderland, and I didn't want to get out of the water.

Tarzan waited patiently by the side of the pool, holding my dress in his hands. Eventually I began to feel selfish for making him wait for me so long. I swam to the edge and got out.

Once out of the pool I began to freeze as the water on my body started to evaporate. My teeth began chattering.

"I'm freezing! Quick! Give me the dress."

I grabbed my white cotton sundress from him and vigorously rubbed it all over myself. But even after all the wetness disappeared, I felt frozen. My teeth continued to chatter.

"Tarzan, I'm freezing to death. What should I do?"

"Come here," he said, taking me in his arms. "If we huddle together, the warmth of my body will be transferred to yours."

There we were, hundreds of feet below the ground, hugging each other. But it wasn't a romantic embrace, you know. It was more like first aid.

Finally I warmed up and we separated. I couldn't put my dress back on because it was damp and it would have made me cold again.

"While we're waiting for my dress to dry," I said, "let's talk about active and passive voice."

"Okay."

We sat back down on the rocks.

"It's really pretty simple," I said. "Let me give you two sentences as examples. The first one is 'Tarzan gathers fruit.' The second one is 'The fruit is gathered by Tarzan.'"

"What's the difference? They both mean the same thing."

"Well, it all has to do with whether the subject of the sentence *performs* the action or *receives* the action."

"What do you mean?"

"Well, take the first sentence. What's the subject of that sentence?"

"It's *Tarzan. Tarzan* gathers fruit."

"Right. And in that sentence, Tarzan performs the action. He gathers fruit. A sentence in which the subject performs the action is said to be in the *active* voice."

"Oh."

"Now take the second sentence: 'The fruit is gathered by Tarzan.' What's the subject of that sentence?"

"It's *fruit.* The *fruit* is gathered by Tarzan."

"Right. And in that sentence, the fruit doesn't actually do anything; instead, the fruit has something happen to *it.* The fruit *receives* the action. A sentence in which the subject receives the action is said to be in the *passive* voice."

"Well, I understand that," he said, "but I don't see why it's important. First of all, you're talking about whether a *sentence* is in the active or passive voice. I thought you were going to tell me that *verbs*—not sentences—were in the active or passive voice."

I had to think about that for a second. "You're right," I said. "It's actually a *sentence* that's expressed in either the active or passive voice. But do you see that the verb form changes depending on the voice? In active voice we used *gathers* and in passive voice we used *is gathered.* So verbs are *affected* by voice."

"But what does that have to do with good grammar or bad grammar? Both of the sentences you used are grammatically correct, right?"

"That's true. It's just that some people think it's better to usually use the active voice. It just sounds more direct and clear. On the other hand, sometimes, for one reason or another, you really *need* to use the passive voice, and that's okay too."

"When would you need to use the passive voice?"

"Well, let's say that I said 'Abraham Lincoln was elected President of the United States in 1860.' I think most people would agree that

that sounds better than 'The people of the United States elected Abraham Lincoln President in 1860.'"

"Why?"

"It's a matter of emphasis. You want to put the emphasis on Lincoln, not on the people of the United States—because it's Lincoln that you're really talking about. So you make Lincoln the subject of the sentence and use passive voice."

"Oh." He thought about that awhile, then asked, "Does every sentence exist in both active and passive voice?"

"That's a very interesting question," I said. I thought about it for a while and then I realized something. I realized that only sentences with *transitive* verbs can be changed to passive voice.

"Do you remember when we spoke about transitive and intransitive verbs?"

"Yes. A transitive verbs has an object and an intransitive verb doesn't."

"Good. Now, a sentence in the active voice with a transitive verb can be switched to the passive voice. Let's try it. I'll give you a sentence in the active voice with a transitive verb, and you change it to the passive voice."

"Okay."

"Let's see . . . How about this one: 'Jane brought food to the table.'"

"That's easy. To make that passive voice you'd say 'The food was brought to the table by Jane.'"

"Very good. And do you see that in the active voice the verb is *brought,* but in the passive voice the verb is *was brought?* They're different."

"I see."

"Okay, now let's see what happens if we try to change a sentence in the active voice with an *intransitive* verb to passive voice. Try this one: 'Tarzan sleeps.'"

Tarzan thought for a while then said, "You can't switch that to passive voice. It doesn't work."

"Right, because there's no *object* to talk about. There's no *thing* to bring to the front of the sentence to become a new subject. In that other sentence, "Jane brought *food* to the table,' *food* is the object. By bringing the word *food* to the front of the sentence it becomes the subject: 'The *food* was brought to the table by Jane.' It works. Do you understand?"

"Yes. Any transitive verb has an object. And once you have an object, you can switch the sentence to passive voice by making that object the subject. Is that it?"

"Yes!"

"I like the idea," he said, "of you bringing food to the table and me sleeping. When can we do that?"

"Those were just examples."

"Oh."

"Do you think my dress is dry yet? I think we should go back." I felt my dress and it was mostly dry. I put it on.

We started to walk back the way we had come and I said, "It's amazing that this whole place is lit up by glowworms!"

"We're lucky they're here. Otherwise, we wouldn't be able to see."

We walked back through all the chambers we had passed through on our way down. Along the way it occurred to me that we might make a wrong turn and get lost, but that didn't happen. Tarzan was an excellent guide.

When we emerged from the cave the sun was starting to set.

"Let's hurry," I said. "I want to get back to the cabin before dark."

We walked in the twilight through the jungle hand in hand. Some fireflies—ones with wings—flickered here and there.

"Did I ever mention the fat rats?" he said.

"Fat rats? Is this going to be a joke? Are you telling me a joke?"

"No, I mean real rats. Rats that have eaten too much and have become fat."

"I've never heard of such a thing. What about them?"

"Well, rats eat just about anything—any kind of plant or animal. And they feed mostly at night."

"So?"

"Well, a lot of rats live right around here. Maybe because we're close to a cave; I don't know. Anyway, sometimes they like to eat leaves. So they climb these trees around here and eat. But there are so many leaves that they overeat. They don't seem to know when to stop. They get fat."

"So?"

"So, because they're fat, they're not very good at jumping from tree to tree."

"Why do they jump from tree to tree?"

"To get more leaves; to keep eating."

"So? Will you get to the point?"

"So, because they're fat, and therefore not very good jumpers, they often fall when they try to leap from one tree to another." Then Tarzan looked up.

"You mean they're above us right now!" I shrieked.

"They might be. Any moment, it might start raining rats."

"Do you swear that you're telling me the truth? This isn't a joke?"

"No, really."

Just then, a fat rat fell to the ground at my feet and scampered away. My blood stopped circulating.

"Let's get out of here!" I screamed. "Run!"

We both started running. Fat rats began dropping from the trees all around us. Luckily, none landed directly on us.

When we arrive at the door to the cabin, I was completely out of breath. "Why didn't you tell me about the rats before?" I cried, pounding Tarzan's chest with my fists. I was out of control.

"I forgot," he said. "I didn't think of it. I'm sorry."

He put his arms around me to comfort me and whispered, "You're safe now. Nothing's going to hurt you."

I wiped some tears from my eyes and whimpered, "Next time tell me ahead of time, so I'll know."

"I will."

"Promise?"

"I promise."

"Okay. Well, I'm going in now. Let me go."

He didn't let me go right away. He held me an extra second or two. Then he gave me a little hug and let me go.

"I'll see you tomorrow morning," I said. "Good night."

"Good night."

"Tomorrow morning you have to underline all the verbs in the first paragraph of Article 2. Don't forget."

"Okay."

I turned around and went into the cabin. From the window I watched him walk away.

Chapter 10: Tarzan and Jane Go to the Beach

The next morning, after a breakfast of berries—I'd decided not to eat any more bananas—I put my notebook on the table and turned to Article 2. However, something was on my mind.

"Tarzan, where did you get that outfit you wear?"

"You mean this loincloth?"

"Is that what you call it, a loincloth?"

"Yes. I made it."

"How?"

"From a piece of the sail from the ship my parents came here on."

"Well, you know the bathing suit I always wear? The white one? I don't like it."

"Why?"

"It so . . . I don't know . . . American. It's out of place. You look like you *belong* here. You look like a real man of the jungle. I want to look like a jungle girl."

"Why?"

"Because I love it here. I wish I never had to go back to America."

We were quiet awhile, thinking our private thoughts.

"Could you make me an outfit like yours? Shape it pretty much like my bathing suit, but make it out of the same material your loincloth is made of. Could you do that?"

"Sure. I can do it today. Right now."

"Well, let's have you underline those verbs first, and then you can make it."

"Okay."

"Here, take this." I gave him the notebook and pointed to the first paragraph of Article 2. "Underline all the verbs in this paragraph."

He looked at it and said, "This is so easy. I could underline all the verbs even if the only thing I knew was that a verb is an action word. But now I know all about person, number, and mood. And I know about tense. And I know about transitive and intransitive verbs. And I know about active and passive voice. And I know about a verb's principle parts. And I know about gerunds. Why did I have to learn all that?"

"Well, you're right. This exercise will be pretty easy for you. But you have to know all those things so that when you start writing articles yourself, you'll understand what I'm talking about when I explain your grammatical errors—if you make any, that is."

"Oh."

"All right. Now underline the verbs."

Tarzan drew some underlines and handed the notebook back to me. The first paragraph looked like this:

My father's first thought <u>was</u> to <u>arrange</u> a sleeping shelter for the night—something that <u>might serve</u> to <u>protect</u> them from prowling beasts. He <u>opened</u> the box <u>containing</u> his rifles. He <u>handed</u> one to my mother and <u>kept</u> one for himself, so that they <u>might</u> both <u>be armed</u> against possible attack while at work. Then together they <u>searched</u> for a suitable spot for their first night's sleeping place.

"Tarzan," I said, "if I were a real teacher and I had to give you a grade, I'd give you one hundred percent."

Tarzan beamed.

"Now, before we begin discussing the next part of speech, the adverb, will you make me that outfit we spoke about?"

"Sure."

I decided to wait outside while Tarzan worked on a female version of his outfit. I had no idea how he would make it. He didn't have a sewing machine or anything like that. I guess he must have had scissors and a needle and thread.

I paced back and forth in front of the cabin. I don't have to tell him anything about shoes, I thought, because I'd stopped wearing shoes soon after I arrived in Africa. He knew that. If you've never tried it, I can tell you that it's fun to run around in bare feet.

While I waited for Tarzan to finish my outfit, I thought about the whole idea of bringing him to New York and putting him on display. Why should I do that? He isn't a circus animal or a freak. It wouldn't be fair to him. It wouldn't be right. But my boss told me that's what we were going to do. Well, we'll see about that. Maybe I should quit my job and stay here in Africa with Tarzan. We have fun here, most of the time. Well, I guess I have a lot to think about.

Suddenly a felt something rub against by leg and I looked down. It was a cat! Not a cat like the ones people keep as pets in America, but a tiger cub. It must have been only about five or six weeks old. It was so *cute!* It had cute little ears and a cute little nose and soft fur. As I bent down to pet it, I spotted another one—a brother—peeking at me from behind a tree.

"Come here, little kitty," I called to it in a high voice.

The second cub came forward and rubbed against my other leg. This one was as cute as the other.

"Tarzan!" I yelled. "Come look at this!"

Tarzan came to the doorway with a piece of cloth in this hand. "What?"

"Look at these kittens. Aren't they the cutest?" The cubs nuzzled against me.

"Those are tigers."

"I know, but they're so cute. Can we keep them as pets?"

"Their mother might come around looking for them. I don't think you want to get into a fight with an angry tiger."

"But—"

"And what will you do when they grow up? They'll be dangerous."

"I know; you're right. But can we keep them as pets for just one day? Today? If their mother doesn't come?"

"Why don't you play with them while I finish making your outfit. But stay near the cabin and watch out for the mother."

"Okay."

For the next twenty minutes I played with the tiger cubs. I petted them, picked them up, kissed their fur, and tickled them. I even stroked their bellies. I think they liked it. Maybe they're orphans, I thought. Maybe no mother will come around. And maybe if we keep them, they won't be dangerous to us when they grow up, because they'll know us and love us. I'll have to speak to Tarzan again about keeping them.

"Here's your outfit," Tarzan said, walking out of the cabin.

I took the outfit and said, "I'll go in the cabin and put it on. You stay out here and play with the cubs."

Before he had a chance to answer, I disappeared into the cabin. I hoped that he'd fall in love with the kittens and not want to give them up.

The outfit fit me nicely. I thought to myself: Tarzan could have been a tailor! It felt good to wear it. I walked outside and said, "What do you think? Do I look like a jungle girl?"

Tarzan looked at me and his mouth started moving, as if to speak, but no words came out.

"Well," I said, "I feel like a jungle girl."

"I think you look wonderful," he finally managed.

"Why, thank you."

81

Do you know how sometimes when you get a new outfit it takes a while to get used to? Well, I felt used to my jungle outfit immediately. I felt that I was born to wear it.

"How do you like the kittens?" I asked.

"They're cute."

"Well?"

"But Jane, we can't keep them as pets. What do you want to do, lock them in the cabin? That wouldn't be fair to them."

"You're right; I wouldn't do that. But they could be our pets outside, and they could run around as they please."

"If they can run around as they please, then they're not really pets."

"You're right. But I'm going to *think* of them as pets anyway. And if I give them names, that makes them more like pets."

"What do you want to name them?"

"I don't know. One is yellowish and the other is orange-ish. We could call them Yellowy and Orangey."

"Those are terrible names."

"What do *you* think we should call them."

"I don't want to give them names. They're not pets."

"But if you *had* to give them names."

"What about Fang and Claw."

"No, that sounds too violent. I guess we'll have to think about it some more." Then I said to the cubs, "Okay Yellowy and Orangey, go play now. Daddy and I have to talk about adverbs."

"Daddy?" Tarzan said.

"Well, if their our pets, then I'm the mother and you're the father."

"But they're not our pets."

"They are."

Just then the cubs ran off. Soon they were out of sight. I yelled to them, "Don't go too far from home! Love you!"

Tarzan looked at me as if I were crazy.

"I love this outfit!" I said. "From now on, I'm not even going to wear my sundress. I'm just going to wear this outfit. It's all I need in this hot weather." I felt like a real jungle girl.

"Okay," I said, "today we have to talk about another part of speech, the adverb. Should we sit inside at the table?"

"No, let's go someplace outside."

"Where should we go?"

"Do you want to go to the ocean?" he offered.

The Atlantic Ocean was not far. Tarzan's parents had been put ashore on the west coast of Africa and traveled only a little bit inland before they'd built their cabin. Now I thought back to how much fun it had been to go to the Maryland beaches on the other side of the Atlantic—sun bathing, riding the waves, collecting seashells . . .

"That's a great idea," I said. I wondered if I should ask him if he had any towels to bring, but I knew he didn't. Well, the sun would dry us.

"Okay, let's go," he said. He took my hand and we started walking west.

Soon I heard the roar of waves and smelled the salty air. Then we were at the beach—a strip of white sand along the water. It was amazing to think that now I was gazing west across the same ocean that, from Maryland, I used to look east across. The *same ocean!*

I walked to the water and put my foot it. It was nice; not too cold. The waves were nice and big.

We had nothing to sit on, so we just sat on the sand—facing the water, of course.

"The sun feels good," I said. Isn't it funny that if you're near water that you can swim in, the hot sun feels good, but if you're not near water, then it feels bad? "Let's just enjoy the sun and sea awhile before we start talking about adverbs, okay?"

"Okay."

We lounged on the beach awhile, the way people do who go to the beach in America. But in America, there would have been a lot of other people on the sand; here, we had it all to ourselves.

"I've been here many times before," Tarzan said.

"You have?"

"Sure. I come here to swim. Sometimes I take a hollow reed and use it as a breathing tube. That way I can keep my face below water and still breathe while I explore the ocean floor."

"In America we call that *snorkeling.*"

"You do?"

"Yes. What do you look for on the ocean floor?"

"Different things to eat, like crabs and snails."

"You eat those?"

"Sure."

"Do you cook them first?"

"Sometimes. It depends on how hungry I am."

I didn't have an answer for that. I watched the waves roll in. Some gulls flew overhead.

"Also," he continued, "I look for octopuses on the ocean floor. They're good to eat too."

"That's disgusting!"

"No it isn't."

"Well, how big are these octopuses?"

"Only about as big as my fist."

"Oh. But aren't some of them much bigger? I've heard about octopuses that are bigger than men. I've heard about octopuses that can kill men."

"I've never seen anything like that, but if you say so . . ."

I started to wonder whether or not I should go in the water. "Is it safe to swim here?" I asked.

"I'd say so. There are only two things you might be concerned about."

"What?"

"Well, sharks, for one. Did you know that they have very sharp senses? They can detect a single drop of blood from a quarter of a mile away."

"I'll try not to cut my toe on anything before I go in, then. What's the other thing I should be concerned about, a barracuda?"

"No, they don't come around here. The other thing is the undertow."

"I know what that is. It's that reverse tide that pulls you out to sea. When I was a kid and we'd go to the beach, my mother would always say to me, 'Only go up to your ankles because there might be an undertow.' But then I wouldn't listen and I'd go all the way in. Then she'd yell to me, 'You're out too deep; come back!' Well, today I'm not taking any chances. Yesterday I came close enough to drowning for one lifetime. And I don't want to take any chances with sharks either, blood or no blood. I think I'll just stay put right here on the sand."

"But we'll get too hot here. We'll *have* to go in."

"Well, let's see how we feel after we get too hot."

He didn't answer, so I said, "Okay, let's talk about adverbs."

"Okay."

Even before I started talking, I was beginning to feel hot. The water looked good.

"Do you remember when we talked about adjectives?" I began. "I said that an adjective modifies a noun."

84

"I remember. An adjective usually describes something; for example, if I say 'We're sitting on a sandy beach,' the word *sandy* is an adjective describing—I mean modifying—the noun *beach.*"

"Good. That's right. Now, an adverb is a word that modifies a *verb.*"

"How does it do that?"

"Well, remember, a verb is an action word—like *walk, swim,* or *run.* An adverb often modifies a verb by describing in what manner or to what extent an action is performed."

"What do you mean?"

"Well, if I say 'Tarzan runs quickly,' I'm describing *how* you run. The word *quickly* is an adverb modifying the verb *runs.* Do you see?"

"I think so. And if I say 'Jane walks slowly,' then *slowly* is an adverb modifying the verb *walks,* right?"

"Right . . . Do you think I walk too slowly?"

"No, that was just an example. Well, maybe sometimes."

"Well, I can't help it. Your legs are longer than mine!"

"You walk fine. Now, your swimming, on the other hand—"

"What's wrong with my swimming?" I demanded.

"Take it easy. I was only teasing. You swim fine."

"But you're an *excellent* swimmer. You're amazing."

"I've had a lot of practice."

We were quiet for a while. I picked up a pebble and threw it toward the water. It fell on the sand a few feet before the waves.

"It seems," he said, "that adverbs are words that end in *ly.* Is that it?"

"Not exactly. A lot of adverbs *do* end in *ly.* Sometimes to make an adverb you can simply take an adjective and add *ly* to it. For example, *brave* becomes *bravely.*"

"As in 'He bravely fought the shark'?"

"Right. But sometimes when you make an adverb by adding *ly* to an adjective, you have to change the spelling of the adjective a little; for example, *true* becomes *truly* and *happy* becomes *happily.*" I spelled out the words letter by letter so that he could see how the *e* was dropped in *truly* and how *y* changed to *i* in *happily.*

"Aren't you getting hot?" he said. "We're baking here. The sun is so hot."

I was hot, but I didn't want to admit it. I was scared of sharks and of the undertow. I was scared of octopuses, too. "I'm okay," I lied. One thing I didn't worry about was getting a sunburn because I'd already developed a deep tan.

"Now, getting back to that *ly* business," I said, "you have to understand that not every word that ends in *ly* is an adverb."

"Why not?"

"Because some *adjectives* just happen to end in *ly*. I'll give you some examples. In each of these sentences, the *ly* word is an *adjective*. It's a *lovely* day. It's a *silly* idea. He's a *jolly* fellow. Do you see why?"

"Yes, because each of those words modifies a noun. *Lovely* describes *day*, *silly* describes *idea*, and *jolly* describes *fellow*. They're all adjectives."

"Right. Now, the other thing you have to understand is that not every adverb ends in *ly*."

"Why not?"

"Well, for one thing, an adverb can describe more than just *how* an action is performed. It can also describe *when* or *where* an action is performed."

"How does it do that?"

"Well, let's say that I say 'Yesterday it was raining rats.' The word *yesterday* is modifying the verb *was raining* by telling *when*. So *yesterday* is an adverb—an adverb that doesn't end in *ly*."

I gave Tarzan time to absorb this concept. Meanwhile, I became conscious of how hot I was. I didn't know how much longer I could stay out of the water. I forced myself to continue with the lesson.

"Also," I said, "an adverb can modify a verb by telling *where* an action is performed, or in what direction something happens. For example, if I say 'Look up,' the word *up* is an adverb that modifies the verb *look* by telling *where*. And *up* doesn't end in *ly*."

Tarzan looked up.

"No, you don't have to look up. That was just an example."

"I couldn't help it. When you said 'Look up,' I had to look up." He looked up again.

I looked up too. I couldn't help it.

"Stop looking up," I said. "You're making me crazy."

Tarzan turned his gaze from the sky to my face; then he smiled. Whether he smiled from embarrassment or in an attempt to be ingratiating, it was hard to tell.

I smiled back, not really knowing why.

"Are you ready to swim?" he said.

I was so hot that I couldn't resist. "What do you think the chances are that a shark or the undertow will get me?"

"I'd say less than one in a million."

As I contemplated this he said, "If you want you can go in just up to your ankles."

"Who are you, my mother?"

"Me?"

"Never mind." I don't think he got the joke—or rather, the sarcasm. "All right, come on. I can't stand this heat."

Hand in hand we ran to the water's edge. I let the waves pour over my feet. Tarzan let go of my hand and ran into the waves. When he was waist high, he dove in all the way. Then he stood up facing me, about chest deep, and wiped the hair from his eyes. "Come on in!" he yelled.

I walked slowly toward him. I couldn't help but think of that sentence he used before as an example: *Jane walks slowly.* I didn't want him to think I was a slow walker, so I started to run. Then I dove into the waves as he had done. When I surfaced, I was right next to him. I wiped the hair from my eyes.

"Watch this!" he cried. Suddenly he submerged. Where was he? The next thing I knew, he was on the other side of me!

"How did you get there?" I said.

"I swam underwater. Didn't you see me?"

"No." He must have swum around me.

"You try it," he said. "See if you can swim around me underwater."

"Okay." I took a deep breath and started swimming around him underwater. As I passed him, I felt him grab my waist and lift me out of the water. Then he threw me high in the air. I landed with a big splash. Then I stood up again. He was right next to me.

"What did you do that for?" I demanded.

"I don't know."

I couldn't be mad at him. At the beach in Maryland I'd seen young men and women engage in such activities. It was a kind of play. It meant that he liked me.

"Okay," I said, "I'm cool enough now. Let's go back out."

"A little longer," he said.

"What about the undertow?"

"There's no undertow here."

"Then what about the shark or an octopus?"

"There's nothing here. It's safe."

I guess I believed him. "Okay," I said. We stayed in the water another five minutes. We splashed, dove, and did somersaults. He threw me in the air a few more times.

87

Finally, we ran back to our spot on the sand and shook ourselves off.

"The sun feels good," I said, still standing.

"The water feels good, too," he answered.

"Okay, so where were we with adverbs?"

"You said that adverbs don't always end in *ly* and that sometimes they tell when or where, not just how."

"Right. You have a good memory."

He didn't answer. We sat back down on the sand.

"Okay," I said, "the next thing you should know about adverbs is that they can modify not only verbs, but also adjectives and other adverbs."

"How can they do that?"

"Well, let's look first at how an adverb can modify an adjective. Let's take the sentence 'Tarzan is smart.' In that sentence, the word *smart* is an adjective."

"I know why," he interrupted. "Because it modifies Tarzan; it describes him."

"Right. Now, let's say I change the sentence to 'Tarzan is *very* smart.'"

When I said that, he started to blush a little. Or maybe it was just that his face was getting a little sunburned. That was probably all.

"In that sentence," I continued, "the word *very* modifies the adjective *smart*; it tells *to what degree* Tarzan is smart. Because it's telling *to what degree*, the word *very* is an adverb—and adverb that modifies an *adjective*. Do you see?"

"Yes. And it's another adverb that doesn't end in *ly*."

"Right. Now, here are some other adverbs that modify adjectives by telling to what degree: *extremely, quite, too,* and *more,* as in *extremely quiet, quite remarkable, too tall,* and *more interesting.*

"I see. And of those adverbs, one of them ends in *ly* and the other three don't."

"That's right. But you don't have to be so obsessed with whether or not an adverb ends with *ly*. It's not so important, really."

"*Really* ends in *ly*."

"Okay, but stop. That's enough about *ly*. It's just that a lot of adverbs—but not all—end in *ly*. Let's just leave it at that, okay?" I was getting a little annoyed.

"Okay," he said sullenly.

"Now let's look at how an adverb can modify another *adverb*. Let's say that I say 'Tarzan is easily fooled.' In that sentence, the word *easily* is an adverb. It tells to what extent Tarzan is fooled."

"And *easily* ends—"

I cleared my throat to cut him off. I didn't want to hear any more about that *ly* business. "Now let's say I change the sentence to say 'Tarzan is *very* easily fooled.' In that sentence, the word *very* modifies the adverb *easily*. It tells *how* easily he is fooled—*very* easily. Do you understand?"

"I understand the part about an adverb modifying another adverb, but I don't know why you think I'm easily fooled. I'm not easily fooled."

"I know you're not." Right after that I thought to myself that at some point soon I would try to fool him into accepting the two tiger cubs as pets.

"Then why did you make up that example? Why didn't you make up a different example about me *not* being easily fooled?"

"Don't be so sensitive. I was only fooling around."

He sat glumly without saying anything.

"Okay," I said, "next time I'll try to make up a complimentary example. Okay?"

"Okay," he murmured. Then he said, "Let's go back in the water."

"Not yet. I have some more things to tell you about adverbs. Let me tell you one thing now, and then we'll go back in."

"Okay, but tell me fast because I'm getting hot."

"I can't tell you fast. I have to tell you so that you understand."

He didn't answer. We both stared at the water. The surface glistened where the sun hit it.

"Okay," I said, "I want to talk about an adverb's position in a sentence."

"Its position?"

"I mean where it's placed in a sentence. Is it placed at the beginning, at the end, in middle—"

"Does it make a difference?"

"Sometimes it makes a big difference. You see, usually an adverb is placed as close as possible to the word it modifies. So if I say 'Tarzan is very brave,' the adverb *very* is right next to the adjective *brave*, which it modifies."

"But that seems obvious," he said. "Where else could you put it? You couldn't say 'Very Tarzan is brave' or 'Tarzan is brave very.' It wouldn't make sense."

"You're right. But sometimes you *can* put an adverb in various places in a sentence without really changing the sentence's overall meaning. For example, I could say 'Quickly Tarzan ran into the water' or 'Tarzan quickly ran into the water' or 'Tarzan ran quickly into the water' or 'Tarzan ran into the water quickly.' In each example you ran into the water and you did so quickly. The overall meaning is the same in each case."

"Do you have to make up examples about me running into the water? It reminds me of how hot I am sitting here on the sand."

"I'm sorry. Let me tell you one more thing about an adverb's position in a sentence, and then we'll go back in for another swim. But not too deep, okay?"

"Okay."

I saw a rather large crab walking along the sand near the water. It looked a little scary, like a gigantic spider. But it wasn't too close to us, so I tried to ignore it. "What you have to understand," I said, "is that sometimes you have to put an adverb in a certain place in a sentence; otherwise, the meaning of the sentence will be different from what you intended."

"What do you mean?"

"For example, let's compare the sentences 'Tarzan only swims here' and 'Tarzan swims only here.' They're the same, except for the position of the adverb *only*. The first sentence, 'Tarzan only swims here,' means that you do nothing but *swim* here. You don't fish here, you don't dive here, you don't go boating here; you only *swim* here. But the second sentence, 'Tarzan swims only here,' means that you don't swim anywhere except *here*. You don't swim in the river or the lake; you swim only *here*. Do you see?"

"Yes. But there you go again making up examples of me swimming. Now let's go in the water, like you promised."

"Okay."

We walked to the water hand in hand. "Come this way," I said, slanting away from where I'd seen the crab.

"You know," Tarzan said, "that I swim other places besides here, right? I *do* swim in the river and in the lake."

"Of course I know that. I was just making up an example."

We splashed each other and generally frolicked in the water the way people who like each other often do.

"I just thought of something else that lives in these waters that we should watch out for," he said.

"What?"

"Electric eels."

I knew that eels were fish that looked like snakes. I'd heard of electric ones, but I didn't know how much voltage they carried. "Are they dangerous?"

"Yes. They carry a lot of electricity. If they touch you, they can give you a powerful shock."

I was immediately worried. "I've always heard that if you get an electric shock while you're in the water, you get electrocuted. Can they do that to you?"

"I don't know," he said, "but I know that the shock is so strong that it can paralyze your muscles. Then you can drown."

The word *drown* sparked a feeling of panic within me, no doubt because of yesterday's near-death experience in the underwater passageway. Looking around me, I saw all sorts of lines and shapes zigzagging in the water. They were only shades of light and dark caused by the sun and waves, but to my mind they were electric eels! I felt a scream welling up inside me.

The next thing I knew, I was lying on the beach next to Tarzan. "What happened?" I said.

"You fainted and I pulled you to shore. I never should have mentioned those electric eels. I didn't know that it would scare you so much."

"It's not your fault, I guess. I overreacted. Let me just lie here a minute."

I told myself that if I wanted to be a real jungle girl, I'd have to become a little braver. Well, that would come with time, I supposed.

Finally I sat back up and said, "Let's continue our discussion of adverbs. Did you know that sometimes a word can be either an adjective or an adverb, depending on how it's used?"

"No."

"Well, it can." I noticed that the crab I'd seen before was getting closer to us, but I was determined to act like a brave jungle girl. I ignored it. "For example, take the word *fast*. If I say 'a fast runner,' then *fast* is an *adjective* modifying the noun *runner*. But if I say 'he runs fast,' then *fast* is an *adverb* modifying the verb *runs*. Do you see that?"

"Yes."

"I'll give you one more example. Take the word *early*. If I say 'an early dawn,' then *early* is an adjective modifying *dawn*. But if I say 'he awoke early,' then *early* is an adverb modifying *awoke*."

The crab was getting even closer. Now a second crab appeared from nowhere.

"Let's take a walk along the beach," I suggested. I didn't want Tarzan to know that I was afraid of a crab.

We strolled southward, hand in hand. The water was to our right and the jungle to our left.

"Now I'm going to tell you something a little tricky about adverbs," I said.

"What?"

"Sometimes when you think that maybe you should use an adverb, you should really use an adjective."

"Really? When?"

"Well, some sentences contain a verb that doesn't really express an action; instead, the verb expresses a state of being."

"What do you mean?"

"Well, if I say 'Tarzan runs quickly,' the verb, *runs*, expresses an action—the action of running. But if I say 'Jane feels happy,' the verb *feels* doesn't express any particular action; instead, it expresses a state of being. In other words, with certain verbs, such as *feel, seem, look,* and *smell*, you don't actually *do* anything; you just *are* a certain way. You *feel good*, you *seem happy*, you *look good*, you *smell good*. With those state-of-being verbs, you don't use an adverb; that is, you don't say 'Jane feels *happily*.' Instead, you use an *adjective* to modify the *subject* of the sentence; that is, you say 'Jane feels *happy*.' Do you understand?"

"I guess so."

"The mistake a lot of people make—people who don't understand the state-of-being rule—is to use the adverb *badly* when they should really use the adjective *bad* in a sentence like 'I feel bad about teasing you sometimes.'"

"When did you tease me?"

"Like when I made up the sentence 'Tarzan is easily fooled.'"

"Oh . . . And I feel bad about scaring you by mentioning the electric eels."

"That's right! I mean, it's right that you said 'I feel *bad* about' and not 'I feel *badly* about'—because when you feel a certain way, you're not actually *doing* anything; you're not performing any action, I mean."

"I understand."

We continued walking southward along the beach. We passed two brightly colored parrots sitting in a tree to our left.

"Let's go back in the water," he said.

"Back where we were, or right here?"

"Here. There's no need to go back."

I scanned the water to our right. I didn't see any sharks, octopuses, or electric eels. It looked clean, clear, and inviting. "Okay," I said.

We ran to the water, dove in, and started to splash about.

"Did you see those parrots we passed?"

"Yes."

"Weren't they beautiful? Such bright colors! They would make nice pets. They could talk to us."

He didn't answer. I think he wanted to avoid any discussion of pets—because he wanted the tiger cubs to run free. I dropped the subject.

We stood waist-deep in the water, facing each other. "Another mistake people sometimes make with adverbs is that they use *unnecessary* adverbs."

"What do you mean?"

"Well, remember that I said that adverbs sometimes express where, or in what direction, something happens or takes place? For example, if you say 'Look down,' the word *down* is an adverb because it tells *where*."

Tarzan looked down.

I was about to tell him that he didn't actually have to look down, but I decided not to bother. Then I realized it was probably good that he looked down—in case a shark, octopus, or electric eel happened to swim between us.

"Anyway, some verbs have a direction built into them. For example, the verb *advance* means to move *forward*. So you could say 'He advanced two steps,' but it would be wrong to say 'He advanced *forward* two steps.' Do you see? You don't need the word *forward* because the direction is already built in to the word *advanced*."

I had a feeling that Tarzan might actually take two steps forward in the water, but he didn't.

"In the same way, you would say 'He dove into the water,' not 'He dove *down* into the water.' And you'd say 'He climbed the tree,' not 'He climbed *up* the tree.' In those sentences, *down* and *up* are unnecessary adverbs."

"Let's take two steps forward and dive into the water," he said.

I knew he was kidding. "And when we get out, let's climb a tree!" I said, adding to the joke, however meagerly.

We both laughed, and then he grabbed me by the waist and threw me in the air again. I landed with a splash and stood back up.

We watched the tide roll in and out. I became aware of how the water felt against my legs as it advanced and receded. Suddenly I wondered if the receding tide was an undertow. I knew I shouldn't get so worried over every little thing, but sometimes I couldn't help it.

"Let's go back to where we were before," I said.

"Why? What's the matter?"

"Nothing. I'd just like a change of scene. That's all."

"Okay. Come on."

We walked back onto the beach and turned northward.

"Are we almost finished with adverbs?" he asked.

"I have a few more things to tell you. Why?"

"I'm hungry."

"I don't think it's lunchtime yet. It's still early."

"But I'm hungry anyway."

I didn't know what to say. If he was hungry, he was hungry. To tell the truth, I was a little hungry too.

"Why don't we catch those crabs that were walking around where we were before," he said. "Those would make a nice lunch."

The thought was disgusting to me, even though back in Maryland I'd once eaten crab's legs. "Oh, I think I'd rather have fruit," I said.

"Okay, why don't you have fruit, and I'll have crabs."

"Well, why don't we finish talking about adverbs, and then we'll see."

We arrived back at our original spot. To my relief, the crabs were nowhere to be seen.

"The crabs seem to be gone," Tarzan said. "Maybe later I'll hunt for them."

Maybe later I'll go back to the cabin by myself, I thought.

"Okay," I said, "let's finish talking about adverbs. "Do you know what a *double negative* is?"

"A double negative? I don't even know what a single negative is."

"Well, in grammar, a negative is a word like *no, not, don't, didn't, can't, won't, neither,* or *nothing*—a word that expresses a denial or contradiction. A sentence like 'I don't want crabs for lunch' is considered a *negative* sentence."

"And what do you consider a sentence like 'I want crabs for lunch'?"

"That would be considered a *positive*—or *affirmative*—sentence. Anyway, sometimes people use two negatives in the same sentence."

"Is that wrong?"

"Well, sometimes it's wrong and sometimes it's not, depending on what they're trying to say."

"I don't understand."

"Well, the thing is, two negatives actually cancel each other out; in other words, two negatives make a *positive*."

"How?"

"Well, if I say, 'You can't just do nothing,' that means you *should* do *something*."

"And that's correct?"

"Yes. But if I say 'I don't want no crabs for lunch,' I'm using two negatives—*don't* and *no*."

"And that's wrong?"

"It's wrong because what I really mean is that I don't want crabs. But since I used a double negative, the sentence becomes a positive. But I didn't *mean* it as a positive, because I really *don't* want crabs."

"So what should you have said?"

"I should have said, 'I don't want *any* crabs.' That way, I'm using a single negative, *don't*, which expresses what I really mean."

"I get that, but what does that have to do with adverbs?"

"Well, there are certain adverbs that are considered negatives, and when you use them, you have to be careful about using double negatives."

"Which adverbs?"

"Well, words like *hardly, scarcely,* and *barely.*"

"Why are they negative?"

"Because of the idea they convey. For example, the word *hardly* means 'almost not at all'—'almost *not* at all.' Do you see? It conveys the idea of *not*; it's a negative."

"I guess I see that."

"So, the mistake some people make is using another negative along with a word like *hardly, scarcely,* or *barely.*"

"Like what?"

"Well, if I say, 'I can hardly remember what it's like to live in American,' that would be correct. That sentence has a single negative—*hardly*. But if I say 'I can't hardly remember what it's like to live in America,' that would be incorrect. That sentence has a double negative—*can't* and *hardly*."

"Okay, I get that. Now are you ready to have crabs for lunch."

95

"But I just told you that I don't want crabs for lunch."

"I thought that was just an example of a single negative."

"Well, it is, but I'm not having crabs."

"Well, I am."

Tarzan walked near the water's edge and began to search for crabs.

"Just a minute!" I yelled. I walked closer to where he was and said, "I'm not done telling you about adverbs yet. And besides, you have to underline all the adverbs in the next paragraph of Article 2. Come back to the cabin with me and I'll finish telling you about adverbs on the way. Then you'll do your underlining, and then we'll have lunch."

"Okay, but I'm bringing this crab with me." He had a squirming crab in his right hand.

As he approached me I said, "Keep that thing away from me." I stayed to his left so that I wouldn't have to see the crab." After we'd crossed the beach and entered the jungle, he said, "I guess I don't want crabs for lunch after all. It's too much trouble to break the shell." He dropped it to the ground and it immediately headed toward the water. I don't know if Tarzan had really changed his mind or if he was just being considerate of my feelings. We kept on walking.

"That's good," I said. "I'll make a fruit salad."

"Okay."

"All right. Just one more thing about adverbs. Do you remember what an infinitive is?"

"It's the most basic form of a verb, like *swim*."

"Right. But it can also include the word *to* before it—*to swim*."

"I remember."

"Anyway, some people think it's wrong to place an adverb in the middle of an infinitive. They call that *splitting* the infinitive. For example, if the infinitive is *to swim*, they think it's wrong to say something like *to quickly swim*. Instead, they would say *to swim quickly*."

"Why do they think it's wrong?"

"Well, I think it's because in Latin a word like *quickly*—or the Latin equivalent of *quickly*—always goes before or after an infinitive because in Latin an infinitive is always just one word, not two. So it's impossible to split it. Anyway, some people think that because in Latin you can't split an infinitive, you shouldn't be allowed to in English either."

"Do you think that?"

"I don't know. Sometimes you have to split an infinitive because if you don't, what you're trying to say doesn't sound right. But other times you can make perfect sense without splitting it, and in those cases you probably shouldn't."

"I don't understand."

"Well, let's take the verb *to think*. If I say 'I want you *to seriously think* about adopting Orangy and Yellowy as pets,' I'm splitting the infinitive *to think*. But I think that's okay because if I put the word *seriously* anywhere else in the sentence, it wouldn't sound right." I gave Tarzan time to think about what the sentence might sound like if *seriously* were placed elsewhere.

"But if I say 'I want to choose permanent names for them quickly,' I'm not splitting the infinitive *to choose*, and the sentence sounds good."

"So what's the rule?"

"Well, not everyone agrees on what the rule is. I guess that if you have to split an infinitive, that's okay. But if you can avoid splitting it, you probably should. Okay?"

"Okay, but their names aren't Orangy and Yellowy."

"What are they, then?"

"They don't have names because they're not pets."

I could see that I still had a lot of work to do to get Tarzan to accept those cute little tiger cubs as our pets.

We arrived back at the cabin.

"Where's that notebook?" I said, more to myself than to Tarzan. In a moment I found it and turned to Article 2. We sat at the table in our usual seats.

"Okay," I said, "take a look at the second paragraph of this article and see if you can underline all the adverbs."

Tarzan took the notebook, studied the paragraph awhile, and then began to draw underlines. He handed it back to me. It looked like this:

A hundred yards from the shore was a little level spot, <u>fairly</u> free of vegetation. Here they decided to construct a little platform in the trees <u>out</u> of reach of the larger beasts. My father selected four trees that happened to form a rectangle about eight feet square. Cutting long branches from other trees, he <u>soon</u> built a framework around them about ten feet above the ground, <u>securely</u> fastening the ends of the branches to the trees by means of a rope that was among their supplies. Across this framework he placed other smaller branches <u>quite</u> close together. <u>Finally</u>, he paved this platform with the huge, thick leaves of the jungle.

"Tarzan, that's excellent!" I said. "Why did you underline the word *fairly?*"

"Because it modifies the adjective *free*. It tells to what extent the spot was free of vegetation."

"Good. And why did you underline *out?*"

"Because it helps tell *where*—out of reach of the larger beasts."

"What about the word *soon?*"

"That tells *when* he built a framework—soon."

"Why did you underline *securely?*"

"It modifies the verb *fastening*; it tells *how* he fastened the ends of the branches to the trees."

"How about *quite?*"

"That modifies the adjective *close*. It tells *how* close, *to what extent* close."

"Good. And what about *finally?*"

"It modifies the verb *paved*."

"If that's so, then why aren't the words *finally* and *paved* next to each other. Why is *finally* at the beginning of the sentence?"

"I don't know."

"Well, an adverb is placed *first* in a sentence if it's meant to qualify the entire sentence rather than just a particular word. For example, if I say 'Fortunately, Tarzan and Jane rescued Orangy and Yellowy and gave them a good home,' the word *fortunately* qualifies the entire sentence. Do you see?"

"Yes. But we didn't rescue them."

When I didn't answer right away, Tarzan said, "In the paragraph, I underlined six adverbs. Three ended in *ly* and three didn't."

"So what?" I asked.

"I don't know. I was just saying—"

"It's not that important. I already told you: Not all adverbs end in *ly*. Okay?"

"Okay."

"All right," I said, "we've finished our discussion of adverbs, but there's something else I want to talk to you about."

"What?"

"Well, I know that you don't like the names Orangy and Yellowy, but I thought of better names."

He frowned. Finally he said, "Okay, what?"

"Oman and Yemen."

He didn't answer.

"Those are actually the names of countries, but I think they're good names for the cubs."

"Why?"

This was good. At least he was taking an interest. "Well," I said, "first of all, they start with the right letters. Orangy and Oman each start with the letter O. And Yellowy and Yemen each start with Y. So there's a connection with the old names, see? But also, those two countries are very close to Africa, and on a map, the two little countries look kind of like brothers."

"That doesn't make sense. How can countries look like brothers?"

"I'll show you." On the shelf I found one of Tarzan's father's books that contained a map. I opened to the proper page and pointed out the general area of northeast Africa, near Egypt. "Look," I said, do you see this land just east of Africa. It's called Arabia—some people call it the Arabian Peninsula. Now look at it carefully. The biggest country there is Saudi Arabia. But just below that, side by side, are two littler countries, Oman and Yemen. Do you see them?" I pointed to them.

He looked where I was pointing, but he didn't say anything.

"To me," I continued, "it looks like the big country, Saudi Arabia, is the daddy, and the two little countries below it, Oman and Yemen, are the children—the brothers."

Again he didn't answer.

"I think the names are perfect! If you don't mind, we'll call them that from now on. Oman is the orange one and Yemen is the yellow one."

"You can call them anything you like," he said, "because it doesn't matter what you call them. They're not our pets."

"Well, we'll see."

I left it at that, and so did he.

Chapter 11: Jane Rescues a Tiger Cub

After lunch I thought about the next part of speech I'd like to teach Tarzan about. I decided it would be the preposition. But after all that talk about adverbs, I didn't feel like starting just yet.

"Tarzan," I said, "going to the beach this morning was fun, wasn't it? In America, people go to the beach for fun, too."

"Really? What else do people in America do for fun?"

"Sometimes they go to the zoo."

"The zoo?"

"Yes. It's a place with lots of animals."

"Like Africa?"

"Not exactly. In Africa, the animals run free. In zoos in America, the animals are often kept in cages—so people can stare at them."

"That's not nice. That's cruel. Animals should be free, not locked up. Don't you agree?"

"Of course I do—" Hey, wait a minute. I think he was trying to trick me into saying that it wouldn't be right to keep Oman and Yemen as pets. I'd better be careful how I put this. "Of course I think animals should be free. And if you're referring to Oman and Yemen, they would be free. We wouldn't put them in cages. We'd just take care of them and make sure they were safe."

He didn't answer.

"Do you know what I'd like to do this afternoon?" I said. "I'd like to go to the zoo. Not really the zoo, but is there someplace where I can see lots of different kinds of animals—you know, all in the same place?"

"The only thing like that would be the watering hole."

"What's that?"

"It's a little pond where all different kinds of animals go to drink."

"That's exactly what I mean!" I exclaimed.

"But it's pretty far from here. And I can't take you there by swinging on vines because we'd have to pass over grasslands that don't have lots of trees."

"How could we get there, then?"

"The best way is to ride on Tantor's back."

"Who's Tantor?"

"He's an elephant. He's a friend of mine."

"You gave him a name? Like you'd give a name to a pet?"

Tarzan gave me an annoyed look and said, "I didn't name him. The ape family who raised me called him that."

"Oh." I didn't know if I wanted to take a long ride on an elephant's back. I'd heard that doing that can make you feel kind of seasick. "I don't know about this," I said. "I want to see the animals at the watering hole, but isn't there any other way to get there?"

"Come outside with me and we'll find Tantor and you can meet him. Then you can decide whether or not you want to ride on his back. You can try it out first and see how it feels."

"Okay." We left the cabin and began walking through the jungle. This time we didn't hold hands.

Suddenly a small orange animal raced across our path. It was Oman!

"It's Oman!" I said. "Where's Yemen?" I looked all around but didn't see Yemen anywhere. Tarzan looked around too.

"Come on," I said. "Let's follow Oman."

I took Tarzan by the hand and he reluctantly allowed me to lead him down the path Oman had taken. I spotted Oman about fifty yards ahead, at the base of a tree. He seemed restless, agitated.

"Come on!" I started to run, and Tarzan followed right behind.

In a moment we were at the base of the tree and I said, "Oman, what's the matter? What's wrong? Where's your brother?"

Oman ran around and around the tree. Then he looked at us. Then he ran around the tree again.

"He's trying to tell us something," I said. I looked up to examine the upper branches of the tree. Tarzan's eyes followed mine.

There he was. Yemen, looking like a frightened little kitten, sat quivering on a high branch.

"He's stuck up there," I said to Tarzan. "He can't get down." Then to little Oman: "Don't worry, little fellow; we'll get your brother down." Then I yelled up to Yemen, "Stay right there, Yemen! We're coming to get you!"

"Tarzan," I said, "can you climb up there and get him down?"

"The trunk of this tree is totally smooth. There's nothing to grab onto. I'll have to climb another tree and then swing over on a vine."

"Okay, but take me with you. As we swing past, I'll grab Yemen."

"That might not work. If you try to grab him, he might get scared and move away. He might even fall. Let me go alone."

"No, I need to be there for him. We have to try it."

"Okay, but be careful when you reach for him."

We found a nearby tree suitable for climbing and made our way to the top. Yemen sat across from us on a thin branch about forty feet away.

"Okay," Tarzan said. "Put your arms around my neck. I'm going to swing us over there. When we get near him, grab him by the scruff of his neck. Ready?"

"I'm ready. Go."

We swung out toward Yemen's tree. I kept my eye on him—the way I used to keep my eye on the ball when I played tennis in Maryland—so that I wouldn't miss. As we swung past, I reached out to grab him, but at the last second he back away. I ended up grabbing the branch.

What happened next is a little hard to explain. For some reason, I didn't let go of the branch right away. I seemed to pull it down with me as we continued swinging downward on the vine. Then suddenly I remembered that I was still holding it, and, without thinking, I let it go. But because the branch was rather thin and flexible, when I let it go it acted like a spring and shot back up. I know this sounds crazy, but when that happened I thought about Sir Isaac Newton and about how once in science class I learned about the laws of motion and about how for every action there is an equal and opposite reaction. Then, with a sense of panic, I realized that Yemen was on that branch and that the poor little guy would be flung into the sky like something shot from a slingshot.

I had to get back on the ground and position myself so that I could catch him when he fell.

"Tarzan! Drop to the ground! Fast!"

We dropped to the ground and I looked up just in time to see Yemen falling toward me. He seemed to be contorting his body this way and that to minimize the impact of the fall.

I kept my eye on him and positioned myself the way a center fielder catching a high fly ball would. As he hit my arms I lowered them a little to try to break his fall. In any case, he hit hard, with a loud whack.

"Yemen!" I said. "Are you okay?" I hugged him close to me." I didn't put him down, and he didn't try to squirm free.

"Do you think he's okay?" I asked Tarzan.

"Put him down and see how he walks."

I put him down. Yemen took a few hesitant step. He seemed to be limping.

"He's limping! He's limping!" I yelled. "Do you think he broke a leg?"

Tarzan felt Yemen's legs, one at a time. "They're not broken," he said. "They're just bruised. He'll be okay. He just needs some rest. He shouldn't be walking around."

"We have to take him back to the cabin," I said. "We have to make him a little bed."

I could see from Tarzan's expression that he'd resigned himself to the idea that we'd have to take care of Yemen. There was no other choice.

"Okay. We'll take Yemen, but only because he's injured. We're not taking him as a pet. But we're not taking Oman. He's healthy."

That was the first time that Tarzan had called them by their names! I think he was getting attached to them.

"But we can't separate two brothers. All they have is each other. They've been together since the day they were born. They play together. They love each other. It would be cruel to separate them. You don't really want to do that, do you?"

There was nothing to say to that. Tarzan saw that if we took Yemen, we'd have to take Oman too. "Okay," he said, "we'll take them both, but only for a few days until Yemen's legs are healed. Then we'll put them both back out."

I agreed, but I had a feeling that after a couple of days Tarzan would grow to love them and want to keep them.

We started back toward the cabin with Yemen still in my arms. "Come on, Oman," I called. "Come on, sweetie. We're going back to the cabin to take care of your brother."

Oman didn't move, so I said to Tarzan, "Pick up Oman and carry him back with us."

Tarzan didn't argue. He picked up the orange cub. The two of us, each with our colorful little bundle, walked back to the cabin.

Once there, I made a little cat bed out of a box and a blanket. I put Yemen into it. "Now you rest right there, sweetheart," I said. "Your brother will keep you company." Then to Oman: "Oman, stay with your brother. That's a good boy." Then to Tarzan: "What can we give them to eat?"

"How do you know they're hungry?"

"Tigers are always hungry."

"Okay, fine," he said. Then to Oman: "Oman, go out and catch a mouse and bring it back to your brother. Better yet, catch two mice—one for you and one for your brother."

103

Oman scampered outside. Whether it was to catch mice or to simply play, it was impossible to tell. I wondered whether they had a mother, and if so, where she was.

"You know," I said to Tarzan, "I think we've had enough excitement for one day. Let's not go to the watering hole. I want to just stay here and take care of Yemen. Tomorrow morning we'll start fresh with another part of speech, the preposition."

"Where?" he said, "At the watering hole?"

"I don't know. Maybe we'll just stay in tomorrow so that we can take care of Yemen."

He didn't answer.

Chapter 12: Tarzan and Jane Visit a Watering Hole

The next morning, Tarzan met me at the cabin earlier than usual. Maybe he was concerned about Yemen's health.

"How's Yemen?" he asked as he entered.

"Not too bad," I said. "He's not really limping anymore."

"He isn't?"

"No. Look." I pointed out the cubs to Tarzan. They were playing on the floor in a corner of the cabin. We stared at Yemen's legs to see if we could detect a limp. At first we couldn't tell whether he had no limp or a very slight limp. But when we compared his leg movements to those of Oman, we couldn't tell a difference.

"I think he's all better," Tarzan said.

"Yemmy, are you all better? Come to Mommy." I put my arms out toward Yemen.

"Yemmy?" Tarzan said. "I thought his name was Yemen."

"It's a nickname. It shows that I love him. Yemmy and Omy."

Tarzan frowned.

Yemmy didn't come to me, but he and Omy began playfully chasing each other around the cabin. Then they ran out the door.

"He's all better," Tarzan said. "Let them go. Let them play outside."

I ran to the door and called, "Yemmy, be careful! Your legs are still healing! Mommy loves you!"

I decided not to say anything else to Tarzan about whether or not Yemmy and Omy were our pets. In my mind they were. Probably in his mind they weren't. But what difference did it make? Either way, I'd given them names and I knew we'd always protect them.

But now that Yemmy and Omy had scampered off, we didn't need to stay indoors. We could have our lesson on prepositions anywhere.

"Do you remember yesterday when I said I wanted to go to the zoo—I mean the watering hole?" I said. "Well, now that Yemmy's better, we can go there. But I don't want to ride on an elephant's back. I'm afraid I'll get hot and sweaty and queasy. Isn't there any other way to get there?"

"Well, there's a river."

"Do you mean the one we went to before, where I was afraid of a crocodile?"

"No, a different one. A much bigger one."

I wondered if he could be referring to the Congo River—that enormous river that runs through central Africa. "Do you mean the Congo River?" I asked.

"I don't know what it's called. I just know that it's very big and that it leads to the watering hole."

"Well, you said that the watering hole is far away. We couldn't swim all that way. Is there a boat we could take?"

"A boat?"

"You know, like a rowboat or a canoe. Something like that."

"I don't know what those are, but there's a tree trunk that I once hollowed out with my knife. You can sit in it and float along the river in it."

"That's what I mean! That's a canoe! Can you steer it?"

"I think so. Once I found a wide, flat branch and cut off all the leaves. If I drag it through the water alongside the trunk—I mean canoe—I can pretty much control which way the thing goes."

"That's called a paddle! That's perfect!" I thought back to my childhood. I used to love to go canoeing with my parents at Deep Creek Lake. This was going to be exciting. "Where do you keep this canoe and paddle?"

"It's right by the edge of the river."

"How far?"

"Not too far. If we take to the trees, we can be there pretty soon."

"Okay, let's go."

We walked outside and into the jungle. The thought of canoeing down the Congo River—if that's what it was—made my heart beat fast.

"Why are you walking so fast?" Tarzan said.

"Am I? I didn't realize. I guess I can't wait to see the river."

"Well, then, come on." He grabbed me around the waist and took to the trees. By means of hanging vines we flew from treetop to treetop. Screeching little monkeys scurried out of our way as we passed them. Finally we dropped to the ground. Before us a wide river—one of the widest I've ever seen—rushed past.

"Come on," he said. "I'll show you the canoe."

He led me to the edge of the river. The canoe sat amid a group of bushes. The paddle sat inside the canoe.

Tarzan dragged the vessel to the water. I followed behind. He put the canoe partway into the water and told me to get in. I got in, and then he pushed the canoe all the way into the water and jumped in himself. He sat in front; I was in the back. There were no seats; we just sat on the bottom, which wasn't very deep. In fact, the bottom was only about six inches lower than the edges. He took the paddle and started to steer us out toward the center of the river. Then he steered the craft into the direction of the current, and we started to move at a moderate pace. A sudden breeze made my hair fly back. It felt good. Whether we were traveling north, south, east, or west, I had no idea. I'd lost my sense of direction. But I didn't care. This was fun!

Finally I remembered our true purpose and I said, "Tarzan, we have to talk about another part of speech, the preposition." I watched the scenery to the left and right pass by. It was all jungle greenery. Well, what else would it be?

"Okay," he said. He was always so agreeable!

"It feels weird talking to the back of your head, though."

"Then come around in front of me and sit backwards, facing me."

I thought it might feel uncomfortable to sit in a canoe backwards, but I decided to give it a try. "Okay, here I come," I said.

I carefully maneuvered around him and sat at the very front of the canoe, but facing backwards, toward him. It felt okay. Our toes were practically touching. Sometimes, if we repositioned ourselves, they did touch.

I thought about how to explain prepositions to Tarzan. I started by saying, "Tarzan, do you know what a *phrase* is?"

"No. What?"

"Well, it's a group of words that make sense together but that is less than a complete sentence."

"I don't understand."

"Well, for example, if I say *on the river*, the words *on the river* make sense together, but they're not a sentence. Do you know why they're not a sentence?"

"I think," he said, "it's because a sentence usually has a subject and a verb. But *on the river* doesn't have a subject or a verb. It's just a group of words that could be *part* of a sentence."

"That's right. And a *phrase* is just that—a group of words that make up a part of a sentence but that can't stand alone as a *complete* sentence."

Just for fun, I leaned over the side of the canoe and dragged my fingers through the water. It felt cool. Then I sat up straight again.

"Okay," I continued, "now, a *preposition* is a word that introduces a phrase and also shows a relationship between that phrase and something else in the sentence."

"What do you mean?"

"For example, let's take the phrase *on the river*. The word *on* is a preposition introducing the phrase *on the river*. Now let's make up a sentence using that phrase. I know: *The canoe floats on the river*. In that sentence, the phrase *on the river* explains *where* the canoe floats."

"But if it tells where, then the phrase must be an *adverb*. You told me that adverbs tell *where*."

Tarzan had such a good memory! And he was so smart. This was a tricky area, but I thought he could handle it. "Tarzan, you're so smart! You're right; that phrase is like an adverb."

Tarzan smiled but didn't say anything.

"Since it's a phrase that acts as an adverb, you can call it an *adverbial phrase*. But since it starts with a preposition, in this case the word *on*, you can also call it a *prepositional phrase*."

"You can call it either one?"

"Yes. But since we're talking about prepositions, let's call it a prepositional phrase, okay."

"Okay."

"Now, one thing you have understand about a prepositional phrase—besides that it starts with a preposition—is that it always contains an *object*."

"What do you mean?"

"Well, in the phrase *on the river*, the preposition is the word *on*, and the *object of the preposition* is the word *river*."

"Why?"

"Because the word *river* tells on *what*. On the *river*. Do you see?"

"I'm not sure."

"Well, sometimes prepositional phrases tell where, as in *on the river, under the canoe, above the clouds*, and so on. In each of those phrases, you could say only the preposition and then mentally ask the question *what*? You can say: on *what*? under *what*? above *what*? And the answer, each time, is the *object* of the preposition. On the *river*. Under the *canoe*. Above the *clouds*."

"I think I see. So in the phrase *above the clouds, above* is the preposition and *clouds* is the object of the preposition."

"Exactly."

Now I leaned over the other side of the canoe and dragged my fingers through the water there.

"I just dragged my fingers through the water," I said.

"I know. I saw you."

"In that sentence that I just said, what's the prepositional phrase?"

He thought a moment and then said, "Through the water."

"Right. And what's the preposition?"

"Through."

"Good. And what's the object of the preposition?"

"Water," he said.

"Good. Now, here are some other prepositions that help tell where, or in what direction, something is: *across, behind, and beneath.* Can you make up prepositional phrases using those prepositions?"

Tarzan thought a moment and then said, "Across the river . . . behind the house . . . beneath the ground. Is that right?"

"That's right! Now, sometimes prepositions help tell not where, but *when.* For example, if I say 'We need to be home *before sunset,'* the prepositional phrase, *before sunset,* tells when we have to be home. *Before* is the preposition and *sunset* is the object of the preposition. Do you see?"

"I do."

"Good! Now, here are some other prepositions that help tell when: *after, during,* and *until.* Can you make up prepositional phrases using those prepositions?"

Again Tarzan thought a moment and then said, "After lunch . . . during the storm . . . until tomorrow."

"Very good. I think you get this."

"Do prepositional phrases always tell where or when?" he asked.

"No. Sometimes they just show a relationship or connection between things—an association that's sometimes hard to explain in words."

"Like what?"

"Well, if I say 'Let me get that *for you,'* the prepositional phrase is *for you.* The preposition is *for,* but it doesn't tell where or when. Or if I say 'He died *of malaria,'* the prepositional phrase is *of malaria.* The preposition is *of,* but it doesn't tell where or when."

"Then how am I supposed to know which words, besides the ones that tell where or when, are prepositions? If words like *for* and *of* are prepositions, then couldn't anything be a preposition? Or is it just short words that are prepositions?"

"Well, it can be tricky. Some people just look at a list of prepositions and try to memorize them—so they'll know them for the future. But you also have to realize that every preposition takes an object, and knowing that can help you figure out whether or not a certain word is a preposition. And not all prepositions are short words.

Some of them are, like *at, to, of,* and *for.* But other's aren't, like *underneath* and *alongside.*"

"Can you tell me all the prepositions now so that I can start trying to memorize them?"

"Well," I said, "I don't think I could name them all off the top of my head. Instead, let's talk about what happened yesterday with Yemmy and Omy. Each thing that happened, the way I'll say it, contains a preposition. I'll emphasize the preposition by saying it louder. Okay?"

"Well—"

"Okay. Yemmy was *in* the tree. He was *on* a branch. He flew *through* the sky. We were *under* the tree. We were *on* the ground. We took him *into* the cabin. We walked *through* the door. Does that help?"

"A little. But what are the other prepositions."

"When we get back to the cabin, we can look in the dictionary. For now, I'll tell you what I can remember off the top of my head. I'm not going to say them in any particular order—just how they occur to me, okay?"

"Okay.

"Okay, here we go: *about, among, through, to, between, around, behind, after, before, in, out, down, up, during, beyond, except, outside, with, without, until, above, across, toward, under, underneath, against, along, alongside, since, past, at, over, onto, on, below, of, off, by, near, like, into, inside, for, from.*" Of course, I didn't spit them all out in a row like that; I had to stop and think between each one. "Okay, that's all I can think of right now."

"Are there more?"

"Yes. But that's all I can think of right now."

Suddenly I felt very warm. Either the sun was becoming very hot or it took a lot out of me to remember all those prepositions. I felt an overwhelming urge to dive into the water and stay there.

"Tarzan," I said, "I'm dying of the heat."

"The prepositional phrase is *of the heat,*" he said.

"No, that wasn't an example. I'm really dying of the heat. I have to go in the water."

"Okay, he said, but once you're in, hold onto the side of the canoe. Otherwise, the current might pull you away."

"Okay."

I stood up and dove over the side of the canoe. The water felt wonderful—nice and cool.

"Tarzan," I yelled, "I dove *over* the side *of* the canoe. I'm *in* the water." I had to yell because he was farther away from me.

"I know," he said. "Prepositions—*over, of, in.* I get it."

I let the water cool my body. I didn't say anything for a while. I watched the scenery pass by. Suddenly it occurred to me that crocodiles might be swimming nearby. But this was an awfully big river. What were the chances that one happened to be right where I was? Still, I didn't want to take any chances.

"Tarzan," I yelled, "I'm going underwater a minute to look around for crocodiles!" I submerged with my eyes open. Then I rotated myself in a complete circle, looking for crocodiles in all directions. I didn't see any. I surfaced and grabbed the side of the canoe.

"Tarzan, why don't you come in? The water's great."

"The canoe might drift away."

"Then hold onto it, like I'm doing."

"Okay."

Tarzan dove over the side—the same side I was on. He held onto the side of the canoe right next to me. The vessel continued downstream with the current. We kicked our feet a little.

"There's something I don't understand," he said. "When we talked about adverbs, you said that the word *up* is an adverb. Now you're saying it's a preposition."

"That's a good point," I said. "Do you remember that I said that a word can be more than one part of speech, depending on how it's used?"

"I guess so."

"Well, let's compare two sentences: 'The spider crawled up the tree' and 'The spider crawled up.' Now, in the first sentence, the word *up* has an object—*tree.* So *up* is part of a prepositional phrase—*up the tree.* The word *up,* in that case, is a *preposition.* In the second sentence, the word *up* has no object. So, it modifies the verb *crawled.* It tells *where* he crawled. So it's an *adverb.* Do you see?"

"I do. But you could say that the whole prepositional phrase—*up the tree*—acts like an adverb, because it tells where."

"Yes, that's right. That's what we were talking about before. We said that sometimes a prepositional phrase is also an *adverbial phrase.* But even so, in the phrase *up the tree,* the word *up*—just the single word, itself—is a preposition, not an adverb."

"Because it has an object, *tree,* right?"

"Right. Very good."

"I have to get back in the canoe," Tarzan said. "We're near the watering hole. I'm going to steer us to shore."

"Okay." I held onto the rim of the canoe while Tarzan hoisted himself over the side. Then he began steering us toward the bank—the same bank we'd started from, but much farther downstream. As we neared the shore, I let go of the canoe and swam the rest of the way in. Tarzan finally jumped out of the craft and pulled it out of the water.

"How far is the watering hole from here?" I asked, shaking water from my body.

"It's not too far. Follow me."

He took my hand and led me away from the river. A vast, grassy plain loomed before us.

"Wow! This looks so different from anything else I've seen in Africa," I said.

"A lot of Africa looks like this," he answered.

We walked and walked and finally came to a small pond surrounded by animals of all sorts. There were rhinos, elephants, lions, tigers, zebras, monkeys, baboons, chimps, gorillas, leopards, cheetahs, giraffes, hyenas, and various kinds of birds.

"Oh my goodness!" I exclaimed. "This is better than any zoo!"

"Let's not go too close," he said. "Some of those animals—the lions and tigers, for example—are dangerous."

"Okay. Let's watch from here." We were about sixty yards from the pond.

We sat on the ground and watched the animals. An ostrich approached the water and began to drink. I turned to Tarzan and said, "Look! An Ostrich! I've never seen one before."

"Where?" he said.

I turned back toward the pond, but the ostrich was gone! "He was right there. Really."

"Are you sure?"

"Of course I'm sure. I just saw him. Where could he be?"

"Well, he couldn't have flown away, because ostriches don't fly. That leave two possibilities. One is that you only imagined that you saw him. The other is that a crocodile lunged at him, grabbed him in his jaws, pulled him into the water, and ate him."

"No! That couldn't be! So fast?"

"That's how crocodiles operate. They sneak up on their victims and then lunge at them. They're gone in an instant."

The thought was too horrible. It was painful to think about. Could I convince myself that I had only imagined the ostrich? No, I had really seen it. I buried my head in Tarzan's shoulder and began to cry. "The poor thing!" I blubbered.

Tarzan patted my back and murmured consoling, reassuring sounds. Finally I stopped crying. I wiped the tears from my eyes. "I don't like it here," I said. "I want to go back to the cabin."

"Okay," he said. "Do you want to take one last look at the animals?"

"No." I couldn't bear to see another one disappear.

We stood up and started to walk back to the canoe. "I just thought of something," Tarzan said, after we'd taken only a few steps. "When we came here, we traveled *with* the current. On the way back, we'd have to travel *against* it. But I'm not just making up examples of sentences with prepositions. I mean that the current is very strong. It's impossible to paddle—is that the right word, paddle?—against it."

"But you're very strong," I said. I wasn't trying to flatter him. I just wanted to get back to the cabin.

"Not strong enough to paddle all the way back against that current."

"Then how will we get back? It's too far to walk. And there are no vines here to swing on."

Tarzan thought for a while. A small lizard walked near us. It was small enough that it didn't scare me. Finally Tarzan said, "Did you see those elephants at the watering hole? We'll have to ride one of them back."

I didn't want to ride on an elephant, but I saw that there was no alternative. "Will they let us do that?"

"I'll tell them that I'm a friend of Tantor's. I'm sure they know him."

"Okay. Go tell them. I'll wait here."

I watched Tarzan run to the watering hole. "Don't get too close to the water!" I yelled.

He approached one of the elephants and spoke into its huge ear. Then the elephant bent his knees to allow Tarzan to climb onto his back. Then they started toward me. As they approached, Tarzan said to me, "This elephant knows Tantor. He's going to give us a ride back to the cabin." The elephant bent his knees again and Tarzan put out his hand to me. I took it and he pulled me up alongside him.

It took a while for me to find a comfortable position. I ended up directly behind Tarzan with my hands around his waist—you know, the way a passenger rides behind a motorcyclist.

The elephant started to walk, and I found that the motion didn't make me queasy after all. Actually, it was kind of fun riding up there.

I looked to my left and right and saw miles of grassland. I looked up and saw a blue sky and some white clouds.

After riding for about a hundred yards I said, "Tarzan, this will give us time to finish our discussion of prepositions. Can you hear me?" I was sure he could; my mouth was only a few inches from his ear.

"Yes, perfectly."

"Okay, do you think you understand what a preposition is?"

"Yes. It's a word like *over* or *under* or *around* or *through* that begins a prepositional phrase. And it takes an object."

"That's right. Now I want to talk about some mistakes people make when they use prepositions."

"What kind of mistakes?"

The elephant continued its journey. We bounced up and down a little, but it wasn't unpleasant.

"Well," I said, "you know that a preposition always takes an object, right? For example, in the phrase *under the table*, the object of the preposition is *table*."

"I know."

"Okay. Now, here's the thing. Sometimes the object of a preposition is a *pronoun* instead of a noun. For example, if I say 'Give it to me,' the prepositional phrase is *to me*. The preposition is *to* and the object of the preposition is the pronoun *me*. Do you understand that?"

"Yes. But why would people make a mistake about that?"

"Do you remember when we first spoke about pronouns? I said that a pronoun can be either in the *subjective*—or *nominative*—case, like *I, he, she,* or *they,* or it can be in the *objective* case, like *me, him, her,* or *them.*"

"I remember. You said that if a pronoun is used as the *subject* of a sentence, it's in the *nominative* case. For example, '*I* like to swim' is correct and '*Me* like to swim' is incorrect. And if a pronoun is the *object* of a sentence, it's in the *objective* case. For example, 'I like *her*' is correct and 'I like *she*' is incorrect."

"I'm glad you have such a good memory! Anyway, whenever a pronoun is the object of a preposition, it has to be in the *objective* case. Why? Because it's an *object*—the *object* of the preposition."

"Okay, but I would naturally say 'Give it to me' because that sounds right. I wouldn't say 'Give it to I.'"

"Right. But it gets trickier if a preposition has two objects."

"Two objects?"

"Yes. For example, if I say 'The elephant is giving a ride to Tarzan and Jane,' the preposition, *to*, has two objects: *Tarzan* and *Jane*. Do you see? A preposition sometimes has more than one object."

"Okay. I see that."

"Now, if I'm talking about myself, I wouldn't use my name; I'd use a pronoun. I'd say 'The elephant is giving a ride to Tarzan and *me*.'"

"So what's the mistake people make?"

"Some people would incorrectly say 'The elephant is giving a ride to Tarzan and *I*.'"

"Why would they say that? Don't they know that *I* is the nominative case?"

"I think some people do that because they have it in their minds that the word *I* is more grammatically correct than the word *me*. But it sometimes is and sometimes isn't. It all depends on how the word functions in the sentence."

Tarzan didn't say anything, so I continued.

"My guess is that what happens is, sometimes when kids are little they sometimes use incorrect grammar and their parents correct them. For example, a child might say something to his parents like 'Jim and me are going fishing.' Then the parent, correcting the child, says 'Jim and *I*.' Well, in that case, *I* is correct because it's part of the subject of the sentence. Then later, the kid comes home and says something like 'The fish were divided between Jim and I.' Why? Because, since he's been corrected so many times, he thinks *Jim and me* is always wrong and *Jim and I* is always right. But that's not true. In the sentence 'The fish were divided between Jim and me,' *me* is correct because it's the object of the preposition."

"I see. If you said 'The fish were divided between Jim and I,' that would be wrong because *I* is in the nominative case, and you can't use the nominative case as the object of a preposition. You have to use the objective case—Jim and *me*."

"Do you know, it actually makes me mad when people make that mistake?"

"Why?"

115

"Because by saying *I* instead of *me,* they're trying to show everyone that they have good grammar. But, in fact, the reverse is true. They're really showing that they *don't* understand grammar."

"Do you mean they're trying to show off?"

"Kind of, yes. And they shouldn't show off if they don't have anything to show off about. So when they say something like *between Jim and I,* they sound not only ignorant, but obnoxious!"

"Well, I'll try to never make that mistake."

"Good." I realized that Tarzan had just split an infinitive, but I didn't think it was really wrong, so I didn't say anything about it.

The elephant continued its steady journey. Far ahead I could see jungle trees. Above us several clouds had formed. They looked dark and threatening. I thought it might rain.

"Do you think it's going to rain?" I said.

"It looks like it."

"I hope we get back before it does."

"Why? We swim in these clothes. A little water won't hurt us."

I guess he was right. Still, I don't like getting caught in the rain.

"There's another mistake people make with prepositions," I said.

"What?"

"Sometimes they use two prepositions in a row."

"What do you mean?"

"Well, if I say 'The turtle fell off the log,' that's grammatically correct. The preposition is *off.*"

"And the object of the preposition is *log!*"

"Right. But if I say 'The turtle fell *off of* the log,' that's incorrect. Why? Because you don't need the word *of.* It's enough to just say *off.* In other words, use one preposition, not two."

"I think I see."

"Here, let me give you an incorrect sentence with a double preposition, and you correct it, okay?"

"Okay."

"Try this one: 'The bird flew out of the window.'"

"That should be 'The bird flew out the window.'"

"Good! Now try this one: 'He arrived in Africa on around January 1st.'"

Tarzan seemed stumped for a moment.

"Well," I said, "there are two ways to fix that."

He thought some more and then said, "I guess you could say either 'He arrived in Africa on January 1st' or 'He arrived in Africa around January 1st.'"

"Exactly! Either *on* January 1st or *around* January 1st. But not both."

"I see! I see! It *is* wrong to use two prepositions."

"Of course, as we talked about before, sometimes it's a little tricky to tell the difference between an adverb and a preposition. For example, if I say 'The bird flew out the window,' the word *out* is a preposition—because it takes an object, *window*. But if I say simply 'The bird flew out,' then *out* doesn't take an object and so it's an *adverb* telling where. Okay?"

"Okay."

"So in a sentence like 'He crawled *up through* the hole in the roof,' it looks as if you have two prepositions in a row—*up* and *through*—but you really don't. *Through* is a preposition because it takes an object, *hole*, but *up* doesn't take an object, so it's actually an *adverb* modifying *crawled*. So in that sentence, *up through* is correct."

"Because *up through* is adverb-preposition, not preposition-preposition."

"Exactly! It's a little tricky. You just have to be aware of whether the first of the two words is really an adverb or a preposition."

"Prepositions are neat. I like them. What other mistakes do people make with them."

"Well, there's one more thing, but not everyone agrees that it's really a mistake."

"What's that?"

I noticed that the air felt suddenly different—kind of electrified. I looked up and saw that the clouds had become darker and meaner looking. It was about to rain hard. The jungle was not too far ahead.

"It's going to rain. I'll try to talk fast so I can explain this before it does. It will be hard for you to hear me once it starts . . . especially if there's thunder. Anyway, some people think it's wrong to end a sentence with a preposition. For example, if I say something like 'What are you afraid of?' they think it's wrong because the sentence ends with a preposition. They think you should say 'Of what are you afraid?'"

"But that sounds wrong."

"I know. That's why a lot of people think it *isn't* a mistake to end a sentence with a preposition."

"But why would *anyone* think it's a mistake?"

"I don't know. It might be because old-fashioned grammar books used to say it was. Or it might be because in Latin you don't do that.

117

Or it might be because the word *preposition* comes from a Latin word meaning 'a putting before.' Anyway, I don't think it's really wrong."

"I don't either," Tarzan concurred.

I felt some raindrops on my arm. "It's starting to rain," I said.

"I know; I feel it too."

Just as we approached the edge of the jungle, it started to pour. Heavy sheets of water pelted us. Tarzan slid off the elephant and then reached up to me to help me down. I slid into his arms. Then he patted the elephant's head and said something to it in a language I didn't understand. The elephant turned and trotted away.

"Come on!" Tarzan said. He took my hand and we ran into the jungle. Then he grabbed me around the waist and took to the trees. Flying through the air in a rainstorm was rather exhilarating. Because his body was wet, he was slippery. I had to hold onto him very tight so that I wouldn't fall.

I heard a boom of thunder.

"Tarzan! Is it safe to be up in the trees? We might get hit by lightning!"

"The lightning is still a few miles from here. I think I can get us back to the cabin before it strikes."

"Hurry!"

We flew from tree to tree faster than ever before. It felt like a wonderful amusement park ride—like some kind of water ride.

Suddenly another burst of thunder assaulted our ears. Then a steak of lightning split the sky.

"Tarzan! Hurry! Please!"

Faster and faster Tarzan swung from vine to vine. It became dizzying. Then, there we were on the ground in front of the cabin. We ran inside.

I was out of breath. "We made it! We made it!" I panted.

We sat down at the table. I noticed that our hands were interlaced in the middle of the tabletop, but I didn't remember doing that.

Suddenly I felt something rub against my leg. What could it be? A scary animal? I looked down. It was Yemmy! And there was Omy rubbing against Tarzan's leg! I picked up Yemmy and put him on my lap. I began to pet him. Tarzan picked up Omy and did the same thing.

Tarzan and I just stared at each other without saying anything. But I think that the look I gave him said: See, isn't it nice to have pets to come home to?

He returned my gaze with an expression that seemed to say: You're right, the pets are nice, but you're not going to get me to admit it.

Well, that was okay. We sat there enjoying our furry friends.

"Tomorrow you're going to underline all the prepositions in the next paragraph of Article 2," I said. "And then we'll talk about another part of speech, the conjunction. Okay?"

"Okay," he said with what looked like a sort of smile.

Chapter 13: Jane Learns to Swing on Vines

The next morning we met at the table, as usual. Yemmy and Omy were nowhere to be seen. They must have been playing outside somewhere.

"Start here," I said, showing Tarzan the third paragraph of Article 2, "and underline all the prepositions in this paragraph." But I noticed that the paragraph was rather short, so I said, "Actually, underline all the prepositions from here through the end of the article."

Tarzan took the notebook and studied the last three paragraphs of Article 2. I noticed that his forehead sometimes became furrowed. Other times he unconsciously curled his lip or stuck out his tongue. Finally he began to draw underlines on the page. It looked like this:

Seven feet higher he constructed a similar, though lighter platform to serve as a roof, and <u>from</u> the sides of this he hung a sailing cloth <u>for</u> walls. When completed, he had a rather snug little nest, <u>to</u> which he carried their blankets and some <u>of</u> the lighter supplies.

All <u>during</u> the day excited birds and chattering monkeys watched these new arrivals and their wonderful nest-building operations <u>with</u> interest and fascination.

It was now late <u>in</u> the afternoon, and the rest <u>of</u> the daylight hours were devoted <u>to</u> the building <u>of</u> a crude ladder <u>by</u> means <u>of</u> which my mother could climb <u>to</u> their new home. Just <u>before</u> dusk my father finished the ladder and the two mounted <u>to</u> the comparative safety <u>of</u> their cozy little tree house.

"Okay," I said, "that's pretty good. Can you show me a preposition—and the prepositional phrase its part of—that helps tell where?"

"One is the word *from*, in the phrase *from the sides*. Another is the word *to*, in the phrase *to their new home*. There are even more. Should I show them to you?"

"No, that's enough. That was very good. Now, how about prepositions—and the prepositional phrases they're part of—that help tell when?"

Tarzan studied the page a moment, then said, "One is *during*, in the phrase *during the day*. Another is *in*, in the phrase *in the afternoon*. Still another is *before*, in the phrase *before dusk.*"

"That's excellent! Now, what about prepositions that don't tell where or when, but simply show a relationship between things?"

Tarzan examined the text again and then said, "One is the word *for*, in the phrase *for walls*. Another is the word *with* in the phrase *with interest and fascination*. And another is the word *of* in the phrase *of their cozy little tree house*. Is that right?"

"Yes, that's very good!"

Tarzan smiled.

"But," I said, "I think there are two prepositions you forgot to underline."

"Where!" Tarzan picked up the notebook and started rereading the paragraphs.

"Well, this is a little tricky," I said. "What about the word *to* in the first sentence—in the phrase *to serve?*"

"But isn't the word *to* part of a verb in that case, because it's part of the infinitive *to serve*. You said infinitives were verbs."

"I know. But for some reason, grammarians consider the word *to*, even when it's part of an infinitive, to be a *preposition*. They say that it's a preposition that helps form the infinitive. They don't consider it a verb."

"But it can't be a preposition in that case, because it has no object," Tarzan protested.

"Well, that's something that has always bothered me, too. Nevertheless, if you look up the word *to* in a dictionary, it tells you that it's a preposition used before a verb to indicate the infinitive.

"That's crazy!"

"Well, I guess I agree with you. That's why, if I were a real teacher and I were grading your work, I wouldn't take off any points for not underlining that word."

Tarzan smiled again.

"There's one other preposition you didn't underline," I said.

"Where!" Tarzan again began rereading the text.

"It's also in the first sentence," I said. "It's the word *as* in the phrase *as a roof*."

"But you never said that the word *as* is a preposition."

"I know. I didn't think of it. Usually it isn't a preposition. *As* is one of those words that can be various parts of speech, depending on how it's used. Sometimes it's an adverb, and sometimes it's a conjunction, which is the part of speech we're going to learn about next. But, if it's used to mean 'in the role of' or 'serving the function of' and it takes an object, as in 'to serve *as* a roof,' then the word *as* is considered a preposition."

"Oh." He seemed a bit dejected. I think he wanted to impress me by having correctly underlined *all* the prepositions.

"And," I said, "if I were a teacher, I probably wouldn't take off any points for not underlining *as*. It was my fault. I forgot to include it in that list I rattled off when we were in the canoe.

Tarzan smiled again and squeezed my hand.

"Okay," I said, "today we're going to learn about another part of speech, the conjunction."

"Don't we have to write Article 3 first? We've already used up Article 2 underlining verbs, adverbs, and prepositions."

"You're right." I took the notebook and pencil and stood up. "Let's work on it somewhere outside."

I was excited about writing Article 3. I wanted to find out what happened to Tarzan's parents in the jungle. Also, it would be fun to write again. After all, I'm really a journalist, not a teacher—not that I minded teaching Tarzan. In fact, I liked it. I liked it a lot.

"Where should we go today?" I asked.

"I don't know. Where do you want to go?"

"I don't know. Do you want to just start walking and see what we see?"

"Okay."

"But," I said, "it's going to be hot, so we'll need somewhere to swim. I hope we come to some water somewhere."

"I know where we can go!" he said.

"Where?"

"Would you like to go to an island?"

"An island? What island?"

"There's a big lake a few miles southeast of here with an island in the middle of it," he said.

"Have you ever been there?"

"I've been to the lake, but not to the island. The island is kind of far from shore. It's too far to swim there."

"Then how would be get there?"

"We'd have to build a raft. While you're writing Article 3, I could build it. Then we could take the raft to the island. Once we get to the island, you can tell me about conjunctions."

"What's on this island?"

"I don't know. I've never been there."

"Is there anything dangerous on it?"

"I don't know. I've never been there."

"This isn't the same lake we ended up in after we swam through the underwater passageway, is it? The one near the underground man-eating plants? The one where I almost drowned?"

"No, no. It's a different one."

"If we go to that island, do you promise to protect me from any animals there?"

"Of course."

The idea of visiting an unexplored island was exciting. And there was the lake to swim in if we got too hot.

"Okay," I said. "Let's go."

We left the cabin and walked into the jungle. Tarzan said, "Do you want to walk to the lake or swing through the trees?"

"Let's swing through the trees," I said. "But instead of you holding me, teach me how to swing on vines myself. Then we can both swing, side by side. It'll be faster."

Tarzan didn't answer right away. I think he was wondering whether or not I could learn to do it. Finally he said, "I was raised by apes, so I've been doing this my whole life. It's natural to me. I don't know if you can suddenly start doing it after you're all grown up."

"But when I was a kid, everyone called me a tomboy. We had a jungle gym in our back yard."

"A jungle gym?"

"Some people call it monkey bars. I call it a jungle gym. It's a contraption of metal poles and bars that kids play on. They climb it, hang from it, hang upside down by their knees from it, swing on it. All kinds of things. I was very good at it."

"Well—"

"Please, Tarzan? Please show me? I want to be a real jungle girl. How can I call myself a jungle girl if I can't even swing from tree to tree on vines?"

"Well, okay. We'll see how it goes. Come over here."

He led me to a tree. "Now, climb halfway up this tree and then grab onto that vine right there."

It was an easy tree to climb. It had low, thick branches. I climbed halfway up. A thick vine hung before me. I looked up to see what it was attached to, but it was impossible to tell. Its top was lost in a tangle of vegetation.

"Now," he said, "hold onto that vine and swing yourself across to that tree there." He pointed to another tree about twenty feet away.

"Try to land on the middle branch. As you're swinging across, keep looking at that branch. Don't take your eyes off it."

I grabbed the vine in both hands and pushed off with my feet. I gently floated through the air toward the second tree. I kept my eyes fixed on the branch I was to land on. I landed on the branch, but because of my momentum, or inertia, or whatever you want to call it, I kept moving forward. Luckily, I hadn't let go of the vine. I ended up hanging in the air, on the vine. I lowered myself to the ground.

"Landing can be tricky," Tarzan said. "You have to feel how much forward movement you have, and take that into account as you try to land. Now try it again."

I climbed halfway up the first tree again. When I was about to grab the vine—which by now was hanging in its original position—I saw what looked like a smaller vine attached to the trunk of the tree about three feet above me. Then with a sudden shock I realized that I was looking at a snake!"

"Hey! There's a snake up here!" I screamed.

"Don't move! I'm coming!"

In a flash Tarzan was beside me. In one motion he pulled the snake from the tree and flung it far into the distance. Then he gave me a reassuring little hug and climbed back down.

"That wasn't a poisonous snake," he said. "It couldn't have hurt you."

"No, but it could scare me."

"You're okay. You want to be a jungle girl, right? You have to get used to things like snakes."

He was right. I have to stop being a baby, I told myself. "Do you think the snake's okay. Do you think it got hurt when it fell?"

"I think it's okay."

"Good. I don't want any animals to get hurt, even if they do scare me."

He didn't seem to know what to say to that, so he said, "Okay, now try to swing across again, and be careful how you land. Remember the forward movement. And keep your eyes on the branch."

I tried again. This time I landed on the branch. I didn't fall, but I wobbled a little. "Let me try it again," I said.

Anyway, what happened was, I kept trying it over and over and over until I could do it perfectly. After that I swung from higher branches. Then, little by little, I swung to trees that were farther away. My confidence grew. I was like a kid on a jungle gym.

We never made it to the lake that day. I became obsessed with swinging from trees. I wanted to practice, practice, practice. All day long, with Tarzan as my patient teacher and guide, I swung from one tree to another.

Toward the end of the day, Tarzan taught me some special swinging tricks and techniques that I couldn't even explain to you. It was a "feel" thing. You had to be there.

The last part of the training was especially fun and interesting. We played a game I called "copycat." Tarzan would execute a swinging maneuver, and then I would repeat exactly what he had done. Usually, on my first try, I wouldn't perform the move perfectly. But I'd keep trying, over and over, until I could. By the end of the day I was swinging through the trees like a real jungle girl—not as well as Tarzan, probably, but almost.

As the sun was setting I said, "It's too late to go to the island today. We'll have to go tomorrow. Now let's swing back to the cabin."

Side by side we swung through the trees to the cabin. At the front door, I said, "Well, goodnight. I'll see you first thing tomorrow morning. We'll go to the island and write Article 3 and then learn about conjunctions."

He didn't say anything. He had that look that guys sometimes have at the end of a date when they don't know whether or not it's okay to kiss you goodnight.

"So," I said, "goodnight." I gave him a tiny kiss on his cheek. It was just a peck.

He smiled and said, "Tomorrow we'll go to the island."

I smiled at him. He turned around and took to the trees, swinging toward wherever it is he sleeps. As I closed the door I heard him give a jungle yell—more of a yodel, actually.

Chapter 14: The Island of the Ants

The next morning was warm and sunny. I met Tarzan outside—notebook and pencil in hand—in front of the cabin. I wanted to get an early start toward the island. I wondered what we'd find there.

We started walking toward the trees and Tarzan said, "Have you seen Yemmy and Omy?"

"No. Why do you ask?"

"I don't know."

"Have *you* seen them?" I said.

"Me? No."

Was Tarzan starting to like the cubs? I hoped so. "I'm sure they're fine," I said.

"I wasn't worried," he said.

When we got to the trees Tarzan said, "Okay, we're going to swing to the lake. Just do exactly what I do." I tucked the notebook and pencil into my waistband.

We began to swing from tree to tree. I think Tarzan went a little slower than he normally would have for my sake. I'm glad he did, because it took everything I had to keep up with him. After a while we landed on a branch and he stopped. "Are you okay?" he said. "Do you want to rest? Am I going too fast?" He was so considerate.

"Let's rest for just a minute," I said. "Then let's keep going at about the same pace. No, on second thought, let's go just a bit slower. I'm still getting used to this."

While we rested I inhaled and exhaled deeply. I massaged my arm muscles a little, too.

"Do you feel it in your arm muscles?" he said.

"I do. I'm not used to using those muscles so much," I said.

"Your arm muscles will get stronger and stronger if you keep swinging on trees."

I guess that was a good thing. I didn't want to look like a muscle man, but I wanted to be strong.

"Are you ready now?" he finally said.

"Yes. Let's go."

We swung the rest of the way to the lake. It took about another half hour to get there.

The lake was gorgeous. It reminded me a little of Deep Creek Lake in Maryland. The water was blue and rippled. The cloudless sky above was a lighter blue. Sure enough, an island, covered with vegetation, sat way out in the middle. It looked like a green mound.

"Let's find someplace to sit," I said, "so you can tell me what happened to your parents next. Then I'll turn what you say into Article 3."

"And while you do that, I'll build a raft to take us to the island."

We found a dead tree trunk lying on the ground. "Let's sit on this," I said. "It'll make a nice bench."

We sat on the trunk. A few ants walked back and forth on it. I watched them awhile.

"Don't ants ever stop to rest?" I said. "Are they constantly in motion?"

"They're looking for food," Tarzan said.

I suddenly felt hungry myself. "We forgot to eat breakfast!" I said. "We must have been too excited about coming to the island. Are you hungry?"

"Yes. You stay here and I'll find some fruit."

"I'll come with you," I said. "I know how to swing on vines."

"I know you do. All right, come on."

We took to the trees, gathering our breakfast—coconuts and some fruits I didn't know the names of. We skipped the bananas because we didn't want to attract mosquitoes.

We returned to the tree trunk, sat down, and started to eat. The ants were still there. When they came too close, I pushed them away, or sometimes I pushed them off the trunk completely. But they seemed to know we had food, and suddenly there were more of them.

"These ants are bothering me," I said. Let's finish eating standing up."

We stood up, walked a few feet from the bench, and continued eating.

"I don't think we should sit on that tree trunk after all," I said. "I'm afraid those ants are going to crawl on me."

"Okay. Where do you want to sit?"

I looked around. "How about on those rocks over there?" I pointed out two large, rather flat rocks near the water's edge.

"Okay."

We walked to the rocks and sat down. I picked up some pebbles and threw them into the lake; they made tiny splashes. Then I got up and put my foot in the water to test the temperature. "It's not too cold," I said.

"That's good."

I sat back down on the rock. We finished our fruit and threw the cores and coconut shells into the water. They drifted away with the tide.

I opened my notebook and poised my pencil. "Okay," I said, "tell me what happened next to your parents. The last thing you said was that they'd built a tree house and climbed into it."

Tarzan began to speak about his parents' adventure, and I took notes. When I thought we had enough for another article, I said, "Let's stop there. I don't think the readers of *American Monthly* can digest more than that at one time. I'll turn these notes into a finished article, and you can start building the raft. Okay?"

"Okay." Tarzan stood up and looked around. "I'm going to have to find some logs and vines. I'll place the logs side by side, and then fasten them with the vines. The raft will have to be pretty big to support both of us—at least ten feet by ten feet, I'd say."

"Okay," I said. "You know best."

He wandered off in search of materials and I yelled to him, "Don't get any logs with ants on them!"

I worked on the article. By the time I was about two-thirds finished, he had accumulated all the logs and vines he needed to make the raft. When I finished the article he had the whole thing tied together.

"Look at this!" he said proudly. There sat a wooden raft. Its edges weren't perfectly even, but it looked pretty much like a raft. Indeed, it was about ten feet by ten feet.

I walked over to it and examined it carefully. "That's a beauty," I said. I pretended that I was admiring it, but I was actually checking it for ants. Thankfully, I didn't see any.

"And look at this!" I said. "Article 3!" I waved the notebook in the air. Come back to the rocks. I want you to read it.

We walked to the rocks and sat down. Tarzan took the notebook and began to read my article, as follows:

Article 3: "The First Night"

It was quite warm during my parents' first night in the tree house, so my father left the side curtains thrown back over the roof. As they sat upon their blankets, my mother, straining her eyes into the darkening shadows of the jungle, suddenly reached out and grasped her husband's arm.

"John," she whispered. "Look! What is it, a man?"

As my father turned his eyes in the direction she indicated, he saw outlined dimly against the shadows a great figure standing upright. For a moment it stood as though listening and then turned slowly and melted into the jungle.

"What was it, John?"

"I don't know, Alice," he answered thoughtfully. "It's too dark to see so far, and it may have been only a shadow cast by the moon."

"Well, if it wasn't a man, then it was some huge and grotesque beast. Oh, I am afraid."

He gathered her in his arms, whispering words of courage and love into her ears, for the greatest pain of their misfortune, to him, was his wife's mental anguish.

Soon after, he lowered the curtain walls, tying them securely to the trees so that, except for a little opening, they were entirely enclosed.

As it was now pitch dark within their tiny house, they lay down upon their blankets to go to sleep. My father lay facing the opening, a rifle at his hand.

Scarcely had they closed their eyes than the terrifying cry of a panther rang out from the jungle. Closer and closer it came until they could hear the great beast directly beneath their tree house. For an hour or more they heard it sniffing and clawing at the trees that supported their platform, but at last it roamed away. For a moment my father saw it clearly in the brilliant moonlight—a great, handsome beast, the largest he had ever seen!

"That's good," Tarzan said, when he finished reading. "I like it."

"Good. We're going to use it for underlining the other parts of speech, starting with the conjunction."

"Okay. Let's go to the island," he said, "and we'll talk about conjunctions there."

"All right. But how are we going to get there?"

"On the raft, of course."

"I know," I said, "but how are we going to propel it through the water? The tide is going in, not out."

"Well, there are three ways. We can make some kind of sail and then sail across. Or we can find long poles and push off against the bottom, or we can make paddles and paddle across."

"I don't think we should use a sail. We don't know which way the wind will blow. And I don't think we should use long poles, either. The water will be too deep for that as we get farther out. I think we have to use paddles."

"I'll have to make them from branches or logs."

"Did you bring your knife?"

"Of course. I always carry my knife. It's too dangerous to travel without it." He pulled a knife from his waistband and held it up for me to see. The blade sparkled in the sunlight. "You wait here and I'll find something to make into paddles." He wandered off to look for appropriate branches.

"Don't get anything with ants on it!" I yelled.

To pass the time, I wandered back to the fallen tree trunk and watch the ants walk back and forth. But I kept my distance; I didn't want any of them getting on me.

After a few minutes Tarzan returned with two pieces of wood that looked kind of like paddles. He handed one to me. I checked it for ants and it was clean.

"If we both paddle, it will be easier to steer and we'll get there faster. Also, paddling will build up your arm muscles and you'll be able to swing from trees even better."

I didn't know what to say to that, so we just walked together to the raft and then pulled it into the water. We both jumped on, paddles in hand. I was on the left side, facing forward, and he was on the right.

"I'm on the port side and you're on the starboard," I said, showing off my knowledge—however limited—of nautical terminology.

"Huh?"

"That means I'm on the left side and you're on the right."

"I know I'm on the right."

"I know you do. I was only saying . . ." I felt a little foolish, so I shut up. We both started paddling toward the island.

"What do you think we'll find on the island?" I said.

"I don't know. Probably different kinds of plants and animals."

"Nothing scary, I hope."

"Probably not. Hey! Do you know what we can do for lunch? We can go fishing! We can catch some fish and eat them for lunch."

That sounded disgusting—putting worms on hooks, eating raw fish. Yuck! Still, if I wanted to be a jungle girl . . .

"Well, we'll see about that," I said noncommittally.

We continued paddling toward the island. We were making good time. Every so often I dragged my hand through the clear water.

Suddenly Tarzan said, "I'm going in for a swim."

"Wait," I objected, "I can't paddle this thing by myself."

"Then just float here." He rolled himself off the edge of the raft into the water.

"Well, if you're going in, I am too," I said. I rolled into the water on *my* side.

We both swam about aimlessly for a while. Then Tarzan said, "Meet me under the raft."

"Under the raft?" I said.

"Yes. Swim under the raft, and I'll meet you there."

Okay, I thought—but I didn't say it out loud. We both submerged and swam under the raft. I kept my eyes open. When we met, we clenched out hands together—I mean we interlaced our fingers. Then we separated and surfaced on our own sides. Then we each did a few underwater somersaults. Finally we climbed back onto the raft.

"That felt good," we both said at the exact same time. We both laughed.

We paddled again, not saying much until we got near the island.

"There it is," I said. "It looks much bigger from here than it did from shore."

"I know. It's huge."

We paddled the rest of the way in. When the raft was a few feet from land, we each jumped into the water, which was about waist-deep at that point, and walked the thing the rest of the way in. Then we dragged it all the way onto the beach.

"We better pull it far from the water," Tarzan said. "Otherwise, if the tide comes in, it will drift away."

My biceps hurt from all the paddling, not to mention the vine swinging, but I helped pull the raft farther inland anyway. Tarzan did most of the work, though. We pulled it a good forty yards from shore, just to be safe. My arms ached, but I didn't complain.

We each looked around awhile, and finally I said, "Let's go exploring." I took his hand and we walked from the beach into the jungle greenery.

At first, nothing looked any different from the jungle near the cabin. But little by little I noticed that there was one difference. There were even more animals here than there. Birds of every color filled the trees and sky. Hundreds of species of insects crawled along the ground. In fact, there were so many bugs that you had to be careful where you stepped.

There was no real path to follow, so we made our own path. Tarzan often had to cut branches out of the way with his knife.

After a while we came to a stream and we followed its bank. Every so often a frog would jump in or out of the water. Most of the frogs were green, but some were brown and some were spotted. Maybe some were actually toads; I don't know. Lots of little lizards scampered about too. I think they were mostly salamanders and chameleons.

"This is fun," I said. "I've never seen so many animals."

Tarzan didn't answer, so I said, "We should try to find someplace to sit so we can talk about conjunctions."

"Let's just follow this stream a little longer," he said.

"Okay."

The stream seemed to be going downhill. After following it for about five or ten more minutes, we saw that it fell over some rocks, forming a little waterfall. At the foot of the waterfall, which was only about five feet below the rocks, was a little pool. It seemed to be about twelve feet in diameter and about three feet deep. It was surrounded by large, flat rocks.

"This is a good spot," I said. "Why don't we sit on these rocks. This pool is pretty."

"Okay," he said.

We sat on the rocks that were opposite the little waterfall. "Do you think we could swim in this pool?" I said.

"I don't see why not. But it looks more like a bathtub than a swimming pool."

"I know. But it's still big enough to go in—when we get too hot, I mean."

"Let me see what it feels like."

Tarzan slid himself into the water. He kept his knees bent so that his body, from the neck down, was underwater. "It's nice and cool," he said.

"Let me see." I slid in also. I kept my knees bent too. I faced him with just my head sticking out of the water. Then I noticed some underwater rocks by the edge of the pool. "See those rocks over there?" I said, pointing. If we sit on them, our heads will be above water, and we won't have to stand with our knees bent.

We waded over to the rocks and sat down. They were just the right size. We were able to sit on them comfortably with just our heads sticking out of the water. "I just realized something," I said. "I forgot to bring the notebook. It's back by the edge of the lake."

"That's okay," he said. "We'll get it on the way back."

I thought that would be okay. I was going to have him underline conjunctions, but he could do that back at the cabin.

"Are you ready to talk about conjunctions?" I said.

"Are you sure we're sitting on rocks and not on turtles?" he said.

I immediately felt what I was sitting on with my hand to reassure myself. They were rocks. "You're mean," I said. "You're trying to scare me."

He gave me a sheepish look.

"If you really wanted to scare me, you should have said something about underwater snakes or something." As soon as I said that, I wished I hadn't. Now I was worried about underwater snakes—and it was my own fault. I examined the water in the pool. It was clear and empty, as far as I could tell.

"Anyway," I said, "about those conjunctions . . ." I thought about how to explain conjunctions to him. Sometimes I put my arms out at right angles and let them kind of float in the water. He sometimes did that too. I watched the waterfall hit the pool.

"Do you remember," I said, "when we talked about what a *phrase* is?"

"Yes. We talked about prepositional phrases."

"That's right, but there are other phrases besides prepositional phrases."

"There are?"

"Yes. Actually any time you have two or more words that make sense together, but don't have a subject and verb, you have a phrase. Sometimes a phrase is a preposition and its object, such as *with you*, and sometimes it's an adjective and noun, such as *wooden canoe,* and sometimes it's an adverb and verb, such as *quickly swim.* Do you see?"

"Yes. But can a phrase be more than two words?"

"Sure. If I say *under the apple tree,* that's four words."

"It's a four-word prepositional phrase, right?"

"Right. Now, sometimes you have a group of words that make sense together, and they *do* have a subject and verb, such as *Tarzan swims.* A group of words like that, with a subject and verb, is called a *clause.*"

"Claws?" He held up his hand and bent his fingers.

I spelled *clause* for him and made him spell it back to me. Then he said, "But I thought a group of words like *Tarzan swims* is called a *sentence.*"

"You're right; it is. But it can be called a sentence *or* a clause. The thing you have to understand is that there are *two kinds* of clauses. One of them is just like a sentence—it has a subject and a verb, and it makes sense all by itself. The other type also has a subject and verb, but it doesn't make sense all by itself."

"Why wouldn't it make sense by itself if it has a subject and verb?"

"Well, for example, if I say *when Tarzan swims,* there's a subject, *Tarzan,* and a verb, *swims,* but the whole clause, *when Tarzan swims,* doesn't make sense by itself as a sentence. It needs something else to complete it. For example, I could say, 'When Tarzan swims, he moves his arms.' That would make sense as a sentence. Do you see?"

"I think so."

"Now, those two types of clauses have names. The first one, the one that makes sense as a sentence, is called an *independent clause.* Some people call it a *main clause,* but I like to call it an *independent clause.*"

"I get that," he said. "It's called *independent* because it can stand alone. I mean it makes sense all by itself. It's just like a sentence."

"Right. And the other one, the one that can't stand alone, is called a *dependent clause.* Some people call it a *subordinate clause,* but I like to call it a *dependent clause.*"

"I get that too," he said. "It's called *dependent,* because it *depends* on something else to make it complete—to make it make sense as a sentence."

"Very good. Now that you understand what phrases and clauses are, we can really start talking about conjunctions. But I feel like I'm getting waterlogged. Let's get out of the water."

"Okay."

We stood up, climbed out, and sat back down on the big, flat rocks at the side of the water. We watched the waterfall spill down. It made a continuous, splashing sound as it hit the pool. Pretty birds flew all around us and above us. I think some might have been parrots.

"A conjunction," I said, "is a word that joins other words together. Sometimes it joins single words, sometimes it joins phrases, and sometimes is joins clauses."

"What do you mean by *joins?*"

"I mean that it *connects* them in some meaningful way. For example, if I say *Tarzan and Jane,* the word *and* connects *Tarzan* with *Jane.* The phrase *Tarzan and Jane* means both of us—Tarzan and Jane. Or I could say *Tarzan or Jane.* There, the word *or* connects *Tarzan* with *Jane.* The phrase *Tarzan or Jane* means just one of us—either Tarzan or Jane, but not both. Now do you see what I mean by *joins?*"

"I guess so."

"Okay, now, the next thing you have to understand is that there are different types of conjunctions."

"How many?"

"There are three. No, four. No, three."

"Which is it, three or four?"

"Well," I said, "technically there are three: *coordinating conjunctions, correlative conjunctions,* and *subordinating conjunctions.*"

"That sounds complicated. But why did you say four."

"There's another one, but grammarians don't consider it a conjunction; they consider it an adverb. But it functions so much like a conjunction that they call it a *conjunctive adverb.* And *I* think it functions so much like a conjunction that I didn't even tell you about it when we talked about adverbs. I decided to save it for when we talked about conjunctions. So, there are sort of four types of conjunctions."

Tarzan made a face—sort of a frown.

"But we'll take them one at a time, okay? We'll start with the first one I mentioned, the *coordinating* conjunction. That's probably the easiest one to understand. See, a coordinating conjunction is one that connects two words, phrases, or clauses that are equal. For example, if I say *Tarzan and Jane, Tarzan* and *Jane* are equal to each other."

"But—"

I think I knew what he was going to say, so I interrupted, "I don't mean that we're *really* equal. I know that you're taller, stronger, and faster than I am. I don't mean that. I mean *grammatically* equal. I mean that in the phrase *Tarzan and Jane, Tarzan* and *Jane* serve the same grammatical function, so they're equal in that sense."

"Oh."

"So, as I was saying, a coordinating conjunction connects things that are equal—I mean grammatically equal. Now, some of the words that are coordination conjunctions are *and, or,* and *but.*"

"As in *Tarzan and Jane* and *Tarzan or Jane,* right?"

"Right. Or as in *not Tarzan, but Jane.* And here's an example of the word *but* joining grammatically equal adjectives: *small but strong.*" Tarzan probably thought I was talking about myself with that last example—but I really wasn't."

"I see." He paused a moment and then said, "You said that conjunctions also join phrases and clauses."

"That's right. Here's one: *Tarzan swims and Jane runs.* In that example, the word *and* is a coordinating conjunction because it joins two independent clauses—*Tarzan swims* and *Jane runs.*"

"And because they're both independent clauses, they're grammatically equal, right?"

"Exactly. Now, there are other words that are coordinating conjunctions."

"Like what?"

"Like *nor, for, yet,* and *so.* Here's an example of each—I'll emphasize the coordinating conjunction when I say it: 'They were not grasshoppers, *nor* were they crickets.' 'We decided to leave, *for* we could see that many ants were about to attack.' 'She cried for help, *yet* no one came to her rescue.' 'There were lots of spiders, *so* we decided to leave.' Do you see how all those coordinating conjunctions connect things that are grammatically equal?"

"Yes, but I have two questions. First, I thought you said that the word *for* is a preposition."

"But I also said that a word can be more than one part of speech, depending on how it's used. In the example I just gave, *for we could see that many ants . . .,* the word *for* doesn't have an object—so it's not a preposition; it's a conjunction. It really means *because.*"

"Right. Now I remember. The other thing is, Why were all those examples about bugs?"

"Were they? I didn't realize. I guess I must have bugs on the brain because of all the bugs we saw on the ground coming here."

"Are you scared of them?"

"A little." I looked around to see if there were any scary bugs nearby. There weren't. Then I said, "Let's go back in the water. It's getting hot again." I really was hot. It wasn't just because I was scared of bugs.

We sat back down on the underwater rocks, with just our heads sticking out of the water, as before.

"Okay," I said, "let's talk about another kind of conjunction, the *correlative* conjunction. Now, correlative conjunctions are actually *pairs* of words that are used to join things that are grammatically equal."

"Pairs of words?"

"Yes. For example, one common pair is *either . . . or.* I could say 'Either Tarzan *or* Jane will kill the spider.' The words *either* and *or* work together as a pair. Do you see?"

"I see that you still have bugs on the brain."

"Okay, but do you see what I mean about *either . . . or?*"

"I guess so."

"Here's another common pair: *neither . . . nor.* I could say 'Neither Tarzan *nor* Jane saw the ants coming.'"

"Come on," Tarzan said. "We're leaving. I can see that you're worried about bugs. Let's go back to the raft and paddle back across the lake." He stood up and put out his hand to me. I stood too. He led me out of the pool.

"Okay," I said, "but as we walk, I'll keep telling you about conjunctions."

He led me back the way we had come. We held hands.

"Here's another pair of correlative conjunctions," I said. "*Both . . . and.*" Then I gave an example: "*Both* Tarzan *and* Jane ran from the ants."

"Jane! That's enough about bugs! What's the matter with you?"

I didn't know what was wrong with me, but I couldn't stop thinking about bugs.

"Here's another one," I said. "*Not only . . . but also.*" Then I gave this example: "We were attacked *not only* by ants, *but also* by spiders, cockroaches, and centipedes."

"Jane!" He started to run. He didn't let go of my hand. I think he wanted to get me back to the raft as soon as possible. "Let's take a shortcut," he said. He led us away from the stream.

"Here's another one," I said. "*Whether . . . or.*" Then I gave the example: "*Whether* we run *or* hide, the bugs will devour us."

"Jane! What's wrong with you? Then Tarzan slapped my face—not to punish me, but to try to snap me out of the trance I seemed to be in. I didn't realize it at the time, but I think a bug must have bitten me and given me some kind of fever. I was delirious.

"Do you understand correlative conjunctions?" I said in a strange voice.

Tarzan didn't answer, but continued walking as fast as he could toward the raft. He pulled me along by the hand. I followed like some kind of zombie.

Then I heard him say, "Jane, can you hear me? Are you okay?"

Something seemed to click off in my brain and I started to feel like myself again. I guess the fever had broken. "Where are we?" I said, suddenly aware of my surroundings.

"We're going back to the raft. How do you feel?"

"Okay, I guess. What happened?"

"You were obsessing about bugs. Don't you remember?"

"A little. I must have been in some kind of daze. But I feel better now."

"Are you sure?"

"Yes."

"Still, I want to get back to the raft as soon as possible. Can you swing from trees?"

"I don't think so. My arms are kind of sore from all that paddling we did. And from swinging on vines all day yesterday. Let's just walk."

I didn't recognize anything around us. But then, everything here looked pretty much the same—trees, vines, twigs, birds, insects. The good thing was that the lake had a certain sound and smell, and I sensed that we were headed in the right direction.

Eventually we came to a kind of clearing. Running across the middle of it, from one side to the other was a hill. It was basically a pile of dirt about four feet high and very steep—steeper than a forty-five degree angle. We'd have to climb over it if we wanted to get back to the raft.

How did that hill get there, I wondered. When we approached it I saw that we wouldn't be able to simply walk over it; it was too steep. We'd have to climb over it on our hands and knees. It took only a few seconds to get to the top. Once there, I saw that there were little openings all along the top of the thing. How did those holes get there, I wondered.

Suddenly ants started pouring out of the holes—thousands and thousands of them. A few got on my hands and feet. I screamed and scampered down the other side of the hill, flicking ants off me as fast as I could. Then Tarzan grabbed my hand and said, "Run! Those are army ants! They'll eat us alive!"

We ran to the other side of the clearing. We checked ourselves and each other for ants. We flicked off the few we found. Then Tarzan grabbed me and took to the trees. I held on tight as he swung from vine to vine toward the raft. Finally he set us down at the edge of the beach, and we began walking toward the raft.

As we approached it, I thought that it looked funny. It looked different. I knew the wood was dark, but now it looked *black*. And it seemed to be in motion, somehow. When we got up close, I saw one of the most disgusting sights I'd ever seen. The raft was teeming with ants—millions of them. Some were small with wings, and some were small without wings. Others were large with wings, and still others were large without wings. They covered ever inch of the raft, but here and there they gathered in concentrated clumps. All were in motion.

I drew back in horror. I felt sick. I don't think it would have been as bad if there were just one kind of ant, but there were four different types—big and small, with and without wings. The raft throbbed. It seemed alive.

Tarzan grabbed my hand and we ran about a hundred yards down the beach. I began to cry. Tarzan tried to console me by putting his arms around me.

"How are we going to get back across the lake?" I sobbed. "We can't go anywhere near that raft."

"I'll build another one."

"I want to get back to the cabin before dark."

"Okay. What do you want to do while I build the raft? Do you want to swim in the lake? Do want to lie on the beach? Sit on a rock?"

"I don't know," I said. I couldn't think. Finally I said, "Don't leave me alone. I want to help you build the raft. And we need new paddles too."

We spent most of the rest of the day searching for materials to build the new raft and make the new paddles. We didn't say much. He did all the work, really, but I helped when I could.

By late afternoon the new raft and paddles were ready. They looked pretty much like the old ones. We pulled the thing into the water and jumped aboard. I didn't say anything about who was on the starboard side or the port side. I didn't feel like talking.

We paddled silently for a while. Then Tarzan said, "Why don't you lie down and rest. I can paddle myself." I felt overwhelmed by fatigue, so I lay down on the raft. I just stared straight up into the sky. The sun was starting to go down. The day was almost over.

In Africa, the sun sets very quickly. There's no long period of dusk. First it's daytime, and then all of a sudden it's night.

As Tarzan paddled, I heard the swooshing noise the paddle made in the water. I breathed deeply. I tried to enjoy the sunset.

Suddenly it was dark, and we were still on the lake. We could see, though, because the moon was out. I tried to relax.

After a while I became aware of how peaceful it is on a lake at night. The water was ridiculously calm—like a sheet of glass. There was practically no sound. I felt like I was in another world. I sat back up and said, "This is beautiful."

"How do you feel?" Tarzan asked.

I actually felt good. The horror of the ants was behind us. "Pretty good," I said.

"Really?"

"Really."

Then we didn't say anything for a while, and finally I said, "Let's stop rowing. Let's just drift here on the lake. It's so peaceful."

We laid the paddles on the raft and stretched out on our backs, staring up at the big round moon. I took his hand.

After lying like that for a while, I said, "Let's finish our lesson on conjunctions right here."

"Really?" he said.

"Sure. Why not? It's nice and quiet. There's nothing to bother us."

"Okay."

"So where were we?"

"You already taught me about coordinating conjunctions and correlative conjunctions."

"Oh, right. Now we have to talk about another type of conjunction, the *subordinating* conjunction." We stopped holding hands. I quickly reviewed subordinating conjunctions in my own mind before starting to speak.

"Well," I began, "remember how coordinating conjunctions connect things that are grammatically equal?"

"Yes."

"Well, subordinating conjunctions connect things that are grammatically *unequal*—usually an independent clause and a dependent clause. Actually, they perform a kind of double duty."

"How do they do that?"

"Well, they introduce a dependent clause—by being the first word of it, I mean—and at the same time they connect that whole clause to an independent clause. For example, take the word *because*, which is a subordinating conjunction. In the sentence 'We stopped paddling *because* we wanted to drift on the lake,' the word *because* introduces the dependent clause *because we wanted to drift on the lake*, and it connects that clause to the independent clause *We stopped paddling*. Do you see?"

"No, I don't. What you're saying doesn't really make sense."

All of a sudden *he* was the grammar expert. "What do you mean?" I said.

"Well, you're saying that the word *because* introduces the dependent clause *because we wanted to drift on the lake*. But what if you don't consider *because* as part of the clause? Couldn't you say that *because* actually joins two independent clauses: *We stopped paddling* and *we wanted to drift on the lake?* That would make *because* a coordinating conjunction, just like the word *for* was in the example you gave earlier."

I remembered the earlier example using the word *for*. Neither of us wanted to say it out loud because it was about ants attacking—something we didn't want to be reminded of. Maybe Tarzan was becoming a grammar expert after all. It seemed to me that he was right that *because* could be thought of as a coordinating conjunction joining two independent clauses. Still, I was explaining things to him the way they were explained to me in high school.

"You're very smart," I told him. "You may be right. One of the interesting things about grammar is that it's not always an exact science. Many things are open to interpretation." I thought a little more about whether the word *because* was a coordinating or a subordinating conjunction in the example I'd given. Finally I said, "I don't know why, but I think grammar experts just like to consider a word like *because* as part of the dependent clause it introduces. Maybe if we switched the order of the clauses, the word *because* would seem more like a subordinating conjunction."

"What do you mean?"

"Well, what if I said 'Because we wanted to drift on the lake, we stopped paddling'? Then *Because we wanted to drift on the lake* feels more like a dependent clause and the word *because* feels like it's actually part of that clause. Can you see that?"

"I think so. I think it's because in that case the word *because* doesn't fall *between* the clauses."

We didn't say anything for a while. I was thinking about my high school English teacher and about coordinating and subordinating conjunctions. I don't know what Tarzan was thinking about.

Finally he said, "What are some other subordinating conjunctions?"

"Well, there are a lot of them. Some of them have to do with expressing a cause or reason for something. For example, besides the word *because*, there's *since*, *as*, and *whereas*. I could say 'Since we didn't get back to the cabin before dark, we decided to make the best of the situation by relaxing on the water.' Do you see? *Since* introduces a dependent clause and connects that clause to an independent clause. And it expresses a reason." I was glad that I picked an example in which the subordinating conjunction, *since*, came at the beginning of the sentence. That way Tarzan wouldn't argue about whether it might really be a coordination conjunction, as he had before.

I was right; he didn't. Instead, he said, "You said that *some* subordinating conjunctions express a cause or reason. What do others express?"

"Well, some of them express a time."

"Like what?"

"Like the words *when*, *as*, *while*, *before*, *after*, and *until*."

"But—"

"I know what you're going to say. You're going to say that *before*, *after*, and *until* are prepositions, right?"

"Well, I was going to, but now I remember that a word can be more than one part of speech. So, how can a word like *before* be a conjunction?"

"Remember that prepositions have objects, which are nouns or pronouns. So if I say *before sunset*, the word *before* is a preposition and the word *sunset* is its object. But if I say *before the sun sets*, then *before* is a subordinating conjunction introducing the dependent clause *before the sun sets*."

"I see—because in that case *before* has no object. Instead it introduces *before the sun sets*, which has a noun, *sun*, and verb, *sets*, and is therefore a clause, right?"

"Exactly. Now, here are some other sentences that demonstrate subordinating conjunctions that express time. I'll emphasize the coordination conjunctions when I say them: *When* we got back to the cabin, Yemmy and Omy were waiting for us. *As* we walked through the door, they looked up at us. They rubbed against our legs *while* we ate breakfast."

"You'll be thinking about the tiger cubs *until* we get back to the cabin," Tarzan offered."

"That's right!" I said. Whether I meant that he'd correctly demonstrated the subordinating conjunction *until* or that I'd be thinking about the cubs until we got back, I didn't specify—and Tarzan didn't ask.

"Sometimes," I said, "subordinating conjunctions—"

All of a sudden we felt a bump against the bottom of the raft and I stopped talking. What was that, I wondered. Then we felt it again. Something had hit us from underneath! We both sat up.

"What's that?" I whispered, suddenly concerned.

"I don't know."

"Well, what *could* it be?"

"I don't know."

I think he did know, but he didn't want to frighten me. I decided that it must be either a very large snake—a thirty footer, probably—or a crocodile.

"If you don't know," I whispered, "why did you just grasp the handle of your knife?"

"Did I?" He looked at his knife and saw that he was holding it. He let it go. "It's probably nothing; just a piece of driftwood, maybe."

"What should we do?" I said.

"There's nothing to do. If I dive in to investigate, I won't see anything. It's too dark. Let's paddle back to shore."

"You don't mean the shore of the island, do you?"

"No, the shore of the lake, where we started from."

Without another word we started paddling. I kept waiting for another bump, but none came—except for the bumps my heart was making inside my chest.

"Paddle faster," I said. I couldn't wait to get back to shore. "I can't think about conjunctions anymore right now. Let's just get off this lake."

It took us about fifteen minutes to paddle to shore. Tarzan made one comment along the way. He said, "It's too bad we got bumped like that and it scared you. I was thinking that it would be nice to take a moonlight swim." I didn't say anything in response.

As we pulled the raft out of the water, he said, "Do you remember that pond we once went to—the one where we dove and jumped off the branches of a tree. We can take a moonlight swim there some night. It will be fun."

I remembered the pond. It was the one with the guppies. I imagined what it would be like to go for moonlight swim there. The idea was exciting.

"I think that's a safe pond," I said. "I remember there were turtles there—but not snapping turtles, right?"

"Right. It's safe. So do you want to go one night?"

"Okay," I said. I felt like I had just made a date. It was exciting.

As we walked away from the lake, I remembered the notebook. "Where's that notebook," I said.

We both looked around and finally I spotted it. As I got close to it the idea that it might be covered with ants occurred to me. I approached it slowly, cautiously. There was nothing on it. It was just how I'd left it. I picked it up. Then it occurred to me that some bugs might be inside it, on the pages. I leafed through it in the moonlight. It was clean.

"Tarzan," I said, "I'm so tired. And my arms are so sore. Can you carry me back to the cabin?"

He grabbed me around the waist, and then I held him around the neck. He took to the trees and after not too long we were standing in front of the cabin. It was the middle of the night. The moon was still up and all the stars were out.

"Well . . ." I said.

"Well . . ." he said.

"I guess we'll finish talking about conjunctions tomorrow," I said.

"I'm sorry I took you someplace that had so many ants."

"It's not your fault. You didn't know. You'd never been there before."

He didn't answer. I gave him a little peck on the cheek and said goodnight.

For no reason we both looked up at the sky. "There sure are a lot of stars out tonight," he said.

"There sure are," I answered.

"Well, goodnight," he said. "I'll see you tomorrow morning. If Yemmy and Omy are inside, say hi for me." Then he turned around and ran into the jungle. I don't know why he ran; he just did.

Chapter 15: Tarzan and Jane Plan a Moonlight Swim

The next morning, we met at the table as usual. Yemmy and Omy were nowhere to seen. Outside, the sky was cloudy; it looked like it might rain.

"Are you hungry?" I said.

"Well—"

"I'm not," I interrupted. I know that it's not really polite to interrupt, but I really wanted to finish talking about conjunctions. I'd intended to finish the discussion the night before, but I got nervous when our raft got bumped. "Let's get those conjunctions out of the way, and then we'll have a nice breakfast, okay?"

"That's fine with me," he said. "I want to finish the discussion too. I like grammar. I really do."

"Good. So where were we?"

"You were talking about subordinating conjunctions. You said that some of them, like the word *because*, express a cause or reason and that others, like the word *when*, express time. And you gave me examples of sentences showing that."

He had such a good memory. "You have such a good memory," I said. "Okay, now, other subordinating conjunctions—the word *where*, for example—express a place. If I say 'We'll take a moonlight swim in the pond *where* we saw guppies and a turtle,' the word *where* introduces the dependent clause *where we saw guppies and a turtle*. It's a subordinating conjunction that expresses a place. Do you see?"

Instead of saying whether or not he understood, he said, "It will be fun to take a moonlight swim." But I knew he understood.

"Now, other subordinating conjunctions," I continued, "express some kind of condition or supposition. Some of the words that do that are *if*, *unless*, and *although*. For example, I could say 'We'll take a midnight swim *unless* it's raining.' In that sentence, the word *unless* introduces the dependent clause *unless it's raining*. It's a subordinating conjunction that expresses a condition—the condition that it's not raining. Do you see?"

Again he just said, "It will be fun to take a moonlight swim." And again I knew he understood what I'd told him.

"And sometimes," I said, "a subordinating conjunction—the word *so*, for example—expresses a purpose. If I say "We took a nap in the afternoon *so* we wouldn't be too tired to take a moonlight swim,' the word *so* introduces the dependent clause *so we wouldn't be too tired to take a moonlight swim.* It's a subordinating conjunction that expresses a purpose—in this case, the purpose of the nap. Do you see?"

"Do you think we should take that moonlight swim tonight?" he said.

"I don't know. It looks like it might rain. Besides, we were up so late last night that we'll be tired."

"But we could each take a nap, like you said in your example."

"But that was just an example."

"It was?"

"Yes. I mean no. I mean I don't know. Let's see if it rains and how we feel. If we don't go tonight, we can always go some other night. Is it so important to you to go tonight?"

"Well, I just thought . . ."

He didn't seem to know how to finish that, so I said, "Come on, let's finish talking about conjunctions and then we'll see what the weather's like and how we feel."

"Okay," he said with a bit of disappointment in his voice.

"Good. Now, we've already spoken about coordinating, correlative, and subordinating conjunctions. The only thing left to talk about is that thing I mentioned that's technically an adverb but that acts like a conjunction, the *conjunctive adverb.*"

"What does that do?"

"Well, like coordination conjunctions, conjunctive adverbs join independent clauses. But they don't simply join them in the way the words *and* and *or* do. They serve as a transition between the clauses that that carries the thought from one clause into the next."

"I don't think I understand."

"Well, it might become clearer if I give you some examples. Conjunctive adverbs are words like *however, therefore, nevertheless, moreover, indeed, likewise,* and *furthermore.* For example, I could say 'We wanted to go for a moonlight swim; *however,* it was raining.' Or 'We weren't very hungry and we wanted to finish our discussion of adverbs; *therefore,* we delayed breakfast.' Or 'Tarzan didn't want to adopt two pets; *nevertheless,* he agreed to.' Do you see?"

"Yes. But maybe it won't rain. And maybe I *won't* agree."

"Those were just examples. You always take everything so literally."

He looked glum all of a sudden. I think I'd hurt his feelings.

"I guess you're right," I said. "I try to pretend that everything I say is just an example. But I *do* try to make up examples that have some truth to them. Or sometimes I make up examples that are intended to tease you a little. I'm sorry. I was just kidding around. Okay?"

He didn't answer.

"Anyway," I said, "that's everything I want to tell you about conjunctions. If there's anything else to talk about, it will come up when you start writing your own articles. Now, should we eat breakfast or do you want to underline the conjunctions in Article 3?"

"Do you promise not to make up any more examples that are meant to tease me?"

"I'll try not to," I said. I couldn't promise, because I sometimes couldn't seem to help myself. I don't know why.

"Let me see Article 3," he said. "I'll underline the conjunctions first, and then we'll eat."

I handed him the notebook. "The paragraphs are kind of short," I said. "Why don't you underline the conjunctions in the first three paragraphs."

"He studied the text and then began to draw underlines. When he handed it back to me it looked like this:

It was quite warm during my parents' first night in the tree house, <u>so</u> my father left the side curtains thrown back over the roof. <u>As</u> they sat upon their blankets, my mother, straining her eyes into the darkening shadows of the jungle, suddenly reached out <u>and</u> grasped her husband's arm.

"John," she whispered. "Look! What is it, a man?"

<u>As</u> my father turned his eyes in the direction she indicated, he saw outlined dimly against the shadows a great figure standing upright. For a moment it stood as though listening <u>and</u> then turned slowly <u>and</u> melted into the jungle.

I checked his work and said, "That's very good! Now, show me an example of a coordinating conjunction."

"Well, the word *and* in the phrase *reached out and grasped.*"

"Good. Now, how about a subordinating conjunction that expresses a reason?"

"The word *so* that introduces the dependent clause *so my father left the side curtains thrown back over the roof.*"

"Very good! And how about a subordinating conjunction that expresses time?"

147

"The word *as* that introduces the dependent clause *As they sat upon their blankets.*"

"Excellent! Now, there's one conjunction that you didn't underline."

"Where!" he said, grabbing the notebook. He studied it silently for a while.

"Well, it's tricky," I said. "There's one thing about conjunctions I forgot to tell you."

"What?"

"Sometimes two words act together as a conjunction."

"I know. You told me about correlative conjunctions like *either . . . or* and *neither . . . nor.*"

"That's not what I mean. I mean two words that act together as a *subordinating* conjunction."

"Like what?"

"Well, look at the last sentence of paragraph 3: 'For a moment it stood *as though* listening and then turned slowly and melted into the jungle.' The words *as though* act together as a subordinating conjunction. They introduce the dependent clause *as though listening.*"

"But that clause doesn't have a—"

"I know what you're going to say. You're going to say that that clause doesn't have a subject. But the subject, though not stated, is understood to be *it*, which is the subject of the first clause, *For a moment it stood*. The second clause really means *as though [it were] listening.*"

"Oh."

"Do you remember we once talked about how a subject can be *understood* instead of actually stated?"

Tarzan thought a moment and then his face brightened. "I do! It was when we were discussing verbs and the imperative mood. You said that in the sentence 'Sit down!' the subject is understood to be *you.*"

"That's right!" He really had an amazing memory.

"So," he said, "what are some other words that act together as a subordinating conjunction?"

"Well, there are a lot of them. Besides *as though*, there's *even if, even though, inasmuch as, except that, if only, in case, provided that, as if, more than, so that, in order that, as long as, ever since,* and *just as.* There are probably others, too, but I can't think of any more right now."

"Well, that's plenty! I understand."

"Good. Well, that does it for conjunctions. Now, are you ready for brunch?"

"Brunch?"

"In America, if we have a meal that's too late to be called breakfast but too early to be called lunch, we call it brunch!"

"Actually, I'm starving. Let's have brunch."

Because my arms were still a bit sore, I stayed in the cabin while Tarzan gathered fruit. When he returned we both ate with gusto until we were full.

"I'm stuffed," I said. "And I feel suddenly exhausted. I guess it's from staying up so late last night. I think I'll take a nap."

"That's a good idea," he said. "I'll go see how the weather is near that pond with the guppies. Don't forget: If it's nice tonight, we'll take a moonlight swim. I'll rest up for it too."

"Good. Now let me sleep. Meet me back here at sunset, and we'll see how the weather is, okay?"

"Okay."

With that he left the cabin and I fell into a deep sleep.

Chapter 16: Tarzan and Jane Get Caught in the Rain

I woke up a little before sunset feeling rested. My arms didn't hurt anymore either. I walked to the window to check the weather. It was cloudy and it looked like it might rain.

I walked outside to see if Yemmy and Omy were anywhere around. I didn't see them, but I saw Tarzan strolling up to the cabin. He gave me a smile and I smiled back.

"Did you have a nice nap?" he said.

"Yes, wonderful. Did you?"

"Yes." Then after a moment: "Well, should we walk over to the pond?"

"I don't know," I said. "It looks like it might rain."

"But it isn't raining now. Maybe it won't." I could tell that he was very eager to go for that moonlight swim. I was eager too, but only if the weather was nice."

Neither of us said anything for a while, and then I said, "Well, we can walk over there and see how it is when we get there. If you want to, that is." I knew he wanted to. I don't know why I said that.

"Okay, come on." He took my hand and we started walking toward the pond. The sun was setting, but a full moon was rising between the clouds.

When we were about halfway there it started to drizzle. "I don't want to get wet," I said. "Let's find some shelter." A tree with thick, wide leaves stood nearby. We ran under it and sat leaning against the trunk. "This is perfect," I said. "The leaves of this tree are a natural roof."

We sat under the tree watching the rain without saying much. The sun finally set completely and the jungle turned dark. Still, we could see each other and our nearby surroundings by the light of the moon. I looked up to make sure there were no snakes or fat rats in the tree. I didn't see any.

"It's so peaceful here at night," I said. "I love the sound the rain makes when it hits the leaves."

He didn't say anything. I guess he was listening to the sound. I listened too. I also heard the rustle of leaves and the chirping sound of insects.

"I guess we can't take that swim tonight," I said. "We'll have to go some other time."

"Tomorrow night?" he asked.

"Sure, tomorrow night," I said. "If it doesn't rain."

150

He didn't say anything. Then I said, "This is the first time we've been together at night, isn't it?"

"Well, last night on the raft."

"Oh, right. But I mean this is the first time that we *planned* to be together at night. It's fun being together at night in the rain. It's kind of cozy. I just wish Yemmy and Omy were here with us. Why don't you call them?"

"Call them?"

"You know, call out something like 'Yoo-hoo' and see if they come."

"I'm not going to call 'yoo-hoo.'"

"Why not?"

"I'd feel foolish. It sounds funny."

"I wouldn't think you were foolish. Won't you do it for me?"

Tarzan called, "Yoo-hoo," but the cubs didn't respond.

Then I called, "Here, kitty, kitty," but they still didn't respond.

"Well," I said, "we can't go swimming because it's raining, and we're not tired enough to go to sleep yet because of our naps. But I know what we can do. Let's stay here under the tree and talk about another part of speech. Do you know that we have only two more parts of speech to talk about, and they're both very easy to understand?"

"What are they?"

"Well, one is the *interjection* and the other is the *article*. Let's start with the interjection.

"Okay, what's an interjection?"

"Well, it's like when you said 'yoo-hoo.'"

"What do you mean? 'Yoo-hoo' doesn't really mean anything."

"Well, interjections are just words—or sometimes sounds—that you just kind of throw into a sentence. They're not really a part of the sentence grammatically; they're more like stand-alone words. They're usually used to get someone's attention or express some emotion."

"What kind of emotion?"

"Well, any kind—like surprise, anger, annoyance, pain, sorrow, relief . . ."

"I'm not sure I understand."

"Well, let me give you an example. If you stub your toe and then say 'Ouch! That hurts,' the word *ouch* is an interjection. It stands alone, and it expresses pain."

Tarzan rubbed his toe as if he'd just stubbed it.

151

"Or," I said, "if I say 'Wow, that's amazing!' the word *Wow* is an interjection. It stands alone—I mean it has no grammatical function in the sentence—and it expresses surprise."

Tarzan silently formed the word *wow* with his lips.

"Do you see what I mean?" I asked.

"I think so. Remember when I was teaching you to swing on vines and you climbed halfway up a tree and you saw a snake above you? You screamed, 'Hey! There's a snake up here!' In that sentence, the word *hey* was an interjection, right?"

"Right. Exactly. I used that word to get your attention and to express surprise. But I didn't really think about using the word; it just came out automatically." I thought about that a moment and then said, "Now that I think about it, lots of interjections are words or sounds you say without really thinking. They just seem to come out when you're genuinely surprised or scared or hurt or something."

"I like interjections," Tarzan said. "What are some other ones?"

I thought for a while and then said, "I just realized something. Interjections are sometimes more than one word. If you say 'oh my,' for example, that's an interjection that's made up of two words. Anyway, here's a list of some interjections that I can think of off the top of my head. Remember, some are actually words, and some are just sounds people sometimes make, such as *whew*."

"People say *whew* to express relief, right?"

"Right. Anyway, here goes: Besides *ouch, wow, hey, oh my,* and *whew*, which we've already mentioned, there's *oh, well, gosh, gee, yikes, yes, no, good grief, hello, good-bye, help,* and *say*."

"Why is *say* an interjection. I thought it was a verb."

"Usually it is. But sometimes people use it as an interjection at the beginning of a sentence. For example, they might say: 'Say, that's a nice outfit.' They don't mean *say* literally; I mean they don't mean that you're supposed to say the words *that's a nice outfit* out loud. They just use the word *say* as an interjection to get someone's attention. They could have said: 'Hey there, that's a nice outfit.' It would mean basically the same thing. Do you see?"

"I think so."

"There are a few other words that are usually not interjections but that are often used as interjections—by being placed at the beginning of a sentence."

"Like what?"

"Like *why, look,* and *now.* You might said, 'Why, I don't know,' or 'Look, I've had enough of this,' or 'Now, here's what I think.' In

152

those sentences, *why*, *look*, and *now* are being used not in their normal senses, but as interjections. Grammatically, they're independent elements."

"I see. Are there any other interjections?"

"Well, let me think." After a moment I said, "Okay, here are some others." But then before reciting them, I said, "In the sentence I just said—'Okay, here are some others'—the word *okay* is an interjection. And I could just have easily have said 'Now, here are some others' or 'Well, here are some others.' I guess I just have a preference for the word *okay*. I never realized that before."

Suddenly it started raining much harder. I had to talk louder so that Tarzan could hear me in the downpour. "Here are some other interjections," I shouted. "*Aha*, *gosh*, and *whoops*. And sometimes people use the words *man* and *boy* as interjections."

"They do?" Tarzan shouted.

"Yes. For example: 'Man, that was a close call' or 'Boy, that was rough.'" Then I continued, "And some interjections are just made-up words that sound kind of funny."

"Like what?"

"Like *phooey* and *gadzooks*."

"Don't forget *yoo-hoo*," he offered.

"What?" I said. Actually, I'd heard him, but I thought that if I pretended that I didn't, he'd say it again louder and maybe Yemmy and Omy would hear him.

"Yoo-hoo," he said again, louder.

"What?" I said again.

"Yoo-hoo," he screamed.

I looked around for the cubs, but I didn't see them. I gave up. "Oh, right," I said.

We sat awhile listening to the rain. Finally I said, "That's all I can think of to tell you about interjections. Tomorrow morning you'll underline them in the article. Then after that we'll talk about one more part of speech, the *article*. So, are you ready to take me back to the cabin? I'm getting tired now."

"But we'll get wet."

"I know, but what choice do we have? We'll just have to get wet."

"We can stay here a little longer. Maybe it will stop raining."

"Okay, a few more minutes. Where do you think Yemmy and Omy are?"

"I don't know. Probably somewhere out of the rain."

"Do you want to try calling them again?" I said.

"Do you mean by yelling *yoo-hoo*? I don't think so."

"I'll try." I called *yoo-hoo* but they didn't come.

We sat and listened to the rain again. Then I said, "It doesn't look like it's going to stop. Take me back to the cabin, okay?"

"Okay." We stood up and walked hand in hand back to the cabin. When we got there we were soaking wet.

"Well, I'll see you tomorrow morning," I said. "Try to stay out of the rain." I gave him another little peck on the cheek. Then, after hesitating, he gave me a little peck on my cheek. Then we smiled at each other without saying anything. Finally he turned around and walked back through the rain into the jungle.

Chapter 17: Tarzan and Jane Re-plan a Moonlight Swim

By sunrise the rain had stopped and the clouds had disappeared. It looked like it would be a nice day.

When Tarzan arrived at the cabin, he was holding his knife in his hand.

"Why are you holding your knife?" I said.

"I just had to kill a poisonous snake. A big one."

"Yikes!" I said.

"Gadzooks!" he answered.

"Okay," I said, "I get it. You're showing me that you know what an interjection is. But hardly anyone actually says *gadzooks*."

"That's good. It sound funny."

"Well, we can just stick to words like *well* and *okay* if we want to use interjections."

"Okay."

"So, are you ready to underline some interjections in the article?"

"Hey, you just used the word *so* as an interjection. And you never even mentioned that one to me last night."

"You're right! That's very good. I can see that you know what an interjection is." I didn't bother pointing out that his last sentence started with *hey*, another interjection.

We sat down at the table in our usual seats and Tarzan picked up the notebook.

"Let's see . . ." he said, turning to Article 3. "Where should I start?"

I looked at Article 3. It was upside down from where I was sitting, but I could still read it. I pointed to the fourth paragraph and said, "Why don't you start here and underline the interjections in the next three paragraphs."

Tarzan drew two underlines and turned the notebook toward me. The three paragraphs looked like this:

"What was it, John?"

"I don't know, Alice," he answered thoughtfully. "It's too dark to see so far, and it may have been only a shadow cast by the moon."

"<u>Well</u>, if it wasn't a man, then it was some huge and grotesque beast. <u>Oh</u>, I am afraid."

Tarzan spoke first. He said, "That's all there are—*well* and *oh*. I guess my parents didn't say a lot of weird interjections like *gadzooks*."

"I guess not," I concurred. I closed the notebook.

"Okay," I said, "we have one more part of speech to talk about—the *article*. That's another easy one, so why don't we talk about it right here, right now. Then you'll underline the articles in the last three paragraphs of Article 3. After that we can celebrate the fact that we've covered all the parts of speech."

"But what about breakfast?"

"Are you hungry now?"

"I guess I can wait. We can have brunch again!"

"That's a good idea. So, anyway, there are only three words that are articles—*the*, *a*, and *an*."

"Those words are so easy. Anyone knows what those words mean."

"They are easy words. They're used to point out or identify one thing—as opposed to two or more things, I mean. For example, if I say *a tree*, I mean *one* tree."

"I know that."

"I know you do. But sometimes when you want to point out *one* of something, you refer to a *particular* one. For example, if I say 'Give me *the* notebook,' I'm referring to the particular notebook that we've been writing in. But if I say 'Give me *a* notebook,' then I'm referring to any notebook; it doesn't matter which one."

"I think I knew that too."

"Okay, but here's the thing: The word *the* is called a *definite* article—because it refers to, or indicates, some *definite* thing you're talking about. For example: *the* notebook, *the* knife. Do you see? Not any notebook, but *the* notebook. Not any knife, but *the* knife."

"I see. You're talking about a definite thing."

"Right. And the word *a* is called an *indefinite* article because it refers to, or indicates, any one of a group of things you're talking about. For example: *a* tree, *a* snake. Not any particular tree or snake, but *any* one tree or *any* one snake."

"I see. And what do you call the word *an*?"

"Well, the word *an* is really the same as the word *a*—an indefinite article. It's just that sometimes it's hard to pronounce a phrase that begins with the word *a*. When that happens, you use the word *an* instead. That's all."

"I don't understand."

"Well, do you know that some letters are called *vowels* and the others are called *consonants*?"

156

"I think so."

"Well, just to review, then, vowels are the letters that you can pronounce with your mouth open—*a, e, i, o,* and *u.* And sometimes *y,* as in the word *by.* Anyway, if a word starts with a vowel sound, it's hard to say it with the word *a* before it. I mean, it's hard to say something like *a eagle* or *a apple.* So in those cases, people substitute the word *an—an eagle, an apple.* But the word *an,* just like the word *a,* is an indefinite article."

"So you're saying that if a word starts with a vowel you should use *an,* but if it starts with a consonant, you should use *a?*"

"Not exactly. It's not a matter of whether the word starts with a vowel or consonant. It's whether or not the word starts with a vowel *sound.* Now, usually, if a word starts with a vowel, it will start with a vowel sound—like *eagle* and *apple.* And usually if a word starts with a consonant it will start with a consonant sound—like *cabin* and *turtle.* But that's not always true. For example, the word *honor* starts with a consonant, *h,* but it starts with a vowel sound—because the *h* is silent. So you would say *an* honor, not *a* honor. And the word *uniform* starts with a vowel, *u,* but the *u* is pronounced like a consonant; it's pronounced like a *y*—like the sound of *y* when *y* is a consonant, I mean. So you would say *a* uniform, not *an* uniform."

"I see. Is that all there is to it?"

"That's it. So, are you ready to underline some articles in Article 3?"

"Sure. But it will be so easy. All I have to do is underline the words *the, a,* and *an.* Anyone could do that. Give me the notebook." He took the notebook. "Where should I start?"

I pointed to the seventh paragraph of Article 3 and said, "Start here and underline all the articles in the next three paragraphs."

As he drew underlines, he kept saying, "This is so easy . . . this is so easy."

He handed back the notebook, and it looked like this:

He gathered her in his arms, whispering words of courage and love into her ears, for <u>the</u> greatest pain of their misfortune, to him, was his wife's mental anguish.

Soon after, he lowered <u>the</u> curtain walls, tying them securely to <u>the</u> trees so that, except for <u>a</u> little opening, they were entirely enclosed.

As it was now pitch dark within their tiny house, they lay down upon their blankets to go to sleep. My father lay facing <u>the</u> opening, <u>a</u> rifle at his hand.

As I checked Tarzan's work, he said, "That was easy. I didn't see the word *an* anywhere, though."

"Well, that's fine," I said. "You got them all."

"Now can we celebrate?" he said.

"But there's one more paragraph in Article 3. We didn't use that for anything. I think we should have a review of all of the parts of speech we've studied."

"A review?"

"Sure. It's been a long time since we talked about nouns and pronouns and adjectives. I want to make sure you haven't forgotten anything."

"But what about brunch?"

"Well, we'll have a short review, and then we'll have brunch."

"And after that can we celebrate?"

"Okay. How would you like to celebrate?"

"I want to celebrate by going for a moonlight swim tonight at the pond."

"Okay, I'll make you a deal. Look at the last paragraph of Article 3. I want you to indicate what part of speech each word is."

"How?"

"After each word, just indicate the part of speech that word is in parentheses—you know, those curved lines you enclose things it. Take it sentence by sentence. You don't really have room to write in the parts of speech, so just recopy the paragraph."

"And if I do that correctly, we'll eat brunch, and then tonight we'll swim in the pond?"

"Unless it rains."

"It won't rain."

"Okay, then, it's a deal." I shook his hand to make it official.

Tarzan took the notebook and read the last paragraph of Article 3. Finally, he began to write. After each sentence he took a little break and then started again. When he was all through, he handed me what he'd written. It looked like this:

Scarcely (adverb) **had** (verb) **they** (pronoun) **closed** (verb) **their** (pronoun) **eyes** (noun) **than** (conjunction) **the** (article)

terrifying (adjective) **cry** (noun) **of** (preposition) **a** (article) **panther** (noun) **rang** (verb) **out** (adverb) **from** (preposition) **the** (article) **jungle** (noun).

Closer (adverb) **and** (conjunction) **closer** (adverb) **it** (pronoun) **came** (verb) **until** (preposition) **they** (pronoun) **could hear** (verb) **the** (article) **great** (adjective) **beast** (noun) **directly** (adverb) **beneath** (preposition) **their** (pronoun) **tree house** (noun).

For (preposition) **an** (article) **hour** (noun) **or** (conjunction) **more** (adverb) **they** (pronoun) **heard** (verb) **it** (pronoun) **sniffing** (verb) **and** (conjunction) **clawing** (verb) **at** (preposition) **the** (article) **trees** (noun) **that** (conjunction) **supported** (verb) **their** (pronoun) **platform** (noun), **but** (conjunction) **at last** (adverb) **it** (pronoun) **roamed** (verb) **away** (adverb).

For (preposition) **a** (article) **moment** (noun) **my** (pronoun) **father** (noun) **saw** (verb) **it** (pronoun) **clearly** (adverb) **in** (preposition) **the** (article) **brilliant** (adjective) **moonlight** (noun)—**a** (article) **great** (adjective), **handsome** (adjective) **beast** (noun), **the** (article) **largest** (adjective) **he** (pronoun) **had** (verb) **ever** (adverb) **seen** (verb)!

I checked his work very slowly and carefully. I wanted to make sure he understood everything about parts of speech. I mean I checked every single word. Finally I said, "You're very good at this. I think you could be a grammar teacher."

He smiled.

"Let's go over one thing," I said. "Some words don't have a part of speech indicated after them. Why not?"

"I know what you're talking about. You're talking about *could hear, tree house,* and *at last.* I didn't put anything after *could, tree,* or *at.* I thought that *could hear* was like one verb. And I thought that *tree house* was like one noun. And I thought that *at last* was like one adverb."

"I agree with you. But could you say that in *tree house* the noun is *house* and that the word *tree* is an adjective describing the kind of house?"

159

"I guess you can say that. But I think of a tree house as its own thing—a tree house."

"And in *at last*, could you say that the word *at* is a preposition?"

"I don't think so. Prepositions have objects that are nouns or pronouns. If *at* were a preposition, the object would have to be *last*—but *last* isn't a noun or pronoun. So I think the whole phrase, *at last*, is an adverb telling when."

"Well, if I were a real teacher, I'd give you a hundred percent on this assignment!"

Tarzan smiled widely then said, "Good! Now we can have brunch!"

"Okay. I'm hungry. What shall we have?"

"Wait here." Tarzan ran out the door.

After about ten minutes he came back with an armful of fruit.

"What's all that?" I said. There were fruits of every color and shape.

"Just different things I found in the jungle."

We ate a leisurely brunch and talked about how we would spend the afternoon. Normally we would have gone swimming and talked about grammar. But we were saving the swimming for our "celebration" tonight, and we'd just ended the first phase of our grammar lessons and it was time for a break.

"What should we do this afternoon?" I said.

"I don't know. What do you want to do?"

"I asked you first." I know that was a babyish thing to say, but it just came out.

"Well, we could swim."

"No, we can't. We're saving that for tonight."

"Well, we can continue our grammar lesson."

"No," I said, "first we have to celebrate the fact that we finished studying all the parts of speech. Then we can talk more about grammar."

"Then what do you want to do?"

"I don't know."

We stopped talking for a while. We nibbled on some more fruit even though we were pretty full.

"How do your arms feel?" Tarzan finally said.

"Better. I think they're okay. I think I can swing from trees again."

"That's good. I have two ideas about what we can do this afternoon. I'll tell you what they are, and you can choose."

"Okay. What?"

160

"The first idea is to go to a place I know where you can see baby birds in nests and lots of huge butterflies flying all around. They're all different colors."

"That sounds good. What's the other idea?"

"Well, we can't swim or talk about grammar. But what if we go to the river and just stand about knee-deep in the water. That won't really be swimming. And while we do that, I can tell you what happened to my parents next so that you can write Article 4. That's not really talking about grammar, and we'll need another article for when you teach me the next thing you want to teach me about grammar."

"Both of those ideas sound good. We can do both. Why don't we go to where the baby birds and butterflies are, and we'll find some water there to stand in. Okay?"

"Okay." He smiled. "And don't forget: Tonight we take a moonlight swim in the pond."

"I didn't forget," I said.

We walked through the cabin door holding hands. It felt like every so often he gave my hand a little squeeze. But it was so subtle, I couldn't be sure. Maybe it was my imagination.

Chapter 18: The Land of Butterflies and Birds

When we got to the trees, Tarzan said, "Follow me." He grabbed a vine and so did I. We both swung from tree to tree. My arms felt okay, and I was able to keep up with him.

After about twenty minutes we came to a sort of clearing and dropped to the ground. We began to walk across it. Small trees were scattered here and there.

"What's this?" I said.

"This is where the butterflies are."

"I don't see any."

"Just wait. You will."

As we approached one of the trees, I noticed that one branch was strangely colored. Instead of brown, it was red and blue and yellow.

"Look at that branch!" I exclaimed. "Why is it a funny color?"

"That branch is covered with butterflies. It's a swarm of them that must have just flown here. They're all resting together on that branch."

"Is it safe to go closer?" I asked.

"Sure."

We walked closer and then Tarzan said, "Watch this." He clapped his hands loudly and the butterflies, hundreds and hundreds of them, flew into the air in all directions. Some were blue, others red, and still others yellow. Some were various shades of those colors, like orange, pink, or purple. Some of their wings were solid in color, but some were striped, streaked, or dotted. Others displayed some kind of fantastic pattern of various colors.

The butterflies ranged in size from very small to enormous. The largest had a wingspan of about ten inches! They flew all around us and we stared at them in wonder.

"This is amazing! It's beautiful!" I cried out.

"I'm glad you like it," Tarzan said, smiling.

Eventually the butterflies gathered together again on the branch.

"Let's not disturb them anymore," I said. "Let's leave them in peace."

"Okay."

We continued walking through the clearing. At one point Tarzan said, pointing, "Okay, do you see that small tree over there? It has a bird's nest on the middle branch."

I saw what looked like a brown mound sitting on a branch that was only about four feet above the ground. We walked over to it.

The nest was made of twigs. Inside were three tiny baby birds. I don't know what kind they were. They must have just hatched, because the eggshells were still in the nest. The babies had their mouths open, pointing upward. They seemed to be blind.

"Can they see?" I asked.

"I think baby birds are blind for the first few days. Then they develop sight."

"They're hungry. They look like they're starving."

"They are. Their mother must be nearby, gathering food. Let's stand back a little; otherwise, the she might be afraid to come near."

We stepped back about twenty feet. Shortly after, the mother, with a worm hanging from her beak, swooped down into the nest and began to feed the babies. They gobbled up the worm.

"That's so cute!" I said. "I'm going to name this place the Land of Butterflies and Birds."

Tarzan didn't say anything, so I guess he agreed to the name.

We kept walking until we had crossed the clearing. As soon as we reentered the jungle we came to a little brook. We stepped into it and the cool, clear water came up to our ankles. We followed it by walking in it, in the direction that the water flowed. The further we walked, the deeper the water became. Now it was no longer a little brook, but a stream—maybe even a small river. When the water was up to our knees we stopped and turned toward each other. I said, "Is this what you had in mind when you said we should stand in water that was knee-deep?"

"Yes. We don't want to swim, because we're saving that for tonight. But it feels good to stand in the water like this." He made the palms of his hands very flat and extended them toward me. I flattened my palms and pressed them against his.

Who would have ever thought that a girl from Maryland would one day be standing knee-deep in a stream in the middle of Africa with her hands pressed against those of an Ape Man? It's just funny how things turn out sometimes.

We kept our hands like that. Neither of us seemed to want to separate. Finally Tarzan said, "I can tell you what happened to my parents next, so you can write Article 4."

"But I don't have my notebook."

"Can you just remember what I say and write it down later?"

"I guess so." Our hands were still pressed together. "After you tell me, we'll go back to the cabin and I'll write Article 4. While I do that, you can gather our dinner. And after that it will be time for our moonlight swim."

"Okay. What's the last thing I told you about my parents?"

"You said they were in their tree house and your father saw a panther."

"Right. Well, here's what happened next." Tarzan told me about how his parents built a cabin—the very cabin I was living in now! I made mental notes as he spoke so that I'd be able to write the article when we got back. At some point during his story we separated our hands because our wrists were beginning to ache a little.

When I thought I had enough material for an article, I said, "Let's stop there. That's enough for the next article." Then I said, "Let's start back now, okay?"

"Okay."

"But let's walk back, I said. There's something I want to talk to you about."

"What?"

"Well, it's something about grammar."

"But I thought we weren't going to talk about grammar again until after we celebrate."

"I know. But this is just something extra. It's not something that I'm going to ask you to demonstrate your knowledge of by underlining words or anything."

Tarzan didn't answer.

"It's just a term I want you to know," I said. "You don't have to do anything with this term, but I just want you to know it—because grammarians mention it sometimes."

"Well, okay. I don't mind talking about grammar now—before we celebrate, I mean. I like grammar. What's the term?"

I took his hand and we walked out of the stream. "The term is *predicate*." We started walking back toward the cabin.

"What does that mean?"

"Well, do you know how sometimes we speak of a sentence as having a subject and a verb?"

"Yes," he said, with an upward inflection.

"Well, just as an example, if I say 'Tarzan swims,' the subject is *Tarzan* and the verb is *swims*, right?"

"Right."

"But usually sentences are more complicated than that. For example, I might say 'The mighty Tarzan swims through the river.' Now, in that sentence, the subject is still *Tarzan* and the verb is still *swims*.

But grammarians sometimes talk about something called the *complete subject* and something else called the *predicate*. The complete subject of a sentence is the subject *and* its modifiers. In other words, it's the entire subject; it's what the sentence is about. In the example I just gave, the complete subject is *The mighty Tarzan*."

"I see," Tarzan said. The complete subject is *The mighty Tarzan* because the words *the* and *mighty* go along with the word *Tarzan*; they modify it, right?"

"That's right. Now, you might think that a verb and all the words that go along with *it* would be called a *complete verb*. But they aren't. Grammarians call the verb and everything that goes along with it—its modifiers, its object, and its object's modifiers—the *predicate*."

"So what you're saying is that I can think of a predicate as a complete verb—even though it isn't called that."

"That's right. For example, in the sentence I gave before, the verb is *swims*, but the predicate is *swims through the river*."

"I think I see. *Through the river* is a prepositional phrase that modifies *swim*. It tells where, so it's an *adverbial* phrase as well as a prepositional phrase. And as an adverbial phrase it modifies the verb."

"Exactly. And since it modifies the verb, it's part of the predicate."

"So," he said, "basically, any sentence can be divided into just two parts—the complete subject and the predicate. And anything that modifies the subject is part of the complete subject and anything that modifies the verb is part of the predicate."

"That's right. Now, let me give you two other terms. The first is *predicate adjective*."

"What's that?"

"Well, it's simple. An adjective that's part of the predicate is called a *predicate adjective*. For example, if I say 'Tarzan is strong,' the predicate is *is strong*. Since the word *strong* is an adjective and it's part of the predicate, it's called a *predicate adjective*."

"But if I just said that it's an adjective, would that be wrong?"

"No, you can say that. It *is* an adjective. But if you wanted to be more specific, you could say that it's a predicate adjective."

"Oh."

"Now, the other term I want you to know is *predicate noun*. Can you guess what that is?"

"Well, I would guess that it's a noun that's part of the predicate."

"You're right. For example, if I said 'Tarzan is a man,' the predicate is *is a man*. The word *man* is a *predicate noun*—because it's a noun that's part of the predicate. And yes, if you wanted to, you could simply call it a noun and that would be correct, too."

"But calling it a *predicate noun* would be more specific, right?"

"That's right."

We were now approaching the clearing with the small trees—I mean we were approaching the Land of Butterflies and Birds. As we walked through it, I noticed that the baby birds were still in their nest with their mouths open and that the butterflies were still resting on the branch. When we crossed the clearing Tarzan took my hand and we continued into the jungle.

"As long as we're talking about terminology," I said, "there are a few more terms I want you to know about."

"Are you sure you want to talk about grammar so much? I thought we were going to celebrate first."

"Well, this isn't something I'm going to test you on. It's just something I want you to know."

"Okay. I don't mind. I like grammar."

"And you're very good at it."

Tarzan smiled.

"Anyway," I said, "I want you to understand what a *compound subject* is. It's pretty simple. A compound subject is one that consists of more than one noun or pronoun."

"What do you mean?"

"Well, if I say 'Tarzan likes to swim,' the subject is *Tarzan*. The sentence is about one person—Tarzan. But if I say 'Tarzan and Jane like to swim,' then the subject is *Tarzan and Jane*. It's about *two* people."

"So that sentence has a compound subject because the subject consists of two nouns—*Tarzan* and *Jane*."

"Exactly. Now, another term you should know is *compound predicate*. Can you guess what that is?"

"I would say that it's a predicate that consists of two or more verbs."

"That's right. Can you make up an example?"

Tarzan thought a moment and then said, "The beautiful jungle girl Jane dove off the branch and swam in the lake in the moonlight."

"I see what you have on your mind. But you're right. Now, what are the two verbs?"

"*Dove* and *swam*."

"Right. And what's the predicate?"

"Well, it would be everything that's not the subject—I mean every-thing that's not the *complete* subject. So the predicate is *dove off the branch and swan in the lake in the moonlight.*"

"Very good."

We continued walking through the jungle toward the cabin. Sud-denly I noticed something on the ground that looked like a brown square about twelve inches on each side. I dropped Tarzan's hand. "What's that?" I said.

"I don't know. Let's take a closer look."

The thing seemed to be in motion. Tarzan drew his knife. When we got up close we saw what it was—hundreds of worms tangled to-gether. They were slimy and shiny. They wiggled every which way.

I stepped back and said, "That's disgusting! Why are they all to-gether like that?"

Tarzan put his knife back in his waistband. "I don't know."

"Maybe we should go back to the clearing and tell the mother bird about this so she can feed her babies."

"I'm sure she can find worms for her babies by herself. Why don't we take them back to the cabin with us. We can use them for bait if we go fishing."

The thought repulsed me. "Let's just leave them here," I said. "I don't think I want to go fishing."

We resumed our trek back to the cabin. We didn't hold hands, though. I wasn't mad at Tarzan or anything. We just didn't happen to hold hands. That's all.

We didn't say anything for a while. I wondered what he was think-ing. Finally I said, "What are you thinking?"

"Nothing," he said.

We walked some more in silence. Then I said, "Since we're talking about terminology, there are a few more terms you should know."

"Am I going to be tested on them?"

"No. They're not difficult terms."

"What are they?"

"Well, I want you to know the difference between what's called a *simple sentence*, a *compound sentence*, and a *complex sentence*. Now, let's start with the simple sentence. A simple sentence is one that has one subject and one predicate. For example, 'Tarzan held Jane's hand' is a simple sentence."

"Can a simple sentence have a compound subject or compound predicate?"

"Yes. The sentence 'Tarzan and Jane held hands,' has a compound subject—*Tarzan and Jane*—but the sentence is still a simple sentence. Why? Because it has a subject—in this case compound—and a predicate."

"So," Tarzan reasoned, "a simple sentence is really the same as an independent clause, right?"

"Very good! That's right!"

Tarzan grinned.

"Now," I continued, "a *compound sentence* is one that consists of two simple sentences joined by a conjunction such as *and* or *but*. Or another way to say it is that a compound sentence consists of two *independent clauses* joined by a conjunction. Here's an example: 'Jane put out her hand and Tarzan took it.' Do you see?"

"Yes. *Jane put out her hand* is a simple sentence—or an independent clause—and *Tarzan took it* is another simple sentence—or independent clause. They're joined by the conjunction *and*, so the whole thing is a compound sentence."

"That's right."

"Can a compound sentence be made up of more than two independent clauses? What if I said 'Tarzan put out his hand and Jane took it, and then they continued walking'? Would that be a compound sentence?"

"Yes. When I defined a compound sentence for you, I should have said that it consists of *two or more* independent clauses joined by conjunctions. It's just that most compound sentences have only two independent clauses."

"How come?"

"It's just that a lot of times if you have more than two independent clauses in the same sentence, the sentence becomes a little confusing—to the listener or reader, I mean."

"Oh."

"Now, what's called a *complex sentence* is one that consists of an independent clause and a dependent clause. Actually, it's a sentence that consists of an independent clause and *one or more* dependent clauses. Here's an example: 'Jane took Tarzan's hand when he extended it toward her.' You see, in that sentence, the independent clause is *Jane took Tarzan's hand*. The dependent clause is *when he extended it toward her*."

"So the whole thing, independent clause plus dependent clause, is a complex sentence, right?"

"That's right!"

Tarzan smiled and took my hand. We continued walking toward the cabin.

"I think we'll be back at the cabin soon," Tarzan said. "Is there anything else you want to tell me about terminology?"

He really was an eager learner. "Actually, there is one other thing it would be good for you to know."

"What's that?"

"It's just that sentences are sometimes classified according to their purpose."

"What do you mean?"

"Well, first let me say that what I'm about to tell you doesn't affect whether a sentence is simple, compound, or complex. These "purpose" classifications are just an additional way of describing sentences." I paused a moment and then said, "Sometimes the purpose of a sentence is to state a fact. Other times the purpose is to ask a question. Still other times the purpose is to give a command or make a request. And still other times it's to express a strong feeling."

Tarzan didn't say anything. He just continued holding my hand as we walked.

"So, grammarians have given each of those types of sentences a name. A sentence that states a fact is called a *declarative* statement. Can you make up an example of a declarative sentence—a sentence that states a fact?"

"I'm hungry."

"That's good." After I said that it occurred to me that maybe he wasn't making up an example. Maybe he was really hungry. But I didn't ask him how he meant it.

"Now," I continued, "a sentence that asks a question is called an *interrogative* sentence. Can you make up an example of one of those?"

"Are you hungry?"

"That's right!" Again, was he making up an example, or was he really asking me if I was hungry? Now that I thought about it, I was getting hungry. But again I didn't ask him how he meant his answer.

"Okay," I went on, "a sentence that gives a command or makes a request is called an *imperative* sentence. Can you make up an example of one of those?"

"Join me for dinner, please."

"That's a good one. Now, one more. A sentence that expresses a strong feeling is called an *exclamatory* sentence. Can you make up one of those?"

"I'm starving!"

"That's very good!"

"No, Jane! I mean I'm really starving."

We were now approaching the cabin. "Well, I guess it's time to eat," I said. "I've built up an appetite, too, after all that hiking. Should we gather some fruit?"

He dropped my hand. "I'm tired of eating fruit all the time," he said. "I need some protein. I really need to eat some meat."

"But to do that, wouldn't you have to kill an animal?"

"Before we met, that's what I used to do. I only stopped because I thought it would upset you. But I really need protein."

"Well, to be honest, back in America, I ate meat, too. But I didn't have to kill it myself."

"You don't have to kill it yourself here either. I'll do it, and you don't even have to see it. In fact, you don't even have to know what it is. It might be a large animal, like a tiger or an ostrich, or it might be something small, like a rat or a snake. I'll cut the meat into small pieces and cook it. It will be delicious, and you won't even have to know what it is."

"You can cook it? You can make fire?"

"Sure. Haven't you ever heard of making fire by rubbing sticks together? I'm expert at that."

"But wouldn't rat meat or snake meat taste disgusting?"

"No, it's good. You just think that because you don't like rats or snakes. But like I said, you won't even know what you're eating— except that it's little cut-up pieces of meat. If you like, you can pretend it's steak."

The thought of a steak dinner sounded awfully good to me. I think my body craved protein too.

"Okay," I said, as we walked into the cabin. "I'll join you for a steak dinner. I'll stay here and work on Article 4 and you can go out and get our dinner. But pick some fruit to go along with the meat. And if you have to kill a tiger, make sure it isn't Yemmy and Omy's mother." I didn't know how he'd be able to tell, but I had to say that anyway.

Tarzan left the cabin and I sat at the table to work on Article 4. About an hour later, just before sunset, he returned with our dinner. I had just finished the article.

"What do you want to do first," I said, "read the article or eat dinner?"

"Eat dinner. I'm starving."

He spread out the food on the table and we sat down. The meat looked like meat. I didn't know what kind of animal it had come from, and I didn't want to ask. It was tasty and tender. Once I started eating it, I couldn't stop. I didn't even bother with the fruit. I noticed that Tarzan did the same. Well, we could have the fruit for dessert, I decided.

We didn't speak. We just devoured the meal. Eventually we slowed down and then stopped. "That was amazing," I said. "I really needed that. I don't know how people can be vegetarians."

By now the sun was setting and it was getting dark. It was probably too dark to read Article 4. That would have to wait for the morning. I suddenly remembered our plan to go for a moonlight swim.

"Tarzan," I said, "I know we're supposed to celebrate by going for a moonlight swim, but right now I'm too full. I have to digest my meal first. You should too. Let's just relax here awhile."

We leaned back in out chairs and didn't say anything. Every so often we looked at each other and then looked away. Sometimes my knee banged into his under the table. It was accidental, probably.

"Let me read Article 4," Tarzan said.

"I think it's too dark."

"There's still a little light left. I'll take it over to the window."

I gave him the notebook and he walked to the window.

"Can you see it?" I asked.

"Yes, just barely."

"Read it out loud to me," I said. "I want to hear what I wrote."

"Don't you know what you wrote?"

"Yes, but I want you to read it to me. I like the sound of your voice."

"Okay," he said. He read Article 4 out loud, as follows:

Article 4: "The Cabin"

My parents slept fitfully during their first night in the jungle, waking up at every strange sound. In the morning they awoke feeling not very refreshed, but they were greatly relieved to see that the sun had finally risen.

As soon as they had eaten a small breakfast, my father began to build a wooden cabin, for he realized that they could have no safety or peace of mind until four strong walls separated them from the jungle animals.

The task was a difficult one and required nearly a month, even though he built only one small room. He constructed his cabin of small logs about six inches in diameter, filling the spaces between with clay that he found a few feet beneath the surface soil.

At one end he built a fireplace of small stones. These also he set in clay, and when the house had been entirely completed he applied a four-inch-thick coating of clay to the entire outside surface.

In the window opening he set small branches about an inch in diameter both vertically and horizontally to form a grating that could withstand the strength of a powerful animal. The A-shaped roof was made of small branches laid close together. These were covered with long jungle leaves.

The door he built of pieces of wooden packing-boxes, which had held their belongings, nailing one piece upon another, until he had a solid body three inches thick. But here the greatest difficulty confronted my father, for he had no means of hanging his sturdy door now that he had built it. After two days' work, however, he succeeded in making two wooden hinges, and with these he hung the door so that it opened and closed easily.

The building of a bed, chairs, table, and shelves was a relatively easy matter, so that by the end of the second month they were well settled, and, except for the constant fear of attack by wild beasts, they were not uncomfortable or unhappy.

"That's a good article," Tarzan said when he'd finished. "I like it. What are you going to make me underline in it? We've already covered all the parts of speech."

"You'll see tomorrow, after our next lesson. But I'm not saying anything about it now, because first we have to celebrate by taking a moonlight swim."

"I know. And now it's dark and the moon is up. Are you ready to walk over to the pond?"

"Yes. I think we've done enough digesting."

We left the cabin, took each other's hand, and strolled toward the pond with the full moon shining down on us.

When we arrived at the water, the moon was high in the sky. But there was one problem. The pond was covered in mist. It was as if a cloud had dropped from the sky and settled on the water. I guess you'd call it a fog—a thick fog. It not only covered the water but it also covered the shore in all directions.

When we walked to the edge of the pond, we found ourselves in the middle of a milky world. We could hardly see each other.

"What should we do?" I said. "I can't see anything. I don't think it's safe to swim."

"But we knew it would be nighttime and that it would be hard to see."

"But we thought we'd be able to see by the light of the moon. But this fog is blocking it."

"So what do you want to do?"

"I think we have to go back. I don't feel safe swimming in this fog."

"But once we're underwater it won't make any difference anyway."

"But we can't stay underwater the whole time."

We didn't say anything for a while. Finally I said, "It's just too dangerous. I can't do it. But let's make a date to come back tomorrow night and try again, okay?"

"Okay," he said weakly. He seemed very disappointed.

He took my hand and we strolled back to the cabin. When we arrived he said, "Do you know what will be fun? Tomorrow night, let's build a fire by the pond. We can cook dinner there. Don't worry, you won't know what kind of meat it is."

"A cookout!"

"Is that what you call it? Okay then, we'll have a cookout. And then we'll swim in the moonlight, okay?"

"Okay—if it doesn't rain and there's no fog and the moon isn't blocked by clouds."

He didn't say anything, so I said, "Well, I guess I'll see you tomorrow morning, okay?"

"Okay." Then, instead of giving me a little peck on the cheek, he gave me a little hug. Then he turned around and disappeared into the jungle.

Chapter 19: Tarzan and Jane Rescue a Chimp

The next morning, when Tarzan met me at the cabin, he said, "What do you want to do today?"

"Why do we always have to do something?" I said. "Why can't we just stay here in the cabin for once?"

He didn't seem to know how to answer that, so I said, "Every time we go someplace, it's beautiful, I admit, but something terrible happens. I almost drown or we get attacked by ants. Always something."

"So you want to stay in the cabin all day? On a nice day like this?"

"We can go outside. But let's stay nearby. Just once I'd like to have a day when nothing bad happens."

He stared at me awhile and then said, "Well, what do you want to talk about?"

"Why do we have to talk about anything? Can't we just sit here if we want to?"

"I just thought—"

"Look, you don't have to entertain me or anything. I know that you live here and I'm a visitor, but I don't want you to think of me as a visitor. I can occupy myself if I want to."

"Um . . ."

I think that Tarzan thought I was mad at him or something. But I really wasn't. It's just that I didn't feel like going anywhere or talking right now.

"I'm sorry," I said. "It's not that I'm mad or ungrateful or anything like that. I just like being with you. We don't have to go anywhere or say anything. Don't you like it when we're together, no matter what we do or say?"

"I guess so."

"Well, that's all I'm trying to say. I really like you a lot, and I'm happy just being with you."

Now that we'd established that we weren't going to go anywhere or speak about anything in particular, Tarzan didn't seem to know what to do with himself. Finally he said, "Tomorrow do you want to climb a mountain that has a volcano at the top?"

Here we go again, I thought. "I don't know. We'll see tomorrow."

"Do you want to give me my next grammar lesson now and then have brunch?"

"Why don't you just relax. Come sit here at the table."

We sat across from each other at the table. I took his hands in mine. "Now stare into my eyes and tell me what you see."

"I see your eyes."

"No, I mean stare into my eyes and tell me what you see about my inner spirit, my soul. Have you ever heard the expression 'The eyes are the windows to the soul'?"

"No."

"Okay, now don't talk. Let's just stare into each other's eyes and see what we see."

We held hands across the table and stared into each other's eyes. Under the table our knees were pressed together. We didn't do that on purpose; it just happened because there wasn't a lot of room under there.

I found sitting like that very pleasant and I think he did too, because neither of us broke away for about sixty seconds. We just kept staring into each other's eyes. I guess you could say it was kind of romantic. Finally I gave his hand a little squeeze and broke away.

We stood up and I said, "Okay, come on. Let's have our next grammar lesson."

"Really?"

"Sure. Just do me one favor. Go to the door and see if Yemmy and Omy are anywhere around. If they're not, try calling them."

"You mean by saying *yoo-hoo*? I'm not going to do that."

"Okay, then just call them by name."

"Tarzan went to the door and looked out. Then he called, in a kind of singsong that went from high to low on each name, "Yem-my . . . O-my."

"There not there," he said, coming back into the cabin.

"Okay. Maybe they'll show up later. Anyway, here's the notebook, so let's sit at the table."

We sat down, but we didn't holds hand and our knees didn't touch.

"Not today," I said, "but tomorrow, I'm going to start talking about punctuation—you know, those little marks you make after a sentence or phrase, like periods, commas, and question marks. But sometimes, in order to know what kind of punctuation to use, you have to understand what's going on in a sentence. You especially have to understand clauses and phrases and different *kinds* of clauses and phrases. So, what I want to do today is review what we've already discussed about clauses and phrases, and then talk about them in a little more detail. Then I'm going to have you identify different types of clauses and phrases in Article 4."

"By underlining them?"

"Yes, by underling them. So, are you ready?"

"I guess so. I guess I'm not that hungry yet."

"Well, we had a big dinner last night. That meat was delicious! I can wait to eat too. So let's start."

We both shifted in our seats a little in preparation for the lesson.

"Now, you remember," I began, "that a phrase is a group of words that make sense together but are less than a sentence."

"And they don't have a subject and verb—otherwise, they would make a clause."

"That's right. But there's something I have to tell you. Some people use the word *phrase* rather loosely."

"What do you mean?"

"I mean that some people call anything that's less than a sentence a *phrase*, whether it has a subject and verb or not."

"You mean they don't make any distinction between a *phrase* and a *clause?* They just call everything a *phrase?*"

"Yes. Some people do."

"Is that wrong?"

"Not really. The word *phrase* has two meanings. Let's say that it has a literal, grammatical meaning and a loose, everyday meaning. If you're talking about the literal, grammatical meaning, a phrase is different from a clause because a phrase doesn't have a subject and verb. But if you're talking about the loose, everyday meaning, then there's really no difference between a phrase and a dependent clause—each is a meaningful *part* of a sentence."

"So which meaning of *phrase* are we going by—literal or loose?"

"Well, since this is a grammar lesson, we'll go by the literal, grammatical meaning. We'll make a distinction between *phrase* and *clause.*"

"Okay," he said. "So we'll call something a *phrase* if it doesn't have a subject and verb. Otherwise, we'll call it a *clause.*"

"Right. Now, you also remember that there are two types of clauses—an independent clause, which is also called a *main* clause, and a dependent clause, which is also called a *subordinate* clause."

"I remember."

"Okay. I know you understand all that. Now, what I want you to do is recopy the first four paragraphs of Article 4. Then, after each clause or phrase, indicate in parentheses what it is; in other words, after each clause or phrase write 'independent clause,' 'dependent clause,' or 'phrase.'"

"I thought you said I would be underlining."

177

"You will, after I teach you something else right after this."

"If I indicate that something is a phrase, do I have to say what kind of phrase it is? Like, do I have to say it's a prepositional phrase, if that's what it is?"

"No, you can just say 'phrase.' Now, here, take the notebook and start working."

I watched Tarzan work on the assignment. It didn't go quickly. After each phrase and clause he stopped to think before he indicated the answer. When he finally finished he handed the notebook back to me and I read it, as follows:

My parents slept fitfully during their first night in the jungle, (independent clause) **waking up at every strange sound.** (dependent clause) **In the morning** (phrase) **they awoke feeling not very refreshed** (independent clause), **but they were greatly relieved to see that the sun had finally risen.** (independent clause)

As soon as they had eaten a small breakfast, (dependent clause) **my father began to build a wooden cabin,** (independent clause) **for he realized that they could have no safety or peace of mind until four strong walls separated them from the jungle animals.** (dependent clause)

The task was a difficult one and required nearly a month, (independent clause) **even though he built only one small room.** (dependent clause) **He constructed his cabin of small logs about six inches in diameter,** (independent clause) **filling the spaces between with clay that he found a few feet beneath the surface soil.** (phrase)

At one end (phrase) **he built a fireplace of small stones** (independent clause). **These also he set in clay,** (independent clause) **and when the house had been entirely completed** (dependent clause) **he applied a four-inch-thick coating of clay to the entire outside surface.** (independent clause)

"Do you know what's so hard about doing this?" Tarzan said.

"What?"

"Sometimes something had a verb, but no subject. So I thought it was a phrase. But then I thought that maybe the subject was understood, so it was really a clause. I wasn't sure."

"Like where?"

"Like the part that says 'filling the spaces between with clay that he found a few feet beneath the surface soil.' I thought maybe the subject of that was understood to be *he*, from the previous clause. I wasn't sure."

"I see what you mean. Maybe that's why some people use the word *phrase* loosely—to apply to *anything* that's part of a sentence, I mean. Because it can be confusing. Or, I should say, because you can look at things in more than one way."

"And something else was tricky, too."

"What?"

"Sometimes a prepositional phrase occurred *within* a clause. I didn't know if I should separate that out and call it a phrase, or if I should just think of it as part of the larger clause."

"Like where?"

"Well, it happens a lot. For example, in the first sentence, 'during their first night' and 'in the jungle' are both phrases—prepositional phrases, I mean—but I treated them as if they were just part of the entire independent clause. But in the second sentence I separated out 'In the morning' and called it a phrase. I guess I did that there because it came at the beginning, so I thought the clause hadn't really started yet."

"I see what you mean. You can look at it both ways, and it can get confusing. Again, I think that's why some people just use the word *phrase* loosely to apply to almost everything."

"Also, sometimes two independent clauses were connected by the coordinating conjunction *and* or *but*, and I didn't think that those words were actually a part of a clause; they merely *joined* two separate clauses. But when there was a *subordinating* conjunction, like *for* or *even though*, I thought of that as actually being a *part* of a dependent clause."

"That's right. That's exactly how grammarians think about those conjunctions."

"So how did I do? Did I get a hundred?"

"Let me see." I studied his work carefully. "I think you did very well. Sometimes you can look at something in more than one way, it's true."

Tarzan smiled.

"Now," I said, "I want to teach you something new about clauses and phrases. This is the part you have to understand if you want to be really good at using punctuation, especially commas.

179

"What is it?"

"Well, some clauses and phrases are *restrictive* and some are *nonrestrictive.*"

"What does that mean?"

"Well, it all has to do with whether or not the clause or phrase in question is necessary to identify who or what you're talking about. Let's compare two sentences. The first sentence is 'Yemmy, who has a yellow coat, is cute.' The second sentence is 'The tiger cub with the yellow coat is cute.' Now, in the first sentence, because it starts with the word *Yemmy*, we know right away who we're talking about. That means that the clause *who has a yellow coat* is merely a description that adds additional information about something that's already been identified. If we eliminated those words, we'd still know who we're talking about—Yemmy. Anyway, a phrase or dependent clause that merely describes something but doesn't *identify* it, is called *nonrestrictive*; I mean it's called a *nonrestrictive phrase* or *nonrestrictive clause*. And whenever you have a nonrestrictive phrase or clause, you put a comma before it and after it."

"A comma?"

"You know, that little curly thing."

"Oh."

"Now let's look at the second sentence: 'The tiger cub with the yellow coat is cute.' Now, in that sentence, the first words are *The tiger cub*. But since there's more than one tiger cub, we don't know yet which one we're talking about. In that case the phrase *with the yellow coat* tells us that we're talking about Yemmy and not Omy. That phrase was *necessary* to identify Yemmy."

"Because you didn't say his name, so we didn't know who it was yet, right?"

"That's right. But the description *with the yellow coat* told us who it was. Now, any phrase or clause like that—I mean any phrase or clause that is *necessary* to identify who or what you're talking about—is called *restrictive*; I mean it's called a *restrictive phrase* or *restrictive clause*. And restrictive phrases and clauses *don't* have commas before or after them."

"Because they're not *extra*; they're *necessary*, right?"

"Right."

"But why are the called *restrictive?*"

"Well, it's because a restrictive phrase or clause not only describes something—the subject of the sentence, for example—but it also limits or *restricts* its meaning. For example, the phrase *tiger cub* is kind of

180

general in meaning. It can refer to *any* tiger cub. But by adding the words *with the yellow coat*, we're limiting or *restricting* the discussion to a *certain* tiger cub—the one with the yellow coat."

"That's Yemmy."

"That's right. Now, what I want you to do is take the fifth paragraph of Article 4 and underline any *restrictive* phrases or clauses you see."

Tarzan took the notebook and examined the paragraph. Then he drew two underlines and handed the notebook back to me. It looked like this:

In the window opening he set small branches <u>about an inch in diameter</u> both vertically and horizontally to form a grating <u>that could withstand the strength of a powerful animal</u>. The A-shaped roof was made of small branches laid close together. These were covered with long jungle leaves.

"Why did you underline *about an inch in diameter?*" I said.

"Because we're talking about branches—small branches, I mean. But there are lots of small branches in the world. The phrase *about an inch in diameter* limits the discussion to just the small branches that are about an inch in diameter and not any other small branches. It's necessary information."

"Good. And why did you underline *that could withstand the strength of a powerful animal?*"

"Well, we're talking about a grating, but it could be any grating. The dependent clause *that could withstand the strength of a powerful animal* restricts the discussion to a certain type of grating."

"Very good! Okay, now let's work on identifying *nonrestrictive* phrases and clauses. Remember, those are the ones that give *extra*, not necessary, information. Take a look at the last two paragraphs of Article 4 and underline all the *nonrestrictive* phrases and clauses."

Again Tarzan took the notebook. After studying the paragraphs in question, he drew a few underlines and then handed the notebook back to me. It looked like this:

The door he built of pieces of wooden packing-boxes, <u>which had held their belongings,</u> nailing one piece upon another, until he had a solid body three inches thick. But here the greatest difficulty confronted my father, for he had no means of hanging his sturdy door now that he had built it. After two days' work, <u>however</u>, he succeeded in making two wooden hinges, and with these he hung the door so that it opened and closed easily.

The building of a bed, chairs, table, and shelves was a relatively easy matter, so that by the end of the second month they were well settled, and, <u>except for the constant fear of attack by wild beasts</u>, they were not uncomfortable or unhappy.

"Why did you underline *which had held their belongs?*" I said.

"Because it's nonrestrictive. We already know that we're talking about my parents' packing-boxes, so the subject has already been identified. The clause *which had held their belongings* is just extra information."

"And why did you underline *except for the constant fear of attack by wild beasts?*"

"Well, again, I thought that was extra information. The basic idea is that they were settled and not uncomfortable. If we eliminated *except for the constant fear of attack by wild beasts*, we'd still know that."

Tarzan suddenly had a funny look on his face, as if he felt guilty about something.

"What's the matter?" I said. "What are you thinking?"

"I think I sort of cheated on that last one," he said, coloring slightly.

"What do you mean?"

"Well, I wasn't really sure if that was a nonrestrictive phrase, but I remembered that you said that nonrestrictive phrases and clauses have commas around them. Anyway, I noticed the commas, so I thought it probably was—nonrestrictive, I mean. That's sort of why I underlined the word *however*, also. It had those commas around it. But on top of that, it *did* seem like it was just something extra. I mean, if the word *however* was removed, the overall meaning wouldn't change."

"But *however* is just one word. Did you really consider it a phrase?"

"Well, I know that you said that a phrase is a two or more words, but I thought that maybe this was a nonrestrictive *word*. And I thought that even though it's only one word, you might think of it as a *one-word phrase*. After all, it means pretty much the same thing as *on the other hand*, and that's a phrase. Do you see what I mean?"

"I do. Isn't it amazing how in grammar you can look at something in more than one way? But you shouldn't feel bad about not being sure whether a certain phrase or clause is restrictive or nonrestrictive. Sometimes it can be hard to tell."

"It can?"

"Yes—especially when someone's talking, not writing, and you can't see any commas!"

"For instance?"

"Well, let me make up an example." I thought a moment and then said, "In the sentence 'The hunter who carried a knife killed a crocodile,' is the clause *who carried a knife* restrictive or nonrestrictive?"

He thought a moment and then said, "I don't know. I can't tell."

"Well, it all depends on whether or not there's more than one hunter. If you know that there's only one hunter, then the subject of the sentence has already been identified—the hunter. In that case the clause *who carried a knife* is *nonrestrictive*. If you wrote that sentence, you'd use commas. You'd write: The hunter *comma* who carried a knife *comma* killed a crocodile."

Tarzan didn't say anything, so I went on: "But let's say that you knew there were *two* hunters and that one carried a knife but the other carried a *shotgun*. In that case, when you say *the hunter*, you might be talking about either of them. But the clause *who carried a knife* identifies which one you're talking about—the one who carried a knife."

"I see," he said. "In that case—if there were two hunters, I mean—the clause *who carried a knife* is necessary—so you'll know that we're talking about the one who carried a knife and not the one who carried a shotgun."

"Exactly. And since it's necessary—or, you could say, because it limits or *restricts* the discussion to that particular hunter—it's a *restrictive* clause. And if you write it, you *don't* use any commas. And if you speak it, you might emphasize the word *knife*. You might say: The hunter who carried a *knife* killed a crocodile."

"I see. By emphasizing the word *knife*, you really mean 'The hunter who carried a knife—and not the one who carried a shotgun—killed the crocodile.' So the answer to whether the clause *who carried a knife* is restrictive or nonrestrictive all depends on whether or not there's more than one hunter. That's amazing!"

"Okay. I think we can stop there," I said.

"Okay. Let's have brunch. I'm hungry."

"Me too."

Tarzan gathered our brunch—no meat this time—and we ate it at the table. When we finished he said, "Tonight we're going to have a cookout and a moonlight swim at the pond."

"I know," I said. "That will be fun. I hope the weather is okay."

"And tomorrow," he said, "we can climb a mountain with a volcano."

"Well, we'll see about that." I didn't really want to do that. I was afraid the volcano might erupt.

"So what do you want to do today?" he said.

"Let's play with Yemmy and Omy."

"But they're not here."

"I know. Let's go look for them. We'll take a walk. Maybe they'll come to us."

We left the cabin and started to walk aimlessly through the jungle. I scanned the surrounding area, looking for them. Every so often I called our their names.

Suddenly Tarzan took my arm and said, "Look!"

I looked where he was pointing and saw a chimpanzee!

"Oh my!" I exclaimed. "A chimp! I love chimps! I was hoping I'd see one. What's it doing?"

The chimp was on the branch of a tree trying to reach something on a higher branch—something that looked like a roundish wad of tan paper about the size of a basketball.

"What is that thing?" I asked Tarzan.

"Oh no!" he said. "That's a hornets' nest. That chimp is going to get stung by hundreds of hornets. He could be killed."

We ran to the tree. "Come down!" we called. "Get away from that nest!" The chimp didn't seem to understand. He'd now reached the nest and was poking at it.

"I'm going to have to climb up there and bring him down," Tarzan said.

"You can't," I said. "You'll get stung yourself."

"I have to."

Tarzan scrambled up the tree. Just as he reached the chimp, the nest broke open and hundreds of hornets swarmed out. They filled the air with a buzzing sound. Tarzan grabbed the chimp and jumped to the ground. Then all three of us began to run like crazy toward the cabin. We waved our hands all around us to keep the hornets away. At one point the chimp must have been stung because he cried out in pain. The further we ran, the less dense the hornets became. Finally we got to the cabin and closed the door. Tarzan and I hadn't been stung. The hornets apparently hadn't followed us. At least we didn't see any.

The chimp whimpered in pain and a protective, motherly impulse overwhelmed me. "Don't worry, little chimp, I'll take care of you," I said. "Now, now, where does it hurt? Show Mommy."

The chimp continued to whimper. "It's on his right leg," Tarzan said. "I see it."

I looked at his leg and saw a swelling. "Tarzan, get me a wet leaf. I want to put it on the swelling." Then to the chimp: "Don't worry. It will only hurt for a little while. I'm going to put a wet leaf on your leg and it'll feel better." The chimp looked at me and puckered his lips. Then he scratched himself under his armpit and made a high-pitched noise.

Tarzan left but soon came back with a large wet leaf. "I dunked this in a brook," he said. "It's nice and cool."

"Thanks," I said. I took the leaf and wrapped it around the chimp's leg, where the swelling was. Then I said to it, "Now, you sit quietly while the pain goes away. And don't play with any more hornets' nests!" The chimp made a high-pitched sound again.

"We're going to have to stay here and take care of him," I said to Tarzan. "If he's not better by tonight, we'll have to postpone our cookout and moonlight swim."

"I think he'll be better by tonight," Tarzan said. "Hornet stings don't hurt for more than a few hours."

"Then we'll stay with him for a few hours." Then to the chimp: "What's your name, little fellow? Do you have a name? Does your mother know where you are?" Then to Tarzan: "Do you think he has a name?"

"I don't know. What difference does it make?"

"If he had a name, we'd know what to call him. Otherwise, we'll have to keep calling him 'chimp.'"

"What's wrong with that? That's what he is, isn't he?"

"It's just so impersonal. I think he'd feel better—more loved—if we called him by a real name."

I knew what Tarzan was thinking. He was thinking that if we named him, I'd think of him as a pet. And Tarzan didn't believe in keeping animals as pets. But we wouldn't keep him trapped or locked up or anything. He'd still be free. It's just that we would take care of him and give him love.

Tarzan didn't say anything, so I said, "What's a good name for him?"

"I don't know."

"But if you *had* to make up a name, what would it be?"

"I don't know."

"I mean if it was a matter of life or death, what name would you pick?"

"I don't know."

This was getting us nowhere. I tried a different tack.

"If you could have any kind of animal for a pet, what would it be?"

"None."

"But if you *had* to."

"Well, then I guess I would choose a cheetah."

"Why?"

"Because a cheetah is the fastest runner in the jungle. It's so fast that it would be able to run away from me and I wouldn't be able to catch it. So I'd really end up with no pet at all. And that's how it should be. Animals should be free."

"So, you'd pick a cheetah. Well, that's a good name." Then to the chimp: "Hear that, little fellow? Your name is Cheetah. Tarzan just picked a wonderful name for you."

"Hey," said Tarzan, "I didn't say that. I was just making a joke."

"Still, I think it's a wonderful name." Then to Cheetah: "How's your leg, Cheetah? Is it starting to feel better?"

Cheetah smiled and scratched himself and made funny noises.

Tarzan frowned.

"I think he's starting to feel better. But let's stay with him here. And listen, do you know what we can do now? Tomorrow morning I'm going to teach you about punctuation. We're going to need to write Article 5 before that so you'll have sentences to demonstrate your knowledge with."

"By underlining again?"

"Not necessarily. We'll see."

"Okay. I guess we can work on that now. But what about him?" he said, pointing to Cheetah, who was now sitting at the table.

"You mean what about *Cheetah?*" I asked. I wanted to make sure that we used his name. It didn't sound nice to refer to him as *him* when he's sitting right there. It was kind of rude. But I didn't bother explaining all that to Tarzan because he'd have said that it didn't make any difference how we referred to him because chimps don't understand English.

Finally Tarzan said, "Okay, what about Cheetah?"

"Well, when you tell me what happened next to you parents—and by the way, I can't wait to hear what happened to them—you can tell *both* of us. I'm sure that Cheetah would love to hear what happened too."

"But he doesn't understand—" He didn't finished the sentence. I guess he decided to humor me for some reason. "Okay," he said.

"Good. But before you start talking, let me fill Cheetah in on what happened so far."

Tarzan rolled his eyes. It was the first time I'd ever seen him do that.

"Now Cheetah, listen carefully. What happened so far is that Tarzan's parents—John and Alice—were stranded in this jungle. They were afraid of being attacked by wild beasts, so they built a cabin—this cabin." Then to Tarzan: "Okay, you can start now."

Tarzan opened his mouth to speak, but I said, "Oh wait. One more thing. I just want to remind you that Article 5 is the last article I'm going to ghostwrite. After that you're going to start writing your own articles. And when we finish talking about punctuation, that will be the end of our discussion of the basics of grammar. There are still lots of little things—little rules—to learn, but I want to take those one at a time as they pop up in the writing you do in Articles 6 through 24, okay?"

"Okay."

Tarzan spoke about his parents' continuing adventure in the jungle. As he talked he looked mostly at me but sometimes he glanced at Cheetah. Whenever Tarzan recounted something scary or exciting, Cheetah made a screeching sound. It may have been just a coincidence, but it seemed as if the little guy actually understood the story.

At one point I said, "Okay, that's enough for an article. Let me write this up now. Tarzan, why don't you play with Cheetah while I work."

I sat at the table and worked on Article 5. Tarzan and Cheetah seemed to hit it off right away. Cheetah liked to imitate whatever Tarzan did. If Tarzan made a funny face, Cheetah copied it. If Tarzan jumped up and down, Cheetah did that.

Once I wanted to ask Tarzan a question about something in the story and he said, "Wait. I'm doing something with Cheetah." For a second I felt that maybe now Tarzan liked Cheetah even more than he liked me. But I wasn't jealous. I loved Cheetah too. And besides, I didn't think that Tarzan *really* liked Cheetah more than me.

It took most of the afternoon to finish the article. When I was done, I noticed that the wet leaf was no longer around Cheetah's leg.

"What happened to the leaf?" I said.

"I took it off. The swelling went down. He's all better now."

"That's wonderful!" I said. Then I said, "Tarzan, come to the table. I want you to read Article 5. I want to know what you think of it."

Tarzan sat at the table and began to read. Cheetah stood by his side. Now, I'm not making this up, and you don't have to believe me, but it looked as though Cheetah was reading over his shoulder!

Anyway, here's what Tarzan—and maybe Cheetah—read:

Article 5: "The Gorilla Approaches"

One afternoon, while my father was searching for materials to build a second room onto their cabin, a number of small monkeys came shrieking through the trees toward him. Every few moments they'd cast a fearful glance behind them, as though afraid of some approaching danger. At last he saw it, the thing the little monkeys so feared—the man-beast my parents had glimpsed in the shadows during their first night in the jungle.

It was quickly approaching in a semi-erect position, now and then placing the backs of its closed fists upon the ground. It was a 300-pound gorilla, and, as it advanced, it wildly swung its arms, roared, and salivated.

My father was at some distance from the cabin, having come to chop down a particular tree for his building operations. Seeing the great ape crashing through the underbrush directly toward him, and from a direction which practically cut him off from escape, he felt a shiver run up and down his spine.

He knew that, armed only with an ax, his chances with this ferocious monster were small indeed. And Alice, he thought, what will become of Alice? There was still a slight chance of reaching the cabin. He turned and ran toward it, shouting an alarm to his wife to run inside and close the door.

My mother had been sitting a little way from the cabin, and when she heard his cry she looked up to see the ape springing with incredible swiftness in an effort to overtake my father. With a low cry she sprang toward the cabin and, as she entered, gave a backward glance that filled her soul with terror, for the brute had nearly reached her husband.

"Close and bolt the door, Alice," he cried. "I can finish this fellow with my ax." But he knew he was facing a horrible death, and so did she.

"That's good," Tarzan said. "That's really good. I hope that when I write my own articles, I write as well as you do."

"I'm sure you will," I said, encouragingly. "This story is getting really scary. I hope your father is okay."

"Well, you'll see what happens when I write Article 6."

"Okay," I said. "So anyway, I think it's time to start thinking about dinner. Cheetah, are you hungry? Do you want to have a cookout with us?"

"Hey, wait!" Tarzan said. "We were going to have a cookout and moonlight swim by ourselves. Cheetah doesn't have to come."

"Cheetah," I said, "Do you hear that? I think Tarzan wants to be alone with me. I think he wants me all to himself. Is that okay with you? Do you want to go out and play now so Mommy and Daddy can go to the pond and cook their dinner?"

"Mommy and Daddy?" Tarzan said.

"Well, you know . . ."

Tarzan rolled his eyes again.

"And tomorrow," I said to Cheetah, "you can meet Yemmy and Omy! Won't that be nice?" Then to Tarzan: "If we can find them, that is. Where do you think they are?"

"I don't know. I'm sure they're around somewhere."

"Okay, Cheetah," I said, leading him to the door, "go play now. We'll see you again tomorrow."

Cheetah stepped outside, then jumped in the air, flipped himself over, and landed on his feet. "Why, you're a regular acrobat!" I said. Then he made a few screeching noises and ran off into the jungle.

"He's so *cute!*" I said to Tarzan. "Now we're like one big, happy family—you, me, Yemmy, Omy, and Cheetah. Isn't this fun?"

"I guess. But having a cookout and swimming in the moonlight will be fun, too. Are you ready to go?"

"I'm all ready. We walked hand in hand out the door toward the pond.

Chapter 20: The Moonlight Swim

When we arrived at the pond, the first thing we did was gather logs, twigs, and leaves to build a fire. Then we piled them all on top of each other at the edge of the water. They formed a mound about three feet high. Then Tarzan made a flame by rubbing two sticks together. But he didn't actually rub them together as you might imagine. He cut out a round indentation in one stick and placed that one on the ground. Then he took the other and placed it vertically onto the indentation and spun it quickly in his hands. As the second stick twirled against the first, it caused friction, which in turn caused heat. Eventually, the sticks began to smoke, then burn. Tarzan used the burning sticks to ignite the leaves, which ignited the twigs, which ignited the logs. Soon, just as the sun set, the entire mound of kindling burst into flame. A huge bonfire blazed before us. A reflection of its red, yellow, and orange flames flickered on the surface of the water.

"That's beautiful!" I said.

"It'll be good for cooking our dinner," Tarzan answered. "You stay here and I'll find some meat."

"How will you see? It's dark."

"By the moonlight. There's a full moon."

"Okay, but be careful. And get some long, thin sticks so we can cook the meat over the fire."

"Okay."

"And bring some big leaves that we can use as napkins."

"Okay."

Tarzan left and I enjoyed the sight of the fire. I hummed a little tune to myself to pass the time. I walked to the edge of the water to feel the temperature with my toes. I wanted to make sure it wasn't too cold. This was our third attempt at a moonlight swim. First it rained, and then it was too foggy. I wondered if we would succeed tonight.

Finally Tarzan returned with the meat, the long sticks, and the big leaves. I didn't ask what kind of animal the meat—which Tarzan had cut into cubes—came from. I was going to pretend that it was steak again.

I took a stick and stuck one end of it into a piece of meat. Tarzan did the same. We held the meat over the flames until it looked well cooked; then we ate it. It tasted different from the meat the night before, but it was very good—crisp and tender.

"Instead of cooking one piece at a time," I said, "let's cook several." I picked up four sticks and jabbed each one into a piece of meat. Then I held two sticks in each hand over the fire. "Look, four pieces at once!" I said.

"Watch this," Tarzan said. He picked up a stick and jabbed it all the way through a cube of meat. Then he pressed a second piece onto the end of the stick, just above the first piece. Then he did this three more times, with three other sticks. He held two sticks in each hand and extended them over the flames and said, "Look, eight pieces at once."

Anyway, we kept cooking and eating the pieces of meat until they were all gone. We were pleasantly full. We watched the fire. It made pleasant crackling noises and gave off a pleasant warmth.

Finally Tarzan said, "Are you ready for our moonlight swim? Remember, this is our celebration for finishing all the parts of speech."

All I could think of—because of my mother's many warnings as I was growing up—was that I had to wait a half hour after eating before I could swim. "Let's wait a little longer," I said.

"Why?"

"I like looking at the fire." It wasn't really a lie.

"Okay, but just a little while."

While I waited for the half hour to pass, I sometimes smiled at Tarzan. Each time, he smiled back and then we both looked down.

"Okay," I finally said, "we can swim now."

We both stood up and walked to the edge of the water, about ten feet to the side of the fire. Our bodies seemed to glow in the firelight. We held hands and took a step into the pond.

Just then a thick cloud drifted in front of the moon. "Wait," I said. "That cloud is making things too dark."

"We can still see by the firelight," Tarzan countered.

"But not when we're out in the middle of the pond. We'll have to wait for the cloud to move away. Let's sit back down in the meantime."

We sat back down near the fire. "I wish we had some marshmallows," I said.

"What are marshmallows?"

"They're a kind of dessert, or treat. They're white, spongy, cubeshaped things made mostly of sugar. People sometimes toast them over an open fire like this one."

"Oh." He didn't say anything for a while and then he said, "When the cloud moves away, instead of walking into the water, I think we should dive in from the branches of that tree that's about a quarter of the way around." He pointed to it. "Remember, the tree you jumped from when we were talking about the moods of verbs?"

"I remember," I said. "The top two branches were too high for me. I jumped instead of dove."

"But now that you're a jungle girl—I mean now that you know how to swing from vines and you've become more used to scary things—I think you can do it."

I thought about it and said, "You know, I think I can too." After swinging from treetops on vines, that seemed simple. The middle branch was only about ten feet above the water and the top one about twenty feet. That wasn't so high. The thought of diving from a twenty-foot branch into a tranquil pond in the moonlight was exhilarating.

"Here's an idea." I said, "I'll dive off the middle branch and you dive off the high branch at the exact same time."

"I have a better idea," he said. "You dive off the high branch and I'll dive off the middle branch."

I thought about that. I guess I wanted to prove to Tarzan that I was brave. "Okay," I said, "I'll do it. As soon as this cloud passes across the moon, that is."

We both looked up at the cloud and watched its progress. It moved excruciatingly slowly. "Hurry up," I said to it in my mind.

After what seemed like an eternity, the cloud finally passed across the moon, which now illuminated the entire pond. We stood up, held hands, and walked to the designated tree. I climbed first, all the way to the top branch. Tarzan followed close behind but stopped at the middle branch.

Now we stood on our respective branches, ready to dive. "Okay," I said, "when I say three, we'll both dive. But you dive to the right and I'll dive to the left so we don't bang into each other."

"Okay," he said from the branch below.

"One . . . two . . . three." On three we both dove. I didn't dive straight down, though. I bent my knees and sprang upward first. Then I arched my back and began my downward trajectory. On the way down I thought to myself: I'm swimming at night!

I heard Tarzan's splash just before I hit the water. Then suddenly I was in an incredibly peaceful, cool, dark, wet world. I felt as if I had no cares at all. I felt completely protected.

I opened my eyes but couldn't see anything. But gradually I was able to make out Tarzan before me. We were both about eight feet below the surface. Neither of us made any move to swim to the top. Instead, we swam toward each other and pressed the palms of our hands together. Then, separating, we did a few underwater somersaults. Finally we were out of breath and we shot to the surface. Our heads broke water at the same time.

"That was great!" I said, treading water. We looked up at the moon. It was still there with no clouds blocking it. "Let's dive again. This time you take the high branch and I'll take the middle."

We climbed the tree again and dove. We swam underwater awhile, then did some somersaults, then swam around on the surface. After that we both dove from the high branch at the same time.

We spent about an hour diving. Sometimes we made up contests and games, such as who can make the least amount of splash when we hit the water or who can execute the most perfect swan dive.

Finally we swam to shore and sat next to the fire, which was still burning. The wetness on our bodies chilled us, but the fire warmed us; it was a strange sensation. Eventually the water on our skin evaporated and we weren't cold at all.

"I really wish we had those marshmallows," I said.

Tarzan didn't answer, so I said, "Well, I guess we should go back now. Don't forget that tomorrow we start on punctuation, okay?"

"Okay. But before we go we have to put out this fire."

"I know," I said. "We don't want to start a forest fire—I mean a 'rain forest' fire."

He didn't seem to realize that I was making a kind of joke, so I said, "What should we use to put it out?"

"We'll have to find something to fill with water and then douse the flames. Let's look around for some hollowed-out logs or curved pieces of bark."

We each found a curved piece of bark. Luckily, the fire was very close to the water, so it was easy to put out. At first the burning logs sizzled and smoked as we poured water on them, but eventually they became completely extinguished.

We walked back to the cabin hand in hand. "Well, we were lucky that cloud drifted away," I said. "Otherwise, we wouldn't have been able to swim."

"I know."

"Isn't it amazing underwater at night? It's so peaceful and quiet."

"I know."

Finally we arrived back at the cabin. "Well, tomorrow's another day," I said.

"I know."

"Is that all you can say—*I know?*"

"I don't know."

"Why are you acting weird? What's the matter?

"Nothing. I mean I don't know."

We stood before the door of the cabin without saying anything for a while. The moon looked down on us. Finally Tarzan said, "Would it be okay if I kissed you goodnight?"

He didn't have to ask me that. I would have kissed him. Instead of answering him out loud I gave him a smile that was intended to say: Sure, I don't mind.

He read the signal and gave me a quick kiss on the lips. It tasted sweet. Then he turned around and started to walk away. But suddenly he turned back, approached me, gave me another little kiss and a little hug. Then he turned again and ran off into the jungle.

Chapter 21: Tarzan and Jane Climb a Mountain

The next morning we met at the table, as usual. Neither of us mentioned anything about the night before; in fact, we didn't say anything at all. But we didn't have to. We seemed to be developing a special closeness that allowed each of us to know what the other was thinking and feeling.

Finally I said, "Did you see Yemmy, Omy, or Cheetah on the way over?"

"No, I didn't. But don't worry; I'm sure they're fine."

"I hope so," I said.

"I know we're going to talk about punctuation today," he said, "but remember my idea about climbing a mountain with a volcano? Let's climb that today and have our lesson there."

"You must be kidding," I said. "A volcano could erupt. The hot lava would burn us to death in a second. And you know as well as I do that every time we go somewhere that's supposed to be beautiful or magnificent, something terrible happens."

"I never should have mentioned the part about the volcano. I should have just said that it's a beautiful mountain. You see, it never erupts; the volcano is dormant."

"But that doesn't mean that it *couldn't* erupt."

"It won't, though. I mean it never has, as long as I've been alive. Look, I could argue that I don't want to sit here at the table because there might be an earthquake and that the ground could split in two right where we're sitting. And then you could say that there won't be an earthquake right here and I could say "But there *could.*"

I didn't answer.

"What I'm trying to say," he continued, "is that I'm sure there won't be an eruption. Really."

"But if there really *was* going to be an eruption, would we have any warning, in case we had to escape?"

"Well, there won't be an eruption, because, as I said, this volcano is dormant. But probably with an active volcano, there'd be some warning–like a rumbling noise or something."

"Probably?"

"Well, I've never experienced an active volcano," he said, "but it stands to reason."

"Well, I don't know. Where is this mountain? How far is it?"

"Well, it's far enough away that you can't really see it from here. But if we take to the trees, it won't take too long to get there."

Suddenly something occurred to me. I remembered something about Africa that I had learned while studying up on the continent in preparation for my trip here. There *were* no volcanoes on the west coast of Africa; only on the east coast.

"Tarzan," I said, "Are you sure this mountain you're talking about is a volcano? I thought that only the east coast of Africa had volcanoes—like Mount Kilimanjaro, for example. Why do you think this one's a volcano?"

"Well, because the top is curved downward, not upward. In my father's picture books, that's what volcanoes look like."

"But I'm telling you that scientists have determined that there are no volcanoes near here. That downward curve could have been caused by anything. The top of the mountain might have collapsed, or maybe eons ago it was hit by a meteor from space. For all we know, the indentation at the top of the mountain might be filled with water! At the top of that mountain might be a mile-deep lake."

"Really?"

"It could be." Now I was getting excited. "Come on, let's go."

"What about breakfast?" Tarzan said.

"We can have brunch along the way. We can pick some fruit or berries."

"Okay."

We left the cabin, entered the jungle, and took to the trees. As we raced from treetop to treetop, birds and chattering monkeys ducked out of our way. After about a half hour we dropped to the ground.

Before us stood an enormous mountain. If must have been about a mile high. It was made of dirt, not stone, and it was mostly covered with vegetation. It was steep, but not too steep to walk up.

"You know what this reminds me of?" I said to Tarzan. "In Maryland, near Deep Creek Lake, there's a mountain called Backbone Mountain. It's the highest mountain in the state. When I was a kid, my parents took me to see it. We tried to climb it, but my parents got too tired." I paused and then said, "Okay, are you ready to see what's really at the top of this mountain?"

"I'm ready," Tarzan said.

We started to climb. It wasn't easy, I have to admit—because of the steepness, I mean. After a while I started to feel a little out of breath. When I'd tried to climb Backbone Mountain in Maryland, I was only about nine years old and seemed to have unlimited energy.

197

"Okay," I said, "we can start talking about punctuation while we climb. First of all, let's talk about what punctuation is. Punctuation is the use of various little marks—or symbols—in writing to make the writer's meaning clear. Each of the different symbols is called a *punctuation mark*. But each one also has its own specific name—and its own particular purpose."

"I think I knew that," Tarzan said. "I've read about punctuation in my father's books. And I've seen it in the articles you've written. But it's still a little confusing."

"I know. Sometimes it can be tricky. So let's break it down into various types of punctuation marks. For example, some of them are used to end sentences. Those are the *period, the question mark,* and *the exclamation point.*" They're all easy to understand.

I looked up the mountain and saw that we still had a very long way to go.

"Anyway," I said, "a period looks like a little dot, and it's used to end a normal sentence. Mh."

I didn't mean to say *mh*. It just came out. It was an involuntary grunt I made from the exertion. But I didn't want to admit to Tarzan that I was getting out of breath because I didn't want him to think I was weak.

"So, if I were to write something like 'We're climbing a mountain,' I'd put a period at the end of that sentence. Ih."

That was another involuntary grunt. I found that if my lips were closed, the grunt came out as *mh,* but if they were open it came out as *ih*. I couldn't help it. The more we climbed, the more I felt like an old lady climbing a flight of stairs.

"Now," I continued, "if I were to write a sentence that's a question, I'd put a question mark at the end of it. Here's what that looks like." I drew a question mark for him in the dirt, like this: ?. Then we continued climbing. "So, can you give me an example of a sentence that would end with a question mark? Mh."

"Are you getting tired?" he said.

"Very good!" I said. I'd decided to take what he said as an *example* of a question rather than as an actual question.

"Now, an exclamation point is used to end a sentence that expresses a strong feeling or emotion. Ih. For example, if I were to write "Boy, this mountain is high!" I'd put an exclamation point at the end of it." I drew an exclamation point in the dirt for him, like this: !.

198

Instead of continuing up the mountain, I turned to him and said, "So, do you see what I mean about those ending marks being easy to understand? That's basically all there is to it." I was really stalling for time because I was tired. "Now, do you have any questions?" I was hoping he'd have a few questions so we could stand still awhile.

"No, I think I understand everything," he said.

"That's good!" I said, hiding my disappointment.

We started climbing again. "Now, the next group of marks I want to talk about are the ones that go *inside* a sentence. They're used to separate words, phrases, and clauses—to make the writer's meaning clear, I mean. The main *interior* punctuation marks are the *comma, colon,* and *semicolon.*"

The comma has so many uses that I didn't think I could teach him about commas and climb a mountain at the same time. "The comma," I said, "is a very special punctuation mark because it's used more than any other—so let's save that one for last, okay? Mh."

"Okay."

"All right. Now, a colon looks like two little dots, one directly above the other. It's used to separate two parts of a sentence in which the second part explains, exemplifies, amplifies, or summarizes the first part. Ih."

"What do you mean?"

"Well, let's say that I write 'We have one goal: to get to the top of this mountain.' I'd put a colon after the word *goal* because what comes next explains what was said in the first part of the sentence. Mh. Another way to look at it is to think of a colon as a little sign that says 'Get ready. Here comes the next part of the sentence, which is going to explain—or illustrate or amplify or summarize—what I just said.'"

"I think I see."

"Here's one more example of a sentence that uses a colon: 'You did everything necessary for a cookout: you hunted meat, gathered kindling, and started a fire.'"

"We put the fire out, too."

"I know. But in writing that sentence, you'd put a colon after the word *cookout.* Mh. By doing that you're saying 'Okay, get ready. Here comes the summarization—or explanation—of what was just said.'"

"I see."

We were now about halfway up the mountain. I touched Tarzan's arm and said, "Stop a minute. We're halfway up. Let's take a break." I think he knew I was tired.

"Okay."

"We can keep talking, though." I inhaled deeply and then continued, "Anyway, a lot of times when you have a colon, you have some kind of list after it—because the list illustrates what you just said. For example, let's say that I wanted to write 'The three longest rivers in Africa are as follows: the Nile, the Congo, and the Niger.' In that sentence I'd put a colon after the word *follows*. Generally, after the phrase *as follows*, you need a colon. Do you see?"

"Yes. You use the colon to indicate 'Get ready; here comes the list.'"

"Exactly. But you need to understand that you don't need a colon *every* time you have a list. You need it only if the list is preceded by an expression such as *as follows* or *the following*."

"Why?"

"Because sometimes a list acts as an object—a compound object—of a verb. And you don't separate a verb from its object with punctuation. For example, if I say 'Tarzan killed a snake,' the verb is *killed* and the object of that verb is *snake*. And it would be wrong to put any punctuation within that sentence. Now, let's say that I wanted to write 'Tarzan killed a snake, a spider, and a crocodile.' There we have a list of what you killed. But we don't need a colon after the word *killed* because the list of animals functions as the object of that verb. Now, can you reword that sentence in a way that *would* require a colon?"

Tarzan thought a moment and then said, "'Tarzan killed the following animals: a snake, and spider, and a crocodile.' In that sentence you'd need a colon after the word *animals*."

"Excellent! Now, one more thing. In the same way that you don't separate a verb from its object with punctuation, you also don't separate a *preposition* from its object—or compound object—with punctuation. So if I were to write 'I'm very fond of swimming, eating, and sleeping,' I wouldn't put a colon after the word *of*, even though what follows is a list."

"Because *of* is a preposition, right? And the list is its object."

"Yes. Exactly."

I gazed up at the top of the mountain and Tarzan said, "Are you ready to climb some more?"

"Okay," I said. I took a deep breath and we continued toward the top.

"Now," I went on, "let's talk about another interior punctuation mark, the semicolon. It looks like a comma—you know, that curly thing—but with a dot directly above it. Anyway, you use a semicolon to separate independent clauses that are *not* joined by a coordinating conjunction like *and* or *but*."

"I'm not sure I know what you mean."

"Well, remember, an independent clause is one that can stand alone as a sentence. It has a subject and predicate. Ih. 'Tarzan swims,' for example, is an independent clause. Now here's an example of *two* independent clauses joined by a coordinating conjunction: 'Tarzan swims and Jane runs.'"

"The two independent clauses," Tarzan offered, "are *Tarzan swims* and *Jane runs*. And the coordinating conjunction is *and*, right?"

"Right. But if I were to write that sentence and leave out the word *and*, I'd have to use a semicolon to separate the clauses. I'd have to write 'Tarzan swims *semicolon* Jane runs.'" I stopped, picked up a stick, and wrote the sentence in the dirt, like this:

Tarzan swims; Jane runs.

"Do you see?" I said. "The semicolon separates the independent clauses."

"I do see, but I'm confused about something. If you have two independent clauses, and each can stand alone as a sentence, why don't you just separate them with a period? Why don't you write 'Tarzan swims *period* Jane runs *period*'?" He took the stick and in the dirt he wrote:

Tarzan swims. Jane Runs.

"That's a very good question," I said. We started climbing again. "Actually, you *could* use periods and it wouldn't be wrong."

"Then why do you use a semicolon?"

"Well, sometimes two independent clauses are very closely related to each other. Sometimes they're so closely related that they feel like they're really one sentence."

"Like what?"

"Well, let's take the sentence 'I tested the water; it was cold.' Of course, if you say that out loud, there *is* no punctuation."

"Because punctuation is used only in writing, right?"

"Right. When people speak out loud, they use other means—pauses, facial expressions, gestures—to make their meaning clear. Ih. So anyway, if I say 'I tested the water; it was cold' out loud, I don't make much of a pause between the two clauses—because I want to show that the clauses are closely related; they're part of the same idea. And if I *write* it, I write: 'I tested the water *semicolon* it was cold.'"

"I see. If you used periods, the two clauses would become too separated. They wouldn't seem like part of the same idea."

"You've got it! Mh."

We were now about three-quarters of the way up the mountain. "We forgot to eat brunch!" I said suddenly as I spotted a nearby bush filled with red berries. "Let's stop awhile and have some of these berries."

We walked to the bush and each picked a handful of berries. "Let's sit," I said.

We sat on the ground and started popping berries into our mouths. The view from our lofty vantage point was amazing. Miles of jungles, plains, rivers, and lakes lay before us. We could even see the blue waters of the Atlantic Ocean!

"These berries are delicious!" I said. We each picked another handful and sat back down.

"While we're eating," I said, "we can talk about more punctuation marks." I said that because I knew I wouldn't get out of breath if we talked here, sitting down.

"Okay," Tarzan agreed.

"Okay, now, like I said, I want to save the comma for last. So let's talk about punctuation marks that you place both *before and after* words, phrases, and sentences."

"Which ones are those?"

"*Quotation marks* and *parentheses*. First let's talk about quotation marks. They look like this. I used a stick to draw a set of quotation marks in the dirt, like this: " ".

"What do they do?"

"Those mark the beginning and end of the exact words of a speaker. The exact words of a speaker are called a *direct quotation;* that's why those marks are called *quotation marks*. Now, in writing—when you're writing a story, for example—you usually have both *narrative* and *dialogue*."

"What does that mean?"

"Well, in a story, the *narrative* is what the author tells the reader. In other words, it's the regular telling of the story. But the *dialogue* is what the characters in the story say to each other out loud."

"You mean it's their conversation?"

202

"Yes. Dialogue is conversation. Anyway, when you write, whenever you want to show what is dialogue—as opposed to narrative, I mean—you enclose it in quotation marks. That way the reader will know the difference between what the author is saying to him and what the characters are saying to each other. Here, let me show you an example. I'm going to write a little story in the dirt here." I took a stick and wrote the following:

Once upon a time a reporter named Jane met a handsome jungle man named Tarzan.
"Hi, my name is Jane," the reporter said.
"My name is Tarzan," the jungle man said.

"Now, do you see how those quotation marks work? Only the part that the characters actually say out loud—the dialogue—is enclosed in quotation marks."
"I see."
"Now, let's change the story a little." I took the stick and wrote another story in the dirt:

Once upon a time a reporter named Jane met a handsome jungle man named Tarzan.
"Hi, my name is Jane," the reporter said.
"Did you say 'Hi, my name is Jane'?" the jungle man asked.

"Okay, now, in the last line of that example, the man says something out loud, but it *includes* a repetition of the exact words of the reporter. A situation like that is called a *quotation within a quotation.* The man is quoting what the woman said within his own quotation."
"That sounds complicated."
"It isn't really. Here's what you have to understand: Some people call quotation marks *double quotation marks* or *double quotes* because each mark is made up of *two* little lines." I pointed to an example of a double quote in the story. "Now, there's another kind of quotation mark—or, I should say, another *pair* of quotation marks—that's called *single quotation marks* or *single quotes.* Those are like double quotation marks, but instead of having *two* little lines, they have only *one* little line." I pointed out the single quotes in the last line of the story. "Now, single quotes are used to mark the beginning and end of a quote *within* a quote. Do you see?"

"I do. In the last line of the story, everything the man says is enclosed in *double* quotes, but the part where he repeats what the woman said is enclosed in *single* quotes."

"And do you see," I asked, "why you can't use double quotes for a quote within a quote?"

"Because then, all together, you'd have *four* quotation marks that all look the same. You wouldn't know where one quote ended and another started. It would be confusing."

"That's right!"

Tarzan popped one last berry into his mouth and said, "Should we keep walking? I want to see if there's really a lake at the top of this mountain."

"Okay." We stood up and started climbing again.

"There are a couple of other times people use quotation marks," I said.

"You mean besides for exact quotations?"

"Yes. Sometimes people place quotation marks—double quotes, I mean— around a particular word or phrase to show that that word or phrase is being singled out for special attention or that it's being used to mean something other than its usual or literal meaning."

"I don't understand."

"Well, I'll give you some examples, and that should make it clearer. Really, there are two different situations I'm thinking of. The first situation involves drawing attention to a certain word or phrase."

"When would you do that?"

"Well, let's say that you're talking about a certain word—as opposed to the actual thing that that word stands for. For example, let's take the word 'cheetah.' If I say 'A cheetah runs fast,' I'm talking about an actual cheetah. But if I say 'The word "cheetah" is spelled with two *e*'s,' then I'm talking about the word that *stands* for that animal and not the actual animal. Mh. Do you see?"

"I think so."

"Good. Anyway, in writing, to show that you're talking about a certain word, and not the actual thing that the word stands for, you place quotation marks around that word. Ih." It occurred to me that in books, words thought of as words are often printed in italics—you know, those letters that slant to the right—instead of indicated by quotation marks. But I decided not to mention that to Tarzan now because it might confuse him—especially since we didn't have any printed books with us to look at. Then, just for fun, or maybe to

204

tease him a little, I said to Tarzan, "Now, do you know the difference between the word 'cheetah' spelled with a small c and the word 'Cheetah' spelled with a capital C?"

"No. What?"

"Well, if it's spelled with a small c, it refers to that very fast-running cat. But if it's spelled with a capital C, it refers to our pet chimp—Cheetah!" I couldn't help but smile.

"Oh."

We continued climbing, and then Tarzan said, "What's the other situation you were talking about—when people use quotes, I mean?"

"Well, sometimes people use a word to mean something other than what the word really means?"

"Why do they do that?"

"Different reasons. Sometimes they're being sarcastic or kidding around. Sometimes they use a word that has a similar meaning to another word they might have used, but they use the alternate word to make a point or to emphasize something."

"I don't understand."

"Well, let me give you an example. Let's say I wanted to write you a note asking you if you've seen Yemmy and Omy. I could write 'Have you seen Yemmy and Omy?' or I could write 'Have you seen the cubs?' or I could write 'Have you seen our pets?' But I might write 'Have you seen the "children"?' You see, in that case, because Yemmy and Omy aren't *really* children, I put the word in quotes—to show that I know that they're not really children. Mh."

Tarzan looked puzzled. "But why," he said, "would you use the word 'children' at all if that's not what they are?"

"Because that's the best word to show how I *feel* about them. I love them as I would my own children. Do you see? I was making a point. I mean, I used the word 'children' in a sense other than its literal sense because that was the best way to show how much I love them. And *because* I was using it in a non-literal sense, I put it in quotes."

"Oh." Tarzan paused and then said, "Is this a discussion about punctuation or about whether or not we're going to keep Yemmy and Omy as pets?"

"Both!" I answered immediately. "Come on, let's keep climbing. Ih."

We were approaching the top of the mountain. "Just one more thing about quotation marks," I said. "If you're writing something and in it you mention the title of a song or poem or short story or something like that, you put the title in quotes. For example, I could write 'After Article 5, which is called "The Gorilla Approaches," you'll start writing your own articles.' Now, in that sentence, I would put quotes around the title of the article. Do you see? Mh."

"Yes. But look! We're almost at the top of the mountain. Come on, let's look over the rim to see if there's really a lake at the top."

I was very glad to be at the top, because I was completely out of breath from all the climbing. With a sense of great anticipation, I climbed the last few feet to the rim of the mountain and peered over the edge.

It was water! It was clear blue water.

The crater at the top of the mountain was about a hundred yards in diameter. But the water didn't come all the way to the top, where we were. The surface of the lake was about thirty feet below us.

"Wow! That's beautiful!" I said.

We stared at the shimmering water for a while without saying anything. The sky above was clear and blue. Finally I said, "We have to swim here. But can we? I mean, the water is so far down. How will we get down there."

"Well, we can just dive in. From here."

"Do you think I can dive that far? It's about thirty feet down."

"Sure you can. You dove twenty feet at the pond. This isn't much more."

"But how do we know how deep it is? What if it's only a few feet deep? We could hit the bottom and be killed. And besides, even if we could dive, how would we get back up here when we were done?"

Tarzan scanned the interior perimeter of the crater. Finally he said, "Do you see that over there?" He pointed to a spot to our left. Protruding from the nearly vertical earth was a series of roots and vines that formed a kind of ladder. "I can climb down those roots that are sticking out, all the way down to the lake. Then I can test the depth of the water by swimming down into it as far as I can. Then I can climb back up the ladder." Then he said, "Hey! Do you know what? If I were writing that last sentence, I might put the word *ladder* in quotes because it's not really a ladder!"

"Very good!" I said.

"Come on," he said. "Let's have a closer look at those roots."

We walked to our left until we were directly above the "ladder."

"I'm going down," he said.

Tarzan climbed down the protruding roots and vines without any trouble. Then suddenly he was in the water. "Okay, I'm going under to test the depth," he shouted to me.

He was under there a long time. I began to get worried about him. Then suddenly his head broke the surface. "It's bottomless," he called. "The water must go all the way down to the bottom. It's a mile-deep lake!"

He swam to the ladder and climbed it. He stood next to me, shaking water from his body and getting me wet. I didn't mind, though.

"So," he said, "it's deep enough, and it's easy to get back out. Let's just dive in from here."

I was still afraid to dive from this height. On the other hand, the idea of it thrilled me. I couldn't decide.

"Wait," I said. "Before we go in, let's talk about that other set of punctuation marks I mentioned—*parentheses*."

"Are you just saying that because you're afraid to dive? If you want, you can climb down the ladder—if you're too scared to dive, that is."

Was he being considerate of my feelings, or was he implying that I was a "chicken"? Well, nobody's going to call me a "chicken."

"I'm not scared!" I said. Truthfully, I was a little scared. But I wanted to dive; I really did. "All right. Let's dive. We can talk about parentheses in the water."

We stood side by side at the edge of the rim. "Wait," I said. "It would be better if there were something large, like a tree trunk, floating in the water down there. That way, if we got tired we could hold onto it—like we did at the pond."

"But there are no tree trunks here—except the ones growing out of the ground."

Neither of us said anything for a while. We just stared down at the water. Finally I said, "Maybe if you go partway down the mountain, you can find a large, fallen tree trunk."

"Do you think I'm going to lug a heavy tree trunk halfway up a mountain?"

"I guess you're right. It would be too heavy. That was a bad idea." I was quiet awhile and then said, "Do you think Tantor could drag it up here?"

"I don't think an elephant is going to climb a mountain."

"I guess you're right."

We stared at the water again. Then I said, "Maybe you can find something smaller. A branch or something. Something just big enough for me to hold on to. You don't get as tired as I do."

Tarzan looked down the mountain and I followed his gaze. We both saw it at the same time: a little tree about fifty feet down. "Okay. Wait here," he said.

Tarzan half walked and half ran down the side of the mountain to the little tree. He took his knife from his waistband and cut a medium-sized branch from it. Several smaller branches covered with leaves grew at various angles from the sides of it. He grabbed the thing in his hands and ran back up to me.

"How's this?" he said, holding it up.

The main branch was about three or four inches in diameter and about six feet long. The smaller branches were each about an inch in diameter. Some protruded about three feet to the left and the others about three feet to the right. "That's perfect," I said. "It will float, and if I grab onto it, it will keep me up. Go ahead and throw it down into the water."

Tarzan flung the thing into the air and we watched it fall. When it hit the water, it made a little splash and a little sound. "If looks kind of like a raft," I said. "I might even be able to lie on top of it, if I want."

"That sounds like a good idea. So are you ready to dive now?"

"I guess so. Why don't you go first," I suggested.

"No, I think you should go first," he countered.

"Um, well, are you sure you don't want to go first?"

"Look, why don't we just both dive at the same time. We'll count to three and then go."

I decided to stop acting like a baby. I was going to do it. "Okay. But let's make sure we don't land on the branch. Come over here a little." We walked about twenty feet to the right. Then we stood side by side on the edge, ready to dive.

Tarzan said, "One . . ." Then he looked over at me. "Two . . ." He looked at me again. I guess he thought I looked okay—not too scared, I mean. "Three!"

On "three" we both sprung from the rim of the mountaintop into the air. We arched our backs and then straightened ourselves. Next we were both completely vertical with our arms extended before us. As we plunged toward the water, two thoughts occurred to me: how cold was it and how hard would we hit it? But I didn't have much time to think about those things because within another second or two I found myself deep underwater.

We'd hit the water kind of hard, but our hands and arms softened the impact. It really wasn't too bad. At first the water felt chilly, but within a few seconds I'd become accustomed to it.

I didn't know how far underwater I'd plunged, but I guessed it was pretty far. I opened my eyes and looked up. The light above told me that I was about twenty feet down. I continued to hold my breath and swam to the surface. I wiped the hair out of my eyes and found Tarzan right beside me. We both smiled at each other. We didn't have to say anything. We both knew that the other was thinking: *That was an amazing dive!*

I looked around for the branch-raft and located it about twenty feet to our left. I swam to it and Tarzan followed. I grabbed onto the main branch and found that it easily supported my weight. But I was curious to see if I could actually climb onto the thing and lie on top of it. I hoisted myself onto the main branch and then lay at about a forty-five degree angle to it so that the smaller side branches would support some of my weight. I found that if I lay in just the right position, or angle, the raft would support me. Then I slid back off into the water and let go. I started to swim around, just for fun. Tarzan did too.

I started treading water and looked around. It was an amazing view and an amazing sensation. Below us was clear, cool water; all around us was an actual mountain; and above us was clear, blue sky. I felt as if I were in another world—a fantasy world.

"So," I said, treading water, "are you ready to talk about parentheses?"

"Let me do an underwater somersault first," he said.

"Okay." He dove under, and I did too. We both did a few somersaults down there and then swam underwater to each other and pressed our palms together. Then we both surfaced. We swam to the raft and both held onto it. We kicked our legs a little.

"Okay. Now, parentheses," I said, "are a set of curved, vertical lines that are placed around something—a word or phrase, usually—in a sentence. When you talk about either one of the curved lines individually, you call it a *parenthesis*. You might call the first one an *opening parenthesis* and the second one a *closing parenthesis*. But when you talk about both of them together, as a set, you use the plural—*parentheses.*"

Tarzan didn't answer.

"I can't draw them for you here," I continued, "because there's nothing to write on in the water." I paused a moment and then said, "Wait. I know. I'll draw them on your arm." I broke a small twig from one of the smaller branches of the raft and "drew" a pair of parentheses on Tarzan's upper arm. I used the twig to make a slight indentation in his skin—so slight that he hardly felt it. "Here," I said, "they look like this." I pressed the stick along his arm to form this: ( ).

"Oh. But what do they do?"

"Well, let's say that you're writing something and in the middle of a sentence you want to add something extra that doesn't really belong to the sentence."

"What do you mean?"

"Well, sometimes you want to add a little explanation or clarification to something you just wrote. Or sometimes you just want to add some extra information about something you just wrote. But let's say that that explanation or extra information isn't really a part of the sentence. Maybe it doesn't fit in grammatically with the rest of the sentence. Or maybe the idea of it is different from the rest of the sentence. Or maybe it's something that's completely unnecessary in the sentence, but you want to write it anyway. Something like that, whether it's a word, a phrase, or a clause, is placed within parentheses—to show that it's not really part of the sentence, but just something extra. Do you see?"

"I guess so."

"Well, let me think of an example, and that should make it clearer." I though awhile and then said, "Let's say that I wrote 'Our two pet cats, Yemmy and Omy (they were named after countries on the Arabian Peninsula) are very cute.' Now, because the part about them being named after certain countries isn't really necessary to the meaning of the sentence. I'd put that part in parentheses."

"Oh."

"Here's another example. If I write 'We're lucky enough to have three pets (two cats and a chimp),' I might put *two cats and a chimp* in parentheses—because it's just extra information that could have been left out."

"I see."

We looked at each other and continued holding onto the raft and kicking our feet. Then Tarzan said, "Why do you always make up examples about pets?"

"Do I? I didn't realize."

"You do. Why?"

"I don't know." I paused and then said, "I think I'll climb back onto the raft and lie on it. That's what people in America do when they want to relax."

I climbed on and positioned myself so that the raft supported me. I was flat on my back staring up into an endless sky. I felt safe. Then for some reason I started to think about crocodiles. "Tarzan," I said, "you don't think that a crocodile could have climbed up this mountain and dropped himself into this lake, do you?"

"Of course not."

"Good." I continued to stare straight up into the sky. A couple of puffy white clouds were visible in the distance. There was nothing else to be seen except the interior of the mountain crater in my peripheral vision.

"Do you think," I said, "that it's possible that a crocodile somehow entered this lake from the bottom, from the base of the mountain?"

"No, I don't think that's possible. There's no entrance at the bottom."

"Good." Then after a moment I said, "I think I'll just lie here awhile. It's relaxing. You can swim around if you want to."

"That's okay. I'll stay here by the raft."

I thought about what other punctuation marks I still needed to tell Tarzan about. Well, of course, we still had the comma to cover, but I was saving that for last. I could teach him about hyphens and dashes next. And after that I could talk about the ellipsis—you know, those three dot (or periods) in a row. That should pretty much do it. After that I could talk a little about italics and about writing numbers—whether to spell them out as words or use numerals, I mean. After that, he should be able to start writing his own articles (once we've covered commas, that is).

"Tarzan," I said, "I want to talk about some more punctuation marks: the *hyphen* and the *dash*. Now, the reason I mention those marks together is that they look a lot alike, and so people sometimes mix them up. Each one looks like a little horizontal line. But the dash is longer than the hyphen."

I was feeling very relaxed. In Maryland I'd sometimes take an inflatable raft to Deep Creek Lake and lie on it in the water. Sometimes I'd almost fall asleep on it. I realized that I was feeling a little sleepy now. I forced my eyes open wide and said, "Let's start with the hyphen. It's just a short little line. You can see hyphens a lot of times in books at the end of a line. Sometimes the last word of a line can't fit on that line. When that happens, the first part of the word appears on that line, then a hyphen is printed, and then the rest of the word continues on the next line. But I don't really count that as punctuation. That's really just a printing device." Then I didn't say anything for a few seconds because I had to yawn.

"Also," I continued, "some words are spelled with hyphens—words like *mother-in-law*, *twenty-one*, and *great-aunt*. But I don't really count that use of the hyphen as punctuation either. That's just how the words are spelled." I paused to yawn again. Then I started feeling myself drifting off to sleep. But I pulled myself out of it and sat up.

"I'm suddenly so sleepy," I said.

"Why don't you get off that raft and swim a bit. That should freshen you up."

"Good idea." I slid off the raft, swam underwater awhile, and then resurfaced. I shook my head back and forth to get the water out of my eyes. Then I took a deep breath. I wasn't sleepy anymore. "You were right," I said. "That was invigorating."

We faced each other across the raft. We each had both hands on the main branch and we kicked our feet gently.

"I'm going to dive again," Tarzan said. "I'll be right back."

He swam to the ladder and scampered up it. Then, without hesitating, he dove off the rim of the mountain. I watched him fly through the air. He hit the water about thirty feet from me and resurfaced across the raft from me, as before.

"Okay," he said. "So when do you consider a hyphen a punctuation mark?"

"When it's used to form a *compound adjective*."

"What's that?"

"Well, sometimes when you describe something, you need two words working together to describe it."

"What do you mean?"

"Well, I could write 'Your father was a well-educated man.' In that sentence, the words *well* and *educated* work together to describe your father. Those two words make up what's called a *compound adjective*— an adjective made up of more than one word, I mean. Anyway, often when you have a compound adjective, you place a hyphen between the words.

"Oh."

"Here's another example: 'American Monthly magazine is a Baltimore-based publication.' Now, in that sentence, the words *Baltimore* and *based* make up the compound adjective, and they are hyphenated. Do you see?"

"Yes, but I thought that the purpose of punctuation is to make the writer's meaning clear. In those sentences, even if you *didn't* use a hyphen, the meaning would be clear."

I thought about what Tarzan said and realized that in a way he was correct. I continued kicking my feet gently and said, "I guess in those cases you're right. But most people use hyphens for compound adjectives anyway."

"Why?"

"Well, I think it's because sometimes when you have a compound adjective, you really *need* a hyphen. I mean that if you didn't have it, the writer's meaning *wouldn't* be clear. The meaning might even be different from what was actually intended. In those cases you *have* to use a hyphen—to make the meaning clear, I mean."

"Like when."

I tried to think of a good example to make my point. Finally I thought of something, but it was kind of silly. But I couldn't think of anything else just then. I said, "Do you know what it means for someone to be *armed?*"

"Doesn't that mean that he has a weapon, like a gun or knife or something?"

"Yes. Exactly. Now, let's say that a gorilla happened to get his hands on your knife."

"How would he do that?"

"If you dropped it or lost it or something."

"I would never lose my knife."

"I know, but let's pretend that you did, for the example."

"Okay."

"So, anyway, let's say that I told you that I saw a hairy armed gorilla. That means that I saw an armed gorilla who was hairy. But if I used a hyphen and I wrote 'a hairy-armed gorilla' (when I said that out loud to Tarzan I said 'a hairy *hyphen* armed gorilla'), then that would mean that I saw a gorilla with hairy arms. Do you see the difference? Do you see how the hyphen works to make *hairy-armed* a compound adjective describing gorilla?"

"I guess so. But all gorillas have hairy arms, so why would you even point that out."

"You're right. They do. So let's change the example a little. Let's say that I wrote that I saw a hairy armed *man*. Now, does that mean that I saw an armed man who's hairy or that I saw a man with hairy arms?"

"I guess it all depends on whether or not there's a hyphen between *hairy* and *armed*. With the hyphen it means that you saw a man with hairy arms—a *hairy-armed* man. Without the hyphen it means that you saw an armed man who happened to be hairy."

"Exactly! Very good!"

"I really get it now!" Tarzan said, smiling.

"Okay, but I have to tell you that in a few situations, even if you have a compound adjective, you don't use a hyphen."

"Why? When?"

"Just a minute," I said. "I want to dive again. Wait here."

I swam to the ladder and climbed to the top of the mountain. I stood on the edge, looked down at the water, and sprang into the air. I hit the water like a bullet and shot down to about twenty or twenty-five feet below the surface. I swam back up and over to the raft. I positioned myself across from Tarzan again.

"Now, as I was saying," I said, "in some situations you *don't* use a hyphen for a compound adjective—at least, most people don't. There are three situations I can think of."

"But why wouldn't you use a hyphen if you have a compound adjective?"

"I don't know. It's just not considered proper in certain cases."

"Like what?"

"Well, for one, the general rule is that you use a hyphen if a compound adjective comes *before* the word it modifies. But you *don't* use a hyphen if a compound adjective comes *after* the word."

"What do you mean?"

"Well, before, I used the example of your father being a well-educated man. In that case the compound adjective, *well-educated*, came *before* the word it modifies—*man*. But let's say that I wrote 'Your father was well educated.' In that case the compound adjective comes *after* the word it modifies—*father*. Anyway, most grammarians believe that when the compound adjective comes after, you don't use a hyphen."

"Why do they think that?"

"I guess they think that when it comes after, there's no possible confusion about meaning."

"I guess I can see that," Tarzan said. In that other example, if you said 'The man was hairy armed,' I would know that he had hairy arms. I wouldn't think he had a knife or gun. I wouldn't be confused."

"You're probably right," I said. "If I were a real grammar teacher, I'd probably know for sure—but what you say sounds right."

"When else don't you need a hyphen in a compound adjective?"

"Well, if the first word of a compound adjective is an adverb that ends in *ly*, you don't use a hyphen. For example, I could write about a 'slowly moving turtle.' Because the first word of the compound adjective is an adverb ending in *ly*—*slowly*—I wouldn't place a hyphen between that word and the word *moving*."

"I think I know why," Tarzan said. "It's the same reason as before. No one would get confused by something like that. It can mean only one thing, I mean."

"I think you're right. Now, there's one other time you don't need a hyphen in a compound adjective. Sometimes a compound adjective is actually a compound noun that's being used as an adjective."

"What do you mean?"

"Well, remember that sometimes nouns can be used as adjectives? I remember that in Article 1 we spoke of *stone instruments*. The word *stone* is usually a noun, but in that case it was being used as an *adjective* describing *instruments*."

"I remember."

"Good. So, sometimes a noun that's made up of *two* words—like *high school*, for example—is used as an adjective, as in *high school student*—which is what I was a few years ago, back in Baltimore. Now, in a case like that, you don't place a hyphen between the two words that make up the compound adjective."

Tarzan didn't say anything. I thought that maybe he wasn't really familiar with the concept of high school. I tried to think of something pertaining to Africa, so he'd understand better. Finally I said, "Here's another example: A tsetse fly bite. In that phrase, I wouldn't put a hyphen between *tsetse* and *fly* because *tsetse fly* is a noun being used as an adjective; I mean a tsetse fly is something that exists in the world; it's something that has its own identity. Do you understand?"

"Are you talking about that African fly that sucks people's blood and causes sleeping sickness?"

"Yes, but just as an example."

"Are you afraid of being bitten by a tsetse fly?"

I hadn't been, but now that he mentioned it . . . Why did I have to make up that example? I started looking around for tsetse flies. It occurred to me that I'd been sleepy earlier. In fact, I'd almost fallen asleep on the branch-raft! Could I have already been bitten? But I would have felt it, wouldn't I? "N-no," I stuttered. "I'm n-not afraid."

"Sleeping sickness symptoms aren't pleasant," he said.

"What are they? Wait! Before you tell me, I want you to know that if you were to write that phrase—*sleeping sickness symptoms*—you wouldn't have to put a hyphen between *sleeping* and *sickness*, because *sleeping sickness* is a noun acting an adjective. There's such a thing as sleeping sickness, I mean. So, what are the symptoms?"

"Well, first, there's headache and fever. Then there's extreme tiredness. After that there's coma."

That wasn't good. I tried to remember if I'd had a headache or felt feverish before I became sleepy on the raft. I didn't, so I guess I hadn't been bitten. Then I heard Tarzan say, "What about a vampire bat attack?"

I wasn't sure if he was asking if I was afraid of a vampire bat attack or if in that phrase—*vampire bat attack*—there should be a hyphen between *vampire* and *bat*. "Do you mean am I afraid, or do you mean punctuation-wise?"

"I know you don't need a hyphen, because a vampire bat is something that exists in the world; it's really a noun. I mean are you afraid of being attacked by it?"

"Well, what is a vampire bat? It sounds scary, but I'm not sure what it is."

"It's a bat that lives on blood. It attacks your feet while you're asleep and sucks your blood."

"That's horrible! Then yes, I am afraid."

"You don't have to be. They don't live in Africa; they live in South America."

"Oh. Well, that's good." I didn't really have anything left to say about hyphens. We stared at each other across the raft.

"Do you want to dive again?" he said.

"Okay."

We swam to the ladder and climbed to the rim of the crater. We glanced at each other and then dove into the water. When we surfaced he said, "Do you want to see how far down into this thing we can swim?"

"Okay."

We both started swimming down as far as we could. I knew that I'd have to save some breath for the trip back up to the surface. To be safe, I should use only half my breath on the way down. I swam deeper and deeper with Tarzan at my side. I thought to myself: I'm in the middle of a *mountain*! In *Africa*!

I started to feel myself running out of breath, so I turned around and headed toward the top. Tarzan noticed and followed me. As I neared the surface, I was almost completely out of breath.

We broke surface together and I inhaled deeply, with a gasping sound. When I could speak I said, "How far down do you think we went? About a hundred feet?"

"No, that was only about thirty or forty feet."

"Really? It felt like a lot more."

He didn't say anything and we swam back to the raft. "I'm going to lie on this again," I said. I pulled myself onto it and positioned myself at an angle again. I lay on my back staring up at the sky.

"Can you hear me?" I said.

"I can hear you," he answered from the water. "I'm right next to you."

"Good. Let's talk about the dash now, okay?"

"Okay."

"A dash looks like a hyphen, except it's about twice as long."

"What does it do?"

"It has a few purposes. For one thing—" I stopped mid-sentence because I suddenly started feeling sleepy again. There was something about lying on that raft that made me feel that way. I couldn't help it.

"Why did you stop?"

"I was afraid I was going to fall asleep. You don't think I have African sleeping sickness, do you?"

"No, you'd be much sicker if you did."

"That's what I think, too. It must be the raft." I slid back into the water and said, "I think I'm getting waterlogged. Let's get out for a while."

We swam to the ladder and climbed to the rim of the mountain. We sat facing the water with our feet dangling over the edge.

"What if we fall?" I said.

"Nothing would happen. We'd land in the water and climb back out."

I knew that, but it still seemed a little scary sitting on a ledge with thirty feet of open air beneath me.

"Anyway, do you remember when I started talking about the dash on the raft and I said, 'For one thing—'? Well, I didn't finish that sentence because I suddenly felt sleepy. If I were writing that, I wouldn't use a period after 'For one thing' because the sentence didn't really end. Anyway, for situations like that, where a thought is interrupted and unfinished, people place a dash after the beginning part of the sentence—after the part of the sentence that was spoken. To show a break, I mean."

"Oh."

I looked down at the water below us and said, "But that's not really the main reason people use dashes."

"Then what is?"

"Well, there are two main reasons. Sometimes people use a dash instead of a colon. Do you remember that a colon is used to separate two parts of a sentence in which the second part summarizes or explains the first?"

"I remember."

"Well, usually, if you want, you can use a dash there instead of a colon."

"You can?"

"Yes. For example, when we spoke about the colon I made up an example about you doing everything necessary for a cookout. Instead, I could have made up this example: 'Tarzan did everything necessary for a cookout—hunted meat, gathered kindling, started a fire.'" (When I said that out loud I pronounced the word *dash* when it came in the sentence.) "Do you see? In a case like that I could use a dash instead of a colon."

"Oh."

"You see, in that case, what comes after the dash *summarizes* what was said before the dash. Now here's an example in which what comes after the dash *explains* or *identifies* what was said before the dash: 'There were two swimmers—Tarzan and Jane.' (Again I said the word *dash* out loud.) "You see? I said there were two swimmers, but I didn't identify them. I used a dash to separate the first part of the sentence from the actual explanation of who the swimmers were."

"So you're saying that in those cases you could use either a dash *or* a colon?"

"Yes."

"I'm surprised you didn't say 'There were two pets—Yemmy and Omy.'"

"Well, I could have said that. I guess I just didn't think of it."

He looked at me to see if I was teasing him, and I just looked down into the water.

"Anyway," I finally said, "now let's talk about the other main reason people use dashes. Do you remember that I said you use parentheses to enclose something that doesn't fit in grammatically with the rest of the sentence or something that's a different idea from the rest of the sentence?"

"I remember. Usually it was something extra that adds information or clarity to the sentence."

"Right. Well, people often enclose those "extra" words with a set of dashes—one at the beginning and one at the end—instead of a with a set of parentheses. I remember that when we talked about parentheses I *did* make up an example about Yemmy and Omy. I said, 'Our two pet cats, Yemmy and Omy *parenthesis* they were named after countries on the Arabian Peninsula *parenthesis* are very cute.' Now, I *could* write: 'Our two pet cats, Yemmy and Omy *dash* they were named after countries on the Arabian Peninsula *dash* are very cute.'"

"So you can use either parentheses or dashes?"

"Yes. But sometimes people throw in something "extra" that doesn't even relate to the sentence at all. I mean there's a complete break in thought in the middle of the sentence. When that happens, you have to use dashes, not parentheses."

"Like when?"

"Well, let's say that I wrote 'Today we're going to talk about—oh my, I can't believe how tired I am—when to use a dash.' You see, in that sentence, the part about my being tired is a complete break in thought. It doesn't relate to the rest of the sentence at all. Anyway, in a case like that, like I said, you have to use dashes, not parentheses."

"Oh."

"Also, one other time I like to use a dash is if I want to show a longer-than-normal pause between words."

"What do you mean?"

"I mean that if I want a pause for dramatic effect, I might use a dash instead of some other punctuation mark."

"Like what?"

"Well, don't take this the wrong way, but let's say that I wrote 'Why don't you make up an example of a sentence that uses a dash all by yourself—if you can think of one, that is.' (I said the word *dash* out loud when it came in the sentence.) Do you see? After the word *yourself* I wanted a pause—for dramatic effect—so I used a dash."

"Well—"

"I mean," I interrupted, "without the dash, the sentence wouldn't have been as sarcastic. It wouldn't have been as funny." I was afraid this might be a little over his head. He'd never had any experience with sarcasm.

"But I *can* make up a sentence with a dash," he said.

"Good! What is it?"

"Jungle girl Jane—who's a slow walker and loves pets—is very pretty."

"Um . . . um . . ."

"Was that right?"

"Um . . . yes. You think I'm pretty?" I was flattered. "You think I'm a slow walker?" I was insulted. I didn't know how to feel.

"That was just an example," he said. "Don't take everything so literally." Then he winked at me and I blushed.

We stared down at the water again and didn't say anything. "Finally Tarzan said, "Do you want to go back to the cabin?"

"Not yet. I want to tell you one more thing about dashes. You see, there are really two different kinds of dashes."

"There are?"

"Yes. The one we've been talking about is called an *em* dash."

"Why is it called that?"

"I think it's because it's about as wide as the letter *m*—a capital M, I mean."

"Oh. What's the other one?"

"The other one is called an *en* dash. That one's not as wide—but it's wider than a hyphen. It's about as wide as a capital N."

"What does that one do?"

"Well," I said, watching the surface of the lake shimmer in the sun, "not everyone knows about en dashes. But because I'm a journalist and I work at a magazine, I know about them. At *American Monthly* magazine we use en dashes for two reasons."

"What?"

"Well, remember when we talked about compound adjectives being connected by hyphens? For example, you'd use a hyphen in the compound adjectives in such phrases as *able-bodied man*, *bad-tempered gorilla*, *far-fetched idea*, *quick-witted mind*, and *Baltimore-based publication*, right?"

"Right."

"Now, let's look at that last example, *Baltimore-based publication*. In that example, the hyphen joins two individual words: *Baltimore* and *based*. But what if *American Monthly* magazine were published in New York instead of Baltimore? If you used a hyphen to connect the city, New York, with the word *based*, it might look like you're connecting just the word *York* with *based*. It would look like this." I picked up a stick and in the dirt I wrote: *New York-based publication*. "You see, because of that hyphen, it might seem like what you're trying to say is—I wrote in the dirt again—*New "York-based" publication*. You see? That doesn't make sense. What you're really trying to say is—I wrote in the dirt again—"New York"-based publication. Anyway, the way we show that both the word *New* and *York* together are connected with the word *based* is by using an en dash instead of a hyphen. We'd write—again I wrote in the dirt—*New York–based publication*. Do you see how that en dash is wider than a hyphen but not as wide as an em dash?"

"I see."

"Good. So, anyway, what I'm saying is that if you have a compound adjective and one of the elements that make it up is *itself* two words, then use an en dash instead of a hyphen."

"But since *New York* is a noun that exists in the world, do you even need a hyphen or dash?"

"Yes, because in my example, the compound adjective isn't *New York*, it's *New York–based*. If I said something like *New York landmark*, then I wouldn't need a hyphen or dash, for the reason you said. But if I say something like *New York–based magazine*, then I need to use an en dash."

"Because there's no such thing in the world as a 'New York based,' right?"

"Right. Now, can you make up an example of a compound adjective in which one of the elements is two words? In other words, can you make up an example of a compound adjective that requires an en dash instead of a hyphen?"

Tarzan thought awhile. "Hmm . . ." he said. Then finally he said, "I think I have one. What about this? An Abraham Lincoln–style beard."

"Very good!" I said. "*Abraham Lincoln* is two words, so you joined it to the word *style* with an en dash. After all, it's not a *Lincoln-style* beard, it's an *Abraham Lincoln–style* beard."

Tarzan smiled. Then he said, "What's the other time you use an en dash at *American Monthly?*"

"The other time is kind of simple. When we connect numbers—that show a duration of time, for example—we use an en dash. For example, we'd write that Abraham Lincoln was President of the United States 1861–1865. Or we'd write that our work schedule is Monday–Friday. Or we'd write that in such-and-such report we're going to examine items 12–15." (In each of those examples I said the words *en dash* out loud.) "Do you see what I mean? In those situations, some people use hyphens and others use em dashes. But at *American Monthly* we use en dashes."

"It sounds like in those cases, the en dash really means *to* or *through*, as in *1861 to 1865*. Or *Monday through Friday*."

"That's exactly what it *does* mean."

"Oh. But the people who use hyphens or em dashes—are they wrong?"

"Well, not everyone agrees on this. But all the editors at *American Monthly*, including me, like en dashes."

"Then I like them too."

We smiled at each other.

"Do you want to dive or swim any more?" Tarzan said.

"No, I've had enough."

"Should we go back to the cabin?"

"Yes. But what should be do about the raft—I mean branch—that we threw in the water?"

"Just leave it there."

"Okay."

We both stood up and started walking down the mountain. It was much easier walking down than up—I can tell you that!

"While we walk," I said, "I want to tell you about another punctuation mark—the *ellipsis*."

"What's that?"

"It looks like three dots—like three periods in a row."

"What's that for?"

"Well, first I want to tell you what the word *ellipsis* means. It means 'an omission of a word or phrase.' Anyway, there are three situations in which people like to use an ellipsis."

I found that even though walking down the mountain was much easier than walking up, it wasn't effortless—because of the effect of gravity, I mean. If I wasn't careful, I would start to run whether I wanted to or not. I had to step in a certain way and hold my body in a certain way to avoid that. Tarzan did, too.

"One time people use an ellipsis," I continued, "is when they're quoting something and they want to show that certain words have been left out."

"What do you mean?"

"Well, for example, let's say I want to quote the first sentence of Abraham Lincoln's Gettysburg Address. It goes like this: 'Fourscore and seven years ago our fathers brought forth on this continent a new nation conceived in liberty and dedicated to the proposition that all men are created equal.' Now let's say that I think that's too much to quote and I want to make it shorter—I want to leave out some of the words, I mean. In that case, if I was writing the shorter version, I might write something like this: 'Fourscore and seven years ago our fathers brought forth . . . a new nation . . . dedicated to the proposition that all men are created equal.'" (When I said that out loud to Tarzan I said the word *ellipsis* each time it came in the sentence.) "Now, that sentence has two *ellipses*. That's the plural of *ellipsis—ellipses*."

"I see. You left out 'on this continent' and 'conceived in liberty' to make the quote shorter."

"Exactly. And to show that I left them out, I replaced them with ellipses."

We continued down the mountain, walking in that odd way so that we wouldn't fall or involuntarily run.

"When else do people use ellipses?" Tarzan asked.

"Well, let's say that you're writing about someone reciting some kind of list, and you want to show that the list actually continues beyond the items actually named."

"What do you mean?"

"Well, for example, you might write something like 'When Jane was in the fifth grade, she stood up and recited the names of all the U.S. Presidents in chronological order: Washington, Adams, Jefferson . . .'"

"Did you really do that?"

"Actually, I did. I also named all the U.S. state capitals."

"Wow!"

"But the point is, if you were writing that sentence about the Presidents, it would be too much—and unnecessary—for you to actually list *all* the Presidents. So you just list three or so and then use an ellipsis to show that the list actually continues."

"Oh."

"In that case, an ellipsis really means 'and so on' or 'et cetera.'"

"Oh."

We continued walking down the mountain in that funny way. We were now about a third of the way down.

"What's the other time people use an ellipsis?" Tarzan said.

"Well, people use an ellipsis to show that a statement has been left unfinished."

"I thought you said that you use a dash for that."

"Well, if a statement abruptly stops in the middle, because the speaker was interrupted, for example, you use a dash—an em dash.

But if a statement just kind of slows down or dies away or stops on its own, then you use an ellipsis."

"Like when?"

I knew he was going to ask me that. "Well, let me think of an example." It was hard to think of an example and walk with an unnatural posture at the same time. Finally I said, "Well, let's say that you're saying something and the ending of what you're going to say is very obvious. It might be *so* obvious that you think it would be boring for the reader to actually read."

"What do you mean?"

"Well, let's say I was going to write about walking up and down a mountain. I might write something like "Walking up a mountain is difficult; walking down, on the other hand . . .' Do you see. It was so obvious that I was going to say 'is easy' that I decided to leave the statement unfinished and use an ellipsis. The reader would be able finish the sentence in his mind."

"Oh."

"Or sometimes you might use a well-known proverb. The proverb is so well known that you might just state the beginning of it and then use an ellipsis. The reader will know what you mean; the reader will fill in the rest of the proverb in his mind."

"Like what?"

"Well, let's say I wanted to write about my jungle outfit. I could write 'I decided to wear a jungle outfit instead of an American bathing suit because when in Rome, do as the Romans do.' But I would probably just write 'I decided to wear a jungle outfit instead of an American bathing suit because when in Rome . . .' Do you see? I'd use an ellipsis after the word *Rome* because the proverb is so famous that the reader can finish it in his mind."

"I see."

"Or you might say 'a stitch in time . . .' or 'finders keepers . . .' If you use an ellipsis, people will know that you've left out the rest of the proverb, but they'll still know what you mean."

"Or 'all work and no play . . .' or 'an apple a day . . .'"

"Exactly. Very good."

We were now about two thirds of the way down the mountain.

"I just thought of another reason people use ellipses, but it's not to show an omission of a word or phrase."

"What is it."

"Well, if you're writing dialogue—you know, conversation—and you want to indicate that the speaker pauses between certain words or phrases, you show that with ellipses."

"I don't understand."

"Well, let's say that someone is speaking in a hesitant manner—you know, he's pausing between certain words or phrases. You could write, for example: He said, "Well (pause) um (pause) I (pause) don't know.""

"You mean you could just insert the word *pause* between the spoken words?"

"You could, if you *set off* the word *pause* from the other words—by placing it in parentheses, for example—to show that it's not part of what's actually spoken. But most writers, instead, indicate pauses between words or phrases with an *ellipsis*. For example, they would write that same sentence as: He said, 'Well ... um ... I ... don't know.'" (When I said that out loud to Tarzan, I said the word *ellipsis* whenever one occurred.) "Do you understand?"

"I think so."

"Good. Well, now we've covered all the punctuation marks except the comma."

"When are we going to talk about that?"

"Let's talk about that back at the cabin. At the table."

"Okay."

"While we're walking, I can tell you about italics and writing numbers. Let's start with italics."

"What's that?"

"Well, you don't use italics when you write something by hand. But it's something you see in printed books. Did you ever notice in printed books that some of the letters appear in a slanted type? A type that slants to the right, I mean."

"Now that you mention it, yes."

"Well, any type—whether it's a letter, a word, a phrase, or whatever—that appears in slanted type is said to be in *italics*."

"But why can't you use italics when you write by hand?"

"Well, a lot of people, when they write, slant their letters a little to the right all the time."

"Why?"

"I don't know; they just do. Maybe they learn to write like that in elementary school. I really don't know. Anyway, in handwriting, it would be hard to tell what is in italics and what isn't." I paused and then added, "But if you're writing by hand and you want to show

225

italics, you *underline* the letters instead of trying to slant them. Underlining a word or phrase means the same thing as putting it in italics."

"Oh." Then after a moment he said, "Well, what do italics do?"

"Well, they have three main uses. First of all, the names of certain things, when they occur in a sentence, are always written in italics."

"What kinds of things?"

"Well, the titles of books, plays, magazines, and newspapers. For example, if I was going to write something about the magazine I work for, *American Monthly*, I'd put the magazine's name in italics."

"Or you'd underline it if you were writing by hand, right?"

"Right. And the names of ships, trains, and planes are printed in italics or underlined. For example, if I wrote that Christopher Columbus's ships were the *Nina*, the *Pinta*, and the *Santa Maria*, I would put the names of those ships in italics."

"Oh."

"Now, there are two other situations—besides names and titles—in which you use italics. Do you remember when I said that if you're talking about a certain word as a *word*—instead of as the thing the word stands for—that you put that word in quotes? I think that as an example I said something like 'the word "cheetah" is spelled with two *e*'s.' Do you see what I mean? In that case I wasn't talking about an actual cheetah—the animal—but about the *word* 'cheetah,' so I put it in quotes. Anyway, when you speak of a word as a *word*, you can either put that word in quotes *or* you can italicize it. I could write 'The word *cheetah* has two *e*'s' and simply put the word *cheetah* in italics instead of in quotes."

"Oh."

We were approaching the bottom of the mountain.

"Okay. There's one other situation in which people use italics. If they want to emphasize or stress a certain word or phrase, they put it in italics."

"What do you mean?"

"Well, when people talk, sometimes they emphasize certain words. I mean they might say them louder or with more intensity. For example, a mother might say to a naughty child, 'Don't *ever* do that again!' Did you hear how I emphasized the word *ever*?"

"Yes. You said it louder."

"Right. And in writing, if you want the reader to know that a certain word should be stressed like that, you put it in italics."

"Oh."

"And sometimes you emphasize a word just to make your meaning especially clear or extra clear. For example, in this next sentence I'm going to stress the word *or*: 'When I spoke about referring to a word as a word, I said that you can put it in quotes *or* italicize it.' Do you see? I emphasized the word *or* to make my meaning extra clear."

"I see. By stressing the word *or* you're making it extra clear that *either* method is okay."

"Right. And I think that you just stressed the word *either*. If you were writing that, you'd italicize it."

"Or underline it."

"Right."

We arrived at the bottom of the mountain and continued walking.

"Wow, it feels good to walk normally again," I said. "That was fun swimming in a mountain lake. We'll have to come back here again sometime."

"Okay." Tarzan was usually pretty agreeable, and he usually didn't have much to say.

"Should we walk or take to the trees?" I said.

"The trees. It's more fun."

We took to the trees and started swinging on vines.

"Can you hear me?" I yelled as we flew through the air. "I want to tell you about writing numbers!"

"I can hear you!" he yelled back.

But I decided that I didn't want to have to yell the whole lesson to him. I'd wait until we both landed on the same tree.

After a few minutes we both swung onto a medium-sized tree. We stood side by side on one of the branches. Other branches crisscrossed in front of us and behind us. We held onto them with our hands. A squirrel scampered down the trunk and ran off.

"Okay," I said, "I want to talk about writing numbers—I mean whether you spell them out in letters or use numerals."

"Don't you just always use numerals?"

"No. Sometimes you spell them out."

"When?"

"Well, for one thing, if a number comes at the beginning of a sentence, you always spell it out, no matter what it is. For example, you'd write 'Three hundred and sixty-five days make a year,' using letters, not '365 days make a year,' using numerals."

"But isn't it easier for people to read the number? It's much shorter."

"It is. And that's why usually, in a case like that, you would use numbers. But, like I said, if a number comes at the very beginning of a sentence, you have to write it out."

"Well, I don't see why, but okay."

"Okay, now let's talk about numbers that *don't* come at the beginning of a sentence."

"Well, then do you always use numerals instead of letters?"

"Well, you do if you're talking about a year, such as 1492; a date, such as July 4; a time, such as 12 o'clock; a temperature, such as 32 degrees; someone's address, such as 101 Maple Street; money, such as $5; mathematical expressions, such as 3 times 2; or things like chapter or page numbers, such as Chapter 3 or page 51. In all of those cases you use numerals. However, if you're using numbers in a general sense, in the middle of a regular sentence, then sometimes you're supposed to spell them out in letters instead of using numerals."

"When?"

"Well, it's a little complicated, because there are two different sets of rules people go by. There's what I'll call the *traditional* rule and what I'll call the *modern* rule. At *American Monthly* we use the modern rule, but in my personal writing I like to use the traditional rule."

"What are the rules?"

"Well, according to the *traditional* rule, you use letters for any number that can be expressed in one or two words, such as nine, fifteen, twenty-five, three hundred, and three million. Do you see? Each of those numbers could be expressed with only one or two words. On the other hand, if you need *more* than two words to express a number, such as three hundred and sixty-five, which is actually five words, including the word *and,* you use numerals. For example, you'd write 'There are 365 days in a year,' using numerals."

"Well, that makes sense."

"It does. But at *American Monthly* and at some other magazines and some newspapers, there's a different rule."

"What?"

"Well, we use letters for the numbers one through ten, and we use numerals for anything higher than ten. So, using the traditional rule, you'd write 'There are twelve months in a year,' spelling out the number twelve in letters. But using the modern rule, you'd write 'There are 12 months in a year,' using numerals. Do you see?"

"I do. So which rule should I use when I start writing my own articles?"

"I'd say that you can use whichever rule you like, but just make sure to keep things consistent. I mean that once you pick one rule, stick with that rule throughout."

"Okay. But I think I'll use the modern rule since I'll be writing these articles for *American Monthly* and that's what they use."

"That's a good idea."

We stood on the branch and didn't say anything for a while. Finally I said, "Well, that's about it for numbers. All we have left to cover is the comma, and then you can start writing your own articles. So let's get back to the cabin, where we can sit at the table, okay?"

"Okay."

We started swinging from tree to tree toward the cabin. When we were nearly there I spotted a small pond I had never seen before.

"Hey, look over there to the left," I said. "I never noticed that pond before. Let's go check it out."

"I've been there before. It's very muddy there. It's not a good place to go."

That didn't stop me. I was already swinging toward it. Tarzan followed.

"Jane," he yelled, "I don't think you should go there. There's a lot of muddy sand there."

I didn't listen. I kept swinging toward the pond. Finally I dropped to the ground about forty feet from its edge and started walking toward it.

The ground there was muddy, as Tarzan had warned. My feet sank down to my ankles. I turned my head to look back at Tarzan. He was on the ground now too, about eighty feet from the edge of the pond, where it was drier and firmer.

"This is so muddy!" I yelled.

"I tried to tell you!"

Suddenly I noticed that I had sunk further into the mud. It was halfway up my calves now. I tried to walk, but I couldn't pull my feet out!

"I'm stuck!" I shrieked. "And I'm sinking!" Then I realized what was happening. I was in quicksand! I remembered seeing movies of people dying in quicksand and waves of panic flooded my mind. I desperately kicked with my legs but that only made matters worse. "Tarzan, help me! Help me!" I shrieked. Then I started to cry.

"Jane, listen to me. I can't get over there without sinking myself. Then I'd be no use to you at all. But I think I can help you from here. Now listen to me very carefully. There's only one way to save yourself."

I couldn't imaging what that was. He was too far away to extend a branch to me and there were no trees above me.

"Jane, you're sinking because all your weight is concentrated in one point—where your feet are. You're going to have to lie down flat on your back and extend your arms out at right angles. That will distribute your weight around a greater area and it might stop you from sinking."

"Might? It *might?*" I squawked.

"It's the only way."

"But what if I lie back and my whole body sinks?" I blubbered. "Then what will I do?"

"You're going to half to take that chance, and soon. If you don't act soon it will be too late. Now just let yourself fall gently backwards onto your back. And hold your arms straight out to the side."

I was so desperate that I was willing to try almost anything. Two thoughts occurred to me from within my panic: (1) I trust Tarzan completely and if he says to do this then it must be right and (2) I had to save myself so that I could teach Tarzan about commas; it was the only thing I hadn't taught him yet.

I put my arms straight out to the side and let myself fall gently backwards. All the while I cried, "Oh! oh! oh!"

Now I was flat on my back on top of the muddy sand. "Am I sinking?" I shrieked.

"I don't think so. I think you're stable now. You're okay."

I tried to feel whether my body was sinking or stationary. It felt stationary and I gave a sigh of relief.

I realized that I couldn't stand back up without sinking again.

"Now what am I supposed to do?" I yelled. "Am I supposed to lie here like this for the rest of my life?"

"Don't stand up. You're going to gently roll yourself off the mud. Bring your arms back to your sides and start rolling toward me."

"But I'll get covered with mud!"

"You can't worry about that now. Besides, you can always wash it off later."

He was right. If I didn't want to lie there forever, I was going to have to get dirty. I'd wash off the mud later. But my body wasn't at the correct angle to roll toward Tarzan. It was ninety degrees the wrong way. "I can't roll toward you!" I yelled. "I'm lying in the wrong direction!"

"I want you to roll toward me because it's the shortest distance to firm ground. Just wiggle yourself around and then start to roll."

I have to tell you that wiggling yourself around in quicksand without sinking is not easy. I had to somehow wiggle myself and remain flat with my arms out all at the same time. Finally I managed to rotate myself to the proper angle. Then I drew my arms in to my sides and started rolling myself toward Tarzan. Every time my face pointed down, I held my breath so that I wouldn't inhale mud.

I became covered with sticky mud. Every inch of my body, including my face and hair, was covered with it.

"Come on," Tarzan encouraged. "You're doing fine. Just keep on rolling. You're almost out."

While I rolled I thought about how lucky I was that Tarzan knew this trick about lying flat and rolling. Otherwise . . ."

The ground began to feel firmer and firmer under me, and I knew that I wouldn't die. I rolled faster and faster. All of a sudden I felt Tarzan lift me up and stand me up next to him.

I threw my arms around him. I didn't care that I got mud all over him.

We stood like that, holding each other, for a while. Then we broke apart and I looked down at myself. I couldn't see my skin—only mud.

"Come on," Tarzan said. "We have to get cleaned off."

"Where?"

"The pond—where we took the moonlight swim. Let's go." He took my hand.

I knew that the pond wasn't far from where we were. We both started to run, hand in hand. I couldn't wait to get the mud off me.

When we arrived at the pond we both simply ran into it until the water was up to our necks. Tarzan cleaned himself off easily because he wasn't nearly as dirty as I was. I had to deal with my hair, my face, and my entire body.

I started with my face. I lowered myself so that my head was underwater and I vigorously rubbed my face with my hands. I came up for air and then went back under to work on my hair. As I ran my fingers through it, I felt the mud start to come off. I kept doing that, sometimes coming up for air, until my hair felt clean. Next I went to work on my body, rubbing the mud from every inch of me. When I felt that I was relatively clean, I started to swim around underwater. I figured that the motion of my body against the water would get me even cleaner.

Finally, Tarzan and I swam to the edge of the pond and got out. "How do I look?" I asked. "Am I clean?"

Tarzan inspected me and said, "You're clean, but your jungle outfit looks a little dirty."

I looked down at my outfit. He was right; it was still dirty.

"I'm going to have to wash it," I said. "You should go back to the cabin and wait for me there."

"Why?"

"I need privacy."

"Oh. Okay, I'll wait for you at the cabin. But be careful when you walk back. The jungle is a dangerous place."

As if I didn't know that, I thought.

Tarzan walked off toward the cabin. I went back into the water, up to my neck again. I removed my jungle outfit and vigorously rubbed the material back and forth against itself in the water. Every so often I'd lift it out of the water to see how clean it looked. When I was finally satisfied, I put it back on, swam to the edge of the pond, and got out. I started walking back to the cabin.

It felt weird to be walking in the jungle by myself. I was so accustomed to being with Tarzan—my protector. Well, the cabin was nearby. I could get back there safely. Or so I thought.

On the way, no animals attacked me; it was nothing like that. What happened was that I happened to notice a pretty parrot in a tree to my left. I turned to gaze at it and suddenly I found myself flat on the ground with a pain in my right ankle. I had tripped!

I sat up and examined the ground behind me and noticed a kind of indentation there. It was about a foot across and about three inches deep. Who knows how it got there. Anyway, because I was distracted, I hadn't noticed it.

I stood back up and started walking toward the cabin again. I think I might have been limping a little.

When I arrived, Tarzan was standing in the doorway. "What happened to you? Why are you limping?"

"Am I? I tripped. I think I sprained my ankle."

Tarzan came to me and lifted me in his arms. "Don't walk on it," he said.

He carried me into the cabin and placed me on the bed. "Let me see it," he said.

I extended my ankle to him; he felt it with his fingers. (Wow! He's like a doctor, I thought.)

"I don't think it's broken," he said. "It feels like you only bruised it. But you need to stay off it for a while."

"How long?" I didn't want to have to stay off it. How could I have fun in Africa if I couldn't run around freely?

"I don't know. Probably just a day or two. We'll have to see if it starts getting better or worse."

"What if it gets worse?"

"Then we'll have to make you a pair of crutches until it heals. But I don't think that will be necessary."

"I hope not."

We didn't say anything for a while. I noticed that it was starting to get dark outside. It had been a long day: mountain climbing, swimming and diving, rolling in quicksand. Suddenly I felt exhausted. I yawned and said, "As long as I'm already in bed, I think I'll go to sleep now. Why don't we meet again tomorrow morning. I'll hop over to the table on my good leg and we'll talk about commas. Okay?"

"Okay. It's been a long day and you should get your rest. I'll be back first thing tomorrow morning."

He walked to the door, turned around, and said, "Goodnight, then." Then he was gone. A moment later I was fast asleep.

Chapter 22: Jane Rests Her Sprained Ankle

When I awoke the next morning, I sat on the edge of the bed with my feet on the floor. Then I slowly put pressure on my right ankle to see if it still hurt. It did. I'd better stay off it, I thought.

I hopped to the table on my left leg and sat down. Tarzan hadn't arrived yet, so I decided to make some notes on comma usage in my notebook. I thought back to my high school English class and tried to remember all the reasons for using commas. I knew that there were a lot of them. All together I was able to think of sixteen different reasons. I jotted them down in my notebook and numbered them. I figured I'd just go through the list and explain the reasons to Tarzan one by one.

Just then I head Tarzan at the door. But when I looked, it wasn't Tarzan—it was Cheetah.

"Cheetah, sweetie, come sit with Mommy at the table," I cooed. "Come on."

Cheetah waddled over and sat across from me in Tarzan's chair.

"That's a good boy," I said. "While we're waiting for Tarzan, let's practice our commas, okay?"

Cheetah scratched his neck and yawned.

"Do you know what a comma is? It's a little curly thing, like this." I drew a comma in the notebook, but Cheetah didn't look at it. "Cheetah, if you don't pay attention, you're not going to get a good grade in school," I joked, for my own benefit.

Just then Tarzan really did arrive. "Hey, little fellow," he said to Cheetah as he strolled in, "what are you doing in my chair? Here, let me get you your own chair." Tarzan took a chair from the corner of the room and placed it at the edge of the table to my left. Then he sat down in his customary seat across from me.

"How's your ankle?" he asked.

"It still hurts."

He took my hands in his and looked deeply into my eyes. "I'm so sorry. I never should have left you alone yesterday."

"Don't feel bad about that. I insisted. I needed my privacy, you know. I had to clean my outfit."

"Still . . ."

"Well, let's not dwell on it," I said. "I'm sure it will heal before too long. Now let's make the best of it. We can sit here quietly and talk about commas."

"Okay. I guess you're right."

234

"I made some notes in my notebook. Do you know how many reasons I thought of to use commas?"

"How many?"

"Sixteen!"

"Yikes! It will probably take us all day to go over that many."

"I know," I said. "The good thing is, we *have* all day."

"But what about food? With sixteen rules to learn, we're going to need something to eat."

"You're right. Going over these sixteen rules might become tedious. Why don't we have a snack after every four rules."

"You mean as a reward?"

"Yes. And just to break up the tedium, too. Why don't you go out and find us some fruit—enough for four separate snacks for each of us. And for Cheetah too. And when you're out, see if you can find Yemmy and Omy. Bring them back with you. We'll make it a "fruit and comma" party, okay?"

"A fruit and comma party?"

"You know, we'll all be here and we'll have snacks and talk about commas. It will be fun."

"Okay. I'll go get the fruit and be back as soon as I can. And while I'm gone, stay off that ankle."

"Don't worry. I will."

Tarzan left. As soon as he'd gone, Cheetah moved back into Tarzan's chair. We stared at each other across the table. I made a silly face and Cheetah imitated it. Then I made a funny body movement and he imitated that. We entertained ourselves like that for a while. Finally I said, "Cheetah, would say that Yemmy and Omy are your brothers or your cousins? What do you think?"

He didn't answer.

"Well, I think they're your brothers. No, I mean your cousins. No, I mean your brothers. I mean I don't know what I mean."

He didn't answer.

"Cheetah, do you think I should take Tarzan to New York and put him on display? Do you think that would be wrong?"

No answer.

"I think it would be wrong."

Silence.

"Cheetah, how long do you think it will take for my ankle to heal?"

No answer.

"Cheetah, do you think that Tarzan is in love with me?"

Cheetah grimaced. Anyway, I talked to Cheetah in that vein until Tarzan came back with the fruit, which he carried inside a huge folded leaf.

"Did you find Yemmy and Omy?" I said expectantly.

"I did. They're right behind me."

The cubs followed Tarzan into the cabin. I started to rush toward them but remembered my ankle just in time. I stayed where I was.

"Where were they?"

"They were playing outside. They were in plain sight."

"I'm so glad they're here!" Then to the cubs: "Hey, fellas! Mommy's so glad to see you! I missed you! Come here and let me pet you."

They came over to me and I petted each of them on the head and the back of the neck. They stared into my eyes.

Tarzan placed the fruit on the table. Then he picked up Cheetah and placed him on the chair to my left. Finally he sat down on his own chair. Yemmy and Omy spotted the bed, jumped onto it, and lay on their stomachs, facing us.

"Isn't this wonderful?" I said. "We're all here together." Then to Cheetah: "Say hi to you brothers. I mean your cousins. That's Yemmy and Omy." I took Cheetah's arm and moved it up and down, forcing him to wave to the cubs. When I released his arm, he grabbed for a piece of fruit. I seized his arm again to stop him. "We're saving that fruit for a reward when we finish talking about the first four reasons for using a comma. You're going to have to wait."

"Why don't you let him have a piece now?" Tarzan said. "*He's* not really talking about commas; we are."

"I guess you're right." Then to Cheetah: "Okay, Cheetah; I'm sorry. You can take a piece. Here." I handed him some fruit. I didn't know exactly what it was. He gulped it down. "Now, let's save the rest for later." I pushed all the rest of fruit to the edge of the table opposite him.

"All right," I said to Tarzan, "are you ready to dig in?"

"Dig in? Are you talking about the commas or the fruit?"

"The commas!"

"I'm ready."

I glanced over at Yemmy and Omy on the bed. They were so cute. "All right, then let's get to work. Now, a comma is used to separate different elements within a sentence. It's kind of like a little pause. Do you know how sometimes when you speak, you pause a moment before or after certain words or phrases? Well, in writing you use a comma to indicate those little pauses."

Tarzan nodded his head.

"Okay, now, one time you might use a comma—Cheetah, you listen to this too—is when you have two independent clauses."

"I thought you said that if you have two independent clauses you separate them with a semicolon."

"I did. But you didn't let me finish. What I was going to say is that if you have two independent clauses joined by a coordinating conjunction, such as *and* or *but*, you can place a comma after the first clause, before the conjunction."

"Now I remember," Tarzan said. "What you said about the semicolon is that it's used between independent clauses that *aren't* joined by a conjunction."

"Right."

"But why did you just say that I *can* use a comma between independent clauses joined by a conjunction? Why didn't you say that I *must* use a comma in that situation?"

Just then Cheetah yawned.

"I think we're boring him," I said. "Cheetah, you don't find punctuation fascinating?"

He yawned again.

"I suppose not," I said.

Cheetah climbed down from his chair and jumped onto the bed alongside Yemmy and Omy. He lay down next to them.

"Look at that," I said. "Isn't that the cutest thing—all of them lying next to each other like that?"

Tarzan looked over at them but said nothing.

"I think they're all going to fall asleep. They look so tired. They must have been awake during the night—not like us."

In a few minutes, all three of them were asleep. "Well," I said, "I guess nobody's going to bother us during our lesson. Anyway, the reason I said that you *can*—not *must*—place a comma between independent clauses separated by a coordinating conjunction is that you don't *always* use one."

"Why not?"

"Well, it depends on how long the clauses are. You see, if the clauses are short, you don't need a comma. For example, if I wrote 'Tarzan swims and Jane runs,' I wouldn't separate the clauses—*Tarzan swims* and *Jane runs*—with a comma."

"Each of those clauses is only two words."

"Right. They're very short. But if I wrote 'Tarzan swims in the river and the ocean, and Jane runs through the jungle and the prairie,' then I'd use a comma, because the independent clauses are longer. Using one would make the meaning of the sentence clearer."

"So, how long do the independent clauses need to be in order for you to use a comma? Is there a certain number of words?"

"There's no rule for that. I mean there's no certain number of words. If you're writing something and the clauses seem long to you, use a comma. Otherwise, don't. You see, it all has to do with making your meaning clear. Usually, if the clauses are long, using a comma helps make the meaning clear. That's all."

"Oh."

"Okay, let's move on to the next situation in which you use a comma. You separate an introductory dependent clause from an independent clause with a comma. Here's an example." In the notebook I wrote: "Realizing the need for protection from wild beasts, your father built a cabin."

"This is the cabin he built!"

"I know. But do you see the comma after the word *beasts*? I used that to separate the introductory dependent clause—*Realizing the need for protection from wild beasts*—from the following independent clause—*your father built a cabin.*"

"I think I see."

"Well, let's test you. Can you make up a similar example?"

Tarzan took the pencil and wrote in the notebook: "When we finish talking about the first four uses of the comma, can we have a snack?"

I didn't know whether or not he was kidding around with me. I mean, was that an example of a comma separating an opening dependent clause from a following independent clause, or was he asking about the snack in earnest?

"That's very good!" I said. "That's a perfect example. And of course we can have a snack after the first four reasons for using a comma. We agreed to, didn't we?"

Tarzan just smiled.

"Okay, now let's go on to another reason for using a comma. If a sentence begins with a prepositional phrase, you sometimes use a comma to separate the prepositional phrase from the rest of the sentence."

"Sometimes?"

"Well, it depends on whether the prepositional phrase is long or short. If it's short, you don't need a comma. For example, in the sentence 'In 1492 Columbus sailed the ocean blue,' the opening prepositional phrase—*In 1492*—is only two words, so you don't need a comma after it. But I have to tell you that there's an exception to that rule about not using a comma after a short opening prepositional phrase."

"What?"

"Opening prepositional phrases that are considered transitional, such as *for example, in fact,* and *on the other hand,* always require a comma after them."

"Why?"

"Just because it helps make the meaning clear."

"Oh."

"Anyway, sometimes you have an opening prepositional phrase that's long. In that case you should use a comma after it. Here's an example." I took the notebook and wrote: "After Tarzan and Jane finished talking about four uses of commas, they had a snack." "You see, in that sentence, the opening prepositional phrase, from the word *After* through the word *commas,* is eleven words long. That's why I placed a comma after it."

"How long does the prepositional phrase have to be to be considered long? What's the cutoff?"

"Well, some people feel that there's no exact number of words it needs to be to be considered long. If you're the writer and it feels long to you, then use a comma. Or if you think your meaning will be made clearer by using a comma, then use it. Or if you want the reader to pause a little bit in his mind after the prepositional phrase, use it."

Tarzan didn't say anything.

"I can tell you this," I continued. "At *American Monthly*—and usually in my personal writing, too—we make five words the cutoff. If the opening prepositional phrase if five words or more, use a comma. If it's less than five, don't." Then I added, "Unless we want the reader to make a little pause in his mind. Then we use a comma anyway."

"Is that what I should do in my writing? Use the five-word rule, I mean?"

"You can. But you don't really have to."

"Well, since I'll be writing these articles for *American Monthly,* I think I'll use the five-word rule."

"That's good. Now let's go on to the next use of the comma."

"And after that we can have a snack."

"Right, because this is going to be the fourth rule. Now, this rule concerns using not *one* comma, but *two*. It concerns using a *pair* of commas to *surround* a word, phrase, or clause."

"Do you mean like parentheses? *Those* surround certain words and phrases."

"Yes, it is like that. In fact, the words that you surround with parentheses are said to be *parenthetical.*"

"Parenthetical?"

"Yes. If you say that a word, phrase, or clause is *parenthetical,* you mean that it's not really a necessary part of the sentence. It's something extra that's been inserted into the sentence. Words and phrases like that are sometimes surrounded by parentheses. And sometimes they're surrounded by dashes—em dashes. But sometimes they're surrounded by commas."

"How do you know if you should use parentheses, dashes, or commas?"

"Well, one answer is that sometimes it just depends on the whim of the writer. But I think a better answer is that it depends on how closely related the inserted words are to the rest of the sentence—either grammatically or meaning-wise. If they're fairly closely related, use commas. But if they're less closely related—or not related—use parentheses or dashes."

"Oh."

"Let me give you an example." I took the notebook and wrote: "Tarzan, who was raised by apes, is good at climbing trees." I turned the notebook toward him. "You see, in that sentence, the parenthetical phrase—or clause—*who was raised by apes* is closely related to the rest of the sentence and I surrounded it by commas."

Tarzan nodded.

"Now watch this." I wrote in the notebook: "Tarzan (he was raised by apes) is good at climbing trees." Under that I wrote: "Tarzan—he was raised by apes—is good at climbing trees." I turned the notebook back to him and said, "Do you see? In these two sentences, the parenthetical clause is not closely related to the rest of the sentence grammatically. So I used parentheses the first time and dashes the second time. Either one—parentheses or dashes—is okay." I paused and then said, "But in my personal writing, I have to admit, I have a preference for dashes over parentheses."

"Oh."

Tarzan wrinkled his forehead as if he were thinking deeply. "Do you know what I think?" he finally said. "I think that any word, phrase, or clause that's considered *parenthetical* is no different from a word, phrase, or clause that's considered *nonrestrictive*. Am I right?"

"Tarzan, that's very good! You're right! Saying that a phrase is parenthetical or saying it's nonrestrictive is pretty much the same thing. It's a phrase that's usually explanatory or descriptive but that can be taken out of a sentence without affecting its meaning. And whatever you want to call it—*parenthetical* or *nonrestrictive*—you enclose it with commas."

Tarzan smiled.

"Let's make up some examples of sentences that use a pair of commas to enclose parenthetical remarks. Let's think of one example of a parenthetical *word* enclosed by commas, another of a parenthetical *phrase* enclosed by commas, and still another of a parenthetical *clause* enclosed by commas."

Tarzan looked at me expectantly.

"Okay, now certain words, such as *however*, *nevertheless*, and *though*, are considered transitional words, and when they come in the middle of a sentence they're also considered parenthetical and they're enclosed by commas. Here's an example." I took the notebook and wrote: "Jane loves pets; Tarzan, however, is still not sure if he loves them." I turned the notebook to Tarzan; he read what I wrote and frowned.

"Do you see?" I said. "There, a single word, *however*, is considered parenthetical and is enclosed by commas."

"You're talking about pets again."

"I'm sorry. It was the first sentence I thought of. If I'd thought of something else I would have used that."

I don't know if he believed me.

"Okay, now here's an example of a parenthetical *phrase* surrounded by commas." I took the notebook and wrote: "Jane, after rolling out of the quicksand, cleaned herself in the pond." I turned the notebook to Tarzan and said, "Okay, in that sentence, what's the parenthetical phrase?"

"After rolling out of the quicksand."

"Right! And why is it enclosed by commas?"

"Because it's nonrestrictive. I mean it's parenthetical. I mean it can be omitted without really changing the meaning of the sentence."

"Very good. Okay, now here's an example of a parenthetical *clause* surrounded by commas." I took the notebook as if to write, but then I changed my mind. "Wait a minute. Let's see if you can make one up yourself." I handed him the notebook.

Tarzan thought a moment and then wrote: "Jane, who tripped and hurt her ankle, has to rest for a few days."

"That's very good!" I exclaimed. "You really get this, don't you?"

"I think so."

"Good. One mistake people sometimes make with commas and parenthetical remarks is that instead of using commas both before *and* after a parenthetical remark, they use only one comma, either before or after."

"Why do they do that?"

"I don't know. Maybe they're just sloppy or lazy in their punctuation. Or maybe they don't really understand the rule about enclosing parenthetical expressions in commas."

"Oh." He paused and then said, "Well, we've finished discussing the first four reasons for using commas. Now let's have a snack!"

"That's fine with me. I'm starving."

I looked over at Yemmy, Omy, and Cheetah. They were all sound asleep. Then I turned my attention to the fruit at the edge of the table. There were four kinds, but I didn't recognize them; I mean I didn't know what they were called. One was yellow, another orange, another red, and another green.

"Look," I said to Tarzan, "the fruits are the same colors as the first four colors of the rainbow—red, orange, yellow, and green. (In eighth grade science I had to memorize the order of the colors in the rainbow by memorizing the acronym ROYGBIV—red, orange, yellow, green, blue, indigo, violet.)

"So?"

"So let's line them up in order," I said.

"Why?"

"I don't know. I feel like it. Just for fun." I lined them up: red, then orange, then yellow, then green. "Let's start with the red ones." I took a piece of red fruit and bit into it. It was succulent and delicious. "Mmm!"

Tarzan reached for a yellow piece, but I grabbed his arm. "We have to eat the red ones first," I said.

"No we don't."

"But they're in order."

242

"But you just made up that order. I could have made up a different order."

"I didn't make it up. It's the order of the rainbow. It's nature's order."

"Oh, all right," he said reluctantly, reaching for a piece of red fruit.

There were six pieces of red fruit, and we each had three. When we'd finished, we licked the juice from our fingers.

"Okay, are you ready to learn about four more reasons for using commas?" I said.

"I guess so."

I looked over at the bed and saw that Yemmy had just awakened. "Come here, sweetie. Come to Mommy." I patted my thigh loudly a few times.

Yemmy jumped to the floor, crossed to the table, and jumped onto my lap. I began to pet his head.

"Yemmy's going to have a comma lesson with us," I said. Then to Yemmy: "Aren't you, Yemmy? That's a good boy." I continued to pet him.

Tarzan rolled his eyes a little.

"Okay, now, if you have a series of elements in a sentence, you have to place a comma after each element."

"What do you mean by *a series of elements?*"

"I mean if you have some kind of list. Each thing in the list can be a word, a phrase, or a clause." I took the notebook and wrote: "There were four kinds of fruit on the table: red, orange, yellow, and green." "Do you see? Each color in the list—or series—has a comma after it— except the last element, green, which has a period after it."

"Oh."

"Actually, some people don't use a comma after the next-to-last element—the one before the word *and.* They'd write—" I took the notebook and wrote: "Red, orange, yellow and green."

"Why do they do that?"

"I guess they think that because the word *and* is there, they don't need a comma. They think that *and* takes the place of the comma." I paused and then said, "But I like to use a comma before *and.* That's how we do it at *American Monthly.*"

"Why?"

"Because the meaning is clearer with the comma. If you didn't use a comma in the example I just wrote, someone might think that the last kind of fruit was a mixture of yellow and green. They might think one type is red, one type is orange, and one type is yellow and green."

"I see. The comma before *and* makes it extra clear that there are two different colors: yellow *and* green."

"Right. And by the way, commas that separate elements in a series are called *serial* commas."

"Because *serial* is the adjective form of *series*, right?"

"Right. Anyway, can you make up an example of a series of phrases or clauses? Write one in the notebook, and remember to separate the elements of the series with commas."

Tarzan took the notebook, thought awhile, and then wrote: "Yesterday you climbed a mountain, swam in a lake, and escaped from quicksand."

"That's very good. And I see that you used commas to separate the elements."

Tarzan smiled with pride, and I petted the back of Yemmy's neck.

"But I have to tell you," I said, "that there's one situation in which you don't use commas to separate the elements of a series."

"When?"

"Well, if all the elements in a series are joined by coordinating conjunctions, then you don't use commas. You just use the conjunctions to separate the words." I took the notebook and wrote: "Yesterday we climbed and swam and dove." "You see? In that sentence, each element of the series—*climbed, swam,* and *dove*—is connected by the coordinating conjunction *and*. So you don't need any commas."

"But in the first example you gave me, the one about the different-colored fruits, you said to use a comma before the word *and* at the end of the series."

"I know. It's only when *all* the elements are connected with coordinating conjunctions that you don't use any commas. And, like I said, *some* people don't use a comma before the word *and* in a regular series—I mean a series of elements *not* connected by coordinating conjunctions."

"Oh."

"Okay. That was the fifth rule. Now here's number six: If you use two or more adjectives to modify the same noun, the adjectives are often separated by commas. Here, look." I wrote in the notebook: "I met a smart, brave, handsome man." Then I said, "Do you see the commas? They separate the adjectives. Smart *comma* brave *comma* handsome. But I didn't put a comma after the last adjective—between *handsome* and *man,* I mean."

"Because you don't need any punctuation between an adjective and a noun, right?"

"Right."

"So, who is this man you met? Is it me?"

"It could be," I teased.

Tarzan smiled and said, "Why did you say that in a case like that the adjectives are *often* separated by commas. Aren't they *always* separated by commas?"

"Well, here's where it gets a bit tricky. You see, you use commas only if the adjectives are equal."

"What does that mean? Do you mean if they're the same number of letters or something?"

No, nothing like that. I mean equal in the sense of how important they are or how closely related they are to the noun that follows."

"I don't understand."

"Okay, watch." I took the notebook and wrote: "The monkey climbed a tall, thick tree." Then under that I wrote: "The monkey climbed a tall oak tree." I turned the notebook toward Tarzan so that he could read it.

Yemmy suddenly stood up, turned 180 degrees, and sat back down.

"You used a comma to separate *tall* and *thick* in the first sentence," Tarzan said, "but you didn't separate *tall* and *oak* in the second sentence."

"Right. You see, in the second sentence, the word *oak* is very closely related to the word *tree*. The two-word phrase *oak tree* signifies something we're all familiar with. So, in that sentence, the two adjectives, *tall* and *oak*, aren't really equal."

"I think I see. It's almost as if there's only one adjective—*tall*—and the noun it modifies is *oak tree*."

"Exactly. But in the first sentence, the two adjectives—*tall* and *thick*—are considered equal. They both modify the noun tree in the same way—so I separated them with a comma."

"I see."

"Good. But sometimes it's a little tricky to tell if multiple adjectives that modify the same noun are really equal. Sometimes it's not as obvious as in the example about a tall oak tree."

"Then how do you tell?"

"Well, there are two little tricks you can use to help you decide whether or not adjectives are really equal. One is to try reversing their order. If you can switch their order and the sentence still makes sense, they're equal."

"I see," Tarzan said. "You could say that the monkey climbed the *tall, thick* tree or that he climbed the *thick, tall* tree. Either way it makes sense. So, the adjectives must be equal, and you need a comma between them. But you couldn't say that the monkey climbed the *oak tall* tree. That doesn't make sense."

"Right! In that case the word *tall* has to come before *oak*. So the adjectives are *not* equal, and you *don't* use a comma."

"What's the other little trick to help you decide whether or not adjectives are equal?"

"The other trick is to see what happens if you mentally insert the word *and* between the adjectives. If the sentence still makes sense with the word *and*, the adjectives are equal, and you need a comma. For example—"

"Wait! I have an example," Tarzan interrupted. "You could say that you met a *smart and brave and handsome* man. That makes sense! It still makes sense!"

"Right. And I could say that the monkey climbed a *tall and thick* tree. That makes sense, too."

"But you can't say," Tarzan continued, "that the monkey climbed a *tall and oak* tree. It doesn't make sense to insert the word *and* between *tall* and *oak*."

"Right. And if it doesn't make sense to insert the word *and*, what does that tell you about whether or not you need a comma?"

"Well, if it doesn't make sense to insert *and*, then the adjectives are *not* equal, and you *don't* need a comma."

"Very good!"

"Let me make up one more example." Tarzan took the notebook and wrote: "I met a smart, pretty, dark-haired girl." As he turned the notebook toward me, he said, "I'm not saying this is about you . . . necessarily . . . but I just wanted to show you that the adjectives in this sentence are equal and so they're separated by commas."

I took the notebook and read out loud what he'd written. "Well, that's very nice," I said. I don't think I was blushing when I said that. Then I looked down at Yemmy and said, "Yemmy, isn't Tarzan nice to say such sweet things?"

Tarzan made that dopey grin that he sometimes makes.

"Okay," I said, "two more rules and then we can have another snack. An orange snack this time, because we're going in order. Remember?"

246

"Okay."

"Now, I'm going to call this one 'rule number seven.' But I have to tell you that the rules don't really have numbers. I'm just counting them so that I can keep track of when we can have a snack. I really could have put these rules in any order."

"Oh."

"Anyway, sometimes in a sentence you have a noun or pronoun—or a phrase that acts as a noun—and then right after it you have another noun—or noun phrase—that means the same thing."

"Huh?"

"Well, for example, you're known as Tarzan. But you're also known as the Lord of the Apes."

"I am?"

"I think you are. Anyway, take a look at this sentence." In the notebook I wrote: "Tarzan, the Lord of the Apes, swung from tree to tree." I turned the notebook around so that he could read it.

"I see that you enclosed *the Lord of the Apes* in commas," he said. But isn't that because *the Lord of the Apes* is parenthetical? I mean, you already identified who the sentence is about, so the phrase is nonrestrictive. We already went over that rule—the one about putting commas around nonrestrictive phrases."

"I know we did, but this is sort of a special case."

"What do you mean?"

"Well, a phrase like *the Lord of the Apes*, when it's used like I just used it in that last example, has a special name. I really just want you to know what the name is."

"Well, what is it?"

"It's called an *appositive*." I pronounced it for him slowly: "*Uh-POZ-ih-tiv.*"

"What does that mean?"

"Well, that's what I'm trying to explain. If you have a noun or noun phrase, and then you have *another* noun or noun phrase—right after it, I mean—that's simply another way of saying the same thing—as in *Tarzan, the Lord of the Apes*—that second noun or noun phrase is said to be in *apposition* to the first, and that second noun or noun phrase is known as an *appositive*. So, in that example, the phrase *the Lord of the Apes* is an *appositive*."

"Oh, I think I see," Tarzan said. "So, if I say 'Jane, the jungle girl, has a sprained ankle,' then the phrase *the jungle girl* is an appositive."

"Right, because it's just another way of saying *Jane*. Anyway, when you have an appositive, you put commas around it."

"Oh."

"Now, even though appositives are *equivalent* to the nouns they follow, they usually actually *add* some information—something explanatory, for example."

"What do you mean?"

"Well, whether you say *Jane* or you say *the jungle girl*, you're talking about me—so in that way they're equivalent. But the phrase *the jungle girl* adds the information that I'm of the jungle. It explains something about me."

"Oh." He paused a moment and then said, "But I still think this is just like the rule about putting commas around nonrestrictive phrases."

"I guess you're right. I just wanted you to know what an appositive it. That's all. And I wanted you to know that you put commas around an appositive."

"Okay . . . How many more rules until our next snack?"

"I think that one was number seven, right? Number five was about separating elements of a series with commas, number six was about separating multiple adjectives that are equal with com—"

"You know, that rule about the multiple adjectives is kind of like the rule about the series. Couldn't you say that the multiple adjectives are like a series of adjectives?"

"I don't know. I think it's a little different. It's not really a *list* of adjective."

"But it could be. You said I was a smart, brave, handsome man. That's like listing my good points."

"Well, I never said that it was you I was talking about, did I? But I guess I see what you mean. But my high school English teacher said the series rule and the multiple adjectives rule were two different rules. And he should know."

"Oh."

"Anyway, the next rule is going to be number eight, so after that we can have another snack."

"Before you tell me what it is, I just want to say that, now that you have a sprained ankle, I'm sorry if I ever teased you about being a slow walker. That wasn't nice."

"That's okay." I gave him a reassuring smile.

Just then Yemmy yawned. "Yemmy, do you want to go back to sleep? Do you want to go back on the bed?" I knew it would be difficult for me carry Yemmy to the bed with a sprained ankle. "Tarzan, here, take Yemmy. He wants to go back on the bed."

Tarzan took Yemmy and placed him on the bed between Omy and Cheetah, who were both asleep. Then he returned to his seat at the table.

"Okay," I said, "rule number eight has to do with when you're talking to someone and you address him or her by name."

"What do you mean?"

"It's simple. If I say 'Tarzan, come here,' then . . . Wait. If I were *speaking*, I wouldn't use any punctuation. But if I were to *write* 'Tarzan, please come here,' then I'd put a comma after *Tarzan*."

"Oh."

"It's called *direct address*. I mean that to call someone by name is to *address* him or her *directly*—that's why it's called *direct address*. Anyway, that's rule number eight. After a noun or pronoun used in direct address, you need a comma."

Tarzan took the notebook and wrote: "Jane, can we have a snack now?"

"Very funny," I said. "The comma after *Jane* is correct—because you're addressing me directly—and yes, we can have a snack now. But only the orange ones."

Tarzan didn't argue with me about the colors. He reached for one of the orange pieces of fruit. There were four in all and we each ate two. I expected them to taste like oranges—like I was used to eating in America—but they didn't. I can't exactly describe what they tasted like, but they seemed to be sweet and sour at the same time. I mean, at first the taste was sour, but then after a while it became sweet. It's hard to explain.

When we'd finished, Omy woke up and jumped to the floor. Then he jumped onto Tarzan's lap. Tarzan didn't react to that one way or the other, but he stroked Omy's neck, as I had done to Yemmy earlier. It made me glad to see Tarzan and Omy bonding like that.

"Okay," I said, "let's move on to rule number nine. This one concerns using commas when you're writing dialogue."

"Do you mean when you're writing a story and you show what the characters say to each other out loud?"

"Well, yes. But it doesn't have to be a story; it could be any kind of writing. And it doesn't have to be fictional characters; it can be anyone who's speaking."

"Like what?"

"Well, for example, you might include dialogue in a newspaper or magazine article you're writing, and the people speaking might be actual persons."

"Persons?"

"That's the plural of *person.*"

"I thought the plural of *person* was *people.*"

"It is. But *persons* is also the plural of *person,* and sometimes it's better to use that word."

"Oh," Tarzan mumbled, with a little frown.

He didn't seem to understand the difference between *people* and *persons,* so I thought I'd better explain.

"You see, the word *people,*" I said, "refers to a large body of individuals collectively—you know, people in general. But if you're talking about a specific, relatively small number of individuals, then you usually refer to them as *persons.* For example, you can say that a crocodile attacked three animals and two *persons.* Or you can say that in governments decisions are usually made by *persons* in a position of authority. Or you can say that the word *combat* refers to fighting between armed groups or *persons.* Or you can say that a noun is a word used to name *persons,* places, or things."

"I know what a noun is."

"I know you do. I was just trying to explain when you use the word *persons* instead of *people.*"

"Oh. But in all those examples, would it be wrong to use the word *people* instead? Couldn't you say that a crocodile attacked two *people?*"

"You could. It wouldn't be wrong. But most grammar experts think that the word *persons* is preferable in the examples I just gave."

"How do you know?"

"Because I'm a professional journalist. I have to know those kinds of things to do my job properly."

"Oh." Tarzan was silent awhile and then said. "I have an example of a sentence using the word *persons.* Do you want to hear it?"

"Of course!" I couldn't wait to hear what he came up with.

"If Tarzan and Jane got married, it would be a marriage of *persons* from different continents. You see, you're a person from North America and I'm a person from Africa. We're two persons."

Oh my goodness! Did Tarzan want to marry me? Or was that just an example? I didn't know how to respond. I didn't know what to say. I looked over at Cheetah and Yemmy, but they were both asleep. Finally I said to Omy, "Omy, do you think Tarzan wants to marry me? Did he just propose?" Then I looked at Tarzan and we both blushed. "Well," I said to no one in particular, "I guess that was just an example." We both looked down and remained silent for a while. Finally, I said, "Okay, that's enough about *people* and *persons*. We're supposed to be talking about commas. Now, where were we?"

"You said that rule number nine had to do with writing dialogue."

"Oh, right. Now I remember. Anyway, if you have a direct quotation—"

"I remember what that is. It's when you write word-for-word what someone says out loud. You enclose it in quotation marks."

"Right. Well, the rule is that if you have a direct quotation and you also have a phrase such as *he said* or *she said* before or after it, you separate the quotation from the phrase with a comma. Here, watch." I took the notebook and wrote: He said, "Let's go swimming." Then, under that, I wrote: "I can't because I have a sprained ankle," she answered.

I turned the notebook toward Tarzan and let him read what I'd written. Then I said, "Do you see? In the first sentence, I placed a comma after the word *said*. That separates the introductory phrase *He said* from the direct quotation." I let that sink in, then I continued, "And in the second sentence, I placed a comma after the word *ankle* to separate the direct quotation from the phrase *she answered*, which follows."

Tarzan continued to pet the back of Omy's neck and said, "I see. But in the second sentence, why did you put the comma before the ending quotes? You wrote ankle, comma, quotation mark. Why didn't you write ankle, quotation mark, comma?"

"That's a good question. I can't really tell you why. That's just the way it's done. Commas always go *before* ending quotes, never *after*. Or you could say that commas always go *inside* quotation marks, never *outside*. It's just a rule. Everyone does it that way."

"Oh." Then after a moment Tarzan continued, "What if a phrase like *he said* doesn't come before or after a direct quotation, but it comes in the middle?"

"Do you mean like this?" I said. I took the notebook and wrote: "Let's go swimming," she said, "after my ankle heals." I turned the notebook toward him.

"That's what I mean. And I see that you used two commas—one before *she said* and one after it."

"Right, because each of those commas is needed to separate the phrase *she said* from the direct quotation."

"Oh."

251

"And there's something else I want you to notice about that last example. Do you see that the word *after* starts with a small *a*, not a capital *A?*"

"Yes," he answered, with a rising pitch.

"That's because the phrases *Let's go swimming* and *after my ankle heals* are both part of the same sentence."

"So?"

"Well, some people make the mistake of beginning anything placed inside quotation marks with a capital letter."

"Why do they do that?"

"I guess they're just used to doing it because in most cases what is placed inside quotation marks *is* a full sentence. But if you break a sentence in two by placing a phrase like *she said* in the middle of it, then the second half of the direct quotation begins with a small letter."

"Because the second half is not a new sentence. I mean it's not a complete sentence, right?"

"Right. Of course, you *could* have a situation in which a direct quotation is split in two with a phrase like *he said* but still use a capital letter to begin the second half."

"How?"

"If the second half of the direct quotation is a complete sentence. Here, look." I took the notebook and wrote: *"Let's go swimming,"* she said. *"Let's go boating, too."*

Tarzan took the notebook and read what I'd written. "I see that each part of the quotation is a complete sentence. That's why the second half starts with a capital letter, right?"

"Right. And that's why I used a period—not a comma—after *she said.*"

"To show that a new sentence is about to begin, right?"

"Right."

"But couldn't you say that in that example you have two separate direct quotations instead of one quotation split in half?"

"I guess you could say that. You can look at it either way."

"Oh."

"That's one of the things that makes grammar so interesting—that you can sometimes see things in more than one way."

He didn't answer that. He continued petting Omy's neck.

"There's one other thing I want you to know about using commas with direct quotations."

"What?"

"If you need to use a question mark or exclamation point, or some other punctuation mark, at the end of a direct quotation, you use *only* that punctuation mark; in other words, you don't use, let's say, a question mark *and* a comma."

"I don't understand."

"Here, look." I took the notebook and wrote: *"Are you hungry?" she asked.* Then under that I wrote: *"You bet!" he exclaimed.* Then I turned the notebook toward Tarzan and let him read what I'd written.

"Do you see?" I said. "After the question *Are you hungry,* I need a question mark. But do you notice that I didn't use a comma after it? I used *only* a question mark."

"I see. And after *You bet,* you used an exclamation point—with no comma after it."

"Right."

"Well," he said, "I know that was just an example, but if you're really asking me if I'm hungry, the answer is yes. Are you?"

"I could eat."

"How many more rules before our next snack?"

"That was rule number nine, right? Then there are three more—numbers ten, eleven, and twelve."

"That's a lot. Come on, let's hurry."

"Now, Tarzan, we can't hurry just because we're hungry. These rules are important."

"I know," he said, with a look of shame.

"And when we do eat, we have to eat the yellow fruit next, because that comes next in the order of the rainbow."

"Okay. So what's rule number ten?"

"Well, do you remember what an *interjection* is."

"Yes. It's a part of speech that's used to express emotion. It's a word like *golly, yikes,* or *gadzooks.*"

"That's right. But hardly anyone actually says *gadzooks.*"

"I know."

"Anyway, interjections usually come at the beginning of a sentence. And after the interjection you need either an exclamation point or a comma."

"How do you know which one to use?"

"It depends on how strong the emotion is—the emotion the word expresses, I mean. Here, look." I took the notebook and wrote: *"Ouch! That hurts!"* Then under that I wrote: *"Gee, that's odd."* I turned the notebook toward Tarzan. "You see, in the first sentence I used an exclamation point after the word *Ouch* because that word expresses a lot of emotion."

"Because whatever it was really hurt a lot, right?"

"Right. But in the second sentence, I used a *comma* after the word *Gee* because that word expresses less emotion—I mean that it expresses only a little emotion."

"Oh."

"Anyway, if you have an opening interjection that doesn't express a great deal of emotion, you follow it with a comma."

"Okay. What's rule number eleven?"

"Not so fast! We can't rush things just because you're hungry. I want to make sure you understand. I want you to make up some examples of sentences that have opening interjections with commas after them. Now, go ahead and write them in the notebook."

Tarzan wrote two sentences in the notebook and then turned it toward me. I read them, as follows: "Boy, am I hungry" and "Oh, what I'd give for a piece of fruit."

"Okay, that's very good," I said, "even if you are a wise guy."

"A wise guy?"

"Never mind. Okay, let's go on to the next rule."

"That would be number eleven. What is it?"

"It has to do with *contrasted elements.*"

"What does that mean?"

"Well, let me show you." I took the notebook and wrote: "Let's eat later, not now."

Tarzan took the notebook and read what I'd written. "I think I see," he said. "You take something that *is,* and you contrast it with something that *isn't* by using a comma and a phrase that begins with a word like *not.*"

"Right! That's what I mean by *contrasted elements.* Anyway, the point is, you need a comma before the phrase that expresses the contrast. Here's another example." In the notebook I wrote: "My name is spelled Jane, not Jayne."

Tarzan took the notebook and said, "I see. This is an easy rule. You just have to place a comma before the phrase that expresses the contrast. Let me try one." In the notebook he wrote: "Omy is on my lap, not yours."

"Very good! The comma after the word *lap* is correct. Now here's one more." I wrote: "We're pet lovers, not pet haters."

Apparently, he was able to read what I'd written upside down. As soon as I finished writing he said, "Okay, I see what you're doing.

I'm not a pet hater! I just don't think they belong indoors. They should be free."

"They are free." Then to Omy: "Aren't you, Omy?"

Tarzan stopped petting the orange cub as if waiting for him to answer. Then he resumed stroking the back of his neck.

"He loves you," I said to Tarzan.

"How do you know?"

"Because he loves to sit on your lap and have you pet him. He wouldn't let you do that if he didn't love you."

"Really?"

"Really."

Tarzan didn't seem to know how to answer that, so he just kept on petting Omy. Finally he said, "Okay, what's rule number twelve? After that one, we can have another snack."

"Well, rule number twelve has to do with avoiding confusion."

"What do you mean?"

"Well, sometimes you need a comma to separate parts of a sentence even though there doesn't seem to be any rule that requires it. That's because sometimes if you *don't* use a comma, a sentence might be confusing; I mean it might be misunderstood or misread."

"Like what?"

I took the notebook and wrote: "To Betty, Sue was a troublemaker." Then, under that I wrote: "To Betty Sue was a troublemaker." Then I said, "You see, Betty thinks Sue is a troublemaker."

"Who are Betty and Sue?"

"Nobody. This is just an example."

"Oh."

"Anyway, by using a comma after *Betty*, I make my meaning clear. But if I don't use a comma—like in the second sentence—you might think the sentence is about someone named Betty Sue."

"Oh, I see. Because it starts out *To Betty Sue* . . ."

"Right. Okay, here's one more example." I wrote: "I prefer tigers to lions, and chimps to gorillas." Under that I wrote: "I prefer tigers to lions and chimps to gorillas." Then I said, "Do you see the difference here? Without the comma, someone reading that sentence might think I was going to say that I prefer tigers to *lions and chimps.*"

"I do see. The meaning isn't immediately clear without the comma."

"Right. And that's why you need one. Now, can you make up an example of a comma that avoids confusion?"

Tarzan thought for a long time. Finally he wrote: "A few minutes after, the yellow fruit was eaten." Below that he wrote: "A few minutes after the yellow fruit was eaten."

"Tarzan! That's an excellent example!" I said.

"I know," he said proudly. "The first example means 'A few minutes after (they finished talking about the twelfth rule), the yellow fruit was eaten.' The second example seems to mean 'A few minutes after the yellow fruit was eaten (something else happened).'"

"That's right! To avoid confusion, or misreading, you need that comma after the word *after.*"

"Okay. That was rule number twelve, and now it really *is* time for a snack."

"Good. I'm hungry."

We each reached for a piece of yellow fruit. But we each reached for the same piece and our fingers touched. "I'm sorry; you take it," we each said at the exact same time. Then we both laughed.

The yellow fruit wasn't bananas. Tarzan knew I wouldn't eat bananas because of the effect banana juice had on mosquitoes. This stuff looked more like pineapple, but it tasted less tangy. You'd have to taste it yourself to know what I mean.

When we finished—three pieces each—Omy jumped down to the floor and then up onto the bed. Just then Cheetah woke up and climbed back onto the chair to my left.

"What is this, musical chairs?" I said.

"Musical chairs?"

"Never mind. Then to Cheetah: "Cheetah, sweetie, are you going to join us for our lesson on commas? We have only four more rules to cover. After that, Tarzan will start writing his own articles for *American Monthly.* Isn't that exciting?"

Cheetah yawned.

"Okay," I said, "this is rule number thirteen—even though the rules don't really have numbers. Anyway, sometimes in a sentence you have the exact same word twice is a row. Here's an example." Out loud, I said, "Whatever you do, do it fast." Then I said, "Now watch this." In the notebook I wrote: "Whatever you do, do it fast." Under that I wrote: "Whatever you do do it fast."

Tarzan read what I'd written and said, "That second sentence looks funny. It looks funny to have the word *do* twice in a row like that."

"I agree. Here's another example." In the notebook I wrote: "Whatever is, is." Under that I wrote: "Whatever is is."

Tarzan read that and said, "It's the same thing. It looks funny having the same word twice in a row."

"I know. That's why you often need a comma to separate identical words standing next to each other."

"Why did you say *often*. Why not *always?*"

"Because sometimes when you have the same word twice in a row the meaning is clear—even without a comma."

"Like what?"

"Well, if I say 'He said that that was the reason,' the meaning is clear. You don't need a comma between *that* and *that*. In fact, using a comma there would make the meaning *less* clear. Cheetah, don't you agree that would be less clear?"

Cheetah didn't answer, but he made a face.

"So," Tarzan said, "how do you know when you use a comma between identical words that are next to each other and when you don't?"

"Well, you can try it both ways and see which way seems more clear. Then do it that way."

"You mean it's up to the writer?"

"I guess so. The important thing is that the meaning is clear, that's all."

"Oh." Tarzan scratched his head and then said, "You know, this rule doesn't seem that different from the last one. In each case you're using a comma to avoid confusion."

"I guess you're right. But in high school I learned those as two separate rules."

"Still . . ."

We both thought about that awhile. Finally I said, "Okay, let's go on. This is rule number fourteen. It has to do with using a comma to show that one or more words have been left out of a sentence."

"I thought you show that with those three dots—an ellipsis."

"Well, an ellipsis is usually used to show that words have been omitted from a direct quotation. But I'm talking about words that are left out in regular writing."

"Like what?"

"Well, for example, have you ever heard the expression 'To err is human; to forgive, divine'?"

"No," he said with a rising inflection.

Well, what that really means is 'To err is human; to forgive *is* divine.' But the second *is* was intentionally left out."

"Why?"

"Because it's understood. It just sounds better without it. It would sound repetitive to say the word *is* twice."

"Oh."

"But to show that the word *is* was omitted, a comma is used. Here, look." I wrote in the notebook: "To err is human; to forgive, divine."

"I see," Tarzan said. "You put a comma between *forgive* and *divine* to show that the word *is* was left out."

"Right. Here's another example." In the notebook I wrote: "In North America there are three countries; in Africa, more than forty." Then I said, "Now, in the second part of that sentence, which words are omitted."

"I think it's 'there are.' The second part of the sentence really means 'in Africa *there are* more than forty.' And you placed a comma between the words *Africa* and *more* to show that those words were omitted."

"Exactly! Cheetah, are you getting this?"

Cheetah bounced up and down a little on the chair.

"Okay," I said, "let's move on to rule number fifteen. This one has to do with using commas when you're talking about places or dates."

"What do you mean?"

"Well, let's talk about places first. Sometimes in a sentence you have the name of a place, and then right after it you have the name of another place that helps explain—or gives extra information about—the first place. Here, look." I took the notebook and wrote: "Philadelphia, Pennsylvania, is the home of the Liberty Bell." Then I said, "Now, the first place mentioned in that sentence is the city of Philadelphia. And after that you have the name *Pennsylvania,* which shows the state Philadelphia is located in."

Tarzan didn't say anything, so I kept on going.

"Now, what you have to understand is that the second place, Pennsylvania, is *enclosed* in commas."

"I see."

"But lots of people make a mistake when they write a sentence like this one."

"What do they do wrong?"

"Well, lots of people think that you're supposed to separate the first place from the second place with one comma. In other words, they'd write"—I wrote in the notebook: "Philadelphia, Pennsylvania is the home of the Liberty Bell." I showed him what I'd written and then said, "Do you see the difference? In this example, I have only *one* comma; it *separates* the city from the state. That's incorrect. But in my first example, I have *two* commas; they *enclose* the second place named—the state. That's correct."

"I see."

"Good. Can you make up an example of your own? And remember to put commas before *and* after the second place named."

Tarzan took the notebook and wrote: "Cairo, Egypt, is the largest city in Africa."

"Very good!" I said. "I'm so glad you put commas before *and* after *Egypt.*"

"That's what you said I should do."

"I know. But so many people forget. Or they just don't understand the rule."

"Well, I don't see what's so difficult about it."

"Me either."

We smiled at each other. Then I said, "Cheetah, that's not such a hard rule, is it?"

He seemed to shake his head, but I can't be sure.

"Of course," I said, "sometimes you can't put a comma after the second place named because the second place comes at the very end of the sentence. For example, let's say that I wanted to write 'I traveled to Paris, France.' In that case, I can't put a comma after *France,* because the sentence is finished. So there, one comma is used to separate the city from the country—I mean the first place named from the second."

"Well, maybe that's why people sometimes make that mistake you were talking about—using only one comma between the two places, I mean. Sometimes you *can't* use two—when the second place named comes at the end of the sentence, I mean."

"I think maybe you're right."

Tarzan smiled.

"Okay, now let's talk about using commas with dates."

"Okay."

"The rule about using commas with dates is similar to the one we just discussed about using commas with places. What I mean is that sometimes in a sentence you have a date, and then right after that you have another date that explains or gives information about the first date. Here, I'll show you." I took the notebook and wrote: "On July 4, 1776, the Declaration of Independence was approved." Then I turned the notebook toward Tarzan so he could read it.

"Who approved it?"

"Delegates from the Thirteen Colonies. But that's not the point. The point is that if you have two dates in a row, like in this example, you have to *enclose* the second date with commas. It's wrong to simply separate the day from the month with one comma."

"I see. You have commas both before *and* after 1776, just like you had commas both before and after *Pennsylvania* in that example about the Liberty Bell."

"That's it. Now here's something a little tricky. Sometimes you write a month and year with out writing the exact day."

"What do you mean?"

"Look." I took the notebook and wrote: "In October 1492 Columbus reached the New World." Then under that I wrote: "In October, 1492, Columbus reached the New World." I turned the notebook toward Tarzan.

"Okay," I said, "if you state a month and year with giving the exact day—as in October 1492—you can leave out the commas completely. I mean that you don't put a comma before *or* after the year. I pointed to the beginning of the first of the two sentences I had just written.

"But some people," I continued, "like to use commas even if the exact day isn't given. In that case, commas are needed both before *and* after the year." I pointed to the commas in the second of the two sentences.

"So, which way should I do it—with or without the commas?"

"Well, most people do it without the commas. And that's how we do it at *American Monthly*. So I think you should do it without the commas."

"Okay. That's what I'll do, then."

"Good."

"What if you have a day and month instead of a month and year? Then what do you do?"

"Do you mean if I were to write you a note that said something like this?" I took the notebook and wrote: "Would you like to meet on Friday, April 9, for another moonlight swim and cookout?" I turned the notebook toward him.

"That's what I mean! I see that you put commas before *and* after the second date—April 9. Do you really want to have another moonlight swim and cookout?"

"Well, we'll see about that. My ankle has to heal first. The point is, in this example, I enclosed *April 9* with commas. I didn't simply separate *Friday* from *April 9* with one comma."

"Because it follows the rule that if you have a date explaining a previous date, you enclose the second date in commas, right?"

"Right."

I looked at Cheetah and made a funny face. He imitated it.

"Tarzan, make a funny face to Cheetah. He'll imitate it."

"I don't feel like it."

"Why not? What's the matter?"

"Nothing," he said sullenly.

"Are you upset because I didn't agree to meet for another moonlight swim? Is that it? It's not that I don't want to. It's just that my ankle has to heal first. You don't want me to make my injury worse, do you?"

"No."

"All right, then. Now, make a funny face to Cheetah."

Tarzan halfheartedly made a funny face.

"Funnier!" I said.

"Okay." Tarzan turned to Cheetah and made a ridiculously silly face. Then Cheetah imitated it and we both laughed loudly. Tarzan was his old self again.

"Okay, now let's talk about the sixteenth rule."

"Good. Then we can have another snack."

I took the notebook and wrote: "You don't want me to make my injury worse, do you?" I let him read it.

"We already finished talking about that," Tarzan said. "I understand about your ankle. I'm not upset anymore."

"No," I said, "you don't understand why I just wrote that. This *is* the sixteenth rule."

"What do you mean?"

"I mean that if you have a statement followed by a short question, but all in one sentence, you separate the statement from the question with a comma. Here are some other examples." I took the notebook and wrote: "Cheetah's cute, isn't he?" Under that I wrote: "You like Yemmy and Omy, don't you?" Turning the notebook to Tarzan, I said, "Do you see how I used a comma to separate the statement from the ending question?"

He nodded.

"You try some," I said.

He wrote in the notebook (I could read it upside down from where I sat): "We'll swim in the pond again, won't we?" Under that he wrote: "You're hungry, aren't you?"

"The answer to the first question is yes," I said, "and the answer to the second question is also yes."

We smiled at each other.

"Good," he said. "Let's eat the green fruit." He reached for a piece but I grabbed his arm to stop him.

"I just thought of something," I said. "I have to tell you a few more things about commas."

"But you said there were only sixteen rules."

"These aren't really punctuation rules."

"What do you mean?"

"I mean that sometimes when you use a comma, it has nothing to do with separating or enclosing elements of a sentence. It's not really a matter of punctuation; it's a matter of convention."

"Do you mean like when you told me that sometimes a hyphen is a matter of spelling and not punctuation?"

"Yes, something like that. Here, let me show you." I took the notebook and wrote: *1,000,000.* Under that I wrote: *Porter, Jane.* Under that I wrote *In 1906, 500 people were killed in the San Francisco earthquake.* I turned the notebook to him and said, "In that first example, I wrote the number 'one million' in numerals. In any number of four or more digits, you use commas the separate the thousands, millions, and so on. In other words, after every three digits, counting from the right—from the 'ones' column,' I mean—you have to place a comma. It just makes the number easier to read; easier to understand."

"Oh."

Tarzan pointed to the second example and said, "Why did you write *Porter, Jane.* Your name is Jane Porter."

"Sometimes a number of names are listed in alphabetical order—by last name, I mean. You might see that in an attendance list at a school or in a list of author's names in a bibliography at the back of a book. In any case, if names are listed alphabetically by last name, the last name is given first, then a comma, and then the first name."

"I think I see. If there was no comma, it might look as if your name really *was* Porter Jane. That's a funny name." Tarzan giggled a little.

"Right. Okay, now let's look at the last example. If you have a sentence with two different numbers in a row, you separate them with a comma so that they're not mistaken for one big number. If I wrote this—" I took the notebook and wrote: *In 1906 500 people* . . . "—It would look confusing."

"I can see that. This is kind of like that rule about using a comma to avoid confusion," he said. "Like when you talked about Betty and Sue, and lions and chimps. I think it was rule number twelve. Do you remember?"

"I do. I guess, if you like, you could say that this rule really *is* a matter of punctuation; that it's another example of rule number twelve."

Tarzan smiled with satisfaction.

"Anyway, that's all I have to tell you about commas."

"That was a lot."

"I know. That's why I didn't want to tell you about commas when we were climbing that mountain."

"Do you mean when you were out of breath and you kept going 'mh' and 'ih' after every few words?"

"Okay, go ahead; make fun of me. You're in better shape than I am. I admit it."

"I didn't mean . . ." Tarzan protested. Then to Cheetah: "Cheetah, tell her I wasn't making fun of her."

Cheetah looked at Tarzan and then at me.

"That's okay," I said. "I know you weren't. Come on, let's have our snack."

There were five pieces of green fruit.

"There are five pieces," I said. "We can't divide them evenly."

"I have an idea," Tarzan said. "Start by eating two."

We each ate two pieces.

"Now," Tarzan continued. "We're going to share this last piece. I'll put half of it into my mouth, and then you'll put the other half in your mouth. Then we'll both bite down."

"But if we do that, our lips will touch."

He stared meaningfully into my eyes.

"Okay," I said. We'd kissed before. This wouldn't be the first time. "Cheetah, close your eyes."

We both stood up. He put the fruit in his mouth. Half of it protruded from his lips. I put my lips around my half and we both bit down. In the process, our lips brushed against each other briefly.

We sat back down and swallowed our fruit.

"Cheetah, you can open your eyes again," I said. It was really for my own benefit; his eyes were never closed.

"Okay," I said, "now we have to test you on commas."

"What do you mean? I already made up my own examples demonstrating the different rules."

263

"But the reason I wrote Article 5 was specifically for a comma test. I'm going to have you look at every comma in Article 5 and tell me the reason it's there."

"You mean which rule applies to each comma?"

"Exactly."

"Well, I guess I can do that. We've already eaten, and we can't really go anywhere because of your ankle. How *is* your ankle?"

"Well, it doesn't hurt when I'm just sitting here. Let me get up and test it when I try to walk."

"Be careful."

I stood but put all the weight on my left leg. Then I gradually put weight on my right leg.

"It hurts only a little. I think I can walk a little."

I took a few steps, keeping most of the weight on my left leg.

"It's not too bad. I think by tomorrow it might be okay."

"That's great!"

"Okay, now let me find Article 5."

I flipped back several pages in the notebook and found it. I glanced at it and remembered that it concerned Tarzan's father being attached by a 300-pound gorilla. This was truly exciting stuff. I couldn't wait to find out what happened next. Well, after this comma test, Tarzan would start writing his own articles, and I'd find out then.

"Okay," I said, "here's what I want you to do. I want you to take this article and number the commas. I mean after each comma, put the numbers 1, 2, and so on, in parentheses. Take it paragraph by paragraph. I mean, start numbering from 1 again at each new paragraph."

I handed the notebook to Tarzan and he numbered all the commas.

"Okay, now, let's look at the first paragraph." I held the notebook sideways near Cheetah so that Tarzan and I could both read it at the same time.

Cheetah started playing with the notebook!

"Cheetah," I said, "go back on the bed with Yemmy and Omy. Mommy and Daddy have to work here." Then to Tarzan: "Take him to the bed, okay?"

Tarzan lifted Cheetah in his arms and carried him to the bed. Cheetah seemed content to stay there, and Tarzan resumed his seat.

The first paragraph, with the commas numbered, looked like this:

One afternoon, (1) while my father was searching for materials to build a second room onto their cabin, (2) a number of small monkeys came shrieking through the trees toward him. Every few moments they'd cast a fearful glance behind them, (3) as though afraid of some approaching danger. At last he saw it, (4) the thing the little monkeys so feared—the man-beast my parents had glimpsed in the shadows during their first night in the jungle.

"Now, what I want you to do," I said, "is tell me the reason for each of those commas."

Tarzan studied the paragraph. Finally he said, "Okay. The first and second commas are there for the same reason. They're enclosing, or surrounding, a nonrestrictive clause. The clause 'while my father was searching for materials to build a second room onto their cabin' could be removed without changing the meaning of the sentence. So it's nonrestrictive. So it needs commas around it."

"Very good! How about comma number 3?"

Tarzan studied the sentence for a long time. Finally he said, "This is a tough one. This sentence has an independent clause— *Every few moments they'd cast a fearful glance behind them*—followed by a dependent clause— *as though afraid of some approaching danger*. Oh, I'm calling the second part of the sentence a clause, not a phrase, because I think it really means 'as though *they were* afraid of some approaching danger.' I think the subject and verb are understood."

"Okay, go on."

"Anyway, I remember the rule about separating an independent clause from a dependent clause with a comma, but I remember that you said that that rule refers to an *introductory* dependent clause. But in this case, the dependent clause comes *after* the independent clause. So I'm not sure why there's a comma there."

"This is a funny thing," I said. "In high school I was taught that the rule—about separating a dependent clause from an independent clause, I mean—applies to *introductory* dependent clauses. But now that I think about it, people often separate independent clauses from *following* dependent clauses. I know we do that a lot at *American Monthly*. So let's amend that rule to say that you should use a comma to separate an independent clause from a dependent clause whenever a comma helps make the meaning clear."

"You mean it doesn't matter which order the clauses come in?"

"I guess not."

"Okay, then the reason for comma number 3 is that it separates an independent clause from a dependent clause."

"Okay, that's right, but you have to understand that you don't *always* use a comma to separate an independent clause from a following dependent clause."

"When *don't* you?"

"You don't if the sentence is short or if the meaning is clear without the comma. For example, let's say that I were to write 'I sat down because my ankle hurt.' In that case I wouldn't use a comma to separate the independent clause—*I sat down*—from following dependent clause—*because my ankle hurt*. You don't need it because the meaning is clear without it. But if I switch the order of the clauses—if I put the dependent clause first, I mean—then I *would* need a comma. Here, look." In the margin of the notebook I wrote: "Because my ankle hurt, I sat down."

"I see," Tarzan said. "If the dependent clause comes first, you *must* use a comma. But if the *independent* clause comes first, you may or may not use a comma, depending on how complex the sentence is. Is that it?"

"That's it. I guess that's why in high schools they make the rule apply to only *introductory* dependent clauses—because that's the situation in which you *must* use a comma. Well! That's a lot of talk about clauses! Let's go on to comma number 4. Why is that there?"

Tarzan studied comma number 4 awhile, then said, "This one is tricky, too. I have two different ideas about why that comma is there."

"What are they?"

"One idea is that it's there just to avoid confusion. I mean it would look weird to read 'At last he saw it the thing . . .'"

"Okay. What's your other idea?"

"My other idea is that since the word *it* and the phrase *the thing the monkeys so feared* both mean the same thing, you can say that they're in apposition. Is that right? Is the phrase *the thing the monkeys so feared* an appositive?"

"I think you could say that. After all, the noun phrase *the thing the monkeys so feared* is an explanatory equivalent of the pronoun *it*, which precedes it."

"But if the noun phrase is an appositive, it should have a comma both before *and* after it. Here, there's a dash after it. Why is there a dash after it?"

"Well, a dash is sometimes used to introduce a kind of summary or explanation of what came before. And that's what's happening here. The following phrase about the man-beast explains what *it* refers to; what the monkeys feared."

"This is complicated. It seems like *the thing the monkeys so feared* starts out as an appositive—because there's a comma before it—but ends up *not* as an appositive because there's *not* a comma after it."

"Maybe you could look at the dash as a kind of substitute for a comma. Maybe you can think of it as a *strong* comma. That way you could still think of *the thing the monkeys so feared* as an appositive."

"I could?"

"I guess so. You see, this is what's so fascinating about grammar and punctuation. Often, you can look at something in more than one way."

"And each way could be correct?"

"Yes."

"Then I'll say that the purpose of comma number 4 is to separate the pronoun *it* from the appositive that follows."

"Okay, I'll accept that."

To be honest, I wasn't one hundred percent sure myself. Maybe *the thing the monkeys so feared* is simply a nonrestrictive phrase. I guess it all depends on how you look at it. When I wrote Article 5, a comma seemed necessary to me there. Maybe I should have used a colon or dash instead. What do you think?

"You know," Tarzan mused, "punctuation in real-life situations is harder that in the little examples you made up while you were teaching me."

"In a way that's true. But you shouldn't get discouraged. Just remember that there isn't always just *one* correct way to punctuate something. Sometimes you have a choice. For example, around a parenthetical remark you might use commas, or parentheses, or dashes. And before a summary or explanation of preceding remarks you might use a colon or a dash—or sometimes even a comma. So in a way, real-life punctuation isn't harder, because you have choices."

He didn't answer, so I said, "Okay, let's keep going. Let's look at the second paragraph of Article 5." I held the notebook so that we could both read it. It looked like this:

It was quickly approaching in a semi-erect position, (1) now and then placing the backs of its closed fists upon the ground. It was a

300-pound gorilla, (2) and, (3) as it advanced, (4) it wildly swung its arms, (5) roared, (6) and salivated.

"Okay, let's start with comma number 1," I said. "Why is that there?"

"That's there to separate the independent clause—*It was quickly approaching in a semi-erect position*—from the following dependent clause—*now and then placing the backs of its closed fists upon the ground.*"

"Right. Now what about comma number 2?"

"Well, in that sentence you have two independent clauses joined by the coordinating conjunction *and*. So you need a comma after the first clause, before the conjunction."

"Very good! How about the next one."

"I think commas 3 and 4 are there to surround the parenthetical remark *as it advanced*. If you took out that phrase, you'd have . . . *and it wildly swung its arms* . . . That still makes sense." Tarzan paused and then said, "But do you know what's funny? If you look at just the second part of the sentence, starting after the word *and*, you could say that *as it advanced* is an introductory dependent clause leading into the independent clause *it wildly swung its arms* . . . In that case, comma number 4 is being used to separate the clauses. Isn't that funny?"

"Yes. I mean, I think that's interesting."

"It seems that you can *often* see things in more than one way."

"That's what I'm trying to tell you. That's why grammar and punctuation are so fascinating. Anyway, let's go on to comma number 5. Why is that there?"

"Well, commas 5 and 6 are both serial commas. You have a series—or list—of things the gorilla did. You have to separate those things with commas. And like you said, you could have omitted comma number 6, because of the word *and*, but we decided that we would always include the final serial comma."

"Tarzan, you have such a good memory. I'm impressed."

He seemed to swell with pride. Then he said, "Let me see the third paragraph."

We both read it. It looked like this:

My father was at some distance from the cabin, (1) having come to chop down a particular tree for his building operations. Seeing the great ape crashing through the underbrush directly toward him, (2) and from a direction which practically cut him off from escape, (3) he felt a shiver run up and down his spine.

"I know why those commas are there," Tarzan said. "Comma 1 separates an independent clause—*My father was at some distance from the cabin*—from a dependent clause—*having come to chop down a particular tree for his building operations.*"

"Good!"

"And commas 2 and 3 enclose the nonrestrictive phrase *and from a direction which practically cut him off from escape.*" You could take out that phrase and the sentence would still make sense."

"Very good! You're on a roll!"

"A roll?"

"Never mind. Let's go on to the fourth paragraph."

We both read it, as follows:

He knew that, (1) armed only with an ax, (2) his chances with this ferocious monster were small indeed. And Alice, (3) he thought, (4) what will become of Alice? There was still a slight chance of reaching the cabin. He turned and ran toward it, (5) shouting an alarm to his wife to run inside and close the door.

"Okay," Tarzan said. "I know why these commas are there too. Commas 1 and 2 are used to enclose the parenthetical—or nonrestrictive—phrase *armed only with an ax.*"

"Right!"

"And commas 3 and 4 are there for the same reason. They surround the parenthetical remark *he thought.*"

"Good!"

"And comma 5 is there to separate the independent clause *He turned and ran toward it* from the following dependent clause, *shouting an alarm to his wife to run inside and close the door.*"

"Very good!"

"This is fun! I like explaining commas. Let me see the next paragraph."

We both read the fifth paragraph. It looked like this:

My mother had been sitting a little way from the cabin, (1) and when she heard his cry she looked up to see the ape springing with incredible swiftness in an effort to overtake my father. With a low cry she sprang toward the cabin and, (2) as she entered, (3) gave a backward glance that filled her soul with terror, (4) for the brute had nearly reached her husband.

"Okay, let's see," Tarzan said. "The sentence with comma 1 has two independent clauses joined by the coordinating conjunction *and*. So you need a comma after the first clause, before the conjunction."

"Good."

"But that sentence has something funny about it. The second independent clause is really made up of a dependent clause—*when she heard his cry*—followed by an independent clause—*she looked up to see the ape . . .*"

"So?"

"So, why isn't there a comma after the little introductory dependent clause—after the word *cry*, I mean? Is it because *when she heard his cry* isn't *really* an introductory depending clause—because in truth it comes in the middle of the sentence?"

"Maybe. Or maybe it's a matter of writer's choice. Maybe when I wrote that sentence I thought it would be clearer if the sentence looked like a two-clause sentence (with one comma separating the clauses) rather than a three-clause sentence (with two commas). It was my choice. Do you see what I mean? When you write Article 6, you can make choices like that too."

"I can?"

"Sure. Now, let's keep going. What about comma 2?"

"Well, commas 2 and 3 are there to enclose the nonrestrictive clause *as she entered.*"

"Good. And comma 4?"

"That's there to separate the dependent phrase at the end—*for the brute had nearly reached her husband*—from the really long independent clause that starts the sentence."

"Very good! Now, let's look at the last paragraph."

We read it together, as follows:

"Close and bolt the door, (1) Alice, (2)" he cried. "I can finish this fellow with my ax." But he knew he was facing a horrible death, (3) and so did she.

"Well," Tarzan said, "comma 1 is there because my father was addressing my mother directly. It's an example of direct address. You use a comma to separate the name of the person being addressed—in this case *Alice*—from the rest of the sentence."

"Right!"

"And comma 2 is there because you have a direct quotation. You use a comma to separate the words quoted from an expression such as *he said*—or, in this case, *he cried.*"

"Very good! What about comma *3!*"

Tarzan looked at that one awhile. "I'm not really sure. I think it's there to separate two independent clauses joined by the word *and*. But is *so did she* an independent clause? If it said something like *she did also* instead, that would be an independent clause. But either way, it means the same thing, so maybe *so did she* really is an independent clause. Is it?"

"I guess you can consider it one. But even if you consider the sentence as having two independent clauses joined by *and*, since the clauses are relatively short, I could have left out the comma anyway."

"You could?"

"Yes. But do you know why I included it?"

"Why?"

"Well, first of all, it wouldn't be wrong to include it—if it separates independent clauses, I mean. But I included it mainly for dramatic effect."

"Dramatic effect?"

"Yes. I want the reader to pause slightly right there. It makes the story more exciting, more gripping. The reader will read it more like this." In the margin of the notebook I wrote: "But he knew he was facing a horrible death . . . and so did she." Then I said, "Do you see what I mean? Isn't that more exciting, more suspenseful?"

"Then why didn't you use an ellipsis if you want him to read it like that?"

"I could have. But I chose a comma. Writer's choice."

"Oh."

"Well, guess what! I've finished teaching you about all the basics of grammar and punctuation. Now you're ready to start writing your own articles. Are you excited?"

"Just a minute," Tarzan answered. "When we first talked about learning grammar and writing articles, you said that first you would teach me grammatical terms and then I would start writing. You said you would teach me the *rules* of grammar by finding mistakes in my writing. But you've already taught me the rules, haven't you?"

"I guess you're right. But when I started explaining the terms to you, I found that I needed to explain some rules at the same time; otherwise, you wouldn't fully understand the terms. Do you see what I mean?"

"I guess so."

"Anyway, this will just make it easier for us. Probably, because you already know a lot of rules, the articles you write won't have a lot of errors. There won't be so much for us to go over."

"Did you already teach me all the rules?"

"Well, you know the basics. But when you start to write, we'll find out exactly what you still don't know. Then we'll go over each point as it arises, okay?"

"Okay. Do you think I'll make any mistakes in my writing?"

"I don't know, but we'll find out soon enough."

"When?"

"Well, look, it's getting dark already. This has been a long day. The time has gone quickly. We must have been having fun."

"I like commas. I had fun."

"Good. Why don't we continue tomorrow morning. You can write your first article, Article 6, then."

Tarzan stood up. "Okay. I'll see you then. I'll take Yemmy, Omy, and Cheetah with me so you can get a good night's sleep. We want your ankle to be all better tomorrow."

Tarzan went to the bed and picked up Cheetah. As he walked to the door he called, "Come on, Yemmy. Come on, Omy." He patted his thigh. The cubs jumped from the bed and followed him out the door.

"Good night!" he called to me from just outside.

"Good night!"

I fell into a deep sleep and dreamt about punctuation marks!

Chapter 23: Diamonds and Gold

The next morning Tarzan arrived bright and early. I was seated at the edge of the bed.

"Where are Yemmy and Omy?" I said. "Where's Cheetah?"

"They're outside somewhere. Don't worry; they're okay."

"Are you sure?"

"Of course; they're fine."

"I wouldn't want anything bad to happen to them."

"Nothing's going to happen. They know how to take care of themselves."

"Okay. As long as you're sure."

Tarzan didn't seem to know how to answer that; he didn't say anything for a while. Finally he said, "How's your ankle?"

"I don't know. I didn't test it yet today. I hopped from the bed to the table. I'll test it now."

I stood up, placing most of the weight on my left leg. I took a few short steps. "Hey! I think I can walk!" I took a few more steps. "It's really not so bad. I think it's going to be fine."

"Good! But don't overdo it right away. I think you should give it time to heal. I think we should stay indoors again today. After we finish our grammar work, we can go outside and take a short walk around the cabin and see how that goes."

"That sounds like a good idea. You would have made a good doctor!"

"Well—"

"You know," I interrupted, "part of me wants to rest my ankle, but another part of me wants to exercise it. See, when I was a kid, if we played sports and someone hurt his foot or sprained his ankle, the coach would say 'Walk it off; walk it off.'"

"What does that mean?"

"The coach thought that a foot, ankle, or knee injury would go away if you walked; if you used whatever was injured in a natural way."

"Oh."

"So part of me just wants to 'walk off' this sprained ankle."

"Oh."

"But I guess that your idea is best. First I'll rest my ankle, and then after our grammar lesson, I'll start to gradually 'walk it off.'"

"Okay. Should we have the grammar lesson first or should we eat first?"

"I'm not that hungry yet," I said. "Let's have brunch a little later. Can you wait?"

"Actually, I had some berries on the way over here, so I can wait."

"I hope they were blueberries."

"Why?"

"Because that's the next color of the rainbow. Yesterday we ate red, orange, yellow, and green fruit, in that order. The next color of the rainbow is blue."

"Are you still following that silly order?" Tarzan said, very much surprised. "It doesn't make any difference."

"The order's not silly. It's natural. Were they blueberries?"

"I guess so. They were blue."

"That's good," I said, very much relieved. "I'm going to have blueberries this morning too—when it's time for brunch, I mean. Do you remember where you found them?"

"I remember."

"Good. Okay, now let's get on with our grammar lesson. What I want you to do is take the notebook and write Article 6."

"What should it be about?"

"Just continue with your life story. Pick it up at the part where your father is about to kill a 300-pound gorilla with an ax."

"Okay."

"The only thing you have to remember is that we don't want the readers of *American Monthly* to be able to tell that the articles were written by two different people. So you're going to have to copy my journalistic style."

"Your journalistic style?"

"Well, I have a certain way that I write magazine articles. I have a certain *style*. Every author has his or her own style—every good author, that is."

"Can't I have my own style?"

"Well, eventually, yes. But you're just starting out as a writer. No one really expects a beginner to have any special style. But more importantly, as I said, we don't want the readers of the magazine to know that two different writers worked on this series of articles. So you're going to have to copy my style. Do you think you can do that?"

"Maybe I can. I've studied your articles for grammar and punctuation, so I know how you write."

"But you also have to copy my syntax."

274

"You mean I have to copy how you put words together to make a sentence?"

"Right—so that your writing sounds just like mine."

"Okay. Let me try. I'll sit here at the table and write. What are you going to do while I'm writing?"

"I'll just sit on the edge of the bed and rest my ankle."

"Okay."

"Oh, one more thing," I said. "Make your article about the same length as each of my articles, okay?"

"Because the readers of your magazine have short attention spans, right?"

"Unfortunately, yes."

Taking small steps, I walked back to the bed and sat down. Tarzan sat at the table and started to write. After about two minutes he said, "What's that song you're humming?"

I hadn't been aware that I was humming! "What song?"

"That song you're humming."

"I was humming?"

"Yes!"

"What did it sound like?"

Tarzan hummed a little tune.

"Oh, I know what that is! It's a song we used to sing in America—"Swanee River."

"Well, can you please stop humming it? I can't concentrate. I'm trying to write."

Why are writers so touchy, I wondered. "I'm sorry," I said. "I didn't realize I was humming. I'll stop so you can write."

About five minutes later Tarzan said, "What's that noise you're making?"

"What noise?"

"That cracking noise."

I realized that I must have been cracking my knuckles. "Oh, I was cracking my knuckles," I explained.

"Cracking your knuckles?"

"It's a habit I have when I'm bored."

"Well, if you're bored, why don't you take one of my father's books from the shelf and read it."

"Okay."

With short steps I walked to the shelf and took down a book about Africa. I returned to the bed and started to read. According to this book, there were gold mines in Africa. Hmm, I thought. I won-

275

der if I should mention this to Tarzan. If we found gold, then if I were to return to America, I'd be rich. Hey! Isn't that funny that I said *if* I return to America and not *when*?

Well, I wasn't in any condition to hike to any gold mines. And besides, didn't gold have to be separated from its ore? We didn't have any equipment to do that. Just then my thoughts were interrupted by Tarzan's exclamation: "I'm finished!"

"Already?" I said.

"That wasn't so fast. You were reading that book for a long time."

"I was?"

"Yes."

"Tarzan, do you know what gold is?"

"Gold?"

"Never mind. Okay, let me see what you wrote." I walked the table. But instead of sitting opposite Tarzan, I sat in the chair to his right.

I started to read Article 6. Every time I came to an error I underlined it so that I would remember which places to draw Tarzan's attention to for our lesson. The difficulty was that the article was so fascinating and exciting that it was hard for me to concentrate on grammar! Nevertheless, I managed to underline all the errors I found.

Before I show you what Tarzan wrote, I want to tell you about Tarzan's writing in general. When I read what he had written I was impressed and, I'll admit it, a little jealous. He succeeded splendidly in copying my style. No one would be able to tell the difference. But I had trained for years to develop that style—my professional journalistic style. Tarzan was able to imitate it exactly immediately. How could that be? Was he a better writer than I was? Was he smarter than I was?

I wasn't really competitive with Tarzan (even though as a kid I was always very competitive in sports and in school). Yet, I couldn't help but feel a bit inadequate in the light of his literary accomplishment. I was now more in awe of Tarzan than ever. Well, I would try not to let my jealousy or competitive streak show.

"Why, Tarzan, that's excellent! You've copied my style perfectly! And the story is so exciting and suspenseful! I can't wait to see what happens in Article 7!"

Maybe I overdid it with all those exclamations, but I didn't want Tarzan to guess that I might be jealous of his literary abilities.

"I'm glad you like it," he said. "I tried to write just like you do. I mean I tried to write as well as you do."

"Do you think I'm a good writer?" I fished.

"I think you're a great writer."

I smiled with pride and gave his hand a little squeeze.

"Well, you're pretty good yourself," I said. "Now, let's go over the errors."

"What are those lines you drew under some of the words?"

"I underlined each error, so that it would be easy for me to remember what to talk to you about."

"I made all those errors?"

"It's not so many."

"Let me see."

I turned the notebook toward Tarzan so that he could see what I'd underlined. The article looked like this:

Article 6: "The gorilla attacks"

The great ape closed in on my father. His nasty, <u>close set eyes</u> gleamed hatred from beneath his shaggy brows, while his great fangs were bared in a horrid snarl as he paused a moment before his victim. <u>He</u> could see the doorway of the cabin, not 20 yards distant.

A great wave of horror and fear swept over him as he saw his young wife emerge, armed with a rifle. She had always been afraid of guns, and would never touch them, but now she rushed toward the ape with the fearlessness of a lioness protecting her young.

<u>Back, Alice!</u> shouted my father. <u>Go back!</u>

Just then the ape charged so that my father could say no more. He swung his ax with all his strength, but the powerful brute <u>grabs</u> it in his terrible hands and <u>hurls</u> it far to one side.

With an ugly snarl he lunged at his defenseless victim. But before his fangs had reached the throat they thirsted for, there was a loud bang and a bullet entered the ape's chest.

<u>Throwing my father to the ground</u> the beast turned upon his new enemy. There before him stood the terrified young woman trying to fire another bullet into the animal's body. But she didn't understand the mechanism of the rifle <u>and,</u> the hammer fell upon an empty cartridge.

Screaming with rage and pain, the ape flew at the delicate woman, who fell to the ground in a dead faint. Almost simultaneously her husband regained his feet, and without thought of the utter hopelessness of it, he rushed forward to drag the ape from his wife's lifeless form.

"Your poor mother!" I exclaimed.

When Tarzan didn't answer, I said, "Well, let's start with the first underline."

"You underlined the title!" he said. "Didn't you like my title?"

"I liked it a lot. And I didn't underline the *whole* title—only two words."

"Why?"

"Because each word of a title should be capitalized."

"I thought you were going to check my grammar and punctuation. I didn't know you were going to check my capitalization too."

"Actually, I'm going to check four things: grammar, punctuation, capitalization, and *usage*."

"What's usage?"

"Well, sometimes when people speak or write, they use the wrong word."

"The wrong word?"

"Well, sometimes two words are similar, and people use one when they should use the other. For example, they might use *affect* when they really mean *effect*. Or they might say *further* when they really mean *farther*. Things like that."

"Oh."

"Those kinds of mistakes aren't really grammatical. They're mistakes in usage. The writer or speaker is *using* the wrong word."

"Oh."

"Anyway, let's get back to the title of your article. It should look like this." In the margin of the notebook I wrote: "The Gorilla Attacks." Then I said, "That's because in a title, you usually capitalize each word."

"Usually?"

"Well, the first word of a title and the last word of a title are *always* capitalized. But some of the other words in a title might not be capitalized, depending on what part of speech they are."

"What do you mean?"

"Well, unless they're the first or last word of the title, articles, prepositions, and conjunctions aren't capitalized. For example, in the title 'Finding a Piece of Gold,' the word *a* isn't capitalized because it's an article and the word *of* isn't capitalized because it's a preposition."

"What's that the title of?"

"Nothing. I just made it up."

"Oh. Well, it looks like in a title the long words are capitalized and the shorts ones aren't."

"It looks like that, but that's not the way the rule works. You have to consider the *part of speech* each word is. For example, the words *is* and *me* are short, but in a title they're capitalized because *is* is a verb and *me* is a pronoun."

"Oh."

"And in the title 'Tarzan and Jane Find Gold,' the word *and* isn't capitalized because it's a conjunction."

"Did you just make up that title too?"

"Yes. But I have to tell you that the rule about not capitalizing conjunctions refers to only *coordinating* conjunctions—you know, the ones that join elements in a sentence that are equal. It refers to words like *and*, *or*, and *but* when they join equal things."

"Then, when *wouldn't* you capitalize a conjunction in a title?"

"Well, let's say that I had a title like "Stronger Than Tarzan." In that title, even though the word *than* is a conjunction, it's capitalized because it's *not* a coordinating conjunction. It *doesn't* connect elements that are grammatically equal."

"Oh. But who's stronger than Tarzan?"

"No one. I just made that up as an example."

"Oh."

"Okay, let's go on to the next underline." I pointed out the phrase 'close set eyes.' "Do you remember," I said, "when we talked about hyphens and I said that they're used to form compound adjectives?"

"I remember. You said that sometimes two words work together to describe a noun or pronoun. You talked about a hairy-armed man. That was funny."

"Well, this is the same situation. The words *close* and *set* work together to describe the word *eyes*. You should have treated those words as a hyphenated compound adjective. You should have written this." In the margin of the notebook I wrote: "close-set eyes."

"I see," Tarzan said. "I should have known that."

"That's okay. Now let's look at the next underline." I pointed to the word *He* at the beginning of the third sentence—the one that began *He could see the doorway* . . .

"What's wrong with that?" Tarzan protested. "It's a pronoun—*He*."

"Remember, whenever you use a pronoun, it must be clear who the pronoun is referring to. In the previous sentence you were talking about the gorilla, so it seems that the word *He*, coming right after that, would refer to the gorilla. But I think that you meant the word

He to refer to your father. You should have written *My father could see the doorway . . .*"

"Let me see that," Tarzan said, taking the notebook. He studied the first paragraph awhile. "I see what you mean. It *is* confusing. I shouldn't have use a pronoun there."

"That's okay."

I had a tendency to tell Tarzan that it was okay for him to made a mistake. I don't know why I did that. Maybe I just didn't want him to feel bad. It's hard to tell someone that he did something wrong, especially someone you lo—I mean, especially someone you're fond of.

"Okay, are you hungry yet, or do you want to keep going?" I said.

"I can wait. I want to see what else I did wrong. Let's keep going."

"Okay, then look at this." I pointed to the phrases *Back, Alice!* and *Go back!* in the third paragraph.

"Wait! I know what I did wrong! Those are direct quotations. Each of those phrases should be enclosed by quotation marks!"

Exactly. That's very good. Also, let me compliment you on your use of the exclamation point. Since those phrases are shouted, it's correct to follow them with exclamation points."

Tarzan smiled proudly.

"Now, do you know what you did wrong in the next paragraph?" I pointed to the words *grabs* and *hurls.*

"Um . . ."

"Well, you switched tenses in the middle of a sentence. You started out with past tense but finished with present tense. You said that your father *swung* his ax. That's past tense—*swung.* You should have finished by saying that the gorilla *grabbed* the ax and *hurled* it far to one side." Before Tarzan could respond, I said, "Sometimes when people tell a story out loud about something that happened to them, they use the present tense instead of the past tense on purpose."

"Why do they do that?"

"To make the story more immediate. To bring the listener into the story. By using present tense, they make it seem as if the story is happening right now instead of in the past. It makes the story more exciting. For example, someone might say: 'Let me tell you what happened yesterday. I walk into a jungle clearing and an elephant comes up to me and sprays me with water.'"

"Do you mean he should have said 'I *walked* into a jungle clearing and an elephant *came* up to me and *sprayed* me with water'?"

"Not necessarily. In conversation, he can choose to tell a story in present tense for dramatic effect. But you're writing an article for publication in a national magazine. Also, you switched tenses within a sentence—and that's never correct."

"Oh."

I forced myself to not tell him that it was okay that he made a mistake. I didn't want to be too lenient.

"Now, look at the sentence that starts the next-to-last paragraph."

Tarzan studied the sentence. "I know what I did wrong!" he said. "*Throwing my father to the ground* is a dependent clause—an *introductory* dependent clause. I should have placed a comma after it to separate it from the following independent clause—*the beast turned upon his new enemy.*"

"That's right. Very good." I wondered if it upset Tarzan to be talking about a fierce beast throwing his father to the ground and then turning upon his terrified mother. I know that *I* would be upset if anything like that happened to *my* parents. But Tarzan seemed to be able to able to discuss these sentences analytically and without any visible emotion—except the emotion he displayed concerning his grammatical abilities. Maybe he was able to do that because he'd never known his parents. Anyway, I decided to keep all those thoughts to myself.

"Okay, there's one more underline to look at." I pointed at the word *and* and the comma that followed it at the end of that same paragraph. "Why did you put a comma after the word *and* there?"

"Because there are two independent clauses joined by *and*. And if you have a situation like that, you place a comma—Oh, wait! You place a comma after the first clause *before* the word *and*, not after the word *and*. I just have to move the comma so that it comes right after the word *rifle*. Is that it?"

"That's exactly it! Very good!"

Tarzan smiled.

"Okay. That takes care of Article 6," I said. "But tell me, when do *you* come into the story? We've finished six articles, and the story is still about your parents."

"I'll come into the story in the next article—Article 7."

"Really?" I was excited.

"Yes. Do you want me to write Article 7 right now?"

I couldn't wait to see what happened next in the story, but I was suddenly starving. "Let's have brunch first. I'm starving. Can you go out and find some more of those blueberries? And see if you can find Yemmy, Omy, and Cheetah when you go out, okay?"

"Okay. In the rainbow, what color comes after blue?" Tarzan asked.

"Indigo."

"What's that?"

"It's kind of between blue and purple."

"Oh. And what comes after indigo?"

"Violet."

"What's that?"

"That's like purple."

"And what's after that?"

"Nothing. That's all there is."

"Well, I don't think there's any indigo or violet food around here. So after we finish eating blueberries, can we go back to eating like normal people?"

"Okay," I said. I couldn't think of any indigo or violet foods either.

"You stay right here and keep resting your ankle. I'll be right back with the blueberries."

Tarzan left and I found myself alone. While he was gone I read a little more about Africa's gold mines. I wondered if there were any possible way that we could find transportable pieces of gold. Then it occurred to me to look in the book's index under *diamonds*. Maybe I'd discover that they were lying around, ready for anyone to just take. Sure enough, the book talked about diamonds. But it said that they were located in the country of South Africa. That was very far from where we were.

I imagined myself returning to America with a bundle of gold in one arm and a bundle of diamonds in the other. I wondered how many I could carry at one time and how much it all might be worth. Maybe I'm being too greedy, I thought. Still, if they're just lying around for anyone to take . . .

Just then Tarzan returned with the berries.

"Let's see them," I said.

He opened his palms to show me. They were blueberries. He gave me one handful and kept the other for himself. He sat down next to me and we each started popping blueberries into our mouths. Then, just for fun, I placed a blueberry in his mouth and he placed one in mine. Then we did that a few more times.

"I'm an Egyptian princess," I joked.

"A what?"

"Never mind." Then after a moment I said, "Tarzan, do you know what diamonds are?"

"Diamonds?"

"Did you know that certain materials—you know, like certain metals or stones—are very valuable? I mean they're worth a lot of money."

"Money?"

"In civilized countries, like America, people use money to buy things."

"Buy things?"

This conversation reminded me of the very first conversations I'd ever had with Tarzan!

"Yes! Buy things!" Then I said, "Sorry, I didn't mean to yell. In America, if people want things, like food, clothing, or houses, they buy them with money."

"Why can't they find food like we do?"

"I don't know. They just can't."

"Oh." Then after a moment: "What does money look like?"

"Usually it's a piece of paper or a metal coin."

"A piece of paper" he said, pointing to a page in the notebook.

"Not regular paper like that—special paper."

"Oh."

I popped the last blueberry into my mouth and wiped my hands against each other. Then I went to the bed, picked up the book about Africa, and returned to the table.

"Have you ever seen anything that looks like this?" I said, turning to a page with a picture of gold. "Or this?" turning to a page with a picture of diamonds.

"I'm not sure. Maybe," he said.

"Where!"

"I don't know. I don't know if I saw that."

"Think!"

"I don't know. I don't remember." Then after a while he said, "Wait. I think I once saw something shiny and yellow at the bottom of a river."

"What was it? Was it gold? Where is the river?"

"I don't know what it was. It was just shiny and yellow. It could have been anything. The river I'm thinking of is about a week's journey from here—and it's infested with crocodiles."

Well, I didn't relish the thought of swimming with crocodiles. Nor did I feel like hiking for a week, especially with my bad ankle.

Besides, who could say what that shiny, yellow thing was. It was most likely worthless.

"Okay," I said, "never mind about that now. Let's get back to our grammar lesson. I need you to sit here and write Article 7."

"Okay."

"I'll sit on the bed and read this book about Africa some more."

"Okay."

I walked to the bed and sat on it cross-legged, facing Tarzan. I thumbed through the pages of the book aimlessly awhile. I glanced at Tarzan and saw that he was working on the article. His tongue stuck out a little.

Suddenly it occurred to me to check the index for *rubies* and *emeralds*. Maybe those precious gems were lying around Africa too. I checked and, sure enough, they were listed. I found pictures of them in the book.

I walked back to the table and showed Tarzan the pictures. "Have you ever seen any of these red or green stones anywhere?"

"Wait. Let me concentrate on this article."

"Just look quickly, and then I'll leave you alone so you can write." I shoved the book between his eyes and the notebook.

"I don't know. I don't remember. Now let me write."

I went back to the bed and sat down again. I looked over at Tarzan and he was writing in the notebook. I wonder, I thought, if there's a way that we can find diamonds, gold, rubies, and emeralds. There must be some way. I could feel my mind in motion. Suddenly it occurred to me that maybe Tantor the elephant could help. I remembered that Tarzan could whisper something into an elephant's ear and the elephant would understand.

"Tarzan, could stop writing for a second?"

Tarzan looked up.

"If you tell something to Tantor," I said, "does he understand you?"

"Yes."

"Well, could you ask him to call a meeting of all the animals of the jungle and then tell them that they should all search for diamonds, gold, rubies, and emeralds? I don't mean that they should go into that river with the crocodiles; they should just find the stuff that's lying around on the ground."

"But Tantor doesn't understand what diamonds are. Or gold or rubies or emeralds."

"But you could show him the pictures in the book!"

"I don't think that would work. Besides, how would he make the other animals understand? He can't hold up the book for them."

"He could explain it to them in animal language. Animals know how to communicate with each other, right?"

"I guess so. But I don't think they can communicate complex ideas, like what you're talking about."

"What's so complex about the idea of looking for a piece of gold on the ground?"

"To an animal, the idea is complex. Animals don't know what gold is."

"But the picture—"

"Still, they probably wouldn't understand. Besides, even if they did understand, there might not be any gold—or any of that other stuff—around here."

"But it *might* be around here and they *might* understand."

"But even if they found it, how would they carry it back? They don't have hands, you know."

"I know. But chimpanzees do. Tell Tantor to include chimps in the big meeting. He should get about a hundred chimps together so they can carry back all the stuff—after they find it, I mean. That would be two hundred handfuls of diamonds, gold, rubies, and emeralds."

"This is the most ridiculous idea I've ever heard!"

"But what do we have to lose? And it could be fun for the animals—like a scavenger hunt. And maybe they'll really find something."

Tarzan didn't answer. I guess there was just no arguing with that kind of logic.

"I figure we should give the animals about a week to find everything there is to find. What do you think?"

"I don't know."

"Hey, wait. I have an idea. How many articles are there left to write? Eighteen, right? And after you finish Article 7 this afternoon, there will be seventeen. If you write two articles a day—one in the morning and one in the afternoon—you'll be finished with all of them nine days from now. Tell Tantor to tell everyone that they should search for nine days. Then the chimps should gather everything into their hands and bring it to us on the ninth day, right after we finish going over your last article, Article 24. It will be like a celebration, or reward, for all the hard work we've done on grammar."

"Are you serious?"

"I am. Now, here. Take this book"—I thrust the book at Tarzan—"and go outside in front of the cabin and call Tantor. When he arrives, show him the pictures that I showed you and explain the plan to him."

Tarzan took the book but didn't get up. He didn't seem to know what to do or say.

"Come on," I coaxed. "Please? For me? Don't you want to give me a gift for teaching you grammar? Please?"

Tarzan stood up and walked to the door, book in hand. I followed.

Outside, Tarzan inhaled deeply and then let forth an earsplitting yell. But it wasn't his regular jungle yell; it was different. This one was the special "calling Tantor" yell.

"How long do you think it will take for Tantor to get here?" I said.

"It depends on how far away he is. Probably not too long."

"I just thought of something," I said. "Don't tell him nine *days*. He probably doesn't understand the concept of days. Tell him nine *suns*—or nine *moons*; whatever you have to say so that the chimps will bring the stuff on the right day."

"I don't speak to him in English. But I know what you mean. I'll try to explain it to him."

"Look! There he is," I said, as Tantor finally approached.

Tarzan walked a few steps to meet him. I watched as Tarzan petted him and then started whispering in his ear. At one point Tantor turned his head and gave Tarzan a questioning look; at least, that's how it appeared to me. Then Tarzan continued whispering into the elephant's ear. After that Tarzan held the book in front of Tantor's eyes and turned to various pages. Finally I saw Tarzan give Tantor a few pats on the back and the beast ran off.

"Did you explain everything to him?" I said, as Tarzan walked back to me.

"As best I could," he said, handing me the book.

"Did you show him all the right pictures?"

"Yes."

"Did you say *suns* or *moons* instead of *days?*"

"As best I could—in elephant talk."

"Oh good! I can't *wait* for the nine days to be up! Isn't this exciting? After nine days we might be millionaires! Or even billionaires!"

Tarzan didn't seem to care one way or another about becoming a millionaire or billionaire. But then, why should he?

"Okay," I said, "thanks for telling Tantor the plan. Now let's go back inside so you can finish Article 7."

We returned to the cabin. Tarzan resumed his seat at the table and I sat on the bed, cross-legged again.

"Okay, now I'm not going to bother you," I said. "Go ahead and finish Article 7."

While Tarzan wrote, I thumbed through the book some more. Suddenly it occurred to me that the colors of rubies, gold, and emeralds were like the colors of the rainbow. Rubies were red; that's the first color. Gold was orangish-yellow, the second and third colors. Emeralds were green, the fourth color. The next color, I thought, is blue. What precious stone is blue? Sapphires! I turned to the index to see if *sapphire* was listed. It was!

"Tarzan?"

"Yes?"

"There's something I forgot to tell you. Another valuable stone is the sapphire. It's blue."

"So?"

"So, do you think it's too late to change the plan?"

"Too late?"

"Do you think there's time to call Tantor back and show him a picture of sapphires?"

"Why?"

"So he can tell all the animals to look for those too."

"Are you serious?"

"Yes."

"I'm not going to do that. He's probably far from here by now. Besides, the whole thing is just silly."

I decided not to argue. I'd probably be rich enough even without the sapphires.

"You mean it's too late?"

"Yes."

"Okay. Then never mind."

Tarzan continued to write. I thumbed through the book some more, but I wasn't really paying attention to it. I was imagining all the animals of the jungle searching for diamonds, gold, rubies, and emeralds. I was wondering if a hundred chimps would be enough to carry everything. Maybe I should have said two hundred.

I don't know exactly how long I daydreamed, but suddenly I heard Tarzan say, "Okay, I'm finished with this article."

"Good!" I said, coming out of my reverie. "Let's see." I walked to the table and sat in the chair to Tarzan's right. My ankle didn't bother me at all.

Tarzan handed me the notebook and I began to read. I underlined a few spots as I went along. When I was finished, the article looked like this:

Article 7: "The Birth <u>Of</u> Tarzan"

My father violently yanked the ape from my mother, and the great bulk rolled upon the ground before him. The ape was dead. The gunshot had done <u>it's</u> work. A quick examination of my mother revealed no marks upon her, and my father decided that the huge brute had died before he could do her any harm.

He gently carried his wife to <u>there</u> little cabin. After <u>2</u> hours of unconsciousness, she finally regained her senses. But her first words filled my father with uneasiness. She gazed wonderingly about the interior of the little cabin, and then, with a satisfied sigh, said, "Oh <u>John</u> <u>its</u> so good to be really home! I've had an awful dream. I thought we were no longer in <u>london,</u> but in some horrible place where great beasts attacked us<u>".</u>

"My darling<u>",</u> he said, stroking her forehead, "<u>Try</u> to sleep again, and do not worry your head about bad dreams<u>".</u>

That night I was born in the tiny cabin. My mother never recovered from the shock of the great ape's attack, and, though she lived for a year after I was born, she was never again outside the cabin, nor did she ever fully realize that she was not in England.

In other ways she was quite normal, and the joy and happiness she took in the possession of her little son and the constant attentions of her husband made that year a very happy one for her, the happiest of her young life.

My father knew that her life would <u>of</u> been troubled by worries and fears had she been in full command of her mental faculties, and there were times when he was almost glad, for her sake, that she could not understand.

"Wow!" I said. "I feel so bad for your mother. But I guess it's best that she didn't understand how dangerous their situation really was. Otherwise, she would have been living in constant fear."

Tarzan nodded with a serious look on his face.

"And thank goodness that ape was dead. Otherwise . . ."

Tarzan nodded again with a thoughtful look.

"Boy, are you a good writer! I would never know that you were an ape-man and not a professional writer."

"I'm just trying to write like you do."

"Well, still, you're very good."

Tarzan smiled a little.

"Okay, anyway, let's go over the errors I found." I angled the notebook so that we both could see it. Tarzan glanced at the article, taking in the various underlines I'd drawn.

Okay," I said, "now, the first error is in the title. You capitalized the word—"

"But you said to capitalize each word in a title. Oh, wait. Now I remember. You said *not* to capitalize the articles, prepositions, and coordinating conjunctions. The word *of* is a preposition. I shouldn't have capitalized it."

"Right. Okay. Now, the next error concerns the word *it's* in the first paragraph, where it says 'The gunshot had done it's work.' This is one of those mistakes in usage that I was talking about. You used the wrong word."

"What do you mean?"

"Well, you have to understand the difference between the word *it's*, with an apostrophe"—I wrote *it's* in the margin of the notebook— "and *its*, without an apostrophe." I wrote *its* in the margin.

Tarzan examined the two words.

"You see, the word *it's*, with an apostrophe, is a contraction. It means *it is*—or *it has*. So, for example, you could write 'It's a nice day.'" In the margin of the notebook I wrote that sentence so Tarzan could see the apostrophe. "That means 'It is a nice day.'"

"What's a *contraction?*"

"It's a word that's made by combining two words into one—with one or more letters left out. An apostrophe is used to show where the letters have been omitted. For example, the word *don't* is a contraction of *do not*, and the word *isn't* is a contraction of *is not*. Do you see?"

"I think so. So, *it's*—with an apostrophe—is a contraction of *it is*. The apostrophe takes the place of the letter *i* in the word *is*, right?"

"Right. But the word *its*, without an apostrophe, is the possessive case of the pronoun *it*. So, for example, you could write 'Every dog has its day.'" I wrote that sentence in the margin of the notebook so Tarzan could see that there was no apostrophe. "In that sentence the word *its* isn't a contraction. It's a possessive pronoun referring to *dog*."

"But I thought you said that to make something possessive, you add an apostrophe and an *s*. For instance, to make the word *dog* possessive, you change it to *dog's*, as in *dog's collar*." Tarzan wrote *dog's collar* in the margin and pointed to the apostrophe. And if that's so, then why don't you add an apostrophe and an *s* to make the word *it* possessive?"

"I'm not sure, but I know that no possessive pronouns ending in *s* use an apostrophe." In the margin of the notebook I wrote the words *hers*, *theirs*, *yours*, and *its* and said each one aloud as I wrote it. "You see, each of those is spelled correctly. Don't they look right? Now, doesn't this look wrong?" In the margin I wrote *her's*, *their's*, and *your's*.

"You're right," Tarzan said. "Those *do* look wrong. There *shouldn't* be an apostrophe."

"Okay. Now let's look at the next underline," I said, "where you wrote '. . . carried his wife to *there* little cabin.' That's another mistake in usage. You used the word *there*,"–in the margin I wrote *there*– "but you should have used *their*." In the margin I wrote *their*. Then I said, "Do you understand the difference?"

"I'm not sure."

"Well, the word *there*, spelled T-H-E-R-E, is usually an adverb telling where, as in 'Sit there.' Or it can be a pronoun that's used to introduce a sentence, as in 'There are plenty of fish in the sea.' But the word *their*, spelled T-H-E-I-R, is a *possessive* pronoun; it's the possessive form of *they*. In your article, you're talking about your mother and father's cabin; the cabin that belongs to *them*; *their* cabin."

"I see. It's *their* cabin. It's *possessive*."

"Right. Okay, now let's see what else I underlined. Okay, in the next sentence I underlined the number 2."

"I know what I did wrong. I should have spelled that out in letters. I should have written *two*."

"Right. Why?"

"Well, you gave me two rules for when to spell out numbers. One rule said that if a number can be stated in one or two words, you should spell it out. This number can be expressed in one word. Also, you told me that at *American Monthly* you spell out the numbers from one to ten and use numerals for eleven and above. And this number is between one and ten. So, according to *either* rule, I should have spelled it out. I'm sorry."

"That's okay." After I said that, I remembered that I was trying to keep myself from telling him that too much. But now it was too late.

I looked at the other underlines and suddenly felt like I needed a break from all the grammar talk.

"Tarzan, let's take a little break. I want to see how my ankle feels when I walk. Let's go outside and take that walk around the cabin, like you suggested.

"Okay."

We both stood up and walked outside, in front of the cabin.

"You should put your arm around my shoulder," Tarzan said, "in case your ankle suddenly gets weak and you start to fall."

I was standing at Tarzan's left, so I put my right arms around his shoulders. He put his left arm around my waist, and we started to walk.

My ankle felt fine, actually, but I didn't admit that to Tarzan right away. I liked walking arm in arm. It was kind of romantic—even though we both knew that our embrace was for medical purposes only.

"How does your ankle feel?" he inquired.

"I'm not sure yet," I lied. "Let's keep walking some more."

Finally we arrived back at the front of the house and we let go of each other.

"Well?" he asked.

"It feels good. I think it's okay. Let's just test it a little more."

We put our arms around each other like before and took a few more steps.

"Well?" he asked again.

"It's good. It feels fine. Let me see if I can run." I started running away from the cabin. When I'd covered about twenty yards I circled back. "It's good."

"You're sure?"

"Yes. I think I can even swing from a vine and land on a branch with my right foot. Come on, let's try it."

We walked to the trees and started swinging on vines. I had no trouble pushing off from or landing on stiff branches.

"It's all healed," I said, as I landed next to Tarzan on a branch. "You know, I've been indoors so long that I really miss being outside."

"Then why don't we get the notebook and finish our lesson outdoors?"

"Good idea. I'll race you to the cabin."

We both started swinging as fast as we could toward the cabin. When the trees ended, we ran the rest of the way. He beat me by about three steps. I didn't mind.

We went inside and I took the notebook and pencil from the table. Then we went back out.

"Where should we go?" Tarzan asked.

It suddenly entered my mind that if all the animals of the jungle were out searching for diamonds and gold, we wouldn't see any about. Or, to put it another way, if we *did* see a lot of animals, that meant that my plan probably wasn't working.

"I think I'd like to just take a walk through the jungle."

"You want to have our lesson while we're walking?"

"No, we'll walk for a while and then find a place to sit for our lesson. I want to exercise my ankle," I lied. (I didn't want to admit to Tarzan that the real reason I wanted to take a walk was to ascertain how many animals were still in the vicinity. I was afraid he might think I was crazy—if he didn't *already* think so, that is.)

I didn't say much as we walked; I was looking around for animals. I didn't see any. This is good, I thought to myself; they all must be out searching. But then suddenly I saw a squirrel climb down a tree. Hmm, I thought, why is that squirrel there? Why isn't he out searching? Did he miss the big meeting? Did Tantor even call a meeting? I was about to ask Tarzan what he thought the squirrel's presence meant, but then I remembered that I didn't want him to know what I was thinking.

"Well, let's look for a good place to sit," I finally said. "Someplace shady, okay?"

"If you want someplace shady, let's look for a tree tunnel."

"A tree tunnel?"

"A place where there are two parallel rows of trees with overhanging branches."

"Oh, I think I know what you mean. The branches of the two rows interlace with each other overhead and form a kind of roof. And the space between the trees, under the roof, is like a tunnel."

"Right. And it's very shady in there."

"Okay," I said, "let's look for one of those."

As we searched for a tree tunnel, I made note of each animal I spotted. There weren't a lot, but there were a few. I saw a frog and a snake. Do those count? I mean, would Tantor have even included frogs and snakes in the meeting? I didn't know.

Eventually we found something that was a little like a tree tunnel—except the rows of trees were very short and not exactly parallel. Still, it was a shady spot.

"This looks good," I said. "Let's sit down in the shade here."

We sat on the ground with our backs against a tree and I opened the notebook to Article 7.

"Okay, let's see where we were. All right; here." I pointed to the word *John* in the phrase "Oh John" near the end of the second paragraph.

"That's my father."

"I know. John Clayton. But do you know why I underlined his name?"

"Well, I think it's because I should have put a comma before it. I mean after it. I mean before and after it. I mean I'm not sure."

"Well, why might you put a comma before it?"

"Because the word *Oh* is an interjection. So there should be a comma after *Oh.*"

"Good. That's right. And why might you put a comma *after* it?"

"Because my mother is speaking directly to my father. That's an example of direct address. So my father's name, John, should be separated from the clause that comes after it by a comma."

"Good. That's right. So then why didn't you put a comma before and after it?"

"Because you said that a comma is like a little pause in a sentence. If I put both of those commas there, the reader might read it like this: 'Oh . . . John . . .' I thought that would be too much pausing. I think my mother would have been speaking faster than that."

"Tarzan, you've just raised an interesting point. Some commas, whether the reader is supposed to pause or not, must be used—because of the rules governing commas, I mean. But some commas—whether or not to use them, I mean—can be left to the judgment of the writer. That's what I've been calling 'writer's choice.' I think if I were writing that sentence, I might use just one comma, after *John.*"

"Why?"

"Because, like you said, using both commas slows down the sentence. You could look at the two-word phrase *Oh John* as one big interjection, which would require just one comma, after it, or you could look at *Oh John* as one big direct address, which also requires just one comma, after it."

"But would it be wrong to place a comma before *John?*"

"No. You could argue that you need it there for two reasons: to set off the interjection, *Oh*, from the rest of the sentence and to set off your father's name, *John*, from the rest of the sentence."

"So should I have put a comma between *Oh* and *John* or not?"

"Technically, yes. But instead I'll say that it's a matter of writer's choice."

"Oh."

"Anyway, let's keep going. Now, the next—"

"I know why you underlined the word *its* right after that. You already explained it. I should have written the contraction *it's*—with an apostrophe."

"Right. Why?"

"Because I really meant 'It is so good to be really home.' I should have written the contraction of *it is* instead of the possessive form of *it.*"

"Exactly!"

"And I know why you underlined *london*, too. I was just careless. That's the name of a city, so it's a proper noun. So it should be capitalized; I mean I should have used a capital *L.*"

"Right. Okay, now let's look at the places where I underlined quotation marks."

"I see three places where you did that: the end of the second paragraph, the beginning of the third paragraph, and the end of the third paragraph."

"Right. Now, remember when we climbed the mountain and we talked about different kinds of punctuation marks? Well, one thing I didn't talk about is what happens when you have to use two punctuation marks at the same time. That often happens with ending quotation marks. For example, at the end of a word, phrase, or sentence enclosed in quotation marks, you might also need a comma or period—or some other mark. When that happens—when you have two punctuation marks together like that, I mean—you have to know which order to put them in."

"You mean I used the wrong order?"

"You did. See, if you have a period and an end quote, the period always goes first. Also, if you have a comma and an end quote, the comma always goes first."

"So at the beginning of the third paragraph, after the word *darling,* I should have written comma-quote, not quote-comma. It should have looked like this." In the notebook Tarzan wrote: *"My darling," he said . . .*

"That's right."

"And I can see," Tarzan went on, "that it's the same problem in the other two places you underlined. I should have put the comma or period *before* the end quote, not after it."

"Exactly. But the rule is the opposite for colons and semicolons. Those both go *after* an end quote." I took the notebook and wrote: *He didn't want to be called "ape-man"; he didn't like it.* Then I said, "Do you see what I mean? The semicolon is placed *after* the end quote."

Tarzan didn't say anything.

"You don't like being called 'ape-man,' do you?"

"No, I don't. I'm not an ape-man; I'm just a man."

"I know. I won't call you that anymore."

He didn't answer. I think I may have hurt his feelings.

"You're not just a man," I said. "You're a *wonderful* man."

He smiled a little at that, so I decided we could go on with the lesson.

"Okay," I said, "now, sometimes you need to have a question mark or an exclamation point together with an end quote."

"Which order do you use then?"

"Well, that's a little tricky. For those, the order depends on whether the question mark or exclamation point refers to the material within the quotes or to the sentence as a whole."

"What do you mean?"

I took the notebook and wrote: *"Is that a monkey?" he said.* Then, under that I wrote: *Did he say "That's a monkey"?* Then I said, "Okay, look at the first example. There, the material enclosed in quotes is a question—so the question mark goes with *that* material, *inside* the end quote."

Tarzan nodded.

"Now look at the second example. There, the sentence as a whole—but not the material quoted—is a question, so the question mark goes at the end of the entire sentence, *outside* the end quote. Do you see?"

"Sort of. But in the second sentence, couldn't you put a period after the word *monkey?* That would show the end of the quoted statement. So after *monkey* you would have a period, then an end quote, and then a question mark."

297

"I can see why you say that, and it would seem to make sense. But that's not the way it's done. You don't use a period *and* a question mark. In that case, you leave out the period—you use the question mark only, I mean."

"But why?"

"I don't know. You just do. Everyone does it that way."

"Oh."

And the rule for the exclamation point is the same. It goes either before *or* after an end quote, depending on whether it refers to the quoted material or to the sentence as a whole." I took the notebook and wrote: *"Boy, this barbecued meat tastes good!" she said.* Then I said, "You see, here the exclamation point refers to the quoted material, so it goes before—or *inside*—the end quote." Then I wrote in the notebook: *Don't call me "ape-man"!* Then I said, "And here, the exclamation point refers to the sentence as a whole, and not to the word in quotes, *ape-man.* So the exclamation point goes after—or *outside*—the end quote. Do you see?"

"Yes, but I thought you said you weren't going to call me an ape-man."

"I didn't. I was just talking about an ape-man in general, for the sake of the example," I explained. I really was.

"Oh," he said uncertainly.

"All right," I said. "Now, we have only two more underlines to look at in this article. First, look at the word *Try* in the third paragraph, where it says *Try to sleep again* . . . The problem there is that you capitalized it."

"I did that because it's the beginning of something quoted—something spoken."

"But the *real* beginning of the spoken material is the phrase *My darling.* The part that begins with *try to sleep* is simply a continuation of that sentence. It doesn't matter that you have an opening quotation mark before the word *try.*"

"But the words *he said, stroking her forehead* break up the quotation. So it looks like the quote starts over again."

"Well, you always need to see if the quoted material that comes after a phrase like *he said* is a brand-new sentence or a continuation of a previous sentence. If it's a brand-new sentence, then start it with a capital letter. But if it's just a continuation, then use a small letter."

Tarzan didn't say anything.

"Here, look." I took the notebook and wrote: *"Let's have dinner,"* *she said. "Barbecued meat would be good."* Then I said, "You see, in this example, the part about the barbecued meat is a new sentence. Because of that, it starts with a capital letter and there's a period after *she said.* Now watch this." I took the notebook and wrote: *"Let's have a dinner," she said, "of barbecued meat."* Then I said, "Now, in that example, the phrase 'of barbecued meat' *doesn't* start a new sentence. So it starts with a small letter."

"And I see that you used a comma, not a period, after *she said.*"

"Right. Because at that point the sentence—the direct quotation, I mean—wasn't finished."

"I see."

"Good. Okay, one more thing. In the last paragraph I underlined the word *of* in the phrase *would of been troubled.* Do you know why?"

"Wait. Do you want barbecued meat for dinner?"

"I wouldn't mind . . . my darling."

Tarzan hesitated a moment and then said, "Oh, I know what you're doing. You said 'my darling' because my father said that to my mother in the story, right?"

"Maybe," I said coyly.

Tarzan blushed a little.

"Anyway," I said, "let's finish talking about this last underlined spot, and then we'll decide about dinner. Instead of 'would of been troubled,' you should have written 'would *have* been troubled.'"

"But when we speak, it sounds like 'would of.'"

"That's because when we speak, we usually use a contraction for *would have;* we say *would've.*" I wrote the word *would've* in the notebook so that he could see it. "The contraction, does, I guess, when you say it out loud, sound like *would of.* I guess that's why people sometimes make that mistake. But remember, the word *of* is a preposition, and it doesn't make sense to use a preposition between *would* and *been.* You need the verb *have* there. *Would have been.* Do you see?"

"I do. The word *of* is a preposition, so it needs an object. It makes no sense to say 'would *of* been.'"

"Exactly. Anyway, that takes care of Article 7."

Tarzan didn't say anything.

"Are you hungry?" I said.

"Starving!"

Then at the exact same time, we both said, "Barbecued meat?" We both laughed. Then, amazingly, at the exact same time, we both said, "At the pond where we had our moonlight swim?"

We laughed again, and then hand in hand (I had the notebook in my other hand) we strolled to the pond. *Our* pond. We arrived just as the sun set.

Chapter 24: Geological Hazards

The next morning, while Tarzan sat at the table working on Article 8, I sat on the bed thumbing through another book from the shelf. This one was entitled *Geological Hazards and Disasters*. Under the title, in smaller letters, was the subtitle *Including Meteorological Hazards and Disasters*.

The first third of the book discussed such geological hazards as earthquakes, landslides, avalanches, and falling rocks. The second third talked about such meteorological hazards as tornadoes, hurricanes, lightning, and heavy fog. The last third discussed floods, tidal waves, and meteor fireballs.

"Tarzan," I said, "would you consider a flood a geological hazard or a meteorological hazard?"

"Huh?"

"I mean, do you think a flood is a phenomenon of the earth or of the weather?"

"Huh?"

"I mean, do you think a flood is caused by the ground or by the weather?"

"I guess by the weather. Sometimes you have a flood after a big rain."

"I think so too," I said. I wondered why the book didn't include the chapter on floods in the meteorological section of the book.

"What about a tidal wave?"

"What's that?"

"It's a giant wave from the ocean that spills onto the land, flooding it. Do you think that's weather-related or earth-related?"

"I don't know. I'm trying to write. Let me write."

"I'm sorry." I decided not to ask him his opinion of whether meteor fireballs were earth- or weather-related.

What made the book interesting was that for each hazard, there was a story about a group of people whose lives were endangered by that hazard. In each story, the people nearly died, but at the last moment they escaped or were rescued.

"Tarzan, it says here that once a family from South America went camping. They set up camp in a narrow space between two rocky cliffs. Suddenly there was a flash flood that filled the space with water. The family would have drowned, but they were able to float away on their air mattresses."

"That's nice. Now let me write."

I continued thumbing through the book while Tarzan wrote. There were so many hazards mentioned that I started to think that the chances were good that at least one of those hazards would befall us, right here. For example, I started to fear that if we ventured outside, an earthquake would split the ground in two where we stood and we'd fall into the crack and be killed. Or that as we swung from tree to tree, lightning or a meteor fireball would strike and kill us.

Okay, call me paranoid if you want, but if you were to read this book, you'd know what I mean.

"Tarzan, do you think it's safe for us to go outside? I mean, do you think we'll be crushed by falling rocks or anything like that?"

"It's more likely that you'll be attacked by a wild animal, if you want to know the truth."

"But you can protect me from wild animals. But you couldn't protect me from something like a tornado, right?"

"I've lived here my whole life and nothing like that ever happened. So I wouldn't worry about it if I were you."

"Okay," I said. But I couldn't help but worry. Then I said, "Tarzan, only eight more days until the chimps bring the diamonds and gold. Do you think they're finding a lot of it?"

"I don't think they're finding any."

"You're such a pessimist!"

"I'm just being realistic. It's too much to expect from the animals—if there's anything to find, that is. Now, let me finish what I'm doing. I'm almost done with Article 8."

I became silent. I read a little about a man who was attacked by a female bird with a long beak. I don't know why that was included in the book. After all, a bird attack isn't a geological or meteorological hazard. It said that birds usually don't attack humans, but that this man must have inadvertently wandered too close to the nest that housed that bird's babies. I was about to tell Tarzan about this, but I decided to keep quiet so that he could finish his article.

Just then, he said, "Okay, I'm done with Article 8."

I put the book down and stood up. As I walked to the table, I checked to make sure that no birds had flown in the window.

Sitting in the chair to Tarzan's right, I reached for the notebook. As I read Article 8, I underlined the errors Tarzan had made. I found only three. When I was finished, it looked like this:

Article 8: "The Death of Alice Clayton"

During the year that followed, my father decorated our cabin. Skins of lion and panther covered the floor. Cupboards and bookcases lined the walls. Odd vases made by his own hand from clay held beautiful tropical flowers. Curtains of grass and bamboo covered the windows.

In his leisure, <u>father</u> read, often aloud to his wife, from the store of books he had brought from England. Among these were many for little children, for they had known that <u>they're</u> child might be old enough to learn to read before they might hope to return home.

At other times my father wrote in his diary, in which he recorded the details of their strange life. This book he kept in a little metal box.

A year from the day I was born my mother died in her sleep. So peaceful was her end that it was hours before my father realized that she was gone. The horror of the situation came to him very slowly. At last, alarmed by <u>me</u> crying, he called, "My little son is crying for nourishment! Oh Alice, what shall I do?"

For a long time no sound broke the deathlike stillness of the jungle except the pathetic wailing of his infant son.

"Oh my," I said, "I feel so bad for your father, all alone like that with a hungry baby."

Tarzan looked at me but didn't say anything.

"Okay," I went on, "let's look at the spots I underlined."

"You underlined *father* in the phrase *father read* in the second paragraph. What's wrong with that?"

"Well, words like *father, mother, dad, mom, grandma,* and *grandpa* are sometimes capitalized and sometimes not capitalized."

"What do you mean?"

"Well, let's take the word *dad* as an example. Sometimes that word is used as someone's name."

"How? I never heard of anyone named that."

"Well, a child might call his father 'Dad.' What I mean is, if you had known your father, you wouldn't have called him *John*; you would have called him *Dad.* For example, you wouldn't say 'Hi, John'; you'd say 'Hi, Dad.'"

"Why wouldn't I call him John? That's his name, isn't it?"

"Because it's considered disrespectful for a child to call a parent by his or her first name."

"Oh."

"Anyway, you'd be using 'Dad' as a substitute for his real name. To you, his name is 'Dad.'"

"Oh, I think I get it. Because his name is 'Dad,' it's a proper noun—because it's someone's name, I mean. So it has to be capitalized."

Right. But if you use the word *dad* not as a name, but just as a *word*, as in, let's say, 'My dad was an English nobleman,' then you *don't* capitalize *dad*."

"Because in that case *dad* isn't being used as someone's name. So it's not a proper noun; it's a common noun. So it's *not* capitalized."

"Right. So, let's look again at what I underlined in Article 8. If you had written, let's say, *my father read*, then it would be correct to *not* capitalize father—because the word *my* makes the word *father* a regular *word*, not a name."

"I see. But since I wrote simply *father read*, I'm using the word *father* as my dad's *name*—so *father* should have been capitalized there."

"Exactly. Okay, now let's look at the word *they're* in the phrase *they're child* later in that same paragraph."

"I think I know what I did wrong. I should have spelled it T-H-E-I-R—the possessive form of *they*. It's the child that belongs to them; it's *their* child."

"Right. The word *they're*, spelled T-H-E-Y-apostrophe-R-E, is a contraction of *they are*. So, if I'm talking about Yemmy and Omy, let's say, I could say 'They're cute.'" I wrote *They're cute* in the notebook so Tarzan could see the spelling. "Do you see?"

"I do."

"Good. Now, let's look at the last underline. I pointed to the word *me* in the next-to-last paragraph."

"What's wrong with that?"

"Well, let me ask you this: What part of speech is the word *crying* that comes after the word *me*?"

"Isn't *crying* a verb?"

"Sometimes it is. If you say 'The baby is crying,' then it's a verb. But do you remember that I once told you about gerunds?"

"Um . . ."

"I said that a present participle—that is, a word that's an infinitive plus the letters *ing*, such as *jumping* or *eating* or *crying*—sometimes functions as a noun?"

"Oh, I remember. You said that a word like that names some action or activity, so it's a noun—even though it looks like a verb."

"Right. So, in the sentence you wrote in the article—*At last, alarmed by me crying*—the word *crying* is a gerund. It operates as a *noun*. It's the name of the activity or action of crying."

"I see that."

"So to *modify* a noun you need a *possessive* pronoun, not a personal pronoun. Whose crying is it? It's *Tarzan's* crying. It's *your* crying. And from your point of view—if you're the speaker, I mean—you say 'It's *my* crying.' Do you see?"

"I see. It's not someone else's crying; it's *my* crying. I should have written 'alarmed by *my* crying.'"

"Right. Very good."

We both nodded in agreement.

That afternoon, Tarzan sat at the table writing Article 9. I sat on the bed reading yet another book from the shelf. This one was about the famous Scottish explorer and medical missionary David Livingstone—you know, the one who explored Africa in the mid 1800s. Anyway, when he failed to return to Europe, everyone thought he was missing. Years later, a British explorer, Henry Stanley, went to search for him. When Mr. Stanley finally located him, the first thing he said was the now-famous line "Doctor Livingstone, I presume?"

The book read kind of like an adventure novel—even though all of it was based on fact. All sorts of scary and exciting things happened to Dr. Livingstone. He almost fell off a cliff, he got lost for three days, he was bitten by a poisonous snake, he ate poisonous fruit, he fell into a ten-foot-deep hole, he was attacked by a huge lizard, and he heard unexplainable noises during the night.

"Tarzan," I said, "do you think there's any chance that we might fall off a cliff or fall into a deep hole?"

"I don't think so. Now, let me write."

"But we could be bitten by a poisonous snake, right?"

"Not if we're careful."

"Did you ever hear funny noises at night—noises you can't explain?"

"Like what?"

"I don't know."

We lapsed into silence. I continued reading about Dr. Livingstone, and Tarzan continued writing.

"Okay, I'm done with Article 9," Tarzan suddenly announced.

"So fast?"

I walked to the table and sat to Tarzan's right again. I took the notebook and began to read, underlining the errors as I went along. When I was finished, it looked like this:

Article 9: "Kerchak and Kala"

A mile <u>East</u> of our cabin lived a tribe of apes. Their leader, <u>who's</u> name was Kerchak, weighed perhaps 350 pounds. His awful temper and his mighty strength made him supreme among the little tribe into which he had been born some 20 years before. Every ape in the jungle knew that Kerchak would kill <u>whomever</u> dared question his right to rule.

The tribe over which Kerchak ruled numbered some six or eight families, each family consisting of an adult male with his females and their young, numbering in all some 60 or 70 apes.

One day Kerchak suddenly went on a rampage of rage among his people. The younger and lighter members of his tribe scampered to the higher branches of the great trees to escape his anger. The older ones scattered in all directions, but not before the infuriated brute had felt the bones of one snap between his great, foaming jaws.

Then he spied a female named Kala, who, returning from a search for food with her young baby, was unaware of the state of the mighty male's temper until suddenly the shrill warnings of her fellows caused her to scamper madly for safety.

But Kerchak was close upon her, so close that he'd have grasped her ankle had she not made a furious leap far into space from one tree to another. She made the leap successfully, but as she grasped a branch, the sudden jolt loosened the hold of the tiny baby where it clung frantically to her neck, and she saw the little thing hurled, turning and twisting, to the ground 30 feet below.

With a low cry of dismay Kala rushed headlong to its side, thoughtless now of the danger from Kerchak. But when she gathered the tiny, mangled form in her arms, life had left it. With low moans, she sat cuddling the body to her. Kerchak didn't try <u>and</u> hurt her. With the death of the baby, his fit of maniacal rage passed as suddenly as it had begun.

"Oh my," I said, "I feel so bad for Kala. She lost her baby. There's nothing more horrible than that—nothing. What did she do?"

"You'll find out when I write the next article."

"I can't wait!"

We sat silently awhile, reflecting on the fate of Kala. At least, that's what I was thinking about. Finally, I said, "Okay, let's go over the errors in this article."

I angled the notebook so that we could both see it.

"In this first sentence," I said, "I underlined the word *East* in the phrase *A mile East of our cabin.*"

"Why did you do that?"

"Well, normally, the directions of the compass—north, south, east, and west—are not capitalized."

"Oh." Then after a pause: "But why did you say that *normally* they're not capitalized? Sometimes *are* they capitalized?"

"Well, there is one time when you do capitalize those words."

"When?"

"When you're talking about a place—a geographical region, I mean—and you use one of those words as the *name* of the place."

"What do you mean?"

"Well, for example, in America, when we talk about the Civil War, we say that it was fought between the North and the South. The word *North* refers to the northern part of the United States—to that geographical region, I mean. We use the word *North* as the *name* of that region. And *South* is the name of the southern part of the United States."

"I see. Because you're using *North* and *South* as names—names of places—they're considered proper nouns, so they're capitalized."

"Right. But if I say 'Let's travel north,' then I *don't* capitalize *north* because it's just a direction, not a particular place."

"I see."

"Good. Now, in the next sentence, I underlined the word *who's* in the phrase *who's name was Kerchak.*"

"Why?"

"This is a mistake in usage. What you have to understand is the difference between the word *who's*, spelled W-H-O-apostrophe-S, and the word *whose*, spelled W-H-O-S-E."

"What's the difference?"

"Well, the word *who's*, with an apostrophe, is a contraction of 'who is'—or 'who has.' So, I could say 'Who's afraid of the big, bad wolf?' That's the same as saying 'Who is afraid of the big, bad wolf?'"

"What big, bad wolf?"

"Never mind. Now, the word *whose*, without an apostrophe, is a possessive pronoun. It's the possessive form of the pronoun *who* or *which*. So it really means 'of whom' or 'of which.' So, I could say 'A chameleon is a lizard *whose* skin changes color.' That's the same as saying 'A chameleon is a lizard the skin *of which* changes color.'"

"That sounds weird."

"I know. That's why people usually don't say that. Instead, they use the word *whose*. But interestingly, even though *whose* is a possessive pronoun, it actually *functions* as an adjective."

"How?"

"Well, in the example I just gave, in the phrase *a lizard whose skin*, the word *whose* modifies *skin*—so it functions as an adjective."

"That sounds complicated."

"Well, just remember that *who's*, with an apostrophe, means 'who is' or 'who has,' and that *whose*, without an apostrophe, means 'of whom' or 'of which.' If you can remember that, you won't go wrong."

"Okay. I'll try to remember."

"Good. Okay. Now, at the end of that paragraph, I underlined the word *whomever*."

"Why did you do that?"

"Because you should have written *whoever*. You should have written *whoever dared question his right to rule*. You used the wrong case of the pronoun."

"I did?"

"Yes. If you remember, I said that pronouns can be in the subjective case or objective case. If a pronoun is the subject of a sentence or clause, you use the subjective case."

"I remember. For the subjective case you use pronouns like *I, he, she,* or *they.*"

"Right. And if a pronoun is an object—either the object of a verb or the object of a preposition—you use the objective case."

"I remember that too. For the objective case you use pronouns like *me, him, her,* or *them.*"

"Exactly. Now, the pronouns *who* and *whoever* are both subjective-case pronouns, and *whom* and *whomever* are both objective-case pronouns."

"But doesn't that prove that I used the correct word?" Tarzan argued. "Since the word *kill* is a verb, the pronoun that comes after it must be its object. It should be an objective-case pronoun. *Kill whomever*."

"Usually it works that way. But sometimes the object of a verb isn't simply the single word that comes after it. Sometimes the object of a verb is an entire phrase or clause. In this case, the object of *kill* is the entire clause *whoever dared question his right to rule*. And can you see that in that clause, the word *whoever* is actually the *subject*?"

"I can see that. *Whoever* is the subject and *dared* is the verb in that clause—*whoever dared*."

"Right."

"So, are you saying that you can look at the word *whoever* or *whomever* as both the object of *killed* and the subject of *dared* at the same time?"

"No. It's only the subject of *dared*. It's not the object of *killed*. It's the entire clause—*whoever dared question his right to rule*—that's the object of *killed*. And in that clause, *whoever* is the subject."

"And since it's the subject, it's in the subjective case. It's *whoever*, not *whomever*. I see that now."

"You know," I said, "*whomever* is one of those words that people sometimes use to try to sound as if they have good grammar."

"You mean like when people use *I* instead of *me*? When they should really use *me*, I mean."

"Yes, just like that. They think the word *whomever* sounds grammatically advanced, so they use it to show off. But what they're really showing is that they don't understand grammar. I mean, they might even say something that's obviously wrong, such as "Whomever left his keys on the counter, please come and claim them.""

"That's so wrong!" Tarzan protested. "They should have said "*Whoever* left his keys . . .'" Then he added, "Obviously, the word is the subject of the clause and should be in the subjective case."

"Well," I said, "I'm glad *you* understand that."

Tarzan smiled a little.

"Okay," I said, "there's one more spot to look at. In the last paragraph, I underlined the word *and* in the sentence 'Kerchak didn't try and hurt her.'"

"What's wrong with that?"

"It's a mistake in usage. You should have used the word *to*. You should have written 'Kerchak didn't try *to* hurt her.'"

"But sometimes isn't the word *and* correct in a case like that?"

"Well, if you mean a case in which the word *and* falls between two verbs, the answer is sometimes. Remember, *and* is a coordinating conjunction. It connects things that are equal. So, let's say you asked me if it's raining outside. I might say to you 'Go to the door and look outside.' Or for short, I'd probably say 'Go and look.' In that case, it's correct to use the conjunction *and* between the two verbs—*go* and *look*."

"I see. In that case you'd be asking me to do two different actions—to *go* to the door and to *look* outside."

"Right. But in the sentence you wrote, you didn't mean that Kerchak did two separate things: not *try* (to do such-and-such) and also not *hurt* her. You simply meant that he didn't try to hurt her. So, using the conjunction *and* is wrong."

"But isn't the word *to* wrong also? Why would you use a preposition between two verbs?"

"Because sometimes the preposition *to* isn't used as a normal preposition. Sometimes it's used before a verb simply to indicate the infinitive—in this case, *to hurt*. It's just one of those weird things about grammar that you have to accept."

"Okay. I'll try and accept it. I mean, I'll try *to* accept it."

"Good."

Chapter 25: Jane Falls in Love

The next morning when Tarzan arrived at the cabin, I said, "Where should we go today?"

"What do you mean?"

"Well, we've been indoors the last two days while you were writing your articles. I thought you'd want to spend some more time outside."

"I like to write my articles at the table."

"You do? Why?"

"I can concentrate better at the table."

"Oh. Okay." Actually, I was glad that Tarzan wanted to remain indoors. After reading about all those geological hazards in that book—and about all the scary stuff that happened to Dr. Livingstone—I preferred the indoors myself.

I took the book about Africa from the shelf and sat on the bed while Tarzan worked on Article 10 at the table.

"How many more days until the chimps bring the diamonds and gold?" I said.

"I don't know. I'm trying to write."

I did some quick mental arithmetic and said, "It's seven more days. Seven. One week."

He didn't answer.

I thumbed through the book a little. "Tarzan," I said, "it says here that the average person in Africa swallows eight spiders a year without knowing it. Do you think that's true?"

"I don't know."

I couldn't concentrate on the book. I wondered if I had ever unknowingly swallowed a spider. The thought made my skin crawl. Then—I couldn't help it—I started thinking about the sapphires again. Was it really too late to tell Tantor about them and change the plan? Maybe tomorrow, before Tarzan arrived at the cabin, I would go outside and call Tantor myself. I would tell him about the sapphires and show him what they look like in the book. Tarzan wouldn't even have to know.

I watched Tarzan write. Sometimes his forehead became furrowed in concentration. I liked that. Sometimes he bit his lower lip a little with his upper teeth. I liked that too. Sometimes he closed his eyes for a few seconds. I liked that too. I kept watching him. I don't know why. I just liked to.

There was another reason I liked staying indoors—besides my fear of geological hazards, I mean. I liked being in the same room with Tarzan. It made me feel like we were doing something together, even if he was writing his articles and I was reading a book. I mean, indoors we couldn't be physically farther away from each other than the walls of the cabin. Outdoors, we could become separated by who-knows-how-many feet.

As I gazed over at Tarzan again, I sort of thought to myself: "Oh my, there he is!" I suddenly became super-aware of everything about him: his hair, his eyes, his mouth . . ." Everything about him looked so perfect! Suddenly I felt a weird feeling deep within me. It was like a warm current and an exquisite ache at the same time.

"What are you staring at?" Tarzan suddenly said.

"N-nothing," I stammered. I looked down at my book again, but didn't focus.

I'd heard it said that when you find love and it's the real thing, you *know* it. Well, I knew it. I was in love with Tarzan. Deeply in love. I'd always liked him tremendously, but all of a sudden—*whammo!*—it hit me.

I felt kind of weak all over. In my mind I had an imaginary conversation with Tarzan. I say, "Tarzan, I love you," and he says, "Oh Jane, I love you too. I've always loved you." Then I say, "What shall we do?" and he says, "Let's get married and live happily ever after."

For a while I repeated the conversation in my mind—with variations and embellishments—over and over while I pretended to read my book. I wondered if Tarzan really loved me too. Could I just come right out and ask him? No, he might say no. Then what? Maybe he didn't love me. He used to act as if he did, but lately he hadn't been acting that way as much. Or maybe he did love me but was too shy to admit it.

Well, I couldn't spend the rest of my life not knowing whether or not Tarzan was in love with me—not when I felt like this. I would have to take my chances and reveal my true feelings to him. But not just yet. I'll let him finish his article. Then after we finish discussing the errors, I'll just come out with it and tell him. I felt nervous about it, but I decided to act as normal and natural as I could until the moment I told him. I mean, I didn't want Tarzan to think that I was being weird and ask me what was wrong.

I patiently waited for Tarzan to finish Article 10. While I pretended to read my book, Tarzan and I had lengthy conversations—in my mind, of course—about how much we loved each other. I was so preoccupied that I forgot to think about the chimps bringing diamonds and gold and about geological disasters.

"I'm finished," Tarzan suddenly said, holding up the notebook.

"Let's see," I said, walking to the table and acting as natural as could be. (I really wasn't very nervous, because I was determined to say nothing about love until after our lesson.)

Article 10 was especially fascinating, and it took my mind off my own concerns. I underlined the errors I found. When I was finished, it looked like this:

Article 10: "The Death of John Clayton"

An hour after his rage ended, Kerchak called his tribe together. He motioned them to follow him, and <u>altogether</u> they set off westward toward the shore. All the way Kala carried her little dead baby hugged tightly in her arms.

You see, one day in his wanderings, Kerchak had discovered our cabin, and now he wanted to explore the interior of the mysterious den. Slowly, cautiously, and noiselessly the apes crept through the jungle toward our little house.

On and on they came until Kerchak reached the open door and peered within. Behind him <u>was</u> two other males, and then Kala, closely holding her little dead baby.

Inside the den they saw a strange hairless ape—my father— lying half across a table, his head buried in his arms. On the bed <u>laid</u> a still figure covered by a cloth. From a tiny wooden cradle came the wailing of a hairless baby.

Noiselessly Kerchak entered, crouching for the charge. Then my father rose with a sudden start and faced them. The sight that met his eyes must have <u>froze</u> him with terror, for there, within the door, stood three great male apes, and behind them crowded many more. How many he never knew, for his guns were hanging on the far wall and Kerchak was charging.

When the king ape released the limp form that had been my father, he turned his attention toward the little baby. But Kala was there before him. And when he would have grasped the child, she snatched it herself, dropping her own dead baby into the empty cradle. Before he could intercept her, she had bolted through the door and taken refuge in a high tree.

Kerchak soon called to her to descend, and since there was no note of anger in his voice, she dropped lightly from branch to branch and joined him and the others on their homeward march.

"Oh, Tarzan," I said, "I feel so bad about your father. He must have been terrified."

Tarzan looked at me but he didn't seem to know what to say.

"And now I see how it came to be that you were raised by apes. Kala was so distraught about the loss of her own baby that she snatched you from your cradle as a substitute."

Tarzan had a strange expression on his face but didn't speak.

"And when you became aware of yourself and your environment, you never knew that Kala wasn't your real mother! And that you weren't an ape."

Again Tarzan didn't answer.

"Anyway, I must commend you on your writing. This article is excellent!"

"It is?" Tarzan said, beaming.

"Yes. I love how you never actually said that your father was killed, or that he was dead. You said: '. . . the limp form that *had been* my father . . .'"

Now that I was in love with Tarzan, I seemed to be in love with his writing too.

"Let's see what you underlined," he said.

I angled the notebook so we could both see it. "Okay," I said, "in the first paragraph I underlined the word *altogether* in the clause *altogether they set off westward toward the shore.* That's a mistake in usage."

"It is?"

"Yes." I was all business now. "You have to understand the difference between the single word *altogether* and the two-word phrase *all together.*"

"What's the difference?"

"Well, the two-word phrase *all together* means *all of them together.* You use that phrase when you're talking about a group and you're indicating that all the members perform some action collectively. For example, you might say 'Ten birds sat on a rock; all together they flew off.'"

"I see. They *all* flew off *together.* Or, to change the order of the words a little, they flew off *all together.* And in my article, I should have written *all together they set off . . .*"

"Exactly! Now, the single word *altogether* is an *adverb* that means 'entirely' or 'completely.' So, you might say something like . . . oh . . . 'The feeling of loving someone is *altogether* different from the feeling of liking someone.' Do you understand?"

316

"Yes. You mean the feeling is completely different—it's *altogether* different." Whether or not he knew that I was hinting at my own feelings was impossible to tell.

Then Tarzan said, "Here's another example I just thought of: 'I whispered certain instructions into Tantor's ear, but the message he ends up giving the other animals may be altogether different.' Is that a good use of the word *altogether?*"

"Why, yes, it's very good. But do you really think the animals will get the message wrong?"

"I told you; the whole idea is silly. It won't work."

"Well, we'll see," I insisted.

I wondered if I should ask him if he agreed that the feelings of love and like were completely different. Maybe if he talked about that, he'd make some revealing comments about his feelings for me. But before I could decide one way or another, he said, "How come you underlined the word *was* in the third paragraph?"

"Let's see. Oh, it says: 'Behind him was two other males . . .' Okay, the problem there is that the verb—*was*—should agree in *number* with the subject of the clause—but it doesn't. Now, what's the subject of that clause?"

"Him?"

"No, that's the object of the preposition *behind.*"

"Two?"

"No, that's an adjective that modifies *males* by limiting it."

"Males?"

"Right. If you changed the order of the words in the clause, it would be easier to see that *males* is the subject. The clause could have been written *Two other males were behind him.*"

"I see."

"Anyway, a verb must agree with its subject in *number.* Remember, that means that you use one form of a verb for a *singular* subject and another form for a *plural* subject. Now, you used the verb *was,* which goes with a singular subject, as in *I was, he was, it was.* That was wrong. You should have used *were,* which goes with a plural subject, as in *we were, they were.*"

"I see. I should have written 'Behind him *were* two other males' because the subject—*males*—is plural."

"Very good! It was a little tricky because in that clause, the subject comes *after* the verb; usually the subject comes before the verb."

Tarzan nodded thoughtfully.

"Okay," I said. "Now, in the fourth paragraph I underlined the word *laid* in the clause *On the bed laid a still figure* . . ."

"What's wrong with that?"

"Well, you have to understand the difference between the verbs *lay* and *lie*—and you have to know the correct present tense and past tense for each of them."

"What's the difference?"

"Well, do you remember when we talked about transitive and intransitive verbs?"

"Yes. We said that in a sentence like 'Jane brings fruit to the table,' the word *brings* is a *transitive* verb because it has an object—fruit. You're not just *bringing*, you're bringing *something*. And we said that in a sentence like 'Jane sleeps,' the word *sleeps* is an *intransitive* verb because it doesn't require an object to complete the meaning. You're just sleeping."

"Right. Good. Now, the word *lie* is an intransitive verb meaning 'to place yourself at rest in a horizontal position'; in other words, 'to lie down.' So you can say something like 'I like to lie on the ground and look up at the stars.'"

"I *do* like to do that."

"Good. Now, the word *lay* is a transitive verb meaning 'to place or put or set down,' as in *lay the plate on the table*."

"We'll do that when we have brunch after this lesson."

"Right." *But before that I have to declare my love to you*, I thought to myself.

"Anyway," I said out loud, "one reason people sometimes confuse these words is because the past tense of *lie* happens to be *lay*."

"Huh?"

"Well, remember when we spoke about the principle parts of a verb—the present tense, the past tense, and the past participle?"

"Yes."

"Okay. The principle parts of the verb *lie* are *lie, lay, lain*. So you would say, for example, 'today I *lie* on the bed; yesterday I *lay* on the bed; I should have *lain* on the bed.'"

"Lain?"

"Yes. That's the past participle of *lie*."

"Oh."

"And the principle parts of the verb *lay* are *lay, laid, laid*. So you would say, for example, 'today I *lay* the plate on the table; yesterday I *laid* the plate on the table; I should have *laid* the plate on the table.'

One reason people get confused about *lie* and *lay* is that the past tense of *lie* and the present tense of *lay* are the some word—*lay*."

"Oh."

"Now, in the sentence you wrote in Article 10, you should have used the past tense of *lie*, which is *lay*. You should have written 'On the bed *lay* a still figure . . .' Instead, you used the past tense of the transitive verb *lay*, which is *laid*. That doesn't make sense—because nobody was *placing* anybody anywhere, I mean. Do you see?"

"I do."

"Okay, we've talked about the past tense of *lie* and *lay*. Now let's talk about the present tense."

"Do people mix up those too?"

"Yes. They sometimes say *lay* when they should say *lie*. For example, someone might say 'You look tired; you should lay down for a while.'"

"That doesn't make sense," Tarzan volunteered. "They should say 'You look tired; you should *lie* down for a while.'"

"Good. Why?"

"Because of what the words *mean*. *Lie* means 'lie down'; *lay* means 'to place something on something else.'"

"Very good. And people sometimes make the same mistake with the present participles—the *ing* forms, I mean—of those verbs. They might say 'I feel like *laying* down' when they should—"

"When they should say 'I feel like *lying* down,' right?"

"Right. I think you've got it!"

Tarzan smiled at me. I smiled back and gazed into his eyes about two seconds longer than someone normally might in a situation like that.

I glanced at the notebook and saw that there was only one more error to discuss in Article 10. That meant that in a matter of moments I would tell Tarzan that I loved him.

I sighed, then took a deep breath, and then said, pointing, "Okay, now look at this spot here where I underlined the word *froze*."

"Let's see. It says 'The sight that met his eyes must have froze him with terror . . .' What's wrong with that?"

"Well, a moment ago we talked about the three principal parts of a—"

"I remember. The principle parts of a verb are the present tense, the past tense, and the past participle," Tarzan recited.

"Right. And, if you remember, you need to use the past participle—instead of the past tense, I mean—in constructions that include the word *have, has,* or *had.* For example, you know that the past participle of the verb *eat* is *eaten,* right?"

"Right."

"So, you would say something like 'we should *have eaten* breakfast' or 'he *has eaten* breakfast' or 'if we *had eaten* breakfast, we wouldn't be so hungry right now.'"

"Are you hungry?"

"No." I really wasn't because I was starting to feel nervous about confessing my true feelings to Tarzan. "Are you?"

"A little. But I can wait."

"Okay. Anyway, it would be wrong to say something like 'we should have ate breakfast.'"

"I see. Because the verb includes the word *have,* you need the past participle, not the past tense; you need to say 'should have *eaten.*'"

"Right. Now, you wrote the phrase *must have froze.* Because that includes the word *have,* you should have used the past participle of *freeze*—not the past tense. Now, what's the past participle of *freeze?*"

"Um . . ."

"It's *frozen.* The principle parts of *freeze* are *freeze, froze, frozen*—as in 'today I freeze; yesterday I froze; I could have frozen.'" Before Tarzan could answer it occurred to me that it was ironic that I would be talking about freezing in the middle of a steamy tropical jungle.

"I see," Tarzan said. "I should have written 'The sight that met his eyes must have *frozen* him with terror.'"

"That's it. You've got it."

"Well, now that we've finished going over Article 10, are you ready for brunch?"

"Um . . . not yet. First there's something I have to tell you. Something very important that's been on my mind." Suddenly my heart starting pounding like a jackhammer.

"What is it?"

"I have to tell you that I lo-lo-lo . . ." I couldn't get the word out.

"What?"

"I have to tell you that I lo-lo . . . I mean I have to tell you that I think that you're a really nice guy and that I really adore you."

Do you think that saying 'I adore you' is the same as saying 'I love you'? I don't think it really is. I think that for it to really "count," you have to actually use the word *love.* Okay, I chickened out. I mean, what if he didn't say he loved me back? I don't think I could have coped with that.

"I think you're very nice too!" he exclaimed.

He didn't even say that he adored me! Well, maybe that's because he was raised by apes and didn't know the proper way to express his feelings to a girl. That must have been it. That was all.

"I'm starving!" he said. "Let's have brunch."

"Okay," I answered lamely. I promised myself that later that day, after we'd finished discussing Article 11 (which he'd write that afternoon), I'd tell him how I really felt, and I'd use the right word—*love*.

That afternoon, Tarzan sat at the table writing Article 11 and I sat on the bed thumbing through the book on Africa.

"Tarzan, could you stop writing for a second?"

He looked up at me. "What?"

"It says here in this book that once a snake—a python—grew inside the body of a nine-year old girl who accidentally swallowed a snake egg while drinking from a garden hose. Doctors had to remove the snake from her surgically. After that, for the rest of her life, she was terrified of snakes. Do you believe that?"

"What book is that?"

"The book about Africa."

"That doesn't sound right to me. Now let me write."

I put that book back on the shelf and grabbed the one about geological and meteorological hazards and disasters. I returned to the bed and started to thumb through it. I couldn't concentrate, though, because I kept imagining what my "love" conversation with Tarzan would be like later on. What if he didn't say that he loved me back? Once a guy in my high school confessed to a girl in my class that he loved her, and the girl said, "That's *your* problem. I'm going to leave now so that you can think about your problem by yourself." Then she walked away. The guy was so hurt and embarrassed that he never even tried to speak to the girl again. What if Tarzan said something like that to me? But he wouldn't be so mean; not him. In my imagination he'd say: "Oh Jane, I love you too! I've always loved you!"

I forced myself to pay attention to the book.

After a while Tarzan suddenly said, "Could you please stop humming 'Swanee River'?"

"Sorry." I didn't even know I'd been humming.

There was silence for a while.

"Tarzan," I finally said, "could you stop writing for a second?"

He looked up at me.

"It says something really weird about a flood in this book."

"What?"

"It says that once in Boston—that's in Massachusetts, in America—there was a flood, but it wasn't a flood of water. It says that a tank containing over two millions gallons of molasses exploded."

"What's molasses?"

"It's a kind of food. It's like a thick, sticky, sweet syrup. It's dark brown. Anyway, this tank exploded and a giant wave of molasses raced through the streets of Boston. Lot's of people and horses got stuck in the stuff, and then the rescue workers got stuck too. People were killed."

Tarzan didn't say anything. Instead, he went back to his writing.

"Do you believe that really happened?" I persisted.

"I don't know. Why don't you read a *normal* book? Try something else from the shelf."

I really didn't feel like reading anymore. Instead, I sat on the bed and daydreamed about the meaningful conversation I'd soon have with Tarzan and about the diamonds and gold the chimps would be bringing a week from now.

"Okay, I'm done with Article 11," I heard Tarzan say.

I walked over to the table, sat down to Tarzan's right, and angled the notebook toward myself. "Shall I read it out loud to you?" I asked. I thought that if I read aloud to him, we'd be interacting—more so than if I were to read the article silently, I mean.

"Okay."

"All right. I'll underline the errors—if there are any, I mean—as I go along."

When I finished reading, the article looked like this:

Article 11: "Growing Up"

Tenderly Kala nursed me. But she wondered why I didn't gain strength and agility as did the little apes of other mothers. She sometimes talked with the other females about me, but everyone she spoke to just shook their heads in disbelief. No one could understand how a child could be so slow and backward in learning to care for itself. Why, even after two years I couldn't climb trees or find food alone!

One day Kerchak asked that Kala gives up her puny, defective toddler. But my ape mother, who loved me, threatened to run away from the tribe if we weren't left in peace. After that, they bothered her no more, for Kala was a fine young ape, and they didn't want to lose her.

In many ways I differed from my brothers and sisters, and they often marveled at my superior intelligence. But in strength and size I was deficient. At around ten years of age, I noticed that other apes my age were fully grown, some of them towering over six feet in height! But I was still a half-grown boy.

From early childhood I had used my hands to swing from branch to branch after the manner of my mother. As I grew older I spent hour upon hour speeding through the treetops with my brothers and sisters.

After awhile I began to make rapid strides. I could spring 20 feet across space at dizzying heights and grasp with unerring precision a vine swinging swiftly across my path. I could drop 20 feet at a stretch from limb to limb in rapid descent to the ground. I could climb the highest tree with the ease and swiftness of a squirrel. And everyday my strength increased.

My life among these fierce apes was rather happy, for I knew no other life. I didn't know that there existed in the universe anything other then this jungle and the wild animals with which I was familiar with.

"Wow," Tarzan said, "you underlined a lot in this article!"

"It's not so much, really." I patted his arm so he wouldn't feel bad. "And I *love* the way you write!" I really did.

He smiled appreciatively.

"Okay," I said, "let's look at the first underline. I underlined the words *their heads* in the clause 'everyone she spoke to just shook their heads . . .'"

"What's wrong with that?"

"Well, remember that a pronoun must agree with its antecedent—the word it refers to—in *number*. That means that if the antecedent is plural, the pronoun is also plural, as in '*they* took off *their* coats.' And if the antecedent is singular, the pronoun is also singular, as in '*he* took off *his* coat.'"

"I know that. But I still don't see what I did wrong."

"What you have to understand is that there are certain words that seem as if they might be plural, but they're really singular—I mean that they're considered by grammarians to be singular."

"Like what?"

"Like the word you used at the beginning of that clause—the word *everyone*. You see, grammarians point out that *everyone* really means 'every person'—'every *single* person.' So you would say 'every single person took off *his* coat'—not *their* coat—and you'd also say 'every person took off *his* coat' and you'd also say 'everyone took off *his* coat.' Do you see? If you realize that *everyone* means 'every single person,' then you can see that it's really singular. In the same way, words like *everybody, anyone, anybody,* and *each* are also singular."

"Well, I can see that, but—"

"So," I interrupted, "what you should have written is 'everyone she spoke to just shook *her* head . . .'—because *everyone* is singular and *her* is singular."

"Okay, but I still think that a word like *everyone* can be plural. What if I said '*Everyone* thought the snake was dead, and *they* were right'? Is that incorrect? Should it be '*Everyone* thought the snake was dead, and *he* was right'? That sounds wrong to me."

I thought about that for awhile. Gee, my high school English teacher always said that a word like *everybody* was singular, and now Tarzan proved to me that it was sometimes plural.

"Well," I said, "I see what you mean. But in your example, the word *they* isn't in the same clause as the word *everybody*. Your example uses two independent clauses, I mean."

"So? What does that have to do with anything?"

"I don't know." Now I felt like the student.

"Before," Tarzan said, "you were talking about people taking off their coats. What if I said 'Everybody left the room, taking their coats with them'? In that sentence I don't have two independent clauses. And I even used the word *them* at the end, which is plural. I mean, that sentence sounds fine, but it would sound silly to say 'Everyone left the room, taking his coat with him,' wouldn't it?"

"Uh . . . yes . . . it would." Apparently, my high school English teacher didn't tell me the whole story about words like *everyone*. But I still felt that, in general, words like that were singular. So I said, "Well, I see, by your examples, that sometimes a word like *everyone* can be plural, so let's state the rule like this: Treat a word like *everyone* as singular, unless you can't. Now, following that rule, you should have written 'everyone she spoke to just shook her head . . .'"

"Okay," he said agreeably. You see, that was one of the things I loved about Tarzan. He didn't argue too much. He didn't always have to prove he was right about everything.

"Okay," I said, "now let's look at the next underline. I underlined the word *gives* in the sentence 'One day Kerchak asked that Kala gives up her puny, defective toddler.'"

"Why did you do that? Did I use the wrong tense?"

"No, you—"

"I mean, if I used past tense, that would have sounded wrong: 'One day Kerchak asked that Kala *gave* up her puny, defective toddler.' And if I used future tense, that would have sounded wrong: 'One day Kerchak asked that Kala *will give* up her puny, defective toddler.'"

"You didn't use the wrong tense, you used the wrong *mood*. Remember, verbs have three possible *moods*: indicative, which is used in normal sentences; subjunctive, which is used in sentences that express a wish or a supposition; and imperative, which is used in sentences that express a command or request."

"I remember! We talked about that when we were diving off branches at the pond!"

Our pond, I thought.

"Now," I said, "what kind of sentence is this one about Kerchak asking Kala to do something?"

"Well, you just gave away the answer. If he's asking her to do something, he expressing a request."

"And?"

"And that means I should have used the imperative mood."

"And what's the correct verb form for the imperative mood?"

"I remember! You said that you should always use the *infinitive* in the imperative mood. I remember the example you gave. You said something about insisting that somebody *be* on time."

"Very good. Now, you used the word *gives*: 'Kerchak asked that Kala *gives* up her . . . toddler.'"

"The toddler was me."

"I know. Now, as I was saying, you used the word *gives*. What's the infinitive of that verb?"

"It's *give*."

"Right. So what should you have written?"

"I should have written 'Kerchak asked that Kala *give* up her . . . toddler.'"

Tarzan was so smart! Wasn't he smart?

"Very good!" I exclaimed.

Tarzan smiled and then said, "Okay, now, what about this next underline. Why did you underline the words *At around* in the third paragraph?"

"Let's see. It says: 'At around ten years of age . . .' Okay, the problem here is that you used two prepositions in a row, and that doesn't make sense. When you noticed that other apes your age were fully grown, you were either *ten* years old or *around* ten years old. But you weren't both—*ten* and *around ten*, I mean. You should have picked one preposition or the other. You should have written either 'At ten years of age . . .' or 'Around ten years of age . . .'"

"Now I remember! You taught me about that when we were riding back from the watering hole—the one where the crocodile ate the ostrich—on the back of an elephant. You said it was wrong to say that a turtle fell *off of* a log or that a bird flew *out of* a window. And I even made up an example about someone arriving in Africa *on around* January 1st. Those example were all grammatically incorrect because they used double prepositions."

"Right! You have such a good memory!" Didn't Tarzan have a good memory? I guess you can see why I was in love with him. Well, four more underlines to go, and then I'd confess my feelings to him. And this time I wouldn't chicken out.

"Okay, let's keep going," I said. "Now, in the fifth paragraph I underlined the word *awhile* in the phrase *After awhile* . . ."

"Why did you do that?"

"Well, let me ask you this: What part of speech is the word *after*?"

"It's a preposition."

"Right. And a preposition always takes a . . . what?"

"An object."

"Right. But the object of a preposition has to be a noun or pronoun. But what part of speech is the word *awhile?*"

"Uh . . ."

"It's an *adverb.* It kind of tells *when.* It means 'for a short time.' Anyway, you can't have an adverb functioning as the object of a preposition."

"So what *should* I have written? I mean, the sentence *sounds* right, doesn't it?"

"It sounds right when you say it out loud. But when you write it, you have to use the two-word form—*a while;* I mean, you have to have the word *a,* which is an article, and then the word *while,* which is a noun."

"*While* is a noun?"

"Yes. It means 'a period of time.'"

"Oh."

I took the notebook and wrote *After a while.* Then I said, pointing to those words, "You see, in this phrase, you have three separate words—preposition, article, noun. That makes sense, because now the preposition has an object—*while.*"

"Oh. But when *would* it be correct to use the one-word form of *awhile*—the adverb, I mean?"

"Well, what does an adverb do?"

"It modifies a verb—or an adjective or another adverb."

"Right. So, if I said something like *Stay awhile,* I would use the one-word form—*awhile.* Why? Because the word *stay* is a verb . . . and a verb is modified by an adverb . . . and the single word *awhile* is an adverb. It makes sense."

Then I took the notebook and wrote two phrases: *Stay for a while* and *Stay for awhile.*

Pointing to them, I said, "Now, which of these phrases is written correctly?"

Tarzan pondered this awhile. "Well," he finally said, "I think the first one is correct because you have the preposition *for,* and that means you *must* have a noun or pronoun for its object. By making *a while* two words, you have a noun—*while.*

"That's very good. I tried to trick you on that one by using a verb—*stay*—at the beginning. I mean, I tried to trick you into thinking you needed an adverb—*awhile*—to modify it, but you were too smart to be tricked."

"Well, once you put that preposition in there, it made all the difference."

"You know," I said, "you'd make a good grammar teacher yourself! I paused awhile and then said, "I'm finding that by teaching you grammar, I'm improving my own grammar—just by talking about it and thinking about it a lot, I mean. I guess that whenever someone teaches a subject, they—I mean *he*—I mean *he or she*—naturally gets better at it." I wanted to be sure to use a singular pronoun with the antecedent *someone*.

"Really?"

"Really. As a matter of fact, if you want to become really masterful at grammar, you should teach it to someone else. Would you like me to call Cheetah so that you can teach him everything you've already learned?"

Tarzan apparently didn't know whether or not I was kidding, so he just stared at me for a long time.

"Well," I said, "we can talk about that some more later. Anyway, let's go on to the next underline." I glanced at the article. "Okay, at the end of the fifth paragraph, I underlined the word *everyday* in the sentence 'And everyday my strength increased.'"

"Why did you do that?"

"Well, that's another mistake in usage. You have to understand the difference between the single word *everyday* and the two-word phrase *every day*."

"What's the difference?"

"Well, the two-word phrase *every day* means 'every single day; each and every day.' So you can say something like 'We eat brunch and dinner every day' or 'We used to go swimming every day.'"

"Do you want to go swimming now? Do you miss going swimming?"

"No, I don't mind staying in the cabin so you can write your articles."

"Are you sure?"

"Yes."

"Okay." Then after a pause: "And what about the single word *everyday*?"

"Well, as a single word, *everyday* is an adjective. It means 'ordinary'—that is, it means either 'appropriate for ordinary occasions,' as in *everyday clothes*, or 'commonplace; routine,' as in *everyday situations*."

"Oh. So I should have written 'And every day my strength increased.'" He paused between the words *every* and *day* to show me that he understood that it was a two-word phrase."

"Exactly. Okay, let's keep going. Look at the last paragraph. I underlined the word *then* in the phrase *anything other then this jungle.*"

"Why?"

"That's another error in usage. You have to understand the difference between the words *then*—T-H-E-N—and *than*—T-H-A-N."

"What's the difference?"

"The word *then* is an *adverb* usually meaning 'at that time.' So, for example, tonight I could say to you, 'Come back to the cabin when the sun rises, and we'll have our next grammar lesson *then.*'"

"I see. We'll have our grammar lesson *at that time.*"

"Right. Now, the word *than* is a *conjunction* that's used to compare two unequal things. So, for example, I can say 'Tarzan is stronger *than* Jane.' I'm comparing our strengths—our unequal strengths."

"I see. It wouldn't make sense to say 'Tarzan is stronger *then* Jane,' because I'm not talking about time at all. I'm making a comparison."

"Right."

"And in my article I should have written 'anything other *than* this jungle . . .'"

"Exactly!"

There was only one more underline to discuss, and then I would have a serious talk with Tarzan about my feelings for him and about the meaning of our relationship. My heart started to beat a little faster in anticipation, but I tried not to let it show.

"Okay," I said, "one more underline to go. I underlined the word *with* at the very end of the article."

"Why did you do that?"

"Well, you used the preposition *with* twice in the same phrase—*animals with which I was familiar with.* That's redundant."

"Redundant?"

"I mean it's unnecessary; it's repetitious. You should have used the word *with* only once."

"Which one should I have taken out?"

I debated with myself over whether or not to talk to Tarzan about the correctness of ending a sentence with a preposition. My high school English teacher used to say that doing so is wrong, but my boss at *American Monthly* said it's okay. He said that the rule that you shouldn't end a sentence with a preposition is an old-fashioned one and that nobody follows it anymore. He even pointed out that in some situations you can't *help* but end a sentence with a preposition because the alternative sounds silly. For example, he noted that people commonly make such remarks as "What are you afraid of?," "What is it for?," "Who are you mad at?," and "You wouldn't believe what I have to put up with." After that he pointed out, "Now, wouldn't it sound silly to say 'You wouldn't believe up with which I have to put'?"

I decided not to mention any of this to Tarzan because I felt that ending a sentence with a preposition isn't so bad—in spite of my high school English teacher's admonitions.

"Well," I said, "you can leave out either one. You can say 'animals with which I was familiar' *or* 'animals I was familiar with.' But either way, you're using the word *with* just once."

My heart suddenly started beating fast because I knew that today's grammar lesson was over and that it was now time for our special talk—assuming that Tarzan understood that last point I made about redundant prepositions, that is.

"So, do you understand?" I said. "It's another case of 'writer's choice.' You can leave out either *with.*"

"I understand."

Boom-boom-boom. (That was my heart pounding.)

"Tarzan, n-now that we've finished with today's grammar lesson, there's something very important I have to t-talk to you about."

Boom-boom-boom.

"What?"

"Um . . . you see . . . I . . . um . . ."

"What are you trying to say? Is something wrong?"

"No. It's just . . ."

I couldn't do it. I thought I'd be able to, but now that the time had come, I couldn't. I was too scared. My mouth had become completely dry and I couldn't get the words out.

"It's just that I forgot to tell you something I saw in that book about Africa I was reading."

"What"

"It said that right around here, in the Congo Valley, there's an animal called an okapi. It's related to the giraffe, but it's smaller. Anyway, it said that it washes its ears with its tongue."

"How is that possible?"

"It said that its tongue reaches all the way around to its ear."

"Really?"

"That's what it said."

"Oh. Was that all you wanted to tell me?"

"No . . . um . . . the book also said that some animals—large mammals, I mean—have their sense of smell in their hind hoofs."

"Really?"

"That's what it said."

Okay, I admit it: I was a failure at confessing my love. I'd try again tomorrow morning—as soon as we finished going over the errors in Article 12.

Chapter 26: Tarzan Recalls Being Attacked by a Lioness

The next morning, as usual, Tarzan sat at the table writing and I sat on the bed reading. But I wasn't concentrating. Mostly, I was thinking about the "love" conversation I'd have with Tarzan after this morning's lesson. But right now I was trying to add up how much money all the gold and precious stones would be worth. Oh, by the way, I decided against seeking out Tantor on my own and telling him about the sapphires. I really didn't want to do anything behind Tarzan's back. Besides, how would I find Tantor? I imagined myself calling him from the doorway of the cabin by imitating the yell Tarzan used. But I didn't think I could imitate it and, of course, I didn't want Tarzan to hear me (if he happened to be approaching the cabin at that moment, I mean). Maybe within the next few days I'd see Cheetah and explain the sapphires to him and ask *him* to tell Tantor for me. That was a better idea.

I tried to imagine the size of each piece of gold and of each diamond, emerald, and ruby (I ignored the sapphires for now). Then I tried to estimate the ratio of one of the stones to each of the others. Then I estimated how many stones could fit in a chimpanzee's fist. Then I tried to estimate the value of each stone. So much multiplication was involved that I had to use pencil and paper.

"Tarzan," I called, "can you rip out a blank piece of paper from the back of that notebook and hand it to me? And can you please let me have one of those pencils too?"

"What are you doing?"

"I'm just doing some arithmetic problems to pass the time. Multiplication."

"Oh . . . do you want to teach me about arithmetic after I finish learning everything about grammar?"

"Would you like to learn about algebra?"

"Algebra?"

"Never mind."

I took the pencil and paper and set to work. I filled up several pages with calculations. When I was done, I saw that the total value of the diamonds, gold, rubies, and emeralds would be about ten million dollars—based on two hundred chimpanzee fistfuls. Of course, I could have been wrong about the number of chimpanzees I asked for. But I thought that, one way or another, ten million dollars was about right.

"Tarzan, there are only six more days until the chimps bring the diamonds and gold. I figure it will all be worth about ten million dollars."

Tarzan seemed unimpressed. I wasn't sure if that was because money had no meaning for him or because he thought that the animals of the jungle were incapable of executing such a complicated plan.

Six days. Ten million dollars. I couldn't stop thinking about it, even if it all meant nothing to Tarzan.

Finally I turned my attention to the book I'd been reading. It was the one about hazards and disasters—the chapter on floods.

"Tarzan?"

"What?"

"It says here in this book that once in Pennsylvania—this was in the 1880s—a twelve-room house was carried away by a flood. It says that it was deposited a couple of miles away directly on top of the foundation of another house that was about to be built from blueprints identical to those of the first house. Anyway, when the contractor arrived at the site the next morning, he couldn't believe that the house he was *going* to build was already there, completely built."

"I don't believe that."

"That's what it says. There were witnesses."

"Why can't you read a *normal* book to occupy yourself while I write?"

I went to the shelf and found a book called *The World of Animals.* I sat back down on the bed and thumbed through it.

After a while I said, "Tarzan, it says in this book that in Cuba there are giant land crabs that can outrace a horse."

"That sounds impossible. But why would a crab and a horse have a race in the first place?"

"I don't think that they actually race. I think this means that the crab can run faster than a horse."

"That doesn't sound possible."

"Well, that's what it says."

He didn't answer.

Anyway, between browsing through the book on animals, thinking about the ten million dollars, and thinking about what Tarzan's response might be to my imminent declaration of love, I managed to pass the time. Then suddenly I heard Tarzan say, "Okay, I'm done with Article 12."

I walked to my seat at the table, to Tarzan's right. Taking the notebook, I said, "Should I read it to you out loud?"

"Okay."

"I read the article, underlining the errors as I went along. When I was done, it looked like this:

Article 12: "Self-consciousness"

When I was about ten I became ashamed of my body. The reason was because, whereas my brothers and sisters were covered with hair, I was entirely hairless, like a lowly snake. To hide that fact, I use to cover myself from head to foot with mud, but this dried and fell off. Besides, it felt so uncomfortable that I decided that I preferred the shame to the discomfort.

Then one day I saw my face for the first time. You see, in the area where my tribe lived was a peaceful little lake, and it was there that I first saw my reflection in the clear, still water. It was a scorching Summer day, and one of my ape playmates and myself had gone to the pond to drink. As we leaned over, both our faces were mirrored in the water. I was shocked. It had been bad enough to be hairless, but to have such an ugly face.

That tiny slit of a mouth! How it looked beside the mighty jaws of my more fortunate friend! And those puny teeth of mine. I turned red as I saw how much punier they were than my companion. Why, his were powerful fangs!

I was so busy counting my teeth—for it looked as if I had less than my friend—that I didn't realize that a savage lioness, whose name was Sabor, was sneaking up behind us.

"So, what happened with Sabor?" I asked. "Did she attack you?"

"You'll see."

"Oh. Well, anyway, I know exactly how you must have felt when you thought that you didn't look normal. When I was in junior high school, ugly red pimples would sometimes break out on my face. I felt so ugly that I didn't even want to go to school! I didn't want anyone to see me."

He didn't seem to know what to say about that.

"Anyway," I said, "let's start with the first underline. You wrote *The reason was because . . .*"

"What's wrong with that?"

"It's redundant. It's like saying the same thing twice."

"Why?"

"Because the word *because* means 'for the reason that.' So, if you say *the reason was because*, it's like saying *the reason was for the reason that*. It's like using the word *reason* twice."

"Oh . . . So what should I have written?"

"You should have written 'The reason was *that . . .*'"

"I see. So it would be correct to say 'The reason you didn't want to go to school was *that* you had ugly pimples on your face,' and it would be incorrect to say 'The reason you didn't want to go to school was *because* you had ugly pimples on your face.' Is that it?"

"Y-yes." Why was he bringing up my pimples? Was it in innocence, or was it to make me feel bad for some reason? Was it because I'd called him an "ape-man" a few days ago? It was hard to tell with someone like Tarzan. I hoped that after this lesson, when I tell him that I love him, he won't be thinking about my pimples! The ones I *used* to have, I mean.

"Another little mistake people sometimes make with the word *reason*," I said, "is to put the word *why* after it, as in 'The *reason why* I was ashamed of my body was that it was entirely hairless.'"

"Why is that wrong?"

"For the same reason. The word *why*, like the word *because*, means 'for the reason that.' So, if you say 'The reason why . . .' it's like saying the word 'reason' *twice*. It's redundant."

"Oh. So, it's okay to say 'The reason I was ashamed . . .' but it's *not* okay to say 'The reason *why* I was ashamed . . .' Is that it?"

"Yes, exactly," I said. "Okay, now let's go on to the next underline."

"I wrote 'I use to cover myself . . .' What's wrong with that?"

"Well, in that sentence, the word *use* isn't being used in the normal sense of 'make use of.' It's used as part of the expression *used to*." I wrote *used to* in the notebook so that he could see it. "That expression—*used to*—is used to indicate some past or former habit or custom, as in, 'People *used to* live in caves.' The important thing to understand is that in that expression, the first word is *used*, past tense, with a *d* at the end—not *use*."

"Oh."

"The reason people sometimes make the mistake you made is that when they say the phrase out loud, they pronounce it *use to*. They drop the *d*. It sounds as if they're saying: I *use* to do such-and-such."

"Even if they know there's a *d* at the end of the word, they still pronounce it like that?"

"Most people, yes. So it's understandable that when they write it, they might spell it incorrectly."

"Well, is it *ever* correct to say *use to*?"

"One time. That's when the phrase is coupled with the word *did* or *didn't*."

"What do you mean?"

"Well, I could say 'Didn't you *use to* live with apes?' or 'Did you *use to* live with apes?' See, because the word *did* or *didn't* is past tense—of the verb *do*, I mean—you don't need to make the word *use* also past tense. One past tense—*did*—is enough."

"Oh."

"Anyway, let's go on now to the next underline—the word *Summer* in the second paragraph. This is kind of simple to explain. The seasons—summer, fall, winter, spring—aren't capitalized. I mean they're not considered proper nouns."

"But the months are capitalized: January, February, March . . ."

"I know, but the seasons aren't."

"Well, it seems to me that if months are capitalized, then seasons should be too."

"Well, I guess all the grammar experts got together one day and decided that the seasons shouldn't be capitalized."

"Oh."

"Okay, now let's look at the next underline—the word *myself* in that same sentence. You wrote 'one of my playmates and myself had gone to the pond . . .'"

"Is that wrong?"

"Hey, is that the same pond where we had our moonlight swim?"

"No, a different one."

"Oh. I was just curious." I didn't like the idea of Tarzan going to *our* pond with anyone but me. "Anyway, a word like *myself* can be used as an object if you're talking about yourself; for example, you might say 'I accidentally hurt myself.'"

"*Myself* is the object of the verb *hurt*, right?"

"Right. Or you can use the word *myself* as an intensifier—to emphasize some fact, I mean. For example, you might say 'I killed the snake myself.'"

"My father built this cabin *himself.*"

"Right! That's a good use of the word *himself*. Anyway—I think I once mentioned this to you before, when we first spoke about pronouns—if a word like *myself*—or *yourself* or *himself*—is used as an object, it reflects back to the antecedent and is called a *reflexive* pronoun. And if a word like that is used to intensify or emphasize some fact or information, it's called an *intensive* pronoun."

"Oh."

"Anyway, sometimes people incorrectly use a word like *myself* as part of a compound subject. For example, they might say something like 'Jim and myself went fishing.'"

"That's wrong?"

"Of course it's wrong! The pronoun is part of the *subject* of the sentence, so they need a *subjective-case* pronoun. They should say 'Jim and *I* went fishing.'"

"Then why do they say 'Jim and myself . . .'?"

"I think this is another case of people trying to show that they have good grammar. They're trying to show off. I hate that because they're really showing that they don't understand grammar."

"Oh."

"And sometimes people incorrectly use a word like *myself* as part of a compound object—one that's *not* reflexive, I mean. For example, they might say something like 'The fish splashed water on Jim and myself.'"

"That's wrong?"

"Of course! The pronoun doesn't reflect back to *fish*, so it shouldn't be a reflexive pronoun; it should be a regular, objective-case pronoun—*me*. They should say 'The fish splashed water on Jim and *me.*'"

"Why do they—"

"Again, I think they do that because for some reason they think the word *myself* sounds more grammatical than the word *me*. But in the example I made up, it isn't more grammatical; it's just wrong."

"So, in my article I should have written 'one of my ape playmates and *I* had gone to the pond . . .' because in that case the pronoun is part of the subject of the clause."

"Exactly."

We both didn't say anything for a while after that, and I stole a glance at Tarzan's face. I just liked to look at it; I couldn't help it. I mainly liked looking at his eyes. Sometimes his head would be down, looking at the notebook, and I'd say something to him. Instead of lifting his whole head to look at me, he'd keep his head down and just lift his eyes toward me, opening them wide. When he did that I could feel some kind of electric shock go through me—not a bad one, a good one.

Finally I said, "Okay, now, I also underlined the last word of that paragraph—*face.*"

He kept his head down but lifted his big eyes to me, waiting for me to go on.

"Th-there's nothing wrong with the word *face*; the problem is the punctuation at the end of the sentence. When you make a statement like '. . . but to have such an ugly face,' you're being emphatic. So you need an exclamation point—not a period—after it."

"Oh."

How ironic that Tarzan once believed that he had an ugly face, and there I was, thinking that it's the most *handsome* face I'd ever seen!

"Okay," I said, "let's go on to the third paragraph. There you're talking about your teeth and you say that they're punier than your companion. Now, why would you compare the size of your teeth to the size of an ape?" (I knew the answer, but I wanted to see what he would say.)

"I wasn't. I meant that my teeth were punier than his *teeth*, not that they were punier than his whole body."

"Okay, then you should have said that. But you compared your teeth to your *companion*. What you should have written is '. . . how much punier they were than *those of* my companion' or '. . . how much punier they were than my *companion's*'—with an *apostrophe s* at the end. Either way you're showing that you're comparing your teeth to his *teeth* and not to him. Do you see?"

With his head down he lifted his round eyes to me again and said that he understood.

After the electric current passed through my body, I said, "Okay, one more underline to go."

I knew that after we talked about that last error, it would be time for me to declare my love to Tarzan. My heartbeat suddenly sped up. I could feel it inside me. *Boom-boom-boom.*

"Y-you were talking about counting your teeth and you wrote 'it looked as if I had *less* than my friend.'"

"What wrong with that. It *did* look that way. I counted them."

"This is another error in usage. You have to understand when to use the word *less* and when to use the word *fewer.*"

"You mean I should have written 'it looked as if I had *fewer* than my friend'?"

"Yes. The two words are similar, but they're not exactly the same. *Less* means 'not as *much*' but *fewer* means 'not as *many.*' In other words, if you're talking about something you can *count*, you should use the word *fewer*, as in 'the continent of North America has *fewer* countries than the continent of Africa.'"

"Because you can count exactly how many countries there are in each continent, right?"

"Right. But if you're talking about something you *can't* count—you know, like an *amount* of something—then you should use the word *less*, as in 'my mother's lemonade contain less sugar than my grand-mother's.'"

"Because you can't count sugar, right?"

"Right."

Okay, the time had come. *Boom-boom-boom.* We could have brunch first, and then I could tell him I love him. But no, I would do it right now. I couldn't put if off any longer.

"Tarzan?"

"Yes?"

"There's something important I have to tell you."

"Yes?"

Boom-boom-boom.

"I . . . um . . . uh . . . I-I-I . . ."

"What's wrong? What are you trying to say?"

"I have to tell you that I . . . I . . . forgot to tell you something about . . . **about** *grammar!*"

"What?"

"Well, when we were talking about the word *myself* and about compound subjects, it made me think of it, and now I have to tell you."

"What is it? I thought we were going to have brunch now."

"We will—right after I tell you this. Do you know what a *compound subject* is?"

"Isn't that a subject that has more than one part to it—like 'Jim and I' in that sentence you made up about going fishing?"

"Yes. In the sentence 'Jim and I went fishing,' the subject is made up of two parts: *Jim* and *I*. Anyway, sometimes in a compound subject, the parts that make it up are joined by the conjunction *or* instead of the conjunction *and*."

"I know."

"Anyway, I told you that the verb of a sentence has to agree with the subject in number."

"I remember. You said that if the subject is singular, you should use the singular form of the verb, as in *he swims*, and if the subject is plural, you should use the plural form of the verb, as in *they swim*. That's easy."

"Okay. But what if you have a compound subject joined by *or*, and one part of the subject is plural but the other part is singular."

"Like what?"

"Like the sentence 'Neither Tarzan or the apes like lima beans.' The question is, should the verb *like* agree in number with *Tarzan*, which is singular, or with *apes*, which is plural. In other words, should the sentence be 'Neither Tarzan or the apes *like* lima beans' or 'Neither Tarzan or the apes *likes* lima beans'?"

"I don't know. Which is correct?"

"Well, you should make the verb agree in number with the part of the subject it's *closer* to. So, you would say 'Neither Tarzan or the apes *like* lima beans' because *like* is closer to *apes*, which is plural—*apes like*. But if you switched the order of the compound subject, then you would say "Neither the apes or Tarzan *likes* lima beans' because now the verb is closer to *Tarzan*, which is singular—*Tarzan likes*. Do you see?"

"I do. Is that all you wanted to tell me? Is that what was so important?"

"Um . . . yes. That's all."

Well, I'd just have to tell him later, after we finished going over Article 13. Actually, I couldn't wait to read it because I wanted to see what happened when that lioness snuck up behind him.

That afternoon, as was our habit, Tarzan sat at the table writing and I thumbed through a book on the bed. I debated with myself about whether or not to tell Cheetah to tell Tantor about the sapphires. What if Cheetah didn't explain things properly and the hundred chimps brought me nothing but blueberries. I mean, after all, blueberries are small blue objects, like sapphires. It's probably best if I don't say anything about the sapphires at all. I'd still be getting ten million dollars, even without them.

Next I thought about what I could do with the money. I could buy a big mansion. Or maybe I should give the money to a worthy charity. I know: I could give half the money to charity and then buy a small mansion. That was the best idea.

Once I had that settled, I turned my attention back to the book on my lap. It was the one about animals. After a while I said, "Tarzan?"

"Yes?"

"It says in this book that a rat must chew continuously."

"Why?"

"It says that its sharp teeth keep growing, and by constantly chewing, it keeps them ground down. It says that if a rat loses an upper tooth, the lower tooth below that spot will just keep growing upward until it tears into the rat's brain, killing it."

"Really?"

"That's what it says."

Tarzan resumed his writing without answering.

I lost interest in the book and daydreamed about the conversation I would have with Tarzan after that afternoon's lesson. There were two versions of the conversation. In one I'd tell him that I loved him and then he would say, "Oh Jane, I love you too." In the other I would tell him I loved him and then he would say "That's *your* problem." I was *convinced* that those were the only possible responses he could give. One or the other.

Suddenly I heard Tarzan say, "Okay, I'm done with Article 13."

I went to the table, sat next to him, and picked up the notebook.

"I'll read it out loud to you, okay?" I said.

"Okay."

As usual, I underlined the errors as I went along. This time I found only three. With the underlines, the article looked like this:

Article 13: "Sabor Attacks"

All of a sudden, Sabor <u>the lioness</u> sprang at us with an awful scream. But that scream wasn't a warning. A lion screams like that to freeze its prey in terror for an instant. That gives the beast just enough time to dig its mighty claws into its victim's soft flesh and hold him beyond any hope of escape.

My friend crouched trembling for an instant, and that instant was just long enough to prove his undoing. But my higher intelligence gave me powers far beyond those of other apes. The wild scream of Sabor, instead of paralyzing me, roused my brain and muscles into instant action.

Before me lay the deep waters of the little lake and behind me, the jaws of <u>death</u>. I'd always hated water except as a means of quenching my thirst. My ape mother taught me that it's chilly and uncomfortable, and that you can sink into it and never come back up.

But of the two evils, my mind decided that the water was the <u>best</u> choice, and before the great beast had covered half her leap, I felt the cold waters close above my head.

"Tarzan, I really like how you used the phrase *victim's soft flesh*. By placing the word *soft* in there, you really emphasized the difference between the attacker and the victim. And I like the phrase *felt the cold waters close above my head*. It sounds so deadly—and final."

"I'm just trying to copy your writing style," Tarzan said modestly.

"Well, you're still the writer, and you're good! Very good!"

Tarzan beamed with pride.

"Anyway," I said, "there are only three errors to go over."

It didn't seem to me that it would take very long to talk about only three errors. That meant we'd have plenty of time afterward to talk about what was on my mind.

"Okay, let's look at the first underline," I said. "In the first sentence I underlined the phrase *the lioness* in the clause 'Sabor the lioness sprang at us . . .'"

"Now that I'm looking at that, I think I know why you underlined it."

"Why?"

"Because *the lioness* is nonrestrictive. I've already identified who I'm talking about—Sabor. That means that the phrase *the lioness* is just extra information; the sentence would still make sense without it. You could say the phrase is parenthetical. Or you could say it's an appositive. Anyway, it should be surrounded by commas." Tarzan took the notebook and wrote: "Sabor, the lioness, sprang at us . . ."

"That's it exactly," I said. "Very good. Okay, now let's look at the next underline. I underlined the word *death* in the phrase *behind me, the jaws of death.*"

"What's wrong with that?"

"Well, do you know what *personification* means?"

"No."

"Well, sometimes writers talk about objects or ideas as if they are living beings. They give them personalities or human characteristics. They might say something like *As he walked, Danger crept along behind him.* Now, danger isn't something with legs that's capable of creeping, right? But a writer might *pretend* that danger has legs and can creep. Anyway, the giving of human attributes to objects or ideas is known as *personification.*"

"Oh."

"There are some famous characters that are actually personifications. For example, Jack Frost is the personification of cold weather. And Uncle Sam is the personification of the United States."

"Oh."

"Anyway, you spoke of the 'jaws of death.' Now, death doesn't really have jaws. But *people* have jaws. So, even if you didn't realize it, by using the phrase *the jaws of death*, you were personifying death. And the rule is, when you personify something, you capitalize it. You should have written this." I took the notebook and wrote: *behind me, the jaws of Death.* "Do you see? By capitalizing the word *Death* you show that you're personifying it."

"I see."

Only one more underline to go. *Boom-boom-boom.*

"N-now let's look at the last underline, in the last paragraph, where you wrote *the water was the best choice.*

"What's wrong with that. The other choice was the lion. I was only ten years old. Sabor would have eaten me."

"I'm not saying you should have chosen the Sabor over the water. I'm saying that you made a mistake in usage. Instead of saying that the water was the *best* choice you should have said that the water was the *better* choice. You see, if you're comparing only two things, then you use the word *better*—one is *better* than the other. But if you're comparing *more* than two things, you use the word *best*—one of the things is the *best* of all."

"So I would say 'Which is *better*, fruit or meat?' and I would say 'Which is *best*, fruit, meat, or fish?' Is that right?"

"That's right. Are you hungry? It's still early."

"No, I'm not hungry. What do you want to do for the rest of the day?"

I knew what I wanted to do. I wanted to hear Tarzan say "Oh Jane, I love you too." Then we could talk about getting married. Instead I just said, "I don't know. What do you want to do?"

"I don't know."

"Well, actually, there's something I have to talk to you about."

"What?"

Boom-boom-boom.

"Um, d-do you think the chimps will bring the diamonds and gold on schedule? D-do you think they understood the concept of days—or suns or moons?"

"I told you, I don't think the plan will work."

"Well, that's not really what I wanted to talk about."

Tarzan lifted his eyes to me in that way he had.

"It's just that I have to tell you that . . . that . . . that there's something I forgot to tell you about that I saw in that book about animals I was reading."

"What?"

"Well, it said that the nest of a bald eagle sometimes weighs as much as two tons."

"How can that be? A bird's nest?"

"I don't know, but that's what it said."

Chapter 27: Tarzan Recalls Learning to Swim

The next morning, while Tarzan wrote at the table, I sat on the bed in a funk. Why couldn't I tell him that I was in love with him? Why was I so afraid?

When I was in the seventh grade, boys and girls sometimes passed each other notes saying that they liked each other. Maybe I should write Tarzan a little note like that. No, that was too babyish. But I had to do something. Maybe I should simply *hint* that I loved him—you know, tell him indirectly somehow.

When I thought about how to *indirectly* tell Tarzan that I loved him, I realized that I had completely forgotten to teach him something about grammar! I'd never told him about something call an *indirect object*. Now, not only was I a failure at confessing my feelings, I was also a failure as a grammar teacher. Well, the grammar oversight could be easily remedied.

"Tarzan?"

"Yes?"

"I know you're working on Article 14, but could you stop for a minute? I just realized that there's something I forgot to teach you about grammar."

"What?"

"Well, do you remember that I said that in a sentence like 'Jane kicked the ball,' the verb is *kicked* and the object of the verb is *ball?*"

"I remember. You said that the object is whatever the action is being done to. In that example, the kicking is being done to the ball. You already taught me about that."

"I know. But in a sentence like that, you can call the word *ball* a *direct object*—because the ball is *directly* receiving the action of kicking. But some sentences contain both a direct object and an *indirect object*."

"What's an indirect object?"

"Well, an indirect object usually occurs in sentences that contain a verb like *give* or *tell*. It comes before the direct object and names the receiver of whatever is given or told."

"I don't understand."

"Well, I'll give you an example. Let's take the sentence 'Jane gave Tarzan a note.' See, that sentence not only tells what was given—a note—but it also tells who received it—Tarzan."

"Why would you give me a note? Why wouldn't you just tell me something out loud?"

347

"Um, that was just an example. Anyway, in that sentence, the *direct* object is the thing actually given or told—in this case, a note. The *indirect* object names the receiver of whatever is given or told—in this case Tarzan. Do you see?"

"I think so."

"I'll give you another sentence and we'll see if you can identify the direct object and the indirect object. Try this one: 'Jane told Cheetah a secret.'"

"What did you tell him? Tell me!"

"No, that was an example. I didn't tell him anything," I said. *But if I had told him a secret, it would have been that I love you*, I thought.

"Oh. Well, in that sentence, first of all, the verb is *told*," Tarzan said. "The direct object is *secret*, because that's the thing that's actually being told. The indirect object is *Cheetah*, because that's who's *receiving* the secret."

"Good!"

"Actually, it was kind of easy to tell that *Cheetah* is the indirect object because you said that the indirect object comes *before* the direct object."

"That's right."

"But couldn't you change the sentence to say 'Jane told a secret to Cheetah'? Then 'Cheetah' comes *after* 'secret.'"

"Well, in that case, *Cheetah* becomes the object of the prepositional phrase 'to Cheetah,' and the entire prepositional phrase *functions* as the indirect object of the sentence. When you use a prepositional phrase as an indirect object, the prepositional phrase comes *after* the direct object. Isn't that fascinating?"

"I guess."

Silence for a moment.

"Well," Tarzan finally said, "are you sure that there's no secret you want to tell Cheetah and that there's no note you want to give me?"

"Uh . . . um . . . I'm sure."

"Then can I go back to writing Article 14?"

"Okay."

I didn't say anything else to Tarzan after that because I was eager for him to finish Article 14. I couldn't wait to see what happened after the cold waters of the lake closed over his head!

While he wrote, I calculated how many days were left until the chimps brought us the ten million dollars; it was five. After that I thumbed through the book about Africa, which contained an interesting item. Apparently, once when an African man was fast asleep in a tent, a snake slithered down his throat. The next day, the man could feel the snake moving inside him. Instead of going to a doctor to have the snake removed, as you might expect, he simply prepared a bowl of hot milk. Then he hung himself upside down by his feet over the bowl. The snake, attracted by the smell of the milk, crawled back out of him.

I was about to mention this story to Tarzan when he suddenly said, "Okay, I'm finished with Article 14."

I went to the table, sat down, and began to read aloud, underlining the errors as I found them. When I was through, I saw that again there were only three. It looked like this:

Article 14: "Learning to Swim"

I didn't know how to swim, and the water was very deep. But, more by accident than design, I rapidly moved my hands and feet and fell into the stroke that a dog uses when swimming. In a few seconds my nose was above the water and I found that I could keep it there, and make progress through the water, by continuing my strokes.

I was surprised and pleased with this new skill, but I had no time to think about it. I was now swimming parallel to the shore and there I saw Sabor crouching upon the still form of my friend. I felt <u>badly</u> for him, but it was too late to do anything about it.

The lioness intently watched me, evidently expecting me to return to shore, but I had no intention of doing that. Instead, I raised my voice in the call of distress common to my tribe, adding to it the warning that would prevent would-be rescuers from running into the jaws of Sabor.

Almost immediately there came an answer from the distance, and 40 or 50 great apes swung rapidly and majestically through the trees toward the scene of tragedy. In the lead was my ape mother, Kala, for she had recognized the tones of her beloved son, and with her was the mother of the poor little ape who lay dead beneath cruel Sabor.

Though more powerful and better equipped for fighting than the apes, the lioness had no desire to meet these enraged adults, and with a snarl of hatred she sprang quickly into the bushes and disappeared.

I quickly swam to shore and climbed upon dry land. The feeling of refreshment the cool water had given me filled me with grateful surprise. Since then I've loved the water. I especially <u>love:</u> diving into a lake, jumping into a river, and <u>to swim</u> in the ocean.

"Wow! So that's how you learned to love the water! But I feel bad for your poor friend. Did Sabor eat your friend after she killed him? Never mind. Don't answer that. I don't want to know."

Tarzan took me literally and said nothing.

"Anyway, I liked the phrase *a snarl of hatred*. I can just imagine what that sounded like—and what Sabor must have looked like!"

Again Tarzan didn't answer.

"Okay, well, anyway, let's look at these underlines. The first one is in the second paragraph. You were talking about your ape friend, the one Sabor killed, and you said that you felt *badly* for him."

"What's wrong with that? *Badly* is an adverb. It modifies the verb *felt*."

"Well, do you remember that time we took a walk along the beach? Do you remember that I said that some verbs, like *run*, are action verbs, and other verbs, like *feel*, *look*, and *smell*, are state-of-being verbs?"

"Now I remember," he said, nodding. "You said that with some verbs you don't actually *do* anything; you just *are* a certain way. And you said that when you have a verb like that, instead of using an *adverb* to modify the *verb*, you use an *adjective* to modify the *subject* of the sentence."

"Right. So what should you have written in your article?"

"I should have written that I felt *bad* for my friend—not *badly* for my friend. The adjective *bad* modifies the subject, *I*."

"Right. Good. Okay, now let's go on to the next underline—in the last sentence of the article. After the word *love* you put a colon." Saying the word *love* out loud reminded me of the conversation I was going to have with Tarzan after this lesson, and I felt my pulse quicken.

"I put a colon there because I was introducing a list of water activities I love."

"Well, if you had written 'I especially love *the following*,' then it would be correct to put a colon after the word *following* to introduce the list. But without the phrase *the following*—or some other similar phrase—the list of water activities simply functions as the object of the verb *love*. For example, If you write . . . oh . . . let's say . . . *Tarzan loves Jane*, you wouldn't put a colon after the word *loves*, would you?" I didn't give him a chance to answer that. "Anyway, you should never place a colon between a verb and its object."

"Okay." Then after a pause: "And at the end of that sentence, why did you underline the words *to swim*? I *do* like to swim in the ocean."

"I know you do. I underlined *to swim* because you violated the rules of *parallelism.*"

"Parallelism?"

"Sometimes in a sentence you have two or more elements that need to match each other in some way; for example, if they happen to be verbs, they might need to match each other in tense or mood. The use of properly matching grammatical constructions is known as *parallelism.*"

"What did I do wrong? I mean, what did I do that was *un*-parallel?"

"Well, look at the list of activities. In the first two you used a present participle: *diving* into a lake and *jumping* into a river. But in the third activity, you used an infinitive: *to swim* in the ocean. That's not parallel construction."

"So, what should I have written?"

"You need to use the same verb form for all three activities—to make the construction parallel, I mean. So, you could use present participles for all three activities: 'I especially love *diving* into a lake, *jumping* into a river, and *swimming* in the ocean.' Or you could use infinitives for all three activities: 'I especially love *to dive* into a lake, *to jump* into a river, and *to swim* in the ocean.' Either way is okay. The only thing that's not okay is mixing your verb forms in the same sentence. Do you see?"

"I do. So, that's it for that article. Are you ready for brunch?"

"Well ... I ... um ... there's something I have to talk to you about first. *Boom-boom-boom.* Do you remember when I said that ... I adore you?"

"Yes," he answered, with that upward inflection he uses when he knows I have more to say.

"Well, I just want you to know that ... that ... I really meant it."

"Well, I adore you too, Jane. You know that."

"But there's more, Tarzan. I have to tell you something else."

"What?"

But what if I told him that I loved him and then he said, "That's *your* problem"? I wouldn't be able to bear it. I couldn't bring myself to tell him yet.

"It's just that there's something I forgot to say ... about ... that book I was reading about animals."

"What?"

"It said that ... that snails that live in the desert sometimes sleep for *four years* at a time."

"Really? Which desert, the Sahara?"

"I don't know. It didn't say. I guess any desert." Long pause. "But I have to tell you one other thing."

"What?"

"Um . . . It also said that a snail's mouth is only as big as the head of a pin but that it contains over 25,000 teeth."

"How can that be possible? They must be microscopic."

"I guess they are, then."

"Is that all you wanted to tell me?"

"Um . . . yes . . ." I said weakly, trailing off into nothingness.

After brunch, there we were again at our usual places. I glanced over at Tarzan, who was hard at work at the table, and said, "Do you remember this morning when we were talking about snails in the desert? Do you think we should visit the desert?"

"Why should we do that? It's very hot and dry there."

"But we've visited all sorts of other places in Africa—a waterfall, a cave, a mountain, a watering hole, a river, an island."

"So?"

"Well, we never go anywhere anymore. We used to have so much fun exploring different locations. Now all we do is sit around the cabin every day. Don't you ever want to go out?"

"I have to write these articles for *American Monthly*. You know that."

"But we could take a break. The Sahara Desert is the biggest desert in the world, and it's right here in Africa. It would be a shame if I never got to see it."

"If we went there we would die from the heat or from lack of water."

"No, we wouldn't. We could ride on camels and find an oasis. We could even go swimming—like we used to. Come on, let's go there right now."

"Are you serious? It's not near here. It's pretty far north."

"We could ride on an elephant until we got there, and then we could switch to camels."

"Well—"

"I'll tell you what. We can go there and see how we like it, and then if we don't like it we can come back to the cabin. Now, what can be fairer than that?"

"Jane, you can't just go to the desert like that. You have to prepare. You need supplies."

"Like what?"

"Like a canteen filled with water."

"Do you have a canteen?"

"No."

"Well, couldn't you make one? You know, out of some kind of material around here?"

"I don't know."

I decided to read a little about the Sahara Desert in that book about Africa. "Okay, why don't you go back to writing your article," I suggested. "I'll read on the bed."

Tarzan went back to work and I turned to the index of the book on Africa and looked up "Sahara Desert."

I read awhile and then said, "Tarzan, it says here that the Sahara Desert is not all sand dunes. It has mountain ranges and underground streams and everything."

"But it's mostly sand dunes, right?"

"No, it says that only about *fifteen percent* of the desert is sand dunes. Most of it is rocky plateaus and gravelly plains—whatever *that* means. And there are huge mountain ranges. Some of the mountains are over *ten thousand feet high*. They're so high that *snow* sometimes covers the peaks."

"Really?"

"That's what it says."

"Well, we can't go there now. In five days I'll be finished with all these articles. Besides, you need to be here when the hundred chimps arrive with the ten million dollars."

"I thought you don't believe in that."

"I don't, but *you* do."

I didn't know how to answer that. Finally I said, "But I want to go *swimming!*"

"You can go swimming. Why don't you go swim in that river near here—the one where you saw a hippo."

"But I don't want to go alone. I'm scared of the crocodile. I want you to go with me."

"But I'm in the middle of this article."

Silence

"Here's an idea," he said. "If you're bored, why don't you go outside and look for Yemmy and Omy—or Cheetah. That should cheer you up. Besides, if you're not here, I can concentrate even *better* on this article."

Now he was trying to get rid of me!

"Okay," I said, getting up from the bed. I dragged myself to the door, feeling depressed.

I wandered outside and in a rather weak voice called, "Yeeem-my, Ooom-my." I didn't see them anywhere. Then I called, "Cheee-tah." I didn't see him either.

I wandered back into the cabin and sat back on the bed.

"They're not there," I reported.

"Oh. Well, that's okay. I'm just about finished with Article 15. Just wait."

"Okay."

I sat on the bed and did absolutely nothing for the next five minutes. Wait, that's not true. I thought about what in the world I was doing here in Africa. Maybe Tarzan didn't even want me around. Maybe I should just go back to Baltimore right now. Maybe no chimps would arrive in five days. And what about that idea my boss at *American Monthly* had about putting Tarzan on display in New York City. That's ridiculous. Who is he anyway, King Kong?

"I'm finished," I heard Tarzan say.

I dragged myself to the table. I wasn't really in the mood to give another grammar lesson, but I didn't say anything. Then it suddenly occurred to me: What if I feel so down and depressed right now because I'd been bitten by a disease-carrying mosquito. Maybe I had malaria or yellow fever or African sleeping sickness or something.

I sat in the chair next to Tarzan and said, "Tarzan, feel my forehead and tell me if it feels hot."

"Do you think you have a fever?"

"I don't know. Feel it."

He put the palm of his hand on my forehead and kept it there for a long time. Finally he said, "I don't know. It's hot in the cabin, so it's hard to tell if your forehead is hotter than normal."

"Okay, never mind." I felt my own head, but I couldn't tell either. I mean, my forehead felt like the same temperature as my hand. "Let me see the article."

He handed it to me, but it would have required too much effort for me to read it out loud.

"Look," I said, "I can't sit here anymore. I think I'm dehydrated or something. I have to go in the water. We have to go swimming *right now*."

"Okay, okay. Where?"

"I don't care."

I walked to the door. From the table Tarzan said, "Should I bring the notebook?"

"I don't care."

He picked up the notebook and a pencil and followed me out the door.

"Let's go to the closest place," he said. "The first place we ever swam together—the river near here."

"Fine."

We walked in silence all the way to the river. When we arrived it looked exactly as I remembered it.

"Check for crocodiles," I ordered. Then I added, "Please."

Tarzan put down the notebook and pencil, walked into the river, and then submerged himself. After a while he resurfaced and said, "It's all clear."

Like some kind of automaton, I marched into the river. I swam out a way and then completely submerged myself, including my head and my hair. Then I stood up; only my head was above water. Tarzan was a few feet from me.

"Is this water safe to drink?" I asked.

"I think so. I've done it before and nothing happened."

I took a long drink, then another, then another.

"Check for crocodiles again . . . please."

Tarzan submerged himself again and then resurfaced.

"All clear."

"Good." I suddenly felt about a hundred percent better. I don't think I had malaria or anything. I think I was just dehydrated.

We swam around a little—but for some reason we didn't splash each other or perform underwater somersaults or anything like we used to. I don't know why we didn't; we just didn't.

"Do you want to sit by the edge and go over Article 15?" Tarzan suddenly said.

"Okay."

We swam a few feet toward the bank and then stood and walked the rest of the way out. After we shook the water from our bodies, Tarzan picked up the notebook and pencil. We both sat facing the river. I felt pretty healthy again.

I searched the opposite bank and the surface of the river for crocodiles. I didn't see any. Still, one could have been underwater, I suppose. But Tarzan was with me so I felt safe.

"Do you want to read this out loud to me," he said.

"How about if this time you read it out loud to me? I'll sit right next to you so that I can underline the mistakes as you read."

"Okay." He handed me the pencil and I snuggled up right next to him.

He started to read. I liked the sound of his voice; it was soothing. Every so often I underlined a word or phrase in the article. Whenever I did, he slowed down a little in his reading but didn't stop; he understood that we'd discuss all the errors at once.

Anyway, when he was finished reading and I was finished underlining, the article looked like this:

Article 15: "The Hunting Knife"

When I first discovered a cabin by the shore, I had no idea that it was the cabin my father built after he and my mother had been put ashore by a group of mutineers. I loved exploring that cabin, where I found many strange and interesting things-furniture and tools and books and clothing.

One day a shiny blade of steel caught my eye. I picked it up and accidentally cut my finger. It was a hunting knife. Very carefully I experimented with it and found that it could cut chunks of wood from the table and chairs. I decided to bring it with me to show my fellow apes.

I had only walked a few steps into the jungle when a great form rose before me from the shadows. At first I thought it was one of my own people, but in another instant I realized that it was a huge gorilla from a fierce enemy tribe.

He was so close that there was no chance for me to escape, and I knew that I must stand and fight for my life. I met the brute midway in its charge, striking its huge body with my closed fists. But he was so much bigger than me that I might as well have been a fly attacking an elephant!

But in one hand I still clutched the hunting knife I had found in the cabin, and as the brute closed in on me I automatically turned the sharp point toward him. As it sank deep into its body, the hairy beast shrieked in pain and rage.

In that brief second I learned a new use for my sharp and shining toy. As the raging, clawing beast dragged me to the ground, I plunged the blade repeatedly into its chest. At the same time, he struck terrific blows with his open hand and tore at my throat and arms with his mighty teeth.

For a moment we rolled upon the ground in a fierce frenzy. More and more weakly my torn and bleeding arm struck home with the sharp blade. Then suddenly the great gorilla stiffened with a jerk and rolled lifeless upon the dead vegetation that carpeted the jungle. He was stone dead.

"Yikes!" I said. "I can't believe you had to fight a giant gorilla. How *horrible!*"

Tarzan didn't answer.

"I like how you're so descriptive in your writing. You could have said that the gorilla rolled lifeless upon the *ground* or the *floor,* but you said that he rolled lifeless on the *dead vegetation that carpeted the jungle.* I can just *see* that. You're such a good *writer!*"

Tarzan smiled a little.

"Okay," I said, "now let's go over the errors."

It felt good to be outdoors again. Staying in the cabin day after day was making me batty. Why did we do that, anyway? I guess it started when I sprained my ankle and I *had* to stay in. Then we just got into the habit, I guess.

"Why'd you put that underline at the end of the first paragraph?" Tarzan said.

"I was really underlining the hyphen after the word *things.* The list of strange and interesting things you found *explains* what you said earlier in the sentence, so you should have used a *dash*—an em dash, I mean—instead of a hyphen."

It occurred to me that Tarzan might try to claim that he *did* write an em dash but that he just happened to make it kind of short. But all he said was, "Oh. Now I remember."

"Good. Okay, now, in the second paragraph you wrote 'I decided to *bring* it with me . . .'"

"What's wrong with that?"

"It's a mistake in usage. You have to understand the difference between the words *bring* and *take.*" I scanned the area for crocodiles again. Actually, I sort of did that continuously while we sat there.

"What's the difference?"

"Well, it's a little tricky to explain. It has to do with the direction of movement—either toward or away from the speaker or from the person or place you're talking about."

"I don't understand."

"Well, the word *take* really means 'go *there* with that.' Someone's going *there*—to a place other than where you already are. He's going *away.*"

I let that sink in for a second. Then I said, "but the word *bring* really means 'come *here* with that.' Someone's coming *here*—back to the place where you already are. He coming *toward* you."

I let that sink in. Then I said, "So, let's say that you want me to take a message to Cheetah and bring you his response. You see, you'd say *take* a message to Cheetah—because I'd be going *away* from you—and *bring* you his response—because I'd be coming *toward* you. Do you see?"

"I guess so. But what if I—the speaker—weren't involved in the sentence at all? For example, I could say 'Yemmy took a message to Cheetah.' Or I could say 'Yemmy brought a message to Cheetah.' Which one of those sentences is correct?"

"Well, that's where it gets really tricky. Then you have to decide whether you want to describe things from Yemmy's point of view or from Cheetah's point of view."

"What do you mean?"

"Wait. Do you see any crocodiles?"

Tarzan made a full scan of the area. "No."

"Okay. What I mean is, if you're thinking of Yemmy as the focus of the sentence, then from Yemmy's point of view, he's going *away*, toward Cheetah, so you would say 'Yemmy *took* a message to Cheetah.' But if you're thinking of Cheetah as the focus of the sentence, then from Cheetah's point of view, Yemmy is *coming toward him*, so you would say: Yemmy *brought* a message to Cheetah."

"But how am I supposed to know which one is the focus of the sentence?"

"Well, it's not a matter of *knowing*; it's a matter of deciding. You're the writer, so it's whichever one *you* decide is the focus. It's another case of writer's choice."

"Oh."

"All right. Now let's go on to the next underline—at the beginning of the third paragraph. You wrote 'I had *only walked* a few steps . . .' Are you trying to say that you didn't hop, skip, or jump a few steps; that you only *walked* a few steps?" (I knew he didn't mean that; I was just being a smarty pants.)

"No, I meant that it was only a few steps that I had walked."

"Okay, then that's what you have to say. You see, you placed the adverb *only* in the wrong place in the sentence. We talked about this once before—when we were at the beach, I think. Anyway, the problem is that if you place *only* before *walked*, that means that you did nothing but *walk*."

"I understand. I should have written 'I had walked only a few steps . . .' That would have made it clear that it was *only a few steps* that I had walked."

"Good. Okay, now let's look at the last underline. In the fourth paragraph you wrote: 'he was so much bigger than me . . .'"

"What's wrong with that? He *was* bigger."

"I believe you that he was bigger. But you should have said 'bigger than *I.*'"

"Why? Isn't that one of those examples of trying to show off that you have good grammar when you really don't?"

"No. *Bigger than I* is actually correct. You see, you would use the word *me* if it functioned as the object of a verb—as in *hold me*—or the object of a preposition—as in *tell it to me.* But in the phrase *bigger than,* what part of speech is the word *than?*"

"Um . . ."

"It's a conjunction."

"It's not a preposition?"

"Well, probably some people think it is, and that's why they say things like *bigger than me.* But it's really a *conjunction* used to introduce the second element of an unequal comparison. So, in your article, what you're *really* saying is 'he was so much bigger than *I was.*' But the last word—*was*—is left out; it's understood."

"Oh."

"But you can see that if you *were* to include that last word—*was*—then *I* would be the correct pronoun—because it's the subject of *was,* I mean."

"But I still think it sounds like you're trying to show off if you say something like *bigger than I.* It doesn't sound natural."

"Then you can say *bigger than I was.* That sounds natural."

"Okay."

Just then I realized that sometimes you *should* use the word *me* after the word *than.*

"But sometimes," I said, "it's *correct* to use an objective-case word like *me* after the word *than.*"

"It is?"

"Yes. Because sometimes the word *me* really is the *object* of a verb—a verb that was omitted from the sentence because it's understood, I mean."

"Huh?"

"Well, let's say that I said 'You like Cheetah better than *me.*'"

"But that would be wrong. You just explained that. You said that that would really mean 'You like Cheetah better than *I do.*'"

"Well, that's what I would mean if I said 'You like Cheetah better than *I.*' But if I say 'You like Cheetah better than *me,*' I really mean 'You like Cheetah better than *you like* me.' Do you see? In that case, the words *you like* are left out because they're understood, but the word *me* is really the *object* of the verb *like*. So it's in the *objective case—me*."

"I can see that. So, in my article, was it really okay for me to say that the gorilla was *bigger than me?*"

"Well, what do you think? In your article is the pronoun—*I* or *me*—the *subject* of the understood verb *was* or the *object* of some omitted, understood verb?

"It's the subject of the understood verb *was*. The gorilla was bigger than *I was*."

"Then there's your answer. In your article, it wouldn't have been okay to say *bigger than me*."

We sat in silence for a while and then I said, "Well, that takes care of Article 15. Now what should we do? Should we stay here and swim in the river, or should we go back to the cabin?"

"I don't know. What do you want to do?"

"Hey! Look across there on the other side of the river." I pointed. "Is that a log or a crocodile?"

"I think it's a log."

"I think it looks more like a crocodile. He's asleep, I think."

"Do you want me to swim over there and take a look? Then we'd know for sure."

"No! You might get hurt."

"No I won't."

With that, Tarzan stood up, plunged into the river, and swam half-way across.

"It's definitely a log!" he called. "I can see it clearly from here." Then he yelled, "Come in the water."

I got up, walked into the water, and waded to where Tarzan was. We swam around awhile, but it wasn't a lot of fun. He didn't splash me or throw me in the air or anything. Maybe he didn't like me anymore. Maybe he thought that I looked down at him because he still made a few grammatical errors. But he wanted me to teach him, didn't he?

After a while we noticed that the day was ending. "I guess I should walk you back to the cabin," he said.

"Okay."

When we walked back we didn't hold hands or even talk—nothing. Five minutes of silence.

"Well . . ." he said, when we got to the door.

"Hey!" I said, "We forgot to have dinner. What about dinner?"

"Oh, I guess we forgot. I guess I wasn't very hungry. Are you hungry?"

For some reason I wasn't very hungry either. Still, I thought we should have something.

"I'm not hungry either. But we should have something. Otherwise, we'll get hungry later."

"Is there anything left over from brunch?" he said.

"Just some berries."

"That's good. Let's have that."

We walked to the table and each ate a handful of berries, standing up. Then Tarzan said, "Well, goodnight. See you tomorrow morning."

He walked out the door and was gone.

Suddenly I ran to the doorway and shrieked, "Wait! I forgot to tell you something!"

He turned. "What?"

"Something very important that I've been thinking about."

"What?"

"I lo-lo-lo-"

"What?"

"I l-l-l-looked at a map of Africa and saw that the Sahara Desert is about the same size as the entire United States."

"Really?"

"Really."

"Okay, well, I'll see you tomorrow morning."

"Good night."

Dejectedly I turned around, went inside, and went to bed. It took a long time to fall asleep.

Chapter 28: Tarzan Recalls Learning to Read

The next morning, the sound of rain beating on the roof woke me—or, I should say, *half* woke me. I was in that strange, in-between state of sleep and consciousness. Whether the images that ran through my mind were dreams or thoughts is hard to say. First I was telling Tarzan that I loved him and he was saying "Oh Jane, I love you too; I've *always* loved you." Next I saw 100 chimps bringing me ten million dollars worth of sparkling jewels. But then I imagined Tarzan saying "You love me? That's *your* problem." And then I saw only three chimps bringing me nothing but a spider, a snake, and a dead mouse! The images, which somehow blended together, swirled through my half-consciousness.

"Good morning!" It was Tarzan, standing in the doorway. For real.

"Wha . . ."

"Good morning!"

"What? Oh, it's you." Now I was fully awake and I sat up.

Tarzan was all wet from the rain, but he didn't seem to care. But that's understandable—because he'd been raised by animals, I mean. His soaked hair was flattened down and that made his face look odd. But he didn't even know. He shook the water from himself like a dog does and entered the cabin.

"How do you feel?" he asked, concernedly.

"Okay, I guess. I'm just tired. I didn't sleep much last night."

"Why?"

"I was just thinking about things."

"Like what?"

"Well . . . I don't want to say."

"Come on . . . tell me."

Now I was *really* awake. I got up and walked to the table. We each sat in our accustomed seats—our *newer* accustomed seats, I mean, with Tarzan to my left.

We stared into each other's eyes and then Tarzan said, "What's the matter?"

"Well, it's about . . . us."

"What do you mean? Is something wrong?"

"Well, can I ask you a question? What do you think about . . . about . . . me?"

"Jane, you know I like you. I adore you, just like you adore me. We've told each other that."

"But do you lo . . . do you lo . . . I mean, what I want to know is, What do you think about *us*?"

"Us?"

"I mean, what do you think about our *relationship*?"

"Relationship?"

It was so frustrating! How can you have a meaningful "relationship" conversation with someone who has no real social skills—except for social skills with monkeys? I mean apes.

"Okay, look, why don't you sit here and work on Article 16," I said. "I'll sit next to you and read, okay?"

"I think I could concentrate better if you weren't sitting so close to me."

What! Now was he trying to get rid of me again? But wait. Maybe he meant that he wouldn't be able to concentrate because I would be too much of a distraction—because he loves me! Which did he mean? Could I just ask him? No, he would just say something meaningless or ambiguous like "What do I *mean*?"

After a long pause I stood up a took a book at random from the shelf. I sat at the table across from him and said sarcastically, "Is this far enough away?"

He didn't answer. He was already working on his article.

I stayed put in the seat and started aimlessly thumbing through the book. It was one I hadn't read before—about insects.

"How many more days until the chimps bring the money?" I ventured.

"I don't know."

"I think it's four. Something like that."

"That's nice," he answered, as if there were nothing in the world that could interest him less.

It's so hard to know what he's thinking, I thought. I mean, he never acts overly sad or overly happy about anything. He's always the same. Always in the same mood.

"Can I ask you something?" I said.

He stopped writing and looked up at me.

"I think you're very hard to read. I often wonder what you think about. For example, what are you thinking about right now?"

"Thinking about?"

"Yes! What are you thinking right now?"

"I don't know."

"You must know. Now, think! What are you thinking about?"

"I'm thinking . . . I guess I'm wondering: What *am* I thinking about?"

"Okay, forget that. What were you thinking just before I asked you what you were thinking about?"

"Before that?"

"Yes!"

"Um . . . I was thinking about what I was writing in my article."

It was no use. Maybe after we finished going over the errors in Article 16 I would try again. Maybe I would simply declare my love once and for all. What could he say? Then it occurred to me. All along, I thought that he'd give one of two possible responses: "I love you too" or "That's *your* problem." But now I realized that he'd probably just repeat what I said, but as a question. I'd say, "Tarzan, I love you," and he'd say, "Love me?"

"Never mind," I said. "Go back to your writing."

I looked through the book again. Every so often I glanced up at Tarzan. His tongue stuck out a little as he wrote.

After about two or three minutes of silence—except for the beating of the rain on the roof—I said, "Tarzan, here's an interesting fact in this book. How many insects do you think there are in the world for each human being?"

"I don't know. About a thousand?"

"It says that for each human, there are two hundred million insects. *Two hundred million!* That means that if there were a war between people and bugs, each person would be responsible for fighting two hundred million bugs. Do you think you can win in a fight against that many?"

"I don't know. I guess it depends on what kind of bugs I have to fight."

"Well, it says that the biggest bug in the world lives right here in Africa. It's a kind of beetle that weighs a quarter of a pound. It's so big, it can peel a banana."

"Really?"

"That's what it says."

Tarzan continued to write and I scanned the floor of the cabin for banana-peeling beetles. I didn't see any.

Finally I heard Tarzan say, "Okay, I'm finished with Article 16." He handed the notebook to me and I read the article aloud, underlining errors as I spotted them. When I was finished, the article looked like this:

Article 16: "Learning to Read"

One day in my father's cabin I found a shelf of books that included a first grader's "learn to read" book, other <u>childrens'</u> readers, numerous picture books, and a great dictionary. Their pages were filled with mysterious squiggly lines that looked like little bugs. I wondered what they could possibly mean.

In one book I found a picture of a little ape similar to me. Beneath the picture were three little <u>bugs,</u> B-O-Y. I discovered in the text upon that page that these three bugs were repeated many times in the same sequence. I also noticed that there were relatively few individual bugs, but that the same ones were repeated <u>alot</u>, sometimes alone, but more often in company with others.

I slowly turned pages, scanning the pictures and text for a repetition of the combination B-O-Y. I found it beneath a picture of another little ape and a strange little animal <u>who</u> walked on four legs. Beneath this picture the bugs appeared as: A BOY AND A DOG. There they were, the three little bugs that always accompanied the little ape.

Because each of the pictures <u>were</u> accompanied by a set of bugs, I was able to teach myself to read. I didn't accomplish it in a day, or in a week, or in a month, or in a year. But by the time I was 15 I knew the various combinations of letters that stood for every illustration in one or two of the picture books. And by the time I was 17, I could read fairly well.

I no longer felt ashamed of my hairless body and human features, for now my reason told me that I was of a different race than my wild and hairy companions. I was a MAN and they were APES!

"Tarzan," I said, "that is an amazing story. I'm so proud of you for teaching yourself to read like that. You must be very smart. Brilliant!"

He blushed a little.

Just then something occurred to me.

"Tarzan, in your story, you explain how you taught yourself to read, but how did you know what the letters sounded like?" I mean, how did you know that an M sounded like *mmm?* I mean, how did you learn to speak?"

"Well, some time after I taught myself to read, an English explorer passed through this area. Anyway, he was attacked and nearly torn to pieces by a huge ape—not one from my tribe. After I rescued him, I spent a couple of weeks nursing him back to health. We communicated by writing each other messages on paper. During that time he taught me the sounds of all the letters and how to speak English a little. Then when he was up to it, he returned home."

"Very interesting. So I'm not the first human you've ever seen."

"No, but you're the first human female I've seen."

That sounded so unromantic: *human female.* That's all I was to him, I guess: a human female. I might as well be a female dragonfly.

"All right," I said, a little wearily. Let's go over the errors." Then: "Is it okay if I sit next to you so that you can see?"

"Okay." (He didn't even realize that I was being sarcastic.)

I sat in the chair to his right and looked at him a moment. His hair had dried and his face looked normal again.

"Okay," I said, "in the first sentence I underlined the word *childrens'* in the phrase *other childens' readers."*

"What's wrong with that? I put an apostrophe at the end to show that the word was possessive—*childens' readers."*

"Well, you're right that an apostrophe is used to indicate a possessive-case noun, but you put the apostrophe in the wrong place." I took a deep breath because I knew that explaining the use of the apostrophe to show possession was going to be tricky. "Basically, there are three rules you're going to have to memorize about using apostrophes—and sometimes *s's*—to show possession. But the tricky thing is, even though everyone—grammar experts, I mean—agree on the first two rules, they don't all agree on the third one. So, for that third rule, all I can do is tell you how we do things at *American Monthly,* okay?"

"Okay."

"Now, the first rule is that to show the possessive case of a word that *doesn't* end in an s, you add apostrophe followed by an s. For example, the possessive case of *boy* is *boy's*." I wrote *boys* and *boy's* in the notebook so that he could see. "And it doesn't matter if the word in question is singular or plural. Even for *plural* nouns that don't end in s, to show the possessive case you add an apostrophe followed by an s."

"How can a word that's plural not end in an *s*?"

"Well, not every plural ends in s. For example, what's the plural of *man*."

"Men."

"Right. And what's the plural of *woman*?"

"Women."

"Right. And what's the plural of child?"

"Childrens—no, children."

"Right. The plural of *child* is *children*, not *childrens*. You see, all those words—men, women, children—are plurals, but they don't end in s. So to make them possessive, you add an apostrophe followed by an s." In the notebook I wrote—and at the same time said aloud—*men's, women's, children's*. Then I wrote: *men's pants, women's skirts, children's toys*. "Do you see?"

"I do. The word *children* doesn't end in s, so in my article I should have written *other children's readers*." At the same time he spoke the phrase, he wrote it in the notebook so that I could see that he knew that the apostrophe goes after the n, before the s.

"Very good. Now, the second rule is that if you have a plural noun that *does* end in s, to show the possessive case, you add only an apostrophe." In the notebook, I wrote—and said aloud at the same time—*hornets' nest, countries' governments*. "You see? Those words are plural and they end in s—*hornets, countries*. And to make them possessive I don't add an apostrophe and another s; I just add an apostrophe."

Tarzan nodded.

"Okay, now the third rule is the tricky one. This rule is about showing the possessive case of singular nouns that end in s—or that end in an s sound."

"How can a singular noun end in *s*? Wouldn't the s make it plural?"

"Well, for example, lots of people's names end in s. Those names are proper nouns, but they're singular. For example, the first names *Lois* and *Morris* and the last names *Jones* and *Harris* all end in s—and they're singular."

"Oh."

"And then there are singular *common* nouns that end in an *s* sound, such as *conscience*. And there are names that end in an *s* sound, such as *Max*."

"Oh."

"Anyway, the question is, to show the possessive case of a singular noun that ends in an *s* or *s* sound, do you add an apostrophe *and* an *s*, or just an apostrophe?" I took the notebook and wrote: *Lois's* book or *Lois'* book; *James's* book or *James'* book; *Max's* book or *Max'* book."

"Which way is right?" I said.

"I don't know. Which?"

"Well, some grammarians say you should just add an apostrophe—without the extra *s*. But I don't really agree with that."

"You don't?"

"No. And other experts say that the answer depends on the number of syllables in the word. They say that for a one-syllable word you should add an apostrophe and an *s*, but for a word of more than one syllable, you should add only an apostrophe. But I don't really agree with that either."

"You don't?"

"No. I think the way we do it at *American Monthly* is the best. The answer to whether to add an apostrophe *and* an *s* or just an apostrophe depends on *pronunciation.*"

"Pronunciation?"

"Yes. Here, read this out loud." I pointed to the last entry I made in the notebook—the one that started with *Lois's book.*

When Tarzan read aloud, it sounded like this: "Loises book or Lois book, Jameses book or James book, Maxes book or Max book."

"You see," I said, "when you see an apostrophe *and* an *s*, it makes you add an extra *es* sound at the end of the word—when you say it out loud, I mean."

"I *do* see that. You're right."

"Well, if someone's talking out loud about a book that belongs to Lois, do you think he should pronounce it as *Loises* book or *Lois* book."

"*Loises* book."

"I agree. So for that reason, at *American Monthly*, we spell the possessive form of *Lois* with an apostrophe *and* an *s*—so that when people see it they will be more likely to say *Loises* book and not *Lois* book."

"But people who are reading don't say it at all—if they're reading silently, I mean."

"Well, they sort of do. I mean they sort of say it in their minds."

"Oh."

"And if someone's talking about a book that belongs to James, do you think he should pronounce it as *Jameses* book or *James* book?"

"Well, in that case I think it should be pronounced *James* book, without the extra *es* sound at the end."

"I do too. And at *American Monthly* we show the possessive form of *James* without the extra *s* after the apostrophe—so that people reading it will be more likely to say—or think—*James* book, not *Jameses* book."

"I see." Then Tarzan volunteered: "And I would say *Maxes* book, not *Max* book. So I'd spell the possessive case of *Max* with an apostrophe *and* an *s*."

"Good. So would I."

"I see what you mean now about the answer depending on pronunciation. But what if one person wants the possessive case—of a singular noun ending in *s*, I mean—to be pronounced one way but someone else thinks it should be pronounced another way. I mean, what if someone thought that *Jameses* book is the better pronunciation."

"Well, that's a good question. At *American Monthly*, it's a matter of writer's choice. If you're the writer, think of how you want the reader to pronounce the word in his mind. Then, choose the appropriate spelling. If you want him to pronounce an extra *es* sound at the end, use an apostrophe *and* an *s* to show the possessive case. But if you want him to omit that extra *es* sound, then use only an apostrophe."

"Okay. That sounds like a good rule."

The rain continued to strike the roof of the cabin, but not as hard as before.

"Okay," I said, "let's go on to the next underline."

"In the second paragraph you underlined the word *bugs*. That funny because we were just talking about how I was going to have to fight two hundred million bugs."

"I didn't say you would have to fight them. I said that *if* there were a war between humans and bugs, each person—I mean, there's not going to be a war like that, so you don't have to fight any bugs. Anyway, in the article, the problem isn't really the word *bugs*; it's the punctuation after the word—the comma."

"Oh."

"See, the ending of the sentence, B-O-Y, *explains* what you were saying in the first part of the sentence. So instead of a comma after the word *bugs*, you should have used—"

"Now I remember. I should have used either a colon or a dash!"

"Right."

"But which one?"

"Well, either would be okay, but I think—if I were writing the article, I mean—I would choose a colon."

"Why?"

"I guess I think that a colon—more so than I dash, I mean—signifies the idea of 'get ready; here it comes,' and I think that's the concept I'd want to convey. When the reader sees the colon he might think to himself: Here comes something good. And the whole idea of your figuring out that the squiggles—I mean bugs—were letters that formed words is pretty exciting—and special."

"Oh."

"But that's just my opinion. Someone else might prefer a dash. It's another case of writer's choice."

"Oh."

"Anyway, let's keep going. At the end of the second paragraph, you have the phrase *repeated alot*. The only thing that's wrong there is that you made 'a lot' one word. It's two words: a . . . lot."

"It sounds like one word."

"I know. But it's two words. You have to always spell it as two words."

"Okay."

"All right. There's one more underline. In the third paragraph you wrote about 'a strange little animal *who* walked on four legs.'"

"Is that wrong. Should I have said '*whom* walked on four legs'?"

"No. This isn't about *who* versus *whom*. I think you know that *who* is a subjective-case pronoun and *whom* is an objective-case pronoun. In the clause *who walked on four legs*, the pronoun, *who*, is the subject. So it would have been incorrect to say *whom walked* . . ."

"Then what's the problem?"

"It's a question of whether the pronoun should be *who* or *that*. You see, if you're talking about *people*, you use the pronoun *who*. For example, I could say 'Tarzan is the man *who* lives in this jungle.' But if you're talking about things, you use the pronoun *that*. For instance, I could say 'The knife in your waistband is the one *that* killed the snake.'"

"But I was talking about a dog. A dog isn't a person *or* a thing. I mean, it's not a person, but it's alive."

"Well, if you're talking about animals, usually you use the pronoun *that*, as in 'a strange little animal *that* walked on four legs.'"

"Usually?"

"Well, there's an exception. If the animal has been given a name—you know, if it's a pet, for example—you refer to it with the pronoun *who*, not *that*. For example, I could say 'Cheetah is the chimp *who* comes to visit us.'"

"I see. Because he has a name—*Cheetah*—you used the pronoun *who*."

"Right."

"And in my article, because the dog didn't have a name, I should have used the pronoun *that*—'a strange little animal *that* walked on four legs.'"

"Exactly. Okay, now let's look at the last underline. At the beginning of the fourth paragraph you wrote 'Because each of the pictures were accompanied . . .'"

"What's wrong with that?"

"Well, you made an error that people often make. Remember, the verb of a sentence or clause must agree in number with the *subject* of the sentence or clause. But you made the verb agree in number with the object of the prepositional phrase that occurs *between* the subject and verb."

"Huh?"

"Well, let's look at the clause. The subject is *each*. Now, is that word singular or plural?"

"It's singular. It means *each one*."

"Right. Good. And after the subject you have the prepositional phrase *of the pictures*. Now, what is the function of the word *pictures*? Is it the subject of the clause?"

"No, the subject of the clause is *each*. The word *pictures* is the object of the prepositional phrase *of the pictures*."

"Exactly. So which word, *each*, which is singular, or *pictures*, which is plural, should the verb of the clause agree with in number?"

"It should agree with *each*, because that's the subject of the clause."

"Good. And would you say *each was* or *each were*?"

"I'd say *each was*, because *was* agrees with a singular subject. I mean, I would say something like *he was*, not *he were*, right?"

"Right!"

"But still, *pictures were* sounds better that *pictures was*—because the word *pictures* is plural, I mean."

"But in this case it doesn't *matter* that *pictures* is plural. Why? Because it's not the subject of the clause. Do you see?"

"I guess so."

"Well, let me test you on it. Which of these sentences is correct: 'Every one of the apes *was* in a tree' or 'Every one of the apes *were* in a tree'?"

Tarzan thought a moment and then said, "*Was!* It's *was!* Every one of the apes *was* in a tree. The subject of the sentence isn't *apes*, it's *one*. The word *apes* is only the object of the preposition! Every one . . . *was*."

"Very good. Okay, well, that takes care of Article 16."

"Time for brunch," Tarzan announced.

Now I had a decision to make. Should I try to talk to Tarzan about our relationship—about the fact that I loved him, I mean—or should I have brunch without saying anything? Hmm.

"Are you hungry?" I said.

"Starving."

"Okay, then let's have brunch."

"What should we have?"

"Wait," I said, "there's something I have to tell you first."

"What?"

"It's just that . . . I . . . uh . . . I . . . lo-lo- . . . I l-l-looked through that book about bugs before and it said that a scorpion can walk faster backward than it can forward."

"Really?"

"That's what it said."

After a quiet brunch, we were back in our usual places. The rain still beat on the roof.

As Tarzan worked on Article 17 at the table, I sat on the bed with a book in my lap. But I couldn't concentrate because it occurred to me that once the chimps brought me the ten million dollars worth of gems, I'd have to convert them to cash if I wanted to buy a small mansion.

Where could I cash them in, I wondered. I didn't know of any-place in Africa. I'd have to take them back to America, to a reputable gem dealer, I supposed. But how would I know if he was offering me a fair deal? Maybe he'd realize that I was ignorant about the value of precious gems and try to take advantage of me. I'd probably have to get several estimates, just to make sure.

Being rich, it occurred to me, might be more trouble than it's worth. Besides, if, when I declared my love, Tarzan said that he loved me too, I'd probably stay here in Africa and marry him. Then, would I even need the gems? It was all so confusing. Well, I guess everything will come down to how Tarzan feels about me. One thing I was pretty certain about, though: I wouldn't take Tarzan to America and put him on display. I'd quit my job at *American Monthly* before I'd do that.

Eventually I settled into the book on my lap. It was a new one—about different kinds of birds. I read for a while and then said, "Tarzan?"

"Yes?"

"It says here in this book that an ostrich can kill a lion with one well-placed kick."

"No! The lion is the king of beasts. How is that possible?"

"It says that the ostrich is the largest bird in the world. It can grow to eight feet tall and weigh up to 300 pounds. And it can run more than 40 miles per hour. Its legs must be very strong."

"Wow. I've never seen that happen, but I believe you. But tell me more later; I'm almost done with Article 17."

I leafed through the bird book for a few more minutes and then I heard Tarzan suddenly announce, "Okay, I'm done."

I sat at the table next to Tarzan and read his article aloud, underlining the errors as I went along. When I was done, it looked like this:

Article 17: "Kala and the Hunter"

Until I was 18, I had never seen a human being other than myself. But one day, a hunter, a member of a tribe of native inhabitants of this continent, wandered far west of his village. That same day, my ape mother, Kala, in search of food, moved slowly east along an elephant trail.

For 50 yards before her, the trail was straight, and down this leafy tunnel she saw the <u>steadily-advancing</u> figure of a strange and fearful creature. It was the hunter, who carried a bow and arrows.

Kala did not wait to see more, but, turning, moved rapidly back along the trail. Close after her came the hunter. Here was meat. He could make a killing and feast <u>good</u>.

Just as my mother arrived back at the edge of our ape village, the hunter put an arrow to his bowstring, drew the shaft far back, and drove the missile into Kala's back. With a horrid scream my mother plunged forward upon her face before the astonished members of our tribe. She was dead. Roaring and shrieking, the apes dashed toward the murderer, but he had already fled down the trail like a frightened antelope.

I didn't see the killer, but that didn't stop me from leaping into the trees and speeding through the jungle after him. At my side was my sharp hunting knife and across my shoulders a long rope I'd learned to use as a lasso.

When I heard a strange sound I dropped to the ground to examine the soil. In the soft mud on the bank of a tiny stream I found footprints such as I alone in all the jungle had ever made. My heart beat fast. Could it be that I was trailing a MAN—one of my own kind?

I climbed <u>up</u> a nearby tree and scanned the area for a hairless creature, like myself. There he was, passing below me! I sent the lasso flying around his neck and pulled it tight. His cry of alarm was choked in his windpipe. Hand over hand I drew the struggling killer upward until I had him hanging by his neck in mid-air. Then I tied the rope securely to a thick branch, quickly descended, and, for my mother's sake, plunged my deadly hunting knife into the killer's heart.

"Oh my goodness!" I shrieked. "You killed him!"

"I had to. It was for my mother's sake."

"Still . . . it's so horrible."

"Well . . ."

"Oh, what am I thinking? You poor thing, seeing your mother killed before your very eyes like that. You must have been devastated! I'm so sorry!"

No response.

"Anyway, your writing is compelling. I can just see the whole ending scene: the tree, the lasso, the knife . . ."

Tarzan didn't answer. I don't think he was very good at accepting compliments.

"And you were quite the detective, weren't you—finding those footprints, I mean."

Again no answer.

"Well . . . anyway . . . let's go over the errors, okay?"

"Okay."

"All right. Now, in the second paragraph I underlined the words *steadily-advancing* in the phrase *steadily-advancing figure*."

"Why? That's a compound adjective—*steadily-advancing*. You said to join the words of a compound adjective with a hyphen. You *are* talking about the hyphen, right?"

"Yes, but remember that there are exceptions to the rule about joining the words of a compound adjective with a hyphen. One exception concerns compound adjectives that exist in the world as nouns."

"I remember now. You talked about a tsetse fly bite. A tsetse fly is something that exists in the world, so in the phrase *tsetse fly bite*, you don't connect the words *tsetse* and *fly* with a hyphen."

"Right. Good. Also, I said that if the compound adjective is placed *after* the noun—"

"I remember! You said that my father was *well educated*. You said that in that case, since the compound adjective, *well educated*, comes *after* the noun it modifies, *father*, you don't need a hyphen. And now I remember the third exception too! You talked about a *slowly moving turtle*. You said that if the first word of a compound adjective is an adverb ending in *ly*, you don't need a hyphen."

"Right. And so—"

"And so in my article I shouldn't have used a hyphen in the phrase *steadily advancing* because the first word, *steadily*, is an adverb ending in *ly*."

"Exactly. Very good. Okay, let's go on to the next underline. In the third paragraph you wrote 'He could make a killing and feast good.' Now, what's wrong with that?"

"Um . . ."

"You should have written 'He could make a killing a feast *well.*' You have to understand that *good* is an adjective and *well* is an adverb."

"Oh."

"You see, the word in question—*good* or *well*—modifies the verb *feast.* And to modify a verb, you need an adverb, not an adjective. That's why you should have used *well*, not *good*—' . . . make a killing and *feast well.*'"

"But didn't you say that in some cases you *are* supposed to use an adjective after a verb?"

"You're probably thinking of phrases like *You look good* and *I feel good.* Those are special cases because even though the words *look* and *feel* are verbs, you're not actually—"

"I remember now. You said that if you're not actually *doing* anything, but you just *are* a certain way, then you use an adjective, as in *I feel bad.* You wouldn't say *I feel badly.*"

"Right. But you have to understand that when you use an adjective like *good* or *bad* in a case like that, the adjective isn't modifying a verb—adjectives never modify verbs—it's modifying the noun or pronoun that's the subject of the sentence."

"I understand."

"Good."

We had only one more error to discuss. Then we would be finished with grammar for the day. I'd have the rest of the afternoon and all through dinner to declare my love to him—if I could get up the courage, that is. I looked at his face to see if he still had the same electrifying effect on me. Well, he did. Before I could look away, our eyes met! His were so deep, like bottomless pools, that I felt as if I could tumble right into them. I swooned and then turned away.

"What's wrong?" he said. "You just had a weird look on your face."

"Who me? Oh . . . I was just wondering if . . . if . . . if you really think it's too late to tell Tantor about the sapphires."

What a stupid thing to say, I immediately realized. Of course, that's not what I was thinking, and now he's going to think I'm greedy. But I had to say something to throw him off the track, didn't I?

"But never mind," I hurriedly went on. "The sapphires aren't important. Let's go on to the next underline." What a fool I'd made of myself!

I pointed to the beginning of the last paragraph in as businesslike a way as I could muster and said, "You wrote 'I climbed up a nearby tree . . .' Remember, the word *climbed* implies an upward direction, so you should have said simply 'I climbed a nearby tree . . .'"

"I remember now. You told me about that when we went to the beach. You said that some verbs, like *advance*, *climb*, and *dive*, have a direction built into them, so they don't require adverbs like *forward*, *up*, or *down* after them."

"Right."

We were silent for a while. Then I said, "It was fun at the beach, wasn't it? You scared me with a crab."

"You like being scared?"

"I didn't mean that exactly. I mean that it was fun goofing around together."

"Goofing around?"

"You know, playing."

"Oh."

"Well, didn't you think it was fun?" I sounded so desperate and pathetic!

"I guess so."

"Tarzan, can we talk?" I heard myself saying. I didn't decide to say that; it just came out.

"What do you want to talk about?"

"In few days we'll be finished with all the articles and all the grammar lessons. Have you thought about what will happen after that?"

"Happen?"

"I mean, do you think that afterward I'll be staying here in Africa . . . or going back to Baltimore? And what about you? If I go back home, will you come with me or stay here?" I wanted to say *Don't you want us to be together?* but I was too afraid.

"I thought we were going to New York City so I can be put on display."

"You're not a freak, you know. You're not King Kong."

"Who's King Kong?"

"Never mind. Anyway, I've changed my mind about putting you on display in New York. It's not right. It will just have to be too bad

379

for the readers of *American Monthly*. They don't deserve to see you anyway. In fact, I might not even go back to work for that magazine."

"Why not?"

"I like it here . . . with you . . . and with Yemmy and Omy and Cheetah. Besides, the magazine may have already fired me."

"Why do you say that?"

"Well, for one thing, I've never sent in any of the articles we've written."

"You haven't?" he said, with genuine surprise. "Why not?"

"I don't know. There are no mailboxes anywhere around here."

"But I want my story in the magazine . . . especially after all the writing I've done."

"I'm sorry. I know. Your writing is wonderful and it deserves to be published. Well, we'll see." Then after a pause: "So what should we do for the rest of the day?"

"I don't know. What do you want to do?"

"I want to start doing exciting things again! We've spent too much time hanging around the cabin. I want to visit Mount Kilimanjaro!"

"Now?"

"No, not now. The day's almost over. I mean one day soon."

"But it's so far away. It's on the east coast, near the Indian Ocean!"

"Well, we can take a canoe or ride on an elephant. And I still want to see the Sahara Desert, too. Let's *do* something; let's *go* someplace for a change."

"Well, we're almost finished with all the articles. Maybe you'll still find a way to send them in to your magazine and then they can be published. And we're almost done with my grammar lessons too. Let's finish all that, and then we'll see about visiting volcanoes and deserts, okay? Now, what should we have for dinner?"

"I don't care," I said. "You decide."

Chapter 29: Tarzan Recalls Leaving His Tribe

The next morning sunshine streamed through the window and the air smelled fresh from the previous day's rain.

When Tarzan arrived at the cabin, I was sitting on the bed reading about Mount Kilimanjaro in the book on Africa.

"Hi," I said. "This book has a really interesting article about Mount Kilimanjaro."

"That's good. You can read that while I work on Article 18, okay?"

"Okay."

Tarzan sat at the table and started to write in the notebook.

After a while I said, "Listen to this. Mount Kilimanjaro is the highest point on the entire continent of Africa. Did you know that?"

"Um, I guess I never thought about it. I'm trying to write."

"It says that its peak is covered with snow and ice! How can that be when it's so close to the equator? I thought the equator is supposed to be hot. It's sure hot here, I mean."

No answer.

"It says that about two hundred feet of snow and ice cover the top. Isn't that amazing?"

"Tell me later. I'm trying to write."

"Here's something else interesting. The mountain, which is an extinct volcano, actually has *two* peaks."

"That's nice," he said, with no emotion whatsoever.

"It says that the higher peak—that's the one covered with snow and ice—has a crater at the top. Do you remember when we went swimming in the crater of a mountain?"

No answer.

"Anyway, this crater is *six hundred feet deep!*"

"Okay."

"I really want to go there."

"Okay. Now let me write."

I read silently for a while so that Tarzan could finish Article 18. When I was reading about how farmers grow coffee beans on the lower slopes of the volcano, I heard Tarzan say, "Okay, I'm done."

I scurried to the table, sat down, and took the notebook. It was then that I realized that the thought of the chimps bringing diamonds and gold hadn't entered my mind that entire morning. Maybe it was becoming less important to me. Still . . .

"Wait," I said. "Before I read your article, I have to figure out something. How may days until the chimps bring the diamonds and gold?"

"Don't forget the rubies and emeralds," Tarzan answered. I think maybe he was being sarcastic.

I did some quick calculations. "It's only three more days. Imagine, in three days we'll have ten million dollars!"

"That's nice. Now, what do you think of my article?"

"Okay, let me read it."

I read aloud, underlining the errors, as usual. When I was finished, it looked like this:

Article 18: "Sabor"

After I killed my mother's murderer, I took his bow and arrows and set out slowly on my homeward march. Suddenly I saw Sabor, the lioness whom years before had attacked my playmate and me at the lake, standing in the center of the trail not 20 yards from me.

Her great yellow eyes were fixed on me with a wicked gleam, and her red tongue licked at her lips. Slowly she crept toward me with her belly flattened against the earth. I didn't try to escape, in fact, I welcomed the opportunity now that I was well armed.

Quickly I fit an arrow to the bow, and as Sabor sprang, the tiny missile leaped to meet her in mid-air. At the same instant I jumped to one side, and as the great cat struck the ground beyond me I shot another arrow deep into her side.

With a mighty roar the beast turned and charged once more, only to be met with a third arrow in the neck. But this time she was too close for me to sidestep her onrushing body.

I went down beneath the great weight of my enemy, but with gleaming knife drawn and striking home. For a moment we lay there, and then I realized that the motionless mass lying upon me was beyond power ever again to injure man or ape.

Because I'd seen in my picture books that men wear clothes, I used my hunting knife to remove Sabor's skin. I flung it over my shoulders and proudly marched the rest of the way home.

"So, you finally avenged your playmate's death," I observed. "Good for you. That lioness deserved it." Then after a pause: "You know, your story would make a good movie. There's a lot of excitement; a lot of action. Maybe if your story is actually published in *American Monthly*, a movie producer will read it and ask us to star in a movie about your life. What do you think?"

"What's a movie?"

"Well, never mind about that now. Let's look at the grammar in the article. There are hardly any errors at all. Soon I'll have nothing left to teach you!"

No response.

"Well, I'm glad to see that at the end of the first paragraph you wrote 'attacked my playmate and *me*' and not 'attacked my playmate and *I*.'"

"Well, of course. The pronoun is the object of the verb *attacked* and so must be in the objective case—attacked *me*, not attacked *I*."

"That's right. I just wish other people in the world understood that."

He didn't answer.

"But I just thought of something," I continued. "Sometimes you *should* use a subjective-case pronoun after a verb."

"You should? When?"

"After any form of the verb *to be*. You see, that verb—and each of its forms, such as *am, are, is, was, were, has been, might be*, and so on—is called a *linking verb*. Why? Because the verb *to be* can be used to *link together* many different sentence elements. For example, it can link two nouns, as in 'Tarzan *is* a man'; it can link a noun and an adjective, as in "Tarzan *is* handsome'; and so on. Anyway, a pronoun that follows a linking verb should be in the *subjective* case. For example, you should say 'It was *she*,' not 'It was *her*,' and you should say 'It is *I*,' not 'It is *me*.'"

"That sounds wrong," Tarzan objected. "Besides, I don't see what difference it makes whether or not you give *to be* a special name like 'linking verb'; after a verb, a pronoun should be in the objective case, right?"

"Well, in a sentence like 'It was she,' grammarians don't consider the word *she* to be an object. They consider it to be what's called a *complement*."

"What's that?"

"Well, *regular* verbs take *objects*. But *linking* verbs take *complements*, which are either *predicate adjectives* or *predicate nouns*—you know, adjectives or nouns that are part of a sentence's predicate. You remember what a predicate is, don't you?"

"Yes. It's the portion of a sentence that includes the verb along with all its modifiers and objects. It's the 'complete verb' portion of a sentence."

"Right. Anyway, in a sentence like 'It was she,' grammarians consider *she* a predicate noun, which is simply a restatement of the sentence's subject, *it*. And as a restatement of the subject, it's in the subjective case."

"Well, I guess that explains it, but it still sounds wrong to me. For example, if I knock on the door and you say 'Who is it?' I'll say 'It's *me*.' I wouldn't say 'It's *I*.' It sounds too weird."

"You're right, it does. And that's why most people *do* say things like 'It's me' and 'It's us.' And that raises an interesting point. Some people say that there's one set of grammar rules for talking and another set for writing."

"What do you mean?"

"I mean that there's a difference between what's called *informal* usage and *formal* usage. You see, if you're just talking—you know, having a conversation—following all the rules of grammar to the letter isn't always necessary. You can bend the rules a little and no one will care. You can say things like 'It was *her*,' and that's perfectly all right. But if you're doing what's called *formal writing*—you know, serious writing for a book, a magazine, or a school term paper, for example—then you should carefully follow all the rules of grammar. In formal writing you should say 'It was *she*.' Do you see?"

"I think so."

"Good. Now, another thing I was glad to see in your article is that at the end of the second paragraph you didn't hyphenate the compound adjective *well armed*."

"I didn't hyphenate it because it comes *after* the pronoun it modifies."

"Good! Anyway, there are only two errors in this whole article, so let's go over those."

"Okay."

"In the first paragraph you wrote 'Suddenly I saw Sabor, the lioness *whom* years before attacked . . .' Why did you write *whom* instead of *who*? Remember, *whom* is objective case and *who* is subjective case."

"Because *whom*—or *who*—is a pronoun that stands for Sabor. I wrote that I saw Sabor. *Sabor* is object of the verb *saw*. So, I thought that *whom*, which is the same as Sabor, really, would also be the object of the verb *saw*. Was I wrong?"

"You were. See, in the first clause of the sentence, 'Suddenly I saw Sabor,' *I* is the subject, *saw* is the verb, and *Sabor* is the object of the verb—*I saw Sabor*. But after that clause, you have an entirely different clause—with its own subject, verb, and object. In the second clause, *who* is the subject, *had attacked* is the verb, and *my playmate and me* is the object of the verb—*who had attacked my playmate and me*."

"Oh, I see. I need the pronoun *who*—not *whom*—because it's the subject of the second clause, not the object of the first clause."

"Exactly. All right. Now, in the second paragraph, where I underlined the word *escape*, I'm really drawing attention to the punctuation after that word."

"You mean the comma there is wrong?"

"Yes. Do you remember when we spoke about conjunctive adverbs?"

"Uhh . . ."

"I said that conjunctive adverbs—words like *therefore, nevertheless, moreover, however,* and *furthermore*—are technically adverbs, but they function as conjunctions; that is, they join independent clauses—but they also help carry the thought of one clause into the next. I think that as an example I said something like 'We wanted to go for a moonlight swim; however, it was raining.'"

"I remember now."

I wondered if he meant that he remembered what a conjunctive adverb was or if he remembered our moonlight swim. I didn't press the point.

"Anyway, in your article, the phrase *in fact* is a conjunctive adverb. It joins the clause 'I didn't try to escape' with the clause 'I welcomed the opportunity . . .'"

"Then why is the comma before it wrong? You said that if two independent clauses are joined by a conjunction, you place a comma after the first clause, before the conjunction."

"Well, first of all, I said to use a comma between independent clauses joined by a *coordinating* conjunction, like *and* or *but*. And second, a conjunctive adverb isn't even a conjunction! It's an adverb!"

"Oh."

"Anyway, in your article, you have two independent clauses joined by a conjunctive adverb. In a case like that, you should always use a semicolon after the first clause, before the conjunctive adverb. Why? Because you're separating two independent clauses not joined by a coordinating conjunction. And you should use a comma after the conjunctive adverb. Why? Because the conjunctive adverb serves as an introductory phrase to the second clause. So, what you wrote should have looked like this." I took the notebook and in it I wrote: "I didn't try to escape; in fact, I welcomed the opportunity . . ."

Tarzan studied what I'd written. "I see," he said. "A semicolon before the conjunctive adverb and a comma after it. Here let me try one."

He took the notebook, wrote something in it, and handed it back to me. It said: "Tarzan wrote many articles about his life; however, Jane never sent them in."

"Is that a good example of a semicolon before a conjunctive adverb?" he said.

Was he teasing me? I wasn't sure.

"Yes. It's a good example. But you have to understand that words like *however* and *therefore* aren't *always* conjunctive adverbs."

"They're not?"

"No. Sometimes they're just *regular* adverbs. For example, the word *however*, as a regular adverb, means simply 'on the other hand' or 'by contrast.' In that sense it's used parenthetically and is surrounded by commas. For example, I can write something like this." In the notebook I wrote: "Jane likes to visit interesting places; Tarzan, however, likes to stay home." I showed him what I'd written.

"I like to visit interesting places," Tarzan protested.

"That's not the point. The point is that in that sentence, the adverb *however* is being used to mean 'on the other hand.' It's parenthetical—or nonrestrictive—and so it's surrounded by commas."

"Okay, I see. So, if a word like *however* is used as a conjunctive adverb—forming a transition between two independent clauses—it has a semicolon before it and a comma after it. But if it's simply used parenthetically to mean 'on the other hand,' then it has a comma before and after it. Right?"

"Exactly."

"Okay, now we can have brunch. I'm starving. Are you hungry?"

Is that all he ever thought about? Food? Didn't he ever think about love or romance?

"I guess I can eat," I said wearily.

After brunch I said, "Do you want to work on Article 19 outdoors?"

"But I like to work at the table. I can concentrate better."

"But you said that you like to visit interesting places. Was that true?"

"I do . . . but . . ."

"We haven't been anywhere lately. Do you remember that time when we went to a waterfall? And to an island?"

"But you said you didn't like the waterfall because of the underground man-eating plants. And you didn't like the island because of the ants."

"I know, but—"

"And you're afraid of geological hazards, like earthquakes and rockslides."

"But it's boring staying in the cabin all the time," I protested, with a little whine in my voice.

"Well, where do you want to go?"

"I want to go to the Sahara Desert and Mount Kilimanjaro."

"Do you realize how far away those places are? It would take weeks, maybe months, to get there."

"Oh."

We were silent awhile.

"How about this?" Tarzan offered. "We can carry the table outside, in front of the cabin. I'll write, and you can read one of your books there."

"But that's not going anywhere."

"But at least we'll be outside."

I couldn't really think of anything to say, so I just said, "Okay."

Tarzan lifted the table in his strong arms, carried it outside, and placed it on the ground about four feet from the cabin. Then he went back for two chairs.

"Here, you sit facing the trees," he said, motioning me to the seat whose back faced the cabin. "I'll get the notebook and a book for you to read while I'm working. Which one do you want?"

"I guess the one about birds," I said halfheartedly.

In a moment he was back, and he sat in the other chair, which was to my right.

Without saying anything he opened the notebook and started to write. I could have glanced over to see what he was writing, but I didn't. Instead I leafed through the book on birds.

Instead of concentrating on the book, I wondered what would happen if I told Tarzan that I loved him and he told me that he loved me too. We would get married, I supposed. Then we'd stay here in Africa and live happily ever after, as they say.

Hmm. But *how* would we get married? I'd want our marriage to be legal. We couldn't simply announce to each other that we're married. We'd have to find a judge or someone with authority to marry us. But where was such a person? Surely not here in the jungle.

"Tarzan," I said, "What are the biggest cities in Africa?"

"I guess maybe Cairo in Egypt, Casablanca in Morocco, and Johannesburg in South Africa."

"Oh."

"Why?"

"Um . . . I don't know . . . just wondering."

He went back to work.

If we went north to Cairo or Casablanca, we'd get to cross the Sahara. And if we went south to Johannesburg, maybe we could swing east on the way and see Mount Kilimanjaro. Hmm. Then I remembered that ships' captains had the authority to marry people onboard. Maybe we could build a raft and paddle way out onto the ocean. Maybe we'd find a ship and get married on that. Well, I could see that a lot of thought and planning were going to be necessary. The sooner we start, the better. I was going to have to tell Tarzan that I loved him once and for all after this afternoon's grammar lesson. There was no longer any way around it.

Having decided that, I was able to concentrate on the bird book a little better. After reading awhile, I said, "Tarzan?"

"Yes?"

"It says in this book that there's a kind of bird in Australia that builds its nest from human hair."

"That's ridiculous. Where would a bird get human hair?"

"It says that it steals it from the heads of passersby."

Tarzan made a snorting sound that seemed to say: I don't believe that.

I read awhile longer and then Tarzan said, "Okay, I'm finished with this article." Then, handing the notebook to me, he said, "What do you think?"

I read the article aloud, underlining the errors, as usual. When I was finished, it looked like this:

Article 19: "Leaving the Tribe"

As I eventually grew into adulthood, I found that I had grown away from my people. Their interests and mine were far removed. They had not kept pace with me, nor could they understand any of the many strange and wonderful ideas that passed through my active brain. So limited was their vocabulary that I couldn't even speak with them of the many great fields of thought my reading had opened up before my longing eyes—<u>History, Philosophy, Science</u>. Nor could I make known to them the ambitions <u>which</u> stirred my soul.

Among the tribe I no longer had friends as of old. A little child finds companionship in many strange and simple creatures, but a grown man looks for some equality of intelligence in a friend.

<u>If Kala would have</u> lived, I would have sacrificed all else to remain near her. But now that she was dead, and the playful friends of my childhood had grown into fierce brutes, I felt that I much preferred the peace and solitude of my parents' cabin to a life among a horde of wild beasts.

One day I said to my tribe, "If I were an ape, I would stay here. But I am not an ape. My ways are not your ways, so I am going back to the cabin by the shore. I will not return." And thus I took the first step toward the goal I had set—the finding of other human beings like me.

"Well, I can certainly understand your wanting to leave that tribe of apes," I said. "After all, you were so much more intelligent than they were."

No answer.

"Well, I want to commend you for using the subjunctive mood in the last paragraph, where you wrote 'If I *were* an ape . . .' That was good.

Again no answer. I guess Tarzan was a good example of what people call the strong, silent type. Well, we'd see how silent he was when, after this lesson, I told him that I was in love with him and that I wanted us to get married in one of the big cities of Africa.

"Okay," I said, "let's go over the errors." I angled the notebook so we could both see it.

"Why did you underling 'History, Philosophy, Science'?"

"Because fields of knowledge—and school subjects—aren't capitalized."

"Oh. Never?"

"Well, if they refer to proper nouns they are. For example, *England* is a proper noun, so the adjective *English* is capitalized. And the school subject *English* is also capitalized. But only because is refers to a proper noun."

"Oh."

"For example, when I was in high school, I usually studied five subjects each term: English, social studies, math, science, and French. Of those, only English and French are capitalized because they refer to proper nouns: England and France. The other subjects are not capitalized."

"Unless they're part of a title, right? For example, what if the title of the science course is something like *Science for Beginners?* Then wouldn't you capitalize it?"

"Well, then you would, because it's a part of a title. But that's not what we're talking about. If you have a field of knowledge or school subject in a regular sentence, you don't capitalize it."

"Unless it refers to a proper noun . . . or it's the first word of a sentence."

"Right," I conceded. "Except for that."

I didn't say anything for a while. I watched the leaves of the nearby trees sway in the breeze. I looked for birds that might try to steal hair from my head.

"And why did you underline the word *which* in the next sentence?" Tarzan asked.

"Let's see. You wrote '. . . the ambitions which stirred my soul.' You have to understand the difference between the words *which* and *that.*"

"You mean I should have written '. . . the ambitions *that* stirred my soul'? Why?"

"Well, each word, *that* and *which*, is a relative pronoun that's used to introduce a phrase or clause that gives additional information about something already stated. For example, in this case, you're talking about your ambitions, and then you give the *additional information* that they *stirred your soul*, right?"

"Right."

"But there's one important difference between *that* and *which*. You see, the word *which* is normally used to introduce additional information that's *nonrestrictive*. As such, it normally has a comma before it—because commas set off nonrestrictive phrases and clauses, I mean. For example, let's say that we're talking about your hunting knife—your one and only hunting knife." I took the notebook and wrote: "Your hunting knife, which has a sharp blade, is in the cabin." I showed that to Tarzan and said, "You see, we already know that we're talking about your hunting knife. That means that the additional information about its being sharp is nonrestrictive. That's why I used the word *which* instead of the word *that*—because *which* is used to introduce *nonrestrictive* phrases and clauses, I mean—and that's why I placed commas around the entire nonrestrictive—or parenthetical—phrase: *which has a sharp blade.*"

"Oh."

"Now, on the other hand, the word *that* is used to introduce *restrictive* phrases and clauses that give additional information. For example, we have two chairs out here at the table." In the notebook I wrote: "The chair that faces the trees is occupied by Jane." I showed that to Tarzan and said, "You see, since there are two chairs here, if I say 'the chair,' you won't know which one I'm taking about. I have to *explain* which one I'm talking about by giving additional, necessary information. I said that it's the one that faces the trees. Because that information—about its facing the trees, I mean—is necessary, the clause *that faces the trees* is considered *restrictive*. As such, it's introduced by the relative pronoun *that*, not *which*, and it's *not* preceded by a comma."

"Oh."

"Do you see the difference?" In the notebook I wrote again: "Your hunting knife, which has a sharp blade, is in the cabin." After that I

392

wrote: "The chair that faces the trees is occupied by Jane." Then I said, "You see? The word *which* introduces *unnecessary* additional information and it's preceded by a comma; the word *that* introduces *necessary* additional information and it's *not* preceded by a comma."

"I see. In my article, since people won't know *which* ambitions I'm talking about, I *explain* that they're the ones that *stir my soul*. That's necessary information."

"Right. And because it's necessary, you should precede it with the word *that*—the ambitions *that* stir my soul."

"Okay."

One more error to go. Then we would talk about the wedding plans. Wait, I mean talk about our feelings for one another. Actually, I had in mind a little trick to get myself over the hurdle of confessing my true feelings. It's something I once saw in a movie. A woman was in a situation like mine. She wanted to tell a certain man she loved him but was too afraid or shy. Anyway, she didn't tell him, but then a moment after he walked out the door, she ran to the door and called, "Oh, one more thing." Then, when the man turned around, she really told him. As it turned out, he loved her too. It was very romantic.

I decided, since I'd so far failed to admit to Tarzan that I was in love with him, that I'd try the approach used in that movie. This afternoon, after Tarzan leaves, I'll run to the door and call, "Oh, one more thing." Then when he turns around, I'll tell him I love him. Then, if all goes according to plan, he'll tell me the same thing and we can be married. Then we'll just have to decide which city to get married in: Cairo, Casablanca, or Johannesburg.

"In the third paragraph," I suddenly heard Tarzan say, "why did you underline 'If Kala would have . . .'?"

"Oh. Let's see," I said, coming out of my reverie. "Okay. You wrote: 'If Kala would have lived, I would have sacrificed . . .'"

"What's wrong with that?"

"Well, there's something you have to understand about sentences that express a condition—sentences that begin with a dependent clause that starts with the word *if*, I mean."

"What?"

"Well, it concerns the verb tenses in the dependent clause and the following independent clause."

"What do you mean?"

393

"I mean that if a sentence begins with what I'll call a dependent *if* clause, the verb tense in the following *independent* clause will always be different from the verb tense in the *if* clause."

"It will?"

"Sure. For example, I might say something like . . . oh . . . 'If I eat too much, I will feel too full.' Do you see? In that sentence, the *if* clause uses the present tense—I *eat*—and the following independent clause used the future tense—I *will feel*."

"I can see that. It's because the time of the *if* clause and the following independent clause are not the same. What you're really saying is that if you eat too much *now*, you'll feel too full *later*."

"Exactly. That's why you would never use the same verb tense in both clauses of a sentence like that. You wouldn't say 'If I eat too much, I feel too full.' That would be using the present tense in each clause. And you wouldn't say 'If I will eat too much, I will feel too full.' That's using the future tense in each clause."

"I see. And in my article, I used the same tense in both clauses of the sentence. I used *would have lived* in the *if* clause and *would have sacrificed* in the following independent clause. What do you call that tense—the one that starts with *would have?*"

"That's called the *conditional perfect* tense. *Conditional* because whether or not you *would have* done something depends on some condition that has been expressed or implied—such as whether or not you ate too much or whether or not Kala lived. And *perfect* because it expresses action completed prior to a certain point in time. *Conditional perfect.*"

"Oh. And I used the conditional perfect tense—*would have*—in both clauses of the sentence. That has to be wrong. So, what *should* I have written?"

"You should have written 'If Kala *had* lived, I would have sacrificed . . .' That way, the tenses make sense with each other."

"Make sense?"

"Yes. You can tell from the example about eating too much food and being too full that the *present* tense in the *if* clause is balanced, or completed, by the *future* tense in the following independent clause. Every time you have a sentence with an *if* clause, the tenses of the two clauses will be different from each other and will balance each other."

"So, when you said *If Kala had lived*, what tense is that?"

"That's called the *past perfect* tense. If refers to something that happened in the past, prior to a certain point in time. Anyway, the important thing is, in a sentence with an *if* clause, if you use the *conditional perfect* tense in the independent clause, you have to use the *past perfect* tense in the *if* clause. For example, you would say . . . oh . . . 'If I *had known* you were coming, I *would have baked* a cake.' Do you see how nicely those verb tenses balance and complete each other? It would be wrong to say 'If I *would have known* you were coming, I *would have baked* a cake.'"

"I can see now that that wouldn't make sense. You're using the same tense to express two different times."

"Right."

Well, we were finished with grammar for the day, and now it was time to put my plan into action—the plan about waiting for Tarzan to walk out the door and then saying, "Oh, one more thing." There was only one problem. We were already outside, so how could Tarzan walk out the door? I'd have to get him back inside.

"Tarzan, can you please carry the table back inside the cabin? I'll take the chairs."

We carried the stuff into the cabin and placed it in its usual place. Then I abruptly said, "Okay, see you tomorrow morning."

"Wait," he said, surprised. "What about dinner?"

I was so eager to implement my "one more thing" plan, that I'd completely forgotten about dinner.

"Oh . . . I forgot. Okay, go get us something fast. I'll wait here."

While Tarzan was out gathering food, I imagined the entire conversation about to come. We'd each confess our love, and then we'd choose the city to get married in. While weighing the pros and cons of each in my mind, I heard Tarzan return with the food.

We sat down and started eating in silence. Finally, Tarzan joked, "Don't eat too much or you might feel too full."

"What?" I said. What he'd said didn't really register because I was still daydreaming.

After a while I heard him say, "Why do you have that funny look on your face?"

"What funny look?"

"I don't know. A funny look."

I shrugged my shoulders. After I took a few more bites I said, "Okay, I'm done. Well, see you tomorrow."

Tarzan gave me a quizzical look but got up and walked to the door. Then he said good-bye and left.

I decided to count to ten to give him time to cover some distance from the door. Then I would run to the doorway and call out, "Oh, one more thing."

One, two, three, four, five, six, seven, eight, nine, ten.

I ran to the doorway.

"Oh, one more thing!" I yelled a little too loudly.

He turned. "What?"

"I lo . . . I lo . . ."

"What?"

"I have to talk to you."

"What is it?" he said, walking back to me.

"I have to tell you something about Cairo . . . and Casablanca . . . and Johannesburg."

"What?"

"Well, something very important. Something I should have told you but forgot to say."

"You mean something about grammar?"

"No."

"Then what?"

"It's not about grammar . . . it's about . . . about . . . punctuation!"

Okay, I'd failed again. But I was scared.

"What about it?"

"Well, remember when I taught you about the sixteen different reasons to use a comma?"

"Yes."

"Well, there's something I forgot to say about the serial comma."

"You mean the comma that you use to separate the items of a series?"

"Yes. You see, sometimes the items that you want to separate contain commas themselves."

"What do you mean?"

"Well, come back to the table. I'll show you."

We walked to the table and sat down. I opened the notebook and wrote: "Some large cities in Africa are Cairo, Egypt; Casablanca, Morocco; and Johannesburg, South Africa." Then I said, "Do you see? Because a city and the country it's in are always separated by a comma, each item in the list—each city/country combination, I mean—already contains a comma. That's why I separated the actual items with semicolons. You see, that's the rule. If items in a list contain commas of their own, you separate the items with semicolons. Semicolons are considered stronger than commas."

"Oh."

"Here, look." I took the notebook and wrote: "Some large cities in Africa are Cairo, Egypt, Casablanca, Morocco, and Johannesburg, South Africa." Then I said, "Do you see how confusing could be? Someone who doesn't know a lot about African geography might think I'm talking about *six different cities*."

"I see. Is that all you wanted to tell me? Is that why you called me back?"

"Well, do you think that one day you'd like to visit one of those cities?"

"I don't know. Well, goodnight."

He walked to the door and left. I let him go.

Chapter 30: Tarzan Recalls Jane's Arrival in Africa

As I gradually awakened the next morning, I had a nagging feeling that something was wrong—but I was too groggy to remember what it was. Then, as the cobwebs cleared from my mind, I remembered. But it wasn't one thing; it was three. First, I was mad at myself for being too afraid to tell Tarzan that I was in love with him. Second, it would be a lot of trouble to convert ten million dollars' worth of precious gems into cash—not to mentioned the headache of finding just the right small mansion to buy. Third, with so many potential geological and meteorological hazards, the likelihood of at least one of them coming to pass seemed quite high.

I sighed deeply and got out of bed. What shall I do until Tarzan arrives, I wondered. From the shelf I took the book about animals and sat on the bed to read. The book said that a dog's sense of smell is ten thousand times stronger than a human's. I found that had to believe. If that were true, wouldn't a dog detect every disgusting odor for miles around and be constantly sickened? I put that book back and took down the one about geological disasters. Just as I started to read, Tarzan entered the cabin and sat at the table.

"Good morning," he said. "How are you?"

"I'm good. I mean, I'm well. I mean, I'm fine." Since I was Tarzan's grammar teacher, I wanted to always use proper grammar around him. To tell the truth, I wasn't really sure if there was anything wrong with saying 'I'm good' or 'I'm well'; that's why I finally settled on 'I'm fine.' Was I being overly concerned about my own grammar?

"I'm going to start right in on Article 20," Tarzan said. "What are you reading?"

"It's the book about hazards and disasters."

"Why do you read that? You know it makes you nervous."

Not as nervous as the idea of telling you I love you, I thought.

"I don't know," I said. "It's interesting."

For a while Tarzan wrote and I read. Then I said, "Tarzan, it says in this book that there's a lake, not far from where we are right now, that killed a bunch of people."

"Where? How? What do you mean it killed them? You mean they drowned?"

"No, they didn't drown. It says that a lake in Cameroon—that's a country near here, right?—turned upside down, or inside out, or something, and suffocated a lot of people."

"Really? How?"

"It says that a layer of carbon dioxide gas was trapped under the water, at the bottom of the lake."

"How did *that* get there?"

"It says from geothermal sources beneath the lake, whatever that means. Anyway, one day, because of a rockslide or something, the lake 'turned over,' with the bottom layer of deadly gas shooting to the surface. Then the gas spread over the land for about twelve miles in all directions. And because carbon dioxide is denser than air, it sank to ground level and smothered about 1,750 people."

"That's terrible!"

"I know. Now I'm afraid to go near a lake. And I used to enjoy swimming so much!"

"Why don't you put that book back. Read a *nice* book . . . like the one about birds."

I put back the disasters book and took down the bird book. I read silently for a while and then said, "Tarzan, there's something I forgot to tell you."

"What?"

"Only two more days until the chimps bring the diamonds and gold."

"That's nice. Let me write."

I read about different kinds of birds until I heard Tarzan announce that he'd finished Article 20. I went to the table, sat down, and read the article aloud, underlining the errors as I went along. When I was finished, it looked like this:

Article 20: "The Arrival of Jane"

One day, after I'd been living in my <u>mother's and father's</u> cabin awhile, I walked near the shore and a strange and unusual spectacle met my sight. On the calm waters of the harbor floated a great ship, and on the beach a small rowboat was drawn up.

In the boat were people that in many ways were like those of my picture books. I crept closer through the trees until I was quite near them. One member of the party, the only one who disembarked, was a girl of about 19. One of the men stood up and lifted her upon the land. She gave him a brave and pretty smile of thanks, but no words passed <u>among</u> them.

From the trees I watched the scene, but most of all I watched the sweet face and graceful figure of the girl. <u>Looking at her, she</u> was created to be protected, and I was created to protect her.

The men rowed away, and the girl, now alone, walked toward the jungle. She soon came upon my cabin and entered. I peeked through the window. There she was! How beautiful her features! How delicate her snowy skin!

She was writing at my own table. For an hour I gazed upon her while she wrote. How I longed to speak to her, but I dared not try, for I was convinced that she would not understand me, and I feared, too, that I might frighten her away.

At length she stood up. She loosened the soft mass of hair that crowned her head. Like a shimmering waterfall it fell about her oval face, tumbling below her waist in waving lines. I was spellbound.

When I finished reading the article, I didn't know what to say. Based on what I'd just read, Tarzan thought I was beautiful. He longed to speak to me. He was spellbound. But he was afraid.

Maybe what frightened me—that my feelings of love were unrequited, I mean—was what frightened Tarzan. Maybe all along he's wanted to tell me that he loved me but was afraid that I'd say 'That's *your* problem.' Isn't life strange!

On the other hand, maybe he loved me *then*, but doesn't love me *now*. Lately he's been less attentive and complimentary than he used to be. Hmm. What to do . . .

"Aren't we going to go over the mistakes?" I heard Tarzan say.

"Oh . . . sure . . . okay . . . let's see. Um, well, the first thing I underlined is the phrase *mother's and father's* in the first sentence. You wrote *mother's and father's cabin.*"

"What's wrong with that? I formed a possessive by adding *apostrophe s.*"

"I know, but you added *apostrophe s* to both 'mother' *and* 'father.' The cabin belonged to your mother and father *together.* I mean they owned it *jointly.*"

"So?"

"So, the rule is that if you want to indicate that something is jointly owned by two people, you add *apostrophe s* to the second element only. You should have written *mother and father's cabin.* Likewise, if you want to indicate that something is jointly owned by *more* than two people, you add *apostrophe s* to the last element only, as in *mother, father, and Tarzan's cabin.*"

"Oh."

"Of course, if two people own things individually, then you put *apostrophe s* after *each* person, as in *Washington's and Lincoln's presidencies.*"

"Washington and Lincoln *owned* their presidencies?"

"Well, when I say *own,* I don't mean that someone bought something and held it in is hand, necessarily. I just mean that it's theirs. *Washington's presidency. Lincoln's presidency.*"

"Oh."

"Of course, other times, you might use pronouns instead of proper nouns to show joint possession. For example, Yemmy, Omy, and Cheetah are Tarzan and Jane's pets. Now, how would you say that using possessive pronouns instead of our names?"

"I would say that they were *yours and mine pets.* I mean *yours and my pets.* I mean *your and my pets.* I mean *Tarzan's and your pets.* I mean

Tarzan and your pets. I mean *Jane's and my pets.* I mean *Jane and my pets.* I mean . . ." He trailed off.

"It's tricky, isn't it?"

"It is. How would you say that?"

"Well, if you use two possessive pronouns to show joint ownership, or if you use one possessive pronoun and one noun to show joint ownership, the best idea is to *not* place the two possessive words together."

"What do you mean?"

"I mean you should separate them with the noun their modifying. So if you're talking about our pets, you can say *Jane's pets and mine.*"

"Oh, I see. You put the noun *pets* between *Jane's* and *mine.* I like that; it sounds good—*Jane's pets and mine.*"

"Well, where *are* Yemmy, Omy, and Cheetah, anyway?" I said. "We haven't seen them for a long time. I hope they're okay."

"We might not even recognize Yemmy and Omy now. I mean I'm sure they've grown a lot. You know how fast tiger cubs grow."

Actually, I didn't know how fast tiger cubs grew, but he was probably right. I realized that in truth, Yemmy, Omy, and Cheetah weren't really our pets. After all, they didn't live in the cabin; they lived in the wild. We rarely saw them. But for some reason I couldn't get myself to admit to Tarzan that they weren't our pets. I dropped the subject and turned my attention back to the notebook.

"Okay, let's look at the next underline," I said. "Okay, at the end of the second paragraph, I underlined the word *among* in the clause *no words passed among them.* Now, this is an error in usage. You have to understand the difference between the words *among* and *between.*"

"What is it?"

"Well, if you're talking about only two people or things, you should use the word *between.* For example, let's say that we had some meat for Yemmy and Omy. When we give it to them, we might say, "Here, divide this *between* you.""

I thought Tarzan might say something about the cubs not speaking English, but he remained silent.

"On the other hand," I continued, "if you're talking about three or more people or things, you might use the word *among.* For example, if we had some pet treats for Yemmy, Omy, and Cheetah, we might say, "Here, divide these *among* you.""

"Why did you say that I *might* use the word *among* for three or more things? Don't I have to?"

"Well, sometimes you can use *between*, even if you're talking about more than two things."

"You can?"

"Yes. It depends on whether you're thinking of the things collectively or individually."

"What do you mean?"

"I mean that generally you use *among* when you think of the three or more things collectively, and you use *between* when you think of them individually."

"I still don't understand."

"Okay, let me give you an example. Let's say that a classroom teacher has an apple on her desk. When she finishes writing on the blackboard and turns around, she notices that the apple is missing. She knows it had to have been taken by one of the students in the class. Thinking of the class collectively—as one group, I mean—she says, 'There's a thief among us.'"

Tarzan didn't respond.

"Do you see? Because she's thinking of the students collectively, as a group, she uses *among*, not *between*."

"Oh."

"Okay, now here's another example. Let's say that we were planning a surprise party for Yemmy and Omy. Of course, since it's a surprise, we wouldn't want them to know about it ahead of time. But let's say we want to tell Cheetah. I might say to Cheetah, "I'm going to tell you a secret about Yemmy and Omy; of course, this is just between you, me, and Tarzan."

Again Tarzan didn't respond.

"Do you see? Because I'm thinking of the three of us—you, me, and Cheetah—as individuals, I used *between*, not *among*. Do you see?"

"I guess so. If the things are thought of collectively, as a group, you use *among*. But if the things are thought of individually, you use *between*. Is that it?"

"That's it. Of course, if you're talking about only *two* things, then you always use *between*."

"Okay, I get it."

I looked at the notebook and saw that there was only one underline left to discuss. After that, would I have the nerve to confront my feelings? Would I finally confess my love to Tarzan? Or would I simply say that I was ready to eat brunch? We would soon see.

"Okay, one more underline," I said. "You wrote: 'Looking at her, she was created . . .' That's an example of what's called a *dangling modifier*."

"What's that?"

"Well, do you remember that we said that an adjective *modifies* a noun or pronoun, usually by describing it?"

"Yes," he said, with a rising pitch.

"Well, in that sense, to *modify* something is to describe it, to give information about it."

I waited for Tarzan to reply, but he just looked at me expectantly.

"Anyway, in your article, you used the introductory phrase 'Looking at her . . .' Now, the question is, Who is modified by that phrase? In other words, *who* does that phrase describe? *Who* is 'looking at her.'"

"It was me. I was looking at her—at you."

"Okay. That's the point. Since the phrase 'Looking at her . . .' gives information about *you*, or modifies *you*, the *very next word* after that introductory phrase must be about *you* and not about anyone else. So, for example, you could have written 'Looking at her, I could see that she was created . . .' Do you see? That makes sense. Now it's clear that the phrase 'Looking at her' refers to *you*."

"Oh."

"See, the way you wrote it, it seems as though 'Looking at her' refers to *me*—because you wrote 'Looking at her, *she* . . .' Anyway, in your article, the modifier—the descriptive phrase 'Looking at her,' I mean—and the word it actually modifies—the pronoun *I*, which you happened to leave out altogether—aren't placed next to each other. That means that the modifier—'Looking at her'—is not properly resolved; it seems to hang uncertainly. In other words, it seems to *dangle*. That's why a faulty construction like that is called a *dangling modifier*."

"Oh."

"All right. Now, let's see if you really understand this. I'm going to make up a sentence with a dangling modifier, and you tell me what's wrong with it, okay?"

"I already know what's wrong."

"But I didn't make up the sentence yet."

"I know, but from what you said, I already know that the modifier will be modifying the wrong noun. Right?"

"That's right, but don't be so smart all the time. When you're first learning something, it's nice to show a little honest ignorance."

"Oh."

"Anyway, in this sentence, tell me what the modifier is, then tell me which noun or pronoun it *seems* to modify, and then tell me which noun or pronoun it really *should* modify."

"Okay."

"Wait, there's more. Then tell me how to rewrite the sentence *without* a dangling modifier."

"Okay."

I tried to think up a good sentence. I remembered that in high school English, when we talked about this, some of the errors concerning dangling modifiers sounded pretty funny.

"Okay," I said, "here's one: 'Cooking his lunch, a lion attacked Tom.'"

"That's funny! Okay, the modifier is *Cooking his lunch*. It *seems* to modify *lion*, but it *really* modifies Tom. It could be rewritten as 'Cooking his lunch, Tom was attacked by a lion.' Or, the modifier could be changed into a dependent clause: 'While Tom was cooking his lunch, he was attacked by a lion.'"

Wow, he's good, I thought; a natural grammarian. Maybe if I go back to work at *American Monthly* I can hire him as an editor to correct all the journalists' grammar errors.

"That's excellent," I said. "Okay, that's it for Article 20."

Now, should I suggest that we have brunch, or should I talk about *us?*

"Tarzan, before we have brunch, there's something I'd like to talk to you about."

"What?"

"Did you really think my hair was like a shimmering waterfall? Or did you just write that for the sake of the magazine article?"

"Well, it tumbled down from your head."

Was that a compliment, I wondered?

"Well," I said, "let me put it this way. I think you're nice. Very, very nice."

"Why? What did I do?"

"Oh, little things . . . like this morning when you told me not to read the book about disasters because it might upset me. You were concerned about my feelings. You're sensitive."

"I am?"

"Sure. That's why you told me to read a *nice* book—the one about birds."

No reply. A long silence. Finally he said, "Is that all you wanted to tell me?"

"Uh . . ."

"So, did you find out anything interesting about birds in the book?"

"Um, it said that there's this one kind of sparrow in India whose nest is lit up at night."

"You mean someone put a lamp in it?"

"No, the bird puts some moist clay in the nest, and then it catches fireflies and imprisons them in the clay. The fireflies light up the nest!"

"That's amazing. Are you hungry? Are you ready for brunch?"

That afternoon we brought the table and chairs outside again, but instead of in front of the cabin, we placed them in back—you know, for a change of scene. I was reading the book about animals, and Tarzan was hard at work on Article 21.

In two more days, I thought to myself, we'll be finished with all twenty-four articles. Then what? I wonder what Tarzan's writing about right now. In the last article, he wrote that he'd been spell-bound by the sight of me. I discreetly glanced over at the notebook, but all I could see was the title of Article 21: "Tarzan in Love." Wow, I thought, does that mean . . . does that mean . . .

But maybe he was writing about being in love with me back when we first met. Maybe things were different now.

"What's wrong?" he said.

"Nothing."

He must have seen me glance at the notebook. Well, I wouldn't do that again. I'd just sit here patiently until he finished. Then I'd be free to read the whole thing. Meanwhile, I'll just read about different kinds of animals in this book of mine.

All of a sudden Tarzan said, "How come you're not interrupting me with stories about strange animals like you usually do?"

"I don't know. I'm just thinking about things, I guess."

"What things?"

"I don't know," I lied.

I tried to find something interesting in the animals book so that Tarzan wouldn't suspect that I was thinking about love and about us.

"Here's something," I said, a little too enthusiastically. "Remember I told you about giant crabs in Cuba that can outrace a horse? Well, there are giant crabs in India that can climb coconut trees.

They take the coconuts and fling them to the ground, where they crack open a little. Then they crawl back down and use their powerful claws to open the coconuts, which they eat."

"You say that happens in India? Isn't that where those sparrows imprison fireflies? That must be a pretty interesting place, India."

I didn't know whether or not he was being sarcastic, so I didn't say anything.

I thumbed through the book some more, and then I heard Tarzan say, "Okay, I'm done with Article 21."

I couldn't *wait* to read it. I expected it to be about *me* and how he felt about me. I took the notebook and started to read aloud. I was so enthralled that I forgot to underline the errors. But as soon as I finished reading, I went back and underlined them. Anyway, when I was done, it looked like this:

Article 21: "Tarzan in Love"

The next morning the girl, evidently hungry, wandered into the jungle to gather fruit. Her search led her <u>further and further</u> from the cabin. I waited in silence beside the little house until she should return. My thoughts were of the beautiful girl. I couldn't think of <u>nothing</u> else. I was rapidly becoming impatient for her return, that I might gaze upon her and be near her, perhaps touch her hand.

While I waited I passed the time thinking about what I'd like to say to her. I imagined that I'd say "I am Tarzan of the Apes. I will bring you the best fruits, the <u>most tastiest</u> deer, the finest meats that roam the jungle. I will hunt for you. I am the greatest and mightiest of the jungle fighters. I will fight for you. Your name is Jane; I heard a man in the rowboat call you that. Tarzan loves you. <u>Can</u> I kiss you?"

Suddenly I heard a familiar sound. It was the passing of a great ape through the lower branches of the forest. For an instant I listened intently, and then from the jungle came the agonized scream of a girl. I shot like a panther into the jungle.

Oh my, oh my, oh my! According to this article, Tarzan *did* love me. Then why didn't he act like it? A high school friend of mine once said, "If you want to know if a boy likes you, go by how he acts, not by what he says."

"Tarzan," I said, "you know, these articles are for publication in a national magazine. It's not a fiction magazine, you know. This is journalism. Now, is what you wrote the truth?"

"Of course!"

"All of it?"

"I wouldn't make up something."

"You really wanted to take my hand?"

"Yes."

I extended my hand to him. "Well, here it is . . . take it."

He took my hand, brought it to his lips, and briefly kissed the back of it. Then he released it.

"So what errors did I make in the article?" he said.

Was he toying with me? Here was an article in which he proclaims his *love* for me, and yet he wants to discuss what he wrote *academically*. Well, two can play that game, I thought. "Okay, let's look at the underlines," I said, in a no-nonsense tone.

"In the first paragraph you underlined *further and further*," Tarzan said. "What's wrong with that?"

Even though Tarzan's behavior was frustrating, I decided not to let my feelings show during our grammar lesson. After all, maybe he wasn't "playing a game," so to speak. Knowing him, he probably was being completely sincere. I doubt if he knew how to be any other way—having been raised by apes, I mean. Maybe his whole problem was the same as mine. Maybe, just like me, he was simply too shy or afraid to admit his true feelings. Well, one of us was going to have to break the ice. But Tarzan's writing about feelings he'd had months ago didn't count—it wasn't the same as talking about feelings he has now.

"Okay," I said, not feeling angry any longer, now that I'd had that little talk with myself, "this is another mistake in usage. You have to understand the difference between the words *further* and *farther*."

"What's the difference?"

"Well, both words mean 'more far,' and some people use the words interchangeably. However, most people use *farther* to talk about actual distances that can be measured. For example, they might say 'America is *farther* from here than England'—because the actual distances from here to those countries can be measured."

409

Tarzan didn't respond.

"And," I went on, "most people use *further* to talk about immeasurable, nonphysical, or figurative distances. For example, they might say 'Nothing could be *further* from the truth' or 'Let's not discuss it any *further.*' Do you see?"

"I do. So you don't have to explain it any *further.*"

That was Tarzan's idea of a joke. I smiled a tiny bit and said, "So, what should you have written?"

"I should have written 'Her search led her *farther* and *farther* from the cabin' because the distance she—you—traveled from the cabin can be measured."

"Good. Okay. Now, let's go on to the next underline. A few sentences after that you wrote that your thoughts were of the 'beautiful girl' and that you 'couldn't think of *nothing* else.' Now, do you know why that's wrong?"

"The beautiful girl was you."

"Do you really think I'm beau— I mean, do you know why that's wrong?"

"Um . . ."

"Do you remember when we spoke about double negatives? If you're trying to say something negative—you know, like you *can't* or *won't* or *don't* do such-and-such—you should use only *one* negative word, not two. Why? Because if you use two negatives, the second cancels or undoes the first, and you end up with an *affirmative.* See, if you say 'I couldn't think of nothing,' you're using two negative words in the same sentence: *couldn't* and *nothing.* By doing that, the negative is cancelled and what you're really saying is that you *could* think of *something.*"

"So, then what should I have written?"

"Well, you should have used only one negative. So you could have said either 'I couldn't think of *anything*' or 'I *could* think of nothing.' Either way, you're using a single negative and you're expressing what you really mean."

"Oh."

I was flattered that he couldn't think of anything but me, the 'beautiful girl,' but I decided to concentrate on the grammar lesson for now. "Okay, now let's look at the next underline. In the second paragraph you wrote 'the most tastiest deer.' Now, do you remember when we first spoke about adjectives and we talked about comparing things? We said that when you use an adjective to compare two things, you use the *comparative* form, as in 'Tarzan is *stronger* than

410

Jane.' And when you use an adjective to compare *more* than two things, you use the *superlative* form, as in 'Tarzan is the *fastest* runner in Africa.'"

"I remember."

"Good. So, let's talk about the superlative form. Now, you form the superlative form of most short adjectives simply by adding *est*, as in *tallest*, *strongest*, *fastest*, and so on. And you form the superlative form of most long adjectives by add the word *most*, as in *most interesting*, *most desirable*, *most intelligent*, and so on. Do you remember?"

"I remember."

"Well, in your article, when you wrote *most tastiest*, you formed the superlative using *both* methods—adding *est* and adding the word *more*—at the same time. In other words, you formed the superlative *twice*. You should have written either *most tasty* or *tastiest*."

"Which one is better?"

"Well, I think *tastiest* is the better choice because it's an actual word; I mean it's an actual word in the dictionary."

"Oh."

Well, here we were again with just one more underline to go—and it was in a sentence about kissing! Now, if *that's* not a made-to-order lead-in to a discussion about our feelings for each other, I don't know what is.

"Okay, one more underline," I said. "At the end of the second paragraph, you wrote: 'Can I kiss you?' Now, what's wrong with that?"

"There's something wrong with my wanting to kiss you?"

"No, I mean what's wrong with that grammatically—I mean what's wrong with that usage-wise?"

"Uh . . ."

"The question is, What's the difference between the words *can* and *may*—between the sentences 'Can I kiss you?' and 'May I kiss you?'"

"Uh . . ."

All this talk about kissing made my face feel a little hot. I think I was probably blushing a little, but Tarzan didn't say anything. Then I noticed that his face look a bit red. He must be feeling exactly what I'm feeling, I though.

"Well," I said, "*can* is used to express the *ability* to do something, as in 'I *can* lift a fifty-pound weight,' whereas *may* is used to request *permission* to do something, as in 'May I walk you home?'"

"Oh."

411

"So, we know that you have the *ability* to kiss me. But you were asking *permission* to kiss me. So you should have written 'May I kiss you?'"

"Oh."

"But I have to say that a lot of people, especially in conversation—you know, in *informal* usage—use the word *can* to request permission. For example, they might say, 'Can I borrow a pencil?'"

"And that's not wrong?"

"It depends on whom you ask. Grammar experts and schoolteachers might say it is, but I don't think it is—because so many people say it, I mean."

"So then it *was* okay for me to say 'Can I kiss you?'"

"Maybe. It depends on how formal or informal you want your writing to be. But I have to say that, because we know each other so well, and because we're so fond of each other—in fact, we *adore* each other—you don't have to ask permission to kiss me. You can—I mean *may*—kiss me . . . if you want to, that is."

"Oh. But I was writing about the time I first saw you. Back then, we didn't know each other. So imagined that I would ask you."

"But now we know each other. Do you want to kiss me?"

At that Tarzan's face became even redder.

"Well, you don't have to answer that right now. Let's bring the table and chairs back inside and think about what we want to have for dinner, okay?"

Tarzan silently stood up, lifted the table, and carried it around to the front of the cabin and through the door. I glumly followed with the two chairs.

Chapter 31: Tarzan Recalls Becoming Human

As I gradually awakened early the next morning, several thoughts, or wisps of thoughts, or maybe dreams, swirled through my mind, competing for my attention. One concerned the conversation I'd be having with Tarzan later today or tomorrow about how we truly felt about each other. But that was interrupted by the thought of a hundred chimps arriving with clenched fists. But then that was interrupted sometimes by the idea of mosquitoes infecting me with horrible diseases and sometimes by the thought of a lake turning upside down and smothering me.

Whether these were nightmares or daydreams, I can't say, but suddenly I was wide awake and I sat up in bed. I noticed that the sun was shining and I expected Tarzan to arrive shortly.

While I waited, I wondered what the next day or two would bring. So much—my whole future—was at stake. If all went well, Tarzan would admit that he loved me as much as I loved him and that he wanted to marry me. Also, the chimps would arrive with the diamonds and gold, as planned. And, of course, I wouldn't become the victim of any geological or meteorological hazard—nor would Tarzan, Yemmy, Omy, or Cheetah.

I felt that everything was building to some kind of climax. By tomorrow afternoon I might be loveless, poor, and sick. Or I might not. In fact, I might be deliriously in love and ridiculously wealthy. It was amazing to realize that such vast extremes in my fortunes hinged on such seemingly minor factors as chimpanzees' fists, mosquitoes, and a simple yes or no answer from Tarzan.

My thoughts were suddenly interrupted when Tarzan arrived and bid me good morning. He went right to the table and sat down.

"I'm going to start on Article 22 now. Do you have something to read to occupy yourself while I write?"

Is that all he cared about, whether or not I could *occupy* myself?

"Yes," I said. "I'll read the book about animals while you write."

"Okay."

Actually, I couldn't wait for him to write Article 22 because in the last article he wrote that he loved me. Of course, that was then. Still, maybe in this article he would talk more about his feelings for me.

I thumbed through the book on animals, but every so often I stole a glance at Tarzan to see how far along we was on the article. I didn't expect it to take very long for him to write it, because all the articles were pretty short. For once I was thankful that the readers of *American Monthly* had short attention spans!

"Here's something interesting," I said. "It says here that a seventy-pound octopus can squeeze through an opening as small as a silver dollar."

"What's a silver dollar?"

"It's a coin. It's less than two inches across, I'd say."

"And a big octopus can fit through that? How is that possible?"

"It says it's because it has no backbone."

"Oh."

We were silent again and I thumbed through the book some more. Then suddenly Tarzan announced that he had finished Article 22.

"Good!" I said. "Let me see." I walked to the table.

"Aren't you forgetting something?" he said.

"What?"

"Well, this is the first morning that you didn't ask me how many more days until the chimps are supposed to bring the diamonds and gold. And it's only one more day! It's tomorrow! What happened? Did you forget?"

"I guess I did. I guess I had more important things on my mind."

"Like what?"

"Oh, I don't know. Just things."

"Oh."

I sat down next to Tarzan, took the notebook, and started reading Article 22 aloud. This time I remembered to underline the errors. When I was finished, it looked like this:

Article 22: "Jane in Love"

A mile was covered before I overtook them—a giant gorilla with Jane tightly grasped in one great arm. Seeing me, the ape pushed the terrified girl roughly aside to meet my attack.

Like two charging bulls we came together, and like two wolves we sought each other's throat. Against the long fangs of the ape was pitted the thin blade of my knife.

Jane—her graceful, young form flattened against the trunk of a great tree, her hands tightly pressed against her rising and falling chest, and her eyes wide with mingled horror, fascination, and admiration, watched the ape battle me for his prize.

I plunged my sharp knife a dozen times into the ape's heart, and finally the great beast rolled upon the ground. It was dead. Jane—I mean, you—sprang forward with outstretched arms toward the primitive man that had fought for you.

And I? I did what no red-blooded man needs lessons in doing. I took my woman in my arms and smothered her upturned lips with kisses. For a moment you lay there with half-closed eyes. For that moment, I believe, you, too, knew the true meaning of love.

Well, in this article he *sort* of said that he loved me, I guess. I mean, he referred to me as his *woman* and in the last sentence he used the word *too*. He said that I, *too*, knew the true meaning of love. Doesn't that imply that *he* knew the true meaning? And how would he, unless he loved me? But again, that was then . . .

Instead of talking about whether or not he loved me, then or now, I said, "I'm glad to see that you hyphenated red-blooded in the last paragraph."

"It's a compound adjective," he answered.

"Right. And I'm also glad to see that you wrote: 'For a moment you *lay* there . . .' and not something like 'For a moment you *laid* there . . .' or 'For a moment you *lied* there . . .'"

"Because *lay* is the past tense of *lie*. You taught me that."

"Well, I'm glad you remembered. Most people don't."

No response.

"And I like your writing a lot, too. I like how you said: 'outstretched arms' instead of simply 'arms.' It's very visual, very vivid. I can see it. And I like how you said 'toward the primitive man' instead of 'toward me.' It emphasizes the difference between us; it reminds the readers that we're of two different worlds." I thought about saying something about how opposites attract, but I decided against it.

"Thank you," Tarzan answered. Was he learning how to accept a compliment? I hoped so.

"Anyway," I said, "let's go over the errors. There are only two. First, in the third paragraph, I underlined *admiration*. But I'm really referring to the punctuation after that word—the comma. Can you explain why there's a comma there?"

"Well," he explained, "that whole phrase, starting with 'her graceful young form . . .' and ending with '. . . and admiration' is one giant parenthetical phrase. I mean, if I'd left it out, you'd still know I was talking about Jane . . . about you. That's why there's a comma after it."

"But remember, parenthetical phrases can be enclosed by parentheses, dashes, or commas. Once you choose which of those marks you want to use, you have to use that mark at both the beginning *and* the end of the parenthetical phrase. In other words, you can't start with one type of punctuation mark and then switch to another."

"Oh, I see what I did. I started with a dash—at the beginning of the parenthetical phrase, I mean—but ended with a comma—at the end of the phrase. I should have used either two commas or two dashes. But which one should I have used?"

"Well, that's often a matter of writer's choice. But in this case, because the parenthetical phrase contains several commas of its own—internal commas, I mean—I think dashes is the better choice. It's clearer that way. I mean, there's no chance that someone might mix up the phrase's 'enclosing' punctuation with its internal punctuation."

"I agree," Tarzan said. "So, after the word *admiration*, I should have used a dash, not a comma."

"Exactly. Now, let's look at the next error."

"Then we'll have brunch."

"Okay. But look at the end of the fourth paragraph. You referred to yourself as the 'primitive man that fought for you.'"

"I thought you said you liked that line."

"I do. But I'm not talking about the phrase 'primitive man'; I'm talking about the word *that*. It's a mistake in usage. We spoke about this before. Remember, you use the pronoun *that* to refer to things and the pronoun *who* to refer to people. Since the 'primitive man' is a person—"

"I remember now. We talked about this when I wrote about a dog—a strange little creature who—I mean *that*—walked on four legs."

"Right!"

"So, in this article I should have written 'the primitive man *who* had fought for you.'"

"Good!"

Silence for a while.

"Tarzan," I finally said, "I want you to know how much I appreciate your saving me from that giant gorilla. I owe you my life! I'll be forever grateful." I looked at him meaningfully. I'm not sure, but I probably batted my eyelashes a few times—not on purpose, of course.

"If not for that gorilla," he said, "we may never have met."

"Maybe we should have thanked him before you killed him."

Tarzan didn't seem to know how to respond to that.

"Are you glad we met?" I ventured. "Wait! Don't answer that. You don't have to answer that. I had no right to ask—"

"I-I-I . . ." he stammered. He took my hand and kissed it.

"Oh Tarzan," I exclaimed, "what will become of us? Tomorrow you'll finish the last article . . . and then what? Will you come back to Baltimore with me? Will I stay here with you? We have to talk about these things! I have to know."

417

"I don't know. What do *you* want to do?"

I thought to myself: But don't you understand? It all depends on you. If you love me, I'll stay here with you. But if you don't, I'll return to Baltimore alone. I'll see if there's still a job for me at the magazine. Maybe I'll even suggest to my boss that we publish longer articles in order to appeal to readers with longer attention spans. And if I go back home alone, and if the chimps bring the diamonds and stuff, maybe I'll buy that small mansion. But if I stay here with you I won't even care about the diamonds.

But, of course, I didn't say any of this. I wanted Tarzan to reveal his feeling for me of his own volition. I wanted everything to come from *him*. Otherwise, it wouldn't *mean* anything.

"I don't know," I said. "Let's have brunch. We can talk about it later . . . if you want to."

After brunch I said, "It's a nice day. Let's take the table and chairs outside again. But, for a change of scene, let's place them at the *side* of the cabin, okay?"

"Okay . . . Bring a book with you so you'll have something to do while I write Article 23."

Oh my, "Article 23." That had a scary sound to it. I mean, it was the next-to-last article. We were so close to the end of our adventure, our journey . . . our relationship? Just hearing Tarzan say the number 23 out loud gave me a nervous feeling all over my body.

I brought the book on animals to the table and thumbed through it while Tarzan wrote. From this point on I didn't have to wonder about Tarzan's life story, because I had already entered it. I already knew what happened from here on. You remember how I started this story, way back at the very beginning? I said that I first met Tarzan when he rescued me from a gorilla. Well, that's the incident he wrote about in the last article, so now you're all caught up with how everything unfolded.

"Tarzan," I said, "I know I'm interrupting your writing, but here's another interesting thing about animals in this book."

"What?"

"It says that there was once an alligator that had a tree growing out of its back."

"That's impossible!"

"Well, not really out of its back, technically. See, it had a lot of dirt on its back. I guess it didn't go in the water very much. Anyway, a tree started to grow out of that dirt. And the tree just got bigger

418

and bigger. Eventually, this alligator was walking around with an actual tree growing from its back."

"I'd think he'd be embarrassed in front of all the other alligators. I'd think the others would tease him."

"I don't think animals get embarrassed or tease each other."

"I think you're right. So what happened to this alligator?"

"I don't know. It doesn't say."

"Oh."

We were silent awhile, and then Tarzan said that he'd finished the article. I was especially curious to read this one because I was now part of the story. I was *there*. I'd know exactly what happened, and I'd be able to see how accurate Tarzan was in his storytelling.

I took the notebook and read aloud, underlining the couple of errors I noticed.

Article 23: "Becoming Human"

After we kissed, the terror of what you had just <u>went</u> through seemed to suddenly overwhelm you, and you fell into a dead faint. Then I did just what my first ancestors would have done. I took my woman in my arms and carried her into the jungle.

I took to the trees. When I came to a place that looked cool and inviting, I dropped to the ground. As I gently placed you on the soft grass, you awoke and looked up at me.

With a bound I sprang back into the trees and disappeared. You probably wondered what had happened to me. Had I left you there to your fate in the wild jungle? But in a moment I was back, my arms filled with ripe and luscious fruit.

You reeled and would have fallen, had not I, dropping my burden, caught you in my arms. You didn't lose consciousness again, but you clung tightly to me, shuddering and trembling like a frightened deer. I stroked your soft hair and tried to comfort and quiet you. Then I pressed my lips lightly upon your <u>forehead,</u> you closed your eyes and sighed.

Then I gathered up the fruit, and laid it at your feet. Next I sat beside you and, with my knife, opened and prepared the various fruits for our meal. Together and in silence we ate, occasionally stealing sly glances at one another, until finally you broke into a merry laugh in which I joined.

I had long since reached a decision as to what my future procedure should be. I had had time to recollect all that I had read of the ways of men and women in the books at the cabin. I would act <u>like</u> I imagined the men in the books would have acted were they in my place.

Well, I can tell you, having been there, that that's what happened, all right. So, I thought to myself, whatever Tarzan knew about the interaction of men and women he learned from his father's books! Well, where else could he have learned it? Certainly not from Kala or the other apes!

"That's a nice story," I said. "Did you really think my hair was soft . . . and my voice was merry?"

"I . . ."

"Never mind. You were very sweet to take such good care of me and to bring me such delicious fruit."

"I *wanted* to. It made me *happy* to do that for you."

"It did?"

"Of course. I would do *anything* for you."

Will you marry me, I thought.

"That's so sweet!" I exclaimed. "But let's go over the errors in this article. There are only three. Now, in the first sentence you wrote: 'what you had just *went* through . . .'"

"What's wrong with that?"

"Well, do you remember the principal parts of a verb?"

"You mean the present tense, past tense, and past participle?"

"Exactly. Now, what are the principal parts of the verb *go?*"

"*Go, went, gone.* Today I *go,* yesterday I *went,* I should have *gone.*"

"Very good. And when do you use the past participle?"

"When you use a tense that includes the word *have* or *had,* as in 'I should *have seen* . . .' or 'If I *had taken* . . .'"

"Good. Now—"

"Wait! I see what I did. I got mixed up because the word *just* separated the word *had* from the 'go' verb. I should have written 'what you had just *gone* through . . .' because the verb is really *had gone.*"

"Very good! Now, in the last sentence of the fourth paragraph, I underlined the word *forehead,* but I'm really referring to the punctuation—the comma—after that word."

"What about it?"

"Well, that comma makes the whole sentence a *run-on sentence.*"

"What's that?"

"It's is a sentence with two or more independent clauses that are not separated by conjunctions or semicolons. In other words, it's a sentence with independent clauses that are smack up against each other and are separated by only a comma or by nothing at all."

"Oh."

"If independent clauses are not properly separated—by semicolons or conjunctions, I mean—they seem *run into* each other."

"I get it. So I needed to separate the first independent clause, 'Then I pressed my lips gently against your forehead,' from the second independent clause, 'you closed your eyes and sighed,' with either a semicolon or the conjunction *and.*"

"Right. Otherwise you have a run-on sentence, which is an error."

"Okay."

"All right, one more error to go. In the last sentence of the article, you wrote 'I would act *like* I imagined the men in the books would have acted . . .'"

"What's wrong with that?"

"It's a mistake in usage. You have to understand the difference between the words *like* and *as.*"

"You mean I should have written 'I would act *as* I imagined the men in the books would have acted . . .'?"

"Yes. You see, both words—*like* and *as*—are used to make a comparison, but the one that introduces a *clause*—you know, a group of words with a subject and a verb—is *as.* Therefore, you'd say . . . oh . . . 'When I was a youth among the apes, I was embarrassed about my hairless body, *as* anyone in my position would have been.' Do you see? '. . . anyone in my position would have been' is a clause, so it's introduced by *as*, not *like.*"

"Oh."

"On the other hand, the word that introduces a comparison that doesn't contain a verb is *like.* So, you'd say . . . oh . . . 'He eats *like* an ape.' Do you see?"

"Yes . . . You think I eat like an ape?"

"No! No! That was just an example."

"Oh."

"Well! We've finished going over Article 23. Can you believe that by tomorrow we'll have finished all twenty-four articles? That's quite an achievement! We should be proud of ourselves."

No response.

"So," I said, "have you seen Tantor lately? Has he said anything about the plan?"

"No."

"Well, tomorrow's going to be a big day . . . a big, big day. For one thing we'll have to figure out a way to carry all the jewels. I mean, there will be a hundred chimps bringing it, but only two of us carrying it away . . . if we go away together, that is.

All of a sudden my eyes felt wet. I didn't want Tarzan to see me wiping my eyes so I just kept on talking. "I mean if we go away somewhere together like Mount Kilimanjaro or Cairo or Baltimore."

Suddenly a big tear slid off my cheek and plopped right onto the notebook. I looked at it through misty eyes and saw that, amazingly, it had fallen onto the word *eyes* in the phrase 'you closed your eyes and sighed' in Article 23.

"What's wrong," he said, with genuine concern.

"I'm scared . . . I'm scared," I answered in a tiny voice.

"Of what?"

"Of tomorrow. I don't know what's going to happen."

"Happen? You mean about the chimps and the gold?"

"No, not that. With us! I don't know what's going to happen with us. After you finish Article 24 tomorrow morning, there'll be no reason for me to say here any longer. But I don't want to leave." I started to sob—a little at first, and then uncontrollably.

"Now, now, don't cry. Why do you have to leave?"

"Because *American Monthly* will want me back," I whined. "They'll want me to bring the articles. What am I supposed to do, not show up? Tell them I quit, that I don't need to earn a living?"

"Look, maybe you're just hungry. It's time for dinner. I'll get you some delicious fruit. That should make you feel better."

I didn't answer. I tried to control my sobbing.

"Do you want to have a cookout? Do you want to go to the pond?"

"No. I don't feel like going anywhere."

"Should I find Yemmy and Omy? Or Cheetah? That should cheer you up."

"No, I just want to sit here."

We were silent awhile, then I said reluctantly, "Okay, get the fruit. We'll have dinner."

Tarzan ran off and was soon out of sight. I sat all alone at a little table at the side of a little cabin at the edge of a big jungle—a little girl from Baltimore far, far from home.

I can't remember what I thought about while Tarzan gathered our dinner; my mind was too jumbled, I guess. We must have carried the table and chairs back inside the cabin when he returned, because that's where we ended up. I don't remember what kind of fruit we ate, but we must have eaten something because I remember hearing Tarzan say, "That was good," and I remember hearing myself say, "Well, goodnight. See you tomorrow."

That night I couldn't fall asleep. I kept wondering about the day to come. Would I confess my love to Tarzan? If so, what would he answer? Would the chimps bring the diamonds and gold? If so, I'd be so rich that I'd never have to work again. But is that a good thing? What would I do all day? Would I sit around and be bored? Maybe it's good to need to earn a living. It gives you something to do—to fill the hours of the day. I think that animals don't get bored because they spend all their time foraging for food; that gives them something to do. People are kinds of animals, except we—people in civilized countries, I mean—forage for money so we can *buy* food. But if I had ten million dollars, I'd stop foraging. And then what? What purpose would I have? Would I be Tarzan's wife? Is that my purpose? Will we get married in Cairo or Casablanca, or somewhere else?

Those were the thoughts that swirled through my mind for hours until, finally, I drifted to sleep.

Chapter 32: Tarzan and Jane's Future

When I awoke the next morning, the sun was already quite high. I must have slept late, I thought. Where could Tarzan be? Usually he was here by this time. He knew that he still had Article 24 to write.

I got out of bed, went to the table, sat down, and picked up the notebook. I reread Articles 20 and 21. In them Tarzan wrote that I had a sweet face, a graceful figure, beautiful features, and delicate snowy skin. He said he couldn't thing of anything but me and that he wanted to gaze upon me, be near me, and perhaps touch my hand. Then he said that he wanted to kiss me! Now, I ask you, don't those sound like the words of a man in love? Then why does he seem so uninterested in talking about our future together? By the end of today I'll have to decide whether or not to return to Baltimore.

"Good morning!" It was Tarzan at the door.

"Hi. Where were you? It's late."

"I was here earlier, but I saw that you were asleep, so I went to look for Yemmy, Omy, and Cheetah. I thought you'd like to see them."

That was thoughtful, I thought. But I said, "Oh . . . Did you find them?"

"No. But I don't even know if I'd recognize them anymore. They must be big by now."

"Oh, I guess you're right." Then, after a pause: Well, today's the last day!"

I wanted to see how he'd respond to that. I hoped he'd say something like "What do you *mean* today's the last day? Aren't we going to *see* each other anymore?" I mean, that's what *I* would have said.

But all he said was, "I know; today I write the last article: Article 24. So, what are you going to do while I write it. Do you want to read one of your books?"

"Okay," I said dispiritedly.

I grabbed a book at random from the shelf. I didn't care which one it was. It turned out to be the one about animals. I sat on the edge of the bed and tried to read while Tarzan wrote at the table.

Maybe, it suddenly occurred to me, Tarzan will write something in Article 24 that reveals his feelings about our future. Maybe he's too shy to talk about that out loud, and he'll write it in the article! I convinced myself that that was the case, and I patiently waited for him to finish, while I pretended to read the animal book.

"You're awfully quiet today," he suddenly said. "Is anything wrong?"

"No."

"Aren't you going to tell me anything interesting about those animals you're reading about?"

I wasn't even reading. But I glanced at the page the book happened to be opened to.

"Oh. Okay. It says here that if you cut off the head of a rattlesnake, the severed head can still bite people and inject venom for twenty minutes."

"Really? Without the body?"

"That's what it says."

"Why would someone cut off the head of a rattlesnake?"

"I don't know."

We were quiet again. I didn't want to say anything because I wanted Tarzan to finish his article as soon as possible—so I could see what he said about our future, I mean.

After what seemed like an eternity, he finally said, "Okay, I'm done."

"Good."

I went to the table, sat next to Tarzan, and took the notebook. Reading aloud was a bit difficult because I was breathing faster than normal—from the anticipation of seeing what Tarzan wrote about our future, I mean.

The article was entitled "Home." Well, that was a good sign. Maybe he'd talk about making a home together. In my excitement I forgot to underline the errors as I went along—but as it turned out, there was only one! He was getting so good at grammar! Anyway, after I went back and underlined the error, the article looked like this:

Article 24: "Home"

Again I rose and went into the trees (but first I explained that I would return shortly, so that you would not be afraid while I was gone.) I returned in a few minutes with a quantity of soft grasses and ferns. I made two more trips until I had quite a pile of material at hand.

Then I spread the ferns and grasses upon the ground in a soft flat bed, and above it leaned a large amount of branches together so that they met a few feet over its center. Upon these I spread layers of huge leaves, and with more branches and more leaves I closed one end of the little shelter I had built.

It was growing dark now, so I rose and led you to the leafy bedroom I had erected and motioned you to go inside. To assure you of your safety, I removed my hunting knife from its case and handed it to you handle first. You took the knife, entered, and lay down upon the soft grasses, while I stood guard all night before the entrance.

When you awoke the next morning, I was away again gathering fruit. When you saw me return, your eyes brightened. Once more we sat down together to eat. When we had finished our breakfast I went inside the shady hut and recovered my knife.

Motioning you to follow, I walked toward the trees, and taking you in one arm, swung to the branches above. I think you knew that I was taking you back to my cabin. When we arrived there you took me by the hand to lead me to it.

I drew you to me very gently and stooped to kiss you. You threw your arms around my neck and kissed me. "I love you . . . I love you," you murmured.

Nothing. Not one word about our future together. I was fooled by the title, "Home." He was referring to events that happened *months* ago. And then that ending! He said that *I* said "I love you." But he doesn't talk about what *he* said. Well, I probably did say "I love you." Wouldn't you love someone who rescued you from a gorilla, built you a shelter, and brought you a meal? It's understandable.

"Well," I said, in a businesslike tone, "are you ready to go over the errors? You made only two. After this, you won't need any more grammar lessons. You'll be an expert."

He nodded.

"Okay, look at the punctuation at the end of the first sentence of the article. You have two punctuation marks there—a closing parenthesis and a period. The question is, which should come first, the parenthesis or the period?"

"Since you underlined it, I must have done it incorrectly. So, are you saying that whenever you have both a period and a closing parenthesis at the end of a sentence, the parenthesis comes first?"

"No. Actually, it depends."

"On what?"

"It depends on whether the words within the parentheses exist as a part of the previous sentence or as their *own* sentence."

"I don't understand."

"Well, let me show you." In the notebook I wrote *There are 365 days in a year (except leap year, which has 366).* Then under that I wrote *There are 365 days in a year. (That's not always true, though.)* Then I said, "You see, in the first example the words in parentheses are considered a *part* of the original sentence. I mean, the *whole thing* is one big sentence. For that reason, the word *except*, which starts the parenthetical portion, is spelled with a small *e*. Also for that reason—because the whole thing is one sentence, I mean—the period is placed at the end of everything; in other words, it's placed *after* the closing parenthesis."

"Oh."

"But in the second example, the words in parentheses are *not* a part of the previous sentence; they're their *own* sentence. For that reason, the word *That's*, which starts the new, parenthetical sentence, begins with a capital *T*. Also for that reason, the closing parenthesis is placed at the end of everything; in other words, here the period is placed *before* or *inside* the parenthesis. Do you understand?"

"I think so. If the parenthetical part is simply a continuation of the previous sentence, then it starts with a small letter and the period

428

goes at the end of the *entire* sentence—it even goes after the end of the parenthetical part, I mean. But if the part in parentheses *isn't* a continuation of the last sentence—I mean, if it stands alone as its *own* sentence—then that new, parenthetical sentence starts with a capital letter (because it's the beginning of a new sentence, even though it's in parentheses) and the closing parenthesis goes *last* (because it's enclosing the *entire* sentence, including that sentence's period). Am I right?"

"That's it exactly."

"But if I'm writing something, how do I know for sure if something in parentheses is considered part of the previous sentence or its own sentence? For example, let me show *you* two examples." Tarzan took the notebook and wrote *February has 28 days (sometimes it has 29).* Under that he wrote *February has 28 days. (Sometimes it has 29.)* He showed me the examples and said, "According to the rule you gave me, each of those sentences is capitalized and punctuated correctly. So which one is right?"

"They're both right. You see, it's not a matter of *knowing* which one is right; it's a matter of *choosing*—I mean *you* choosing, as the *writer*—whether or not you want the parenthetical part to be its *own* sentence or part of the previous sentence. Then, once you make that choice, you capitalize and punctuate it accordingly."

"You mean it's another case of writer's choice?"

"Yes."

He nodded.

"Okay, now there's just one more error to talk about. Look at the first sentence of the second paragraph. You talk about a 'large *amount* of branches.' That's a mistake in usage. You have to understand the difference between the words *amount* and *number*."

"What is it?"

"Well, remember when we talked about the words *fewer* and *less*? We said that you use *fewer* for things that can be counted, as in *fewer countries*, and *less* for things that can't be counted, as in *less sugar*."

"I remember."

"Good. Well, it's the same idea where the words *number* and *amount* are concerned. You use the word *number* for things that can be counted, as in 'a greater *number* of coconuts,' and you use *amount* for things that can't be counted, as in 'a large *amount* of food.' Do you see?"

"I do. So, I should have written 'a large *number* of branches,' because I could have counted how many branches there were."

429

"That's right."

Silence for a while. Then I said sarcastically—just to kind of bring things to a head, to force the issue—"Well, I guess that's it. You're done with all the articles and we're done with all the grammar lessons. I guess I'll see you around."

"There's nothing else to teach me about grammar?"

"Not really."

"Nothing?"

To be honest, I could have taught him a little more, but only about very inconsequential things—things he really didn't need to know. For example, I could have talked about what to do if a word is in italics and there's a punctuation mark like a question mark or exclamation point after it. I mean, do you make the punctuation italics also to go along with the word, or do you leave it in regular type to go along with the rest of the sentence? I know that not everyone does it the same way, but at *American Monthly* we *do* italicize punctuation in a case like that. But I didn't think Tarzan needed to know something that minor. Do you agree?

Or, what about if you have a phrase or sentence in parentheses and some of the words are in italics? Do you italicize the parentheses themselves, or do you leave them in regular type? At *American Monthly*, we italicize the parentheses only if *every* word within them is in italics. If only *some* of the words are, we leave the parentheses themselves in regular type. But again, I didn't think Tarzan needed to know something like that. After all, he's not going to become a professional editor—at least, I don't think he is.

"No," I said. "There's nothing else for me to tell you."

Silence.

"Well," I said, "I guess that's it. I might as well get this stuff together and get ready to take it to *American Monthly*. Thank you for all your help and cooperation with the articles. And again, thank you for rescuing me from that gorilla." I extended my hand for a handshake.

He silently shook my hand, then turned around and slowly walked out the door.

During the next ten seconds or so, a turmoil of emotions flooded my brain. I think all my circuits short-circuited or something.

Suddenly I found my legs taking me to the doorway—running to the doorway. I hadn't decided to run to the doorway; it just happened. I mean, it was as if my legs had a mind of their own.

At the doorway my voice started working on its own too. I hadn't decided to call out to Tarzan, but my voice had a mind of its own. I heard it call out, "OH, ONE MORE THING ... ONE MORE THING!"

He turned around. "What?"

Then I heard my voice shout, "I LOVE YOU!"

He looked at me a moment and then exclaimed, "Oh, Jane! I love you too! I've always loved you!"

We ran to each other and flung ourselves into each other's arms. Then we hugged passionately, desperately. Finally, we pulled away from each other and looked deeply into each other's eyes. Then he kissed me gently on the lips and said, "What are we going to do?"

"What would you *like* to do?"

"I don't want you to go back to Baltimore," he said. "I want to *be* with you. I want to *marry* you."

He said it! He said it! He *did* love me!

"I want to marry you too."

We just stared into each other's eyes with dopey grins for a long time.

Finally I said, "Let me ask you something. Ever since I sprained my ankle, I was afraid that you didn't really love me. I used to think you did, but then I wasn't sure. Why did you act distant and uninterested?"

"Well, do you remember that time we went to that big waterfall? And I was so in love with you that I kept staring at your hair and your lips and your beautiful eyes? You discouraged me from doing that; you said that I should concentrate on grammar. But I couldn't help myself because I was so in love. Anyway, after you sprained your ankle, I didn't want you to have to worry about anything else, so I *forced* myself to concentrate on grammar and to not act like a lovesick schoolboy."

"Oh, you silly ... thoughtful ... man! And that was the whole reason?"

"Yes."

"But I *wanted* you to love me. I *wanted* you to."

"Well, I did. I mean, I do."

"And I love you too ... with all my heart ... and now we're going to be married!"

"I've read about the marriage ceremony in books, but I don't know how to go about it. Do you?"

"Well, we want the marriage to be proper and legal, so that it's recognized by everyone throughout the world. So, what we have to do is find someone with the legal authority to perform marriages."

"How do you do that?"

"Well, we'll probably have to travel to one of the large cities in Africa."

"You mean like Cairo or—" He skipped a beat. "Wait, is that why you were asking me about the largest cities in Africa the other day?"

I didn't answer, but my playfully guilty expression told him what he needed to know.

"Well," he said, "which one do you want to get married in?"

"Well, I think there are four choices. There's Casablanca and Cairo to the north and Johannesburg to the South. But there's also the possibility of having a ship's captain marry us at sea. Of course, for that we'd have to build a big raft and paddle way out on the ocean. And we'd have to make the raft big enough to hold the two of us, as well as Yemmy and Omy and Cheetah, in case they want to come with us."

"Well, I think we should rule out the ship-at-sea idea because what if no ship happened by? We might float out there forever. Our food and water might run out. And you really want two tigers on a raft like that?"

"I guess you're right. We'll rule out that idea. That leaves the three cities."

"Well," he reasoned, "if the appeal of northern cities is that you get to cross the Sahara, either one will serve the purpose. So we can eliminate one of them from our considerations. Since Casablanca is closer, let's eliminate Cairo."

"Okay," I agreed. "If we end up going to Johannesburg, we can swing by Mount Kilimanjaro on the way—if it's not too far off course, I mean."

"Wait a minute. I just realized something," he said. "If we're getting married and staying in Africa, what about the twenty-four articles for the magazine? Are you going to send them in?"

"I don't know. Maybe I will. It's not really very important to me anymore—now that I know you love me. Do you care whether or not I send them in?"

"I guess not. Maybe we should keep them as a souvenir of our adventure together."

"That's a good idea," I agreed.

"Wait, I just thought of something else. Today is the day that you're expecting the chimps to arrive with the jewels. You planned it so that they'd be arriving right about now."

"Oh my! I forgot all about that! I guess ten million dollars isn't so important to me anymore."

"But we should still look around to see if they're coming—after they went to all that trouble, I mean."

We put our flattened hands above our eyebrows and looked in all directions for any sign of a hundred chimpanzees with clenched fists. We saw nothing.

"Well," I said, "I guess they're not coming. I guess you were right all along."

He didn't answer.

"So," I said, "now all we have to do is decide whether we want to get married in Casablanca or Johannesburg."

"Right. If we go to Casablanca we'll travel mostly by camel, I think. And if we go to Johannesburg we'll go most by canoe, I guess. Which appeals to you more?"

I couldn't decide. "I don't know. Which one do *you* like?"

"I don't know."

"Well," I said, "I have an idea. In America, if we can't decide something, we flip a coin. If it comes up heads, we do one thing, but if it comes up tails we do the other."

"I don't have a coin."

"Wait! I have an idea." I ran into the cabin and got a pencil. Then I ran back outside to Tarzan. I picked up a leaf from the ground. "Okay, now I'm writing H for *heads* on this side of the leaf and T for *tails* on the other side." I marked both sides of the leaf. "I'll throw this in the air. Before it lands, you guess which side will land facing up. If you guess correctly, we'll go to Casablanca. If you guess incorrectly, we'll go to Johannesburg. Okay?"

"But that's leaving it entirely to chance."

"I know. That's what people sometimes do when they can't make a decision."

"Oh. Okay."

"Are you ready? I'm going to throw it."

"I'm ready"

I took a deep breath and threw the leaf as high into the air as I could. When it reached its high point I shouted, "Call it!"

INDEX